ATLANTIS

AND THE

CYCLES OF TIME

"In this important book Joscelyn Godwin has accomplished the nearly impossible, masterfully summarizing and synthesizing widely disparate approaches to the perennial question of Atlantis. Much more than a catalog of possible Atlantis locations, occult Atlantology is finally accorded the importance it deserves, including a cogent analysis of esoteric cycles of time, the Four World Ages, the Yuga Cycle, and the Precession of the Equinoxes, placing Atlantis in a larger temporal context. This is a must-read for anyone who wishes to truly understand the Atlantis debate."

ROBERT M. SCHOCH, PH.D., AUTHOR OF *VOYAGES OF THE PYRAMID BUILDERS* AND *THE PARAPSYCHOLOGY REVOLUTION*

"From the sublime to the ludicrous, from the poetic to the simply mad, Joscelyn Godwin gives us a chart of the many versions of Atlantis (with all their 'glaring lack of consensus') that will last us till the lost continent rises again. Truly Godwin is the Master of Atlantis."

PETER LAMBORN WILSON, COAUTHOR OF *ATLANTIS MANIFESTO* AND *GREEN HERMETICISM: ALCHEMY & ECOLOGY*

ATLANTIS
AND THE
CYCLES OF TIME

*Prophecies, Traditions,
and Occult Revelations*

Joscelyn Godwin

Inner Traditions
Rochester, Vermont • Toronto, Canada

Inner Traditions
One Park Street
Rochester, Vermont 05767
www.InnerTraditions.com

Library of Congress Cataloging-in-Publication Data

Godwin, Joscelyn.
  Atlantis and the cycles of time : prophecies, traditions, and occult revelations / Joscelyn Godwin.
      p. cm.
  Includes bibliographical references (p.   ) and index.
  ISBN 978-1-59477-262-7 (pbk.)
  1. Atlantis (Legendary place) 2. Prophecies (Occultism) I. Title.
  GN751.G63 2011
  398.23'4—dc22

                                                        2010028510

Printed and bound in the United States of America by Lake Book Manufacturing

10   9   8   7   6   5   4   3   2   1

Text design and layout by Virginia Scott Bowman
This book was typeset in Garamnd Premier Pro with Caslon, Gils Sans, Agenda, and Italian Electric used as display typefaces

To send correspondence to the author of this book, mail a first-class letter to the author c/o Inner Traditions • Bear & Company, One Park Street, Rochester, VT 05767, and we will forward the communication.

Contents

Preface and
Acknowledgments

——————— ✳ ———————

Most writers on Atlantis begin with the discouraging news that there are already thousands of books on the subject. Why write another one? Why read one? It is because of an idea, a dream, a theory that will not let go:

That there was high culture in prehistoric times.

This is the core of the Atlantis myth, ever since the Egyptian priest told the story recorded by Plato. The sciences of time prefer to close the curtains on it. They assure us that such things as cities, technology, a leisured class, organized religion, and warfare only arrived within the historic period. The lines of development and influence, they say, are well mapped. Beyond a certain time barrier, there was no high culture anywhere on Earth: only the primitive culture, however ingenious and admirable, of Stone Age peoples and nomads.

The least interesting books on Atlantis are the ones that toe this line, proclaiming that Plato's Atlantis was really somewhere quite normal and recent, like the volcanic island of Santorini that erupted in the second millennium BCE. The first chapter of this book is a worldwide survey of such theories.

Other authors, more bold, cling to the myth and reject the scientists' time barrier. They are suspicious of experts who preserve the status quo by dampening speculation. Just as historical civilizations and empires rise and fall, they ask, why should not the broader waves of human development? Even if our own civilizing wave began with the city cultures of Jericho or the Indus Valley, that does not mean it was the first and only one. There has been plenty of time for other waves, other cultures, even other humanities to come and go.

The "New Archaeology" that holds, for instance, that there was high civilization in pre-dynastic Egypt or the Andes, tries to argue this on rational grounds. It draws on archaeological evidence and aligns it with ancient texts and myths. But the writers of those texts had a worldview as different as possible from scientific materialism. To credit them starts one on a slippery slope that may lead to actually believing them. Then, as some of the New Archaeologists have found, one enters the company of the Damned.

I borrow that word from Charles Fort, author of *The Book of the Damned* (1919) and other chronicles of anomalous phenomena. "So by the damned," wrote Fort, "I mean the excluded." In the present case, this would be all those Atlantologists whose view of human prehistory rests on something other than rational deduction and material evidence. It is wrong to call them irrational, for they do not reject those avenues of knowledge: they just find others supplementary, if not superior. The Traditionalists rely on an esoteric reading of scriptures and sacred authorities. Theosophists and others open to the paranormal call on intuition, initiation, clairvoyance, or mediumship. There is much disagreement among them, just as there is among the rationalists, but they agree that there *was* high culture in prehistoric times and that it holds a lesson that we do well to learn. Chapters 2–10 trace their various strands and influences, with special attention to the national schools and their agendas. No matter how much or little one credits them, they open up vastnesses that are exhilarating to contemplate.

None of the myriad books on Atlantis has dealt comprehensively with this branch of the history of ideas, which we may call "occult Atlantology." Nor has there been a proper study of another topic profoundly linked to it: that of the cycles of time, one phase of which supposedly ended with the Atlantean cataclysm. Both subjects are the preserve of true believers wedded to their own theories, and of careless repeaters of second-hand data.

The subject of esoteric time cycles deserves a book to itself, but it would be one with limited appeal, full of tables and calculations. Chapters 11–12 are a preliminary decluttering of the field. They explain the two main cyclical systems, the Four World Ages and the Precession of the Equinoxes. I have made this summary with a certain sense of urgency, because at the time of writing there is much agitation concerning the coming year 2012. The reader will discover that the present period, even the fateful year, has figured quite prominently in cyclical theories that have nothing to do with the Mayan calendar. It seems important to set out the bases of these and other theories, and also to clarify the controversy about which of the four ages we are living in. My hope and expectation is that long after 2012, others will follow up some of these leads in the same spirit of open-minded curiosity.

Unless otherwise attributed, all translations are mine.

ACKNOWLEDGMENTS

First I must thank Colgate University, especially those in charge of the Scientific Perspectives Core Courses, for their support of "The Atlantis Debate," and the hundreds of students who have passed through this course in ten years. If any of them should read this, I greet them as fellow explorers. Colgate's president and dean of the faculty generously granted me leave in fall 2009. I thank the staff of Colgate's Case Library, especially its Interlibrary Loan Service; also those at Cornell University Library, the British Library, the Cambridge University Library, the Bibliotheca Philosophica Hermetica (Amsterdam), the National Library of Malta (Valletta), and the libraries of the University of Strasbourg and the Theosophical Society (London), to which I paid short but fruitful visits. I thank Phyllis Benjamin of the International Fortean Organization and Walter Cruttenden of the Conferences on Precession and Ancient Knowledge for giving me a forum for some of these ideas. A friend from Portugal supplied me with recondite material and insights into the Traditionalist current. My colleague Anthony Aveni has encouraged me for many years through conversation and his own teaching and research. Others who have given me materials or ideas on these topics include Frank Donnola, Antoine Faivre, Deborah Belle Forman, Patrick Harpur, John Major Jenkins, Gary Lachman, Jean-Pierre Laurant, Ernest McClain, the late John Michell, James Santucci, Guido Mina di Sospiro, Rüdiger Sünner, Jay Weidner, Peter Lambourn Wilson, and the guest lecturers in my course: Paul LaViolette, Robert Schoch, Laird Scranton, and John Anthony West. None of them are responsible for my omissions, errors, or opinions. Lastly I thank my wife, Janet, especially for her piano-playing that accompanied the writing of this book.

JOSCELYN GODWIN
HAMILTON, NEW YORK

ONE

Atlantis of the Rationalists

———————— ✳ ————————

THE ATLANTIC OCEAN

The narrator of Plato's *Timaeus* said that Atlantis was "beyond the Pillars of Hercules," the classical name for the Straits of Gibraltar, and "larger than Libya and Asia combined,"[1] that is, much of North Africa plus present-day Turkey. So the Atlantic Ocean is the obvious place to begin.

The Jesuit polymath Athanasius Kircher (1602–1680) was the first to publish a map of Atlantis, putting it fairly and squarely in the middle of the Atlantic.[2] There was no reason for him to do otherwise. Plato's testimony made sense, did not contradict the Bible, and agreed with Kircher's own experience of the mutability of land and sea. In 1638 he himself had seen the city of Euphemia in Calabria disappear in a volcanic cataclysm, leaving a putrid lake in its place. Noah's Flood, the subject of his book *Arca Noë,* had caused the whole earth to be submerged, then reappear with a different arrangement of land and sea. The followers of Charles Hapgood (see below under "Antarctica") imagine that Kircher based his illustration on some ancient map he had found. Had this been so, Kircher would not have failed to announce the fact, as he did whenever he made some fortunate discovery.[3] While he states his reasons for believing that Atlantis existed, his map is an imaginary reconstruction, just like innumerable other illustrations in his works.

A mid-Atlantic location was the keystone of *Atlantis: The Antediluvian World* (1882), the book by Ignatius Donnelly (1831–1901) that Sprague de Camp calls "the New Testament of Atlantism"[4] (Plato's *Timaeus* and *Critias* being the Old). Donnelly was a U.S. senator from Minnesota who made good use of the Library of Congress: he also wrote on the catastrophist model of prehistory (*Ragnarök: The Age of Fire and Gravel*) and on Francis Bacon's authorship of the Shakespeare corpus (*The Great Cryptogram*). He was a strict diffusionist, treating all cultural phenomena as imports rather than as indigenous inventions. Given that, the similarities on the eastern and western sides of the Atlantic had to have a common source. Donnelly spread his net to include not only pyramids and flood legends, but also metallurgy, agriculture, shipbuilding, language, alphabets, religion, and mythology. Consequently he found so many parallels that he assumed they must have all originated in the vanished continent.

As for Atlantis itself, Donnelly accepted Plato's exuberant description of it as the most wealthy, powerful, and highly cultured of all ancient civilizations, its memory preserved in worldwide myths of a Golden Age, Paradise, Asgard, Avalon, Elysium, and other vanished Utopias. He wrote in conclusion:

> The Atlanteans possessed an established order of priests; their religious worship was pure and simple. They lived under a kingly government; they had their courts, their judges, their records, their monuments covered with inscriptions, their mines, their founderies,* their workshop, their looms, their grist-mills, their boats and sailing-vessels, their highways, aqueducts, wharves, docks, and canals. They had processions, banners, and triumphal arches for their kings and heroes; they built pyramids, temples, round-towers, and obelisks; they practised religious ablutions; they knew the use of the magnet and of gunpowder. In short, they were in the enjoyment of a civilization nearly as high as our own, lacking only the printing-press, and those inventions in which steam, electricity, and magnetism are used.[5]

---

*All quotations preserve the original spelling.

A "modern revised edition" of *Atlantis: The Antediluvian World* appeared in 1949[6] with contributions from Egerton Sykes, who edited it and wrote a foreword; H. S. Bellamy, who wrote "An Appreciation of Donnelly"; and Lewis Spence, who wrote a short introduction that is really more about himself.

This is an interesting trio. Egerton Sykes (1894–1983) was a lifelong Atlantologist who ran a bimonthly, *Atlantis, A Journal of Research,* from 1948 to 1976. He was also drawn to parapsychological and Fortean topics, but from a generally rational approach. As editor, Sykes smoothed out Donnelly's citation system, cut several chapters whose archaeological and linguistic conclusions he considered outdated, and added many postscripts of his own. The publisher was probably to blame for omitting the 128 engravings that enhanced the original book.

Hans Schindler Bellamy (1901–1980) was a contributor to Sykes's *Atlantis* journal and author of eight books published in London from 1936 onward.[7] Bellamy's main object in his books, articles, and in this "Appreciation" was to promote the "World Ice Doctrine" (*Welteislehre* or *WEL*) of Hans Hoerbiger (1860–1931) as the solution to the fall of Atlantis, whose prior existence he accepted in more or less Donnellian terms. "I firmly believe that atlantologists, and all those interested in the Myth of Atlantis, cannot do better than accept Hoerbiger's helpful teachings," he wrote.[8] Bellamy had known Hoerbiger, a fellow Austrian, since the early 1920s and had become convinced that the *WEL* held the secret of Earth's prehistory and that of mankind. The doctrine holds that the moon, which is covered with ice, is but the latest in a series of satellites that have been captured by the Earth's gravity and one by one crashed into its surface, with imaginable results. The present moon, biggest in the series, was previously a planet in its own right; it was gradually drawn into orbit around Earth and "captured" around 12,000–11,500 BCE. The gravity of the new satellite, counteracting that of Earth, allowed humans and animals grow to giant size. It tugged the oceans from the polar to the equatorial zone, causing catastrophic changes in sea level, including the destruction of Atlantis.

It is astonishing that such a prestigious house as Faber & Faber, with T. S. Eliot among their editors, should have published Bellamy's theories, especially in wartime. Although Hoerbiger had died before Hitler came to power, many influential Nazis had favored the *WEL* as an alternative to Einstein's cosmology. It is also hard to believe in an Austrian called Bellamy, but that may have been an assumed surname for English consumption; the "H. S." initials were never spelled out. Someone at Faber's must have had a soft spot for Hoerbiger, for they went on to publish another *WEL* book, *Atlantis and the Giants* (1957) by Denis Saurat (1890–1959), a literature professor of wide and eccentric interests.

Lewis Spence (1874–1955), the third contributor to the reissue of Donnelly's work, was a Scottish mythographer whose five books on Atlantis recast Donnelly's theories in a more modern idiom. Spence began as a skeptic. The entry on "Atlantis" in his *Encyclopaedia of Occultism* (1920) states, "The theory that the Atlantians founded the civilisations of Central America and Mexico has been fully proven to be absurd, as that civilisation is distinctly of an aboriginal nature, and of comparatively late origin."[9] Soon after, he was preaching the contrary, and would become the most popular of twentieth-century Atlantologists. As to whether Spence belongs in this or a later chapter, Paul Jordan, a severe critic, allows that "though Spence's chain of reasoning is full of gaps and baseless assumptions, it is not conducted outside the realm of the possible (if unlikely)."[10]

In contrast to Donnelly's vision of Atlanteans not far behind modern America in technical achievement, Spence's version was content for them to be a magnificent Stone Age people. He was aware of recent discoveries of paleolithic cultures, especially the Aurignacian, which flourished from 40,000 to 20,000 years ago, and its successor, the Azilian. He could appreciate the high artistic quality of these cultures' cave paintings and the refined technique of their flint and bone artifacts. Yet prehistorians could trace no gradual development, nor pinpoint the origin of Cro-Magnon Man, the modern human type to whom those cultures were attributed. Spence saw the perfect solution: the Cro-Magnons had been the dominant race of Atlantis and had come to Europe as refugees from successive catastrophes. As Jordan points out, this showed typical colonial arrogance in the inability to credit any culture with its own inventions:[11] everything had to have come from some superior source. Spence certainly did not credit his own aboriginal people.

> If a patriotic Scotsman may be pardoned the boast, I may say that I devoutly believe that Scotland's admitted superiority in the mental and spiritual spheres springs almost entirely from the preponderant degree of Crô-Magnon blood which certainly runs in the veins of her people, whose height and cranial capacity, as well as other physical signs, show them to be mostly of Crô-Magnon race.[12]

This new wave of Atlantean studies opened with Spence's *The Problem of Atlantis* (1924), *Atlantis in America* (1925), and *The History of Atlantis* (1927). He used similar methods to examine the possibility of another lost continent in *The Problem of Lemuria, the Sunken Continent of the Pacific* (1932), then set the subject aside for a decade.

A journalist by profession, working for the quality press, Spence had always been more of a compiler and an enthusiast than a scholar. His lasting interest and the majority of his books were in myth, beginning with the ancient Americas and eventually covering the whole world. Unlike academic mythographers, who would apply a structuralist method to their material (as Lévi-Strauss) or seek archetypal themes in it (as Joseph Campbell), Spence was essentially in the business of telling stories, and was always tempted to believe them. He admits in his foreword to Donnelly:

> As one almost fatally open to the lure of the subjective, a ready victim to the temptations of fantasy, I still assert with all the emphasis at my command that unless the iron discipline of scientific detachment be recognized in the consideration of such questions as the Atlantean, its study might as well be abandoned. For me there are two Atlantises—the Atlantis of fantasy and imagination and that of

reality. Sometimes these ideas appear to fuse; at others they are as far apart as the poles.[13]

When the Second World War defied any attempt at explanation with the "iron discipline of scientific detachment," Spence abandoned it. Consequently we will meet him again among the British occultists of chapter 6. From then on, scientists in the Western world, shaken by the example of "Nazi science," have shunned subjects that touch on the irrational, such as parapsychology, or on a catastrophist view of history, like Atlantology. Peter James analyzes this persisting "neo-Aristotelian" stance, which goes back to Isaac Newton (who excluded divine intervention in history), Charles Lyell (who founded the uniformitarian theory of geology), and Charles Darwin (whose evolutionary theory required vast tracts of undisturbed time).[14] Besides an emotional aversion, new findings in geology and oceanography put paid to the idea of a large island or two occupying the north Atlantic Ocean. Among the many proofs are the behavior of the mid-Atlantic ridge, which is the junction between two tectonic plates that are being forced apart, and the quantity of undisturbed sediments on the ocean floor. Henceforth any Atlantis in the Atlantic would have to be much smaller and compatible with the underwater topography. This takes some of the thrill out of the hunt, effectively limiting it to where the ocean floor rises above the surface to form the Canary Islands, the Madeira Islands, the Cape Verde Islands, and the Azores.

The next major contribution to Atlantology came from behind the Iron Curtain, where millennialism was still part of the official philosophy. Nicolas Zhirov, a Soviet chemist, made a serious study of the subject during the 1950s and 1960s, and his book *Atlantis; Atlantology: Basic Problems* appeared in English translation in 1970.[15] It carried great conviction with its command of sources in many languages and its maps, tables, and charts. Zhirov's conclusion was that a largish island could have existed on the northeastern slopes of the mid-Atlantic ridge, with the Azores as the remains of its mountain peaks.

Of later Atlantologists who favor this location, none has surpassed Zhirov in the scientific breadth and depth of his work. Science, however, is always on the move, and Zhirov's is now half a century old. Much of it was already superseded in 1981 by another eastern European scientist, Zdeněk Kukal (see below). Moreover, for all his apparent rigor, Zhirov fell into the besetting sin of Atlantologists, rational and otherwise. This concerns the use of Plato's *Timaeus* and *Critias* as evidence. Whenever some detail of Plato's account supports their theory, they welcome it as evidence; when it does not, they dismiss it. To take one pair of examples among many, Zhirov concludes from Plato's report that the Atlanteans enjoyed two harvests a year but had indoor swimming pools that "the country was situated in the south but it had a cool climate due to the elevation of the plateau. Evidence of this kind and the reference to a coconut palm squashes the theory that Atlantis was situated in the northern latitudes."[16] (The theory he was keen to squash was probably that of Jürgen Spanuth; see below.) On the other hand, when Plato makes much of the Atlanteans' use of metals, saying that "they covered the whole circuit of the outermost wall with a veneer of bronze, they fused tin over the inner wall and orichalc gleaming like fire over the wall of the acropolis itself," and that the Temple of Poseidon "was covered all over with silver, except for the figures on the pediment which were covered with gold,"[17] Zhirov treats it as nonsense: "In our opinion, Atlantis was rather in the Stone Age, a land of cyclopean structures and megalithic edifices."[18]

An ephemeral footnote to this section occurred in February 2009, when the Internet resource Google released its maps of the world's ocean floor. Off the coast of Africa, just west of the Canary and Madeira Islands, there loomed a pattern like a grid of city streets some 100 miles square.[19] The media hailed it on their front pages as "lost Atlantis," whereupon two of the scientists who had compiled the maps issued a statement that it was no such thing.[20] The maps were not, as some thought, satellite photographs that had somehow penetrated miles of seawater; they were compilations from satellite radar measurement of sea levels (which are higher above ocean floor rises) and sonar soundings taken by ships. The grid was merely the criss-cross route taken by the ship that had mapped that region, which stood out because of the greater accuracy of its soundings as compared to surface measurements. Needless to say, not everyone was satisfied with this explanation of a feature so pleasingly in accord with Plato's rectangular plane with its grid of canals, and in one of the prime locations, too.

ARCTICA

Jean-Sylvain Bailly (1736–1793), an eminent astronomer and mayor of Paris who fell victim to the French Revolution, placed Atlantis in the Arctic Circle. Already while writing his history of ancient astronomy,[21] he had concluded that humanity, or at least its most important branch, had originated in the far North. His argument was based on some curious numbers found in Greek, Nordic, and Persian mythology, which he interpreted as encoding the number of days of the year when the sun rises. Adonis, for example, is sentenced to spend four months of the year underground with Persephone, which corresponds to the four sunless months at latitude 79°N. The god Odin is absent from his nuptial bed for sixty-five days of the year, which is the case with the sun at latitude 71°N. In the Zoroastrian sacred text, Zend-Avesta, the longest day of the year is said to be twice as long as the shortest, which is the case at 49°N, a latitude far to the north of Persia. Bailly concluded that these and other legends preserved the racial memory of an origin in the far North and a gradual migration to the South.

Bailly next addressed himself to the Atlantis problem. In a correspondence with Voltaire,[22] he built on the Nordic Atlantis theory of Olaf Rudbeck (see next section). Bailly's location of choice was the islands of Spitzbergen, Greenland, and Nova Zemlya. Against the obvious objections based on climate, he explains that when the earth was younger, its interior heat was greater, and life in the Arctic may well have been more tolerable than elsewhere. Besides, he adds, the earth's movement being less rapid near the poles, the atmosphere was probably less turbid, and so the legend of a perpetual spring may well have been true.[23] The "Atlanteans" were the Hyperboreans of classical legend,[24] who originated in the "Garden of the Hesperides" near the pole and left evidence of their once-happy climate in the fossil flora and fauna of the Arctic Circle.[25] Bailly's theory had a permanent effect on French Atlantology, blending easily with the occult stream, as we shall see in the next chapter.

SWEDEN

A recent book by David King[26] has drawn attention to the most persistent Atlantologist of early modern times, Olaf Rudbeck (1630–1702). Rudbeck was a Swedish professor and entrepreneur whose achievements include the discovery of the lymphatic system and the invention of stratigraphy as an archaeological tool. His attention was first drawn by classical references to the Hyperboreans, dwellers in the "land beyond the north wind." He naturally took this to be Scandinavia, and in the long-bearded Swedish peasantry he seemed to see descendants of the mythic race. Next he applied his ingenuity to the voyage of the Argonauts and concluded that Jason's crew, after obtaining the Golden Fleece, had cruised the Russian rivers as far as the Arctic. There, too, was the "Hades" that Odysseus visited. It only remained to find Plato's Atlantis, and Rudbeck's archaeological excavations in old Uppsala provided the clue: it could have been nowhere else; the correspondences were irrefutable. He published his findings in *Atlantica* (Uppsala, 1679). Like his contemporary Kircher, Rudbeck was not the slightest bit mad—only obsessive, and wrong, thus sharing the fate of many Atlantologists: momentary fame, lasting ridicule, and finally incorporation into the history of ideas.

GERMANY

Jürgen Spanuth (1907–1998) spent his life as the Lutheran pastor of Bordelum, a village on the northwest coast of Germany facing the North Frisian Islands. His Atlantis theory, first published in 1953,[27] became known in the English-speaking world through his books *Atlantis: The*

Mystery Unravelled[28] and the weightier *Atlantis of the North.*[29] Spanuth's Atlanteans were really Bronze Age Germans living on a fertile plain in what is now the North Sea. Their capital was Basileia, an island outside the mouths of the four rivers Eider, Elbe, Weser, and Jade. Their civilization ended after a cometary impact in the thirteenth century BCE, correctly dated in Plato except that it happened 9,000 *months,* not years, before Solon's visit to Egypt. Basilea sank into a mess of impassable mud,[30] leaving the island of Helgoland as a solitary witness. The survivors marched through Europe and Asia Minor, some eventually reaching Egypt, where they were already known as the Haunebu, sea people and traders in amber. That substance, says Spanuth, is the true meaning of Plato's "orichalc."[31] His Atlantean theory apart, Spanuth's work is a fair account of Bronze Age culture in his home region and of his own archaeological discoveries.

BRITAIN

In 1902 Beckles Willson (1869–1942), a Canadian journalist and historian, wrote in *Lost England* of the land that once stretched from Land's End to the Scilly Isles.[32] Saint Michael's Mount, now standing amid the tidal sands of Mount's Bay, was then a promontory rising from a dense forest, whose fallen trunks can sometimes be glimpsed through the clear water. This was the fabled land of Lyonesse, known throughout the ancient world for its tin, the indispensable metal that hardens copper into bronze. Phoenicians, Greeks, and Romans in turn depended on it for their tools and weaponry. In the Dark Ages the land began to subside, and by the Middle Ages it was gone.

Willson did not mention Atlantis, but identical observations inspired a book by a Berlin judge who had already written about Odysseus. Hans Steuerwald's *Der Untergang von Atlantis* is crammed with detailed arguments and the usual selective use of Plato. The mysterious orichalc now became Cornish tin ore,[33] the Atlantean empire a region under Cornish control that stretched from Scotland to Libya, which explains the elephants that Plato mentions.³⁴ Alas, the empire was literally built on sand, but the chief reason for its fall was not the subsidence and rise in sea levels affecting the Cornish coast and its royal island: it was the coming of iron, which put the tin trade out of business.³⁵

A new factor enters the picture with Paul Dunbavin's *Atlantis of the West,* a more elaborate blend of local Atlanticism (Atlantis now being in the Irish Sea) with cosmic and geophysical speculations. Dunbavin is an independent researcher whose previous book argued, mostly on linguistic grounds, that the Picts were of Finnish origin. His Atlantean theory is that in 3100 BCE, the earth was struck by a comet, causing the crust to shift 1°–2° relative to the poles of rotation.³⁶ Among the consequences, "from 3100 BC to about 800 BC, the axial tilt continued to oscillate between about 20° and 26° before settling to its modern value"³⁷ [23° 27']. As the bulge around the equator readjusted itself, some regions sank, including the British Isles, while others such as South America rose. Climates changed, and the length of the year increased from its previous 360 days, necessitating a worldwide resetting of the calendar.

Dunbavin's theory emboldened him to discard the scientists' view, based on Ice Age studies, of how and when Ireland, Britain, and continental Europe were split from a single landmass. He writes: "The hypothesis that the Earth's axis has shifted is able to produce a map of the former shorelines around Britain and Ireland which bears a remarkable resemblance to Plato's description of his lost island."³⁸ The citadel of Atlantis rises on a new island south of the Isle of Man; the rectangular plain is east of it, north of Wales. This becomes the hub of a Neolithic Empire whose influence stretched from Libya to Scandinavia until the catastrophe of 3100 BCE.

THE SAHARA DESERT

Albert Herrmann's book *Unsere Ahnen und Atlantis* (Our ancestors and Atlantis, 1935) may have been the last of several efforts to place Atlantis in the present Sahara Desert. There was a wave of enthusiasm for this idea after the bestselling novel *L'Atlantide* (1919) by Pierre Benoit. In the novel, two French officers are whisked away to a hidden realm in the Sahara ruled by a nymphomaniac queen. Herrmann, a professor at Berlin University, was content to stump around in the sand, looking for evidence of a less glamorous but more plausible Atlantis.[39] On his fourth archaeological expedition (1933),[40] he believed that he had found it in the salt pan of Chott el-Djerid, southern Tunisia, and located Poseidon's city on the delta of a former river (Triton), by a former lake.[41] Perhaps as a means of promoting his modest discovery, Herrmann gave his Atlanteans a Nordic origin. He entered the heated debates over the authenticity of the *Oera Linda Book* (see chapter 5), taking the middle position: that it contains genuine information about a matriarchal civilization in a now-vanished northern land but is contaminated by later additions. This Nordic civilization—"our ancestors" of the title—ended around 1680 BCE with floods and conflagrations due to a cometary impact. The information for that came from another disputed source, the Chinese *Bamboo Annals*.[42] The survivors migrated south, passing through the British Isles (where they built Stonehenge), then settling on the banks of the Triton. But their paradise was not to last.

> The more the Triton region dried up, the more tragic was the fate of the formerly happy inhabitants. One group, the forbears of today's Berbers, retreated to the wetter zones of the bordering lands, but the majority were compelled to emigrate. Thus in the course of centuries Philistines and Phoenicians went to Palestine; beside the Amazons, Lyceans, Moscoi, Libyans and Chaldeans to Asia Minor and Armenia; Etruscans to the Aegean and Italy; Gauls or Druids to France and Britain; Iberians to Caucasia and Spain. They all ensured that although Atlantean culture had died in North Africa, it would put out new shoots in other parts of the Mediterranean.[43]

Thus all the most creative people of antiquity, with the exception of the Semites, are endowed with Nordic ancestry! Lastly, Herrmann attributes a common source to all concentric constructions, including the citadel of Atlantis, Stonehenge, labyrinths, and "Troytowns." Derived from Herman Wirth, it is a symbolic diagram created by Stone Age people as they wandered north and noticed the changes in the sun's course.[44]

CRETE AND THERA

Most classicists believe Plato's story of Atlantis to refer to the civilization of Minoan Crete (third to second millennia BCE) and to the destruction of the volcanic island of Thera (now called Santorini). Several writers have described the sequence of events in the rise and fall of this "Minoan hypothesis."[45] Although it had been hinted at in the nineteenth century, its main proponent was the Greek archaeologist Spyridon Marinatos (1901–1974), who had excavated on Crete and discovered on Santorini the city of Akrotiri: a Pompeii-like time capsule buried beneath volcanic ash. In 1939 Marinatos proposed that the eruption of Santorini around 1500 BCE had not only destroyed most of that island, but that its repercussions had put an end to the flourishing Minoan civilization. This explained the sudden decline of that rich and fascinating culture, formerly blamed on raiders from mainland Greece. In 1950 Marinatos gave his theory the golden touch by suggesting that it explained Plato's Atlantis. Very soon after, Wilhelm Brandenstein was promoting the Minoan hypothesis in the German-speaking world[46] and Massimo Pallottino, in a long and favorable review of Brandenstein's book, offered it to the scholars of Italy.[47]

To Marinatos's countryman, the seismologist Angelos Galanopoulos, the Minoan hypothesis verified the statement in the *Timaeus* that Atlantis vanished "in a single dreadful day and night." Galanopoulos published a series of studies from 1960 onward arguing that it was Santorini itself that Plato had in mind. He went on to include in his explanation the myths of Deucalion's Flood, the Fall of Phaeton, and the miracles of the Exodus, thus providing an alternative to the scarier theories of Immanuel Velikovsky.

The year 1969 was the heyday of the Minoan hypothesis, with books published by Galanopoulos and Edward Bacon,[48] James Mavor (a

Woods Hole, Massachusetts, oceanographer),[49] and J. V. Luce (a classicist of Trinity College, Dublin).[50] In 1971 Prince Michael of Greece began his career as a historian by explaining the theory to the Francophone world.[51] For twenty years or more, the hypothesis set the Atlantean question to rest. But critics were quick to see the flaws in it. First, it required an ingenious twisting of Plato's plainspoken account to place Atlantis in the Mediterranean, not the Atlantic, and to have it destroyed 900 years, not 9,000 years, before Solon heard the story in Egypt around 600 BCE. The excuses were that Plato's "Pillars of Hercules" were really Capes Tainaron and Malea, at the south of the Peloponnese; and that Solon had muddled up Egyptian numerical symbols and read thousands for hundreds.

What was worse was the matter of dating. Marinatos assumed that both the Santorini eruption and the fall of Knossos (capital of Minoan Crete) happened around 1500 BCE. Since his time, C-14 and tree-ring dating have separated the two events, pushing the eruption back as far as 1628 BCE, while the destruction of the Knossos labyrinth is dated to 1380 BCE.[52] Scholars are still arguing about the dates of both events, but they agree that the simple cause and effect no longer holds up.

MALTA

A map in the National Library, Valletta,[53] drawn by Giorgio Grongnet in 1854, shows "Atlantis" as one large and several smaller islands filling the whole region from the Gulf of Gabes to the Gulf of Sirte. This is reproduced in *Malta: Echoes of Plato's Island,*[54] one of several publications on Maltese prehistory by the Mifsud family and their colleagues. The Mifsuds, who work as physicians and have no difficulty with scientific data, are an irritant to the official archaeologists, who are unable to explain how such a small area as Malta gave birth, around the middle of the fourth millennium BCE, to the world's earliest architectural civilization, and how it abruptly ended in the middle of the third millennium BCE. While accepting all the adjustments to Plato's text necessary for a Mediterranean Atlantis, the Mifsuds contest the claims of Thera and Crete and present multiple parallels with the more ancient civilization of their own islands. Their theory is that Malta was the center of a much larger region that is now under water. Its destruction came through tectonic and volcanic action, as the African and Eurasian continental plates ground into one another. A subsidence of the Pantelleria Rift left only the Pelagian Islands on one side and Malta on the other, both severely tilted.[55] The cart tracks that break off at the tops of Malta's cliffs and canals cut in the seabed are evidence that this happened in civilized times.[56]

SICILY

Thorwald Franke, an independent researcher, has built on an idea first proposed by Marinatos and seconded by Spanuth: that the Atlantean invasion mentioned by Plato refers to the incursion into Egypt of the "Sea Peoples."[57] Marinatos's Sea Peoples came from Crete, whereas Spanuth's came from the North Sea. Franke's came from Sicily around 1200 BCE. His argument hinges on the fact that Plato is retelling an *Egyptian* story—that the geographical details reflect Egyptian misconceptions and even shifts, such as transferring the name "Pillars of Hercules" from the Straits of Messina to those of Gibraltar. Franke equates Atlas with Italos, the sole named king of Sicily. He locates the Atlantean plain near Catania and its capital on the Rocchicella Hill near Palagonia, site of the Sanctuary of the Palikè, which becomes a relic of the Atlantean cult. As for the total destruction of Atlantis, Franke explains it as Egyptian political propaganda: having defeated the invaders, they had to declare them annihilated.

CYPRUS

Robert Sarmast, an independent writer and mythologist from Los Angeles, starts from the fact that the Straits of Gibraltar have periodically been closed.[58] While geologists date this situation to the prehuman past,

Sarmast believes that it has happened much more recently, and that by 10,000 BCE the Mediterranean Sea had dried up and become a desert. Adjoining the island of Cyprus, toward the coast of Syria, 1,500 meters beneath the present sea level, he finds an ideal site for the plain, and presumably the city, of Plato's Atlantis. The characteristics and mythology of Cyprus serve as corroborative evidence, while the opening of the straits and consequent flooding of the Mediterranean provide for Atlantis's fall, Noah's Flood, and so forth.

TURKEY

Eberhard Zangger holds a Stanford University Ph.D. in geology and has written many articles on "geoarchaeology." His book *The Flood from Heaven* argues that Atlantis was really Troy.[59] It is a bold stroke to link two great Greek myths, and according to Zangger, Plato himself did not make the connection until he was well into writing the *Critias*.[60] That is why he left it unfinished and abandoned his intended Atlantean trilogy. Zangger's interest was aroused by his excavations at the Greek site of Tiryns. Corings revealed that between 1250 BCE and 1200 BCE, the city had been destroyed by a flash flood, probably due to an earthquake that changed the course of a river and left the settlement buried deep in mud. A close analysis of Plato's texts, which is the theme of much of Zangger's book, discredits the "conventional wisdom . . . that Atlantis was destroyed by a single catastrophe and subsequently drowned in the sea."[61] Solon's tale states that after the *Greek* warriors' triumphant return from their conquest of the Atlanteans (i.e., the Trojans), in one day and night earthquakes and floods caused them all to be swallowed up. It adds that Atlantis was destroyed "in like manner." This suggests a scenario very different from the usual one and compatible with local disasters at the end of the Bronze Age. Zangger goes on to explain Plato's words about the straits becoming henceforth unnavigable: it was because the Trojans' knowledge of how to navigate the Dardanelles and Bosporus was lost.[62]

"The Atlantis Mystery Solved" might have been the subtitle of any of the books treated in this chapter. It is, in fact, that of *The Sunken Kingdom* by Peter James, an ancient historian who has already been quoted. James deconstructs the mid-Atlantic and the Minoan hypotheses but allows that there must be some truth behind Plato's account. He credits Zangger with pointing him toward the Bosporus, whose entrance at the Straits of the Dardanelles was apparently known in antiquity as the *other* "Pillars of Hercules."[63] But rather than Troy, James finds clues in another lost city in ancient Lydia, now the west coast of Turkey. It was Tantalis, whose king was the mythical Tantalus and whose chronicler was not Plato but Pausanias. The stories of Tantalus and his kingdom are so similar to those of Atlas and Atlantis that they seem to have been versions of the same topos.[64] On an expedition in 1994 to the area around Smyrna, James found many remains and features that confirmed his suspicions. He concluded that Solon had gathered his material not in Egypt but there in Lydia. It concerned a Bronze Age civilization that had struggled with the Hellenic Greeks and probably perished in one of the frequent earthquakes. The mystery, it turns out, is nothing but an embellished, misattributed story, handed down in Critias's family and used by Plato in all innocence for his philosophical interpretation of history.[65]

THE CARIBBEAN

Most proponents of the Caribbean as the site of Atlantis have been influenced by Edgar Cayce's predictions that the lost continent would be found there, or else they accept dubious evidence such as the "Bimini Road." Two exceptions are Emilio Spedicato, a mathematics professor at the University of Bergamo, and Andrew Collins, an English psychical researcher and prolific author on ancient mysteries. Spedicato argues for the island of Hispaniola (now divided into Haiti and the Dominican Republic),[66] while Collins prefers Cuba.[67]

Spedicato's original essay of 1985 was a landmark in Atlantology because of its scientific integrity and introduction of a known agent of catastrophe, the asteroid-like "Apollo objects" that periodically hit the earth. The only adjustment he makes to Plato's text is to assume an error in transmission:[68] that the dimensions given for the irrigated plain (300 by 200 stadia) are those of the whole island, in this case Hispaniola. He finds two possible situations for the plain itself in the southern part of the present Dominican Republic and makes an ingenious suggestion for the original form of the capital city, now submerged: "The information about the ring structure of the central part of the capital of Atlantis and the colored stones carved there suggests indeed that the site had a coralline atoll structure, exposed when the onset of the glaciation lowered the level of the oceans."[69] But Spedicato does not seriously engage the question of what sort of civilization really existed in the Caribbean 12,000 years ago. His specialty is the impact and its consequences.

> We assume that the catastrophic event of Plato's story was the oceanic impact which terminated the last glaciation, as previously hypothesized. The great Atlantic tsunami devastated America, Europe and Africa. The ocean penetrated possibly for thousand of kilometers into the Amazonian basin and the Sahara. Immense devastation affected the Mediterranean region. No architectural structure, already weakened by the earthquake that preceded the tsunami, could have resisted. A tsunamic wave of the envisaged size would not only flatten a city, but carry away its debris, leaving virtually no trace. The deluge following the magmatic emission would have affected mostly Europe, northern Africa and west-central Asia, bringing havoc where the tsunami could not reach. Finally, the melting of ice and the subsequent elevation of the sea level by 60 meters would have changed the coastline configuration and affected the direction of currents, thereby justifying the claim that Atlantis had vanished and the ocean had become impassable.[70]

Collins and Spedicato acknowledge each other's researches, and neither is dogmatic about his proposed location for Atlantis. Collins's argument for Cuba over Hispaniola is that its western end accommodates a "fertile plain" of Plato's dimensions facing south and shielded by mountains. Before the post-glacial rise in sea levels, this would have included the Gulf of Batabanó, while the present Isola de la Juventud (Isle of Youth) would be a plausible site for the citadel.[71] Cultural evidence is harder to come by, but Collins does find Cuban cave paintings of humans baiting or capturing bulls, as Plato's Atlanteans did. He himself saw a series of petroglyphs in the Seven Caves of the Isle of Youth that looked like targets and comets.[72] As an afterthought, Collins speculates about the oversized, elongated skulls that have been found in Mexico and wonders whether they represent a strain of gigantism among the ruling classes. Donnelly had pointed out the practice of cranial deformation (squeezing and lengthening infant skulls) on both sides of the Atlantic as one of his many proofs of cultural diffusion. Collins had already written a highly speculative work about the "Watchers,"[73] a legendary people in the Kurdish region endowed naturally with such features. Now he wondered whether they could have crossed the Atlantic and set off a parallel set of legends.[74] A curious corroboration will appear below (see "Venezuela").

A recent study by three scientists[75] confirms the catastrophic theories of these Atlantologists, with convergent evidence from many sources pointing to a date of 13,000 years ago, or circa 11,000 BCE. Richard Firestone (a nuclear physicist on the staff of the Lawrence Berkeley National Laboratory) and his co-authors draw on a wealth of material evidence to propose the following scenario: 41,000 BP (Before Present), a supernova exploded close to Earth; 34,000 BP, the first shock wave reached the earth with radiation, comet, and asteroid impacts; 16,000 BP, the second shock wave arrived, with similar results; 13,000 BP, the "main event" occurred, with multiple impacts of cometlike objects hitting the Northern Hemisphere.[76] Besides creating the Carolina Bays and causing earthquakes, ground fires, climate change, magnetic oscillations, and increased radiation,[77] this event brought the Ice Age to an end, with all the associated changes in sea level, flooding, and so forth. If any prehistoric "Atlantis" was flourishing beforehand, this provides an incontrovertible cause of its end.

CENTRAL AMERICA

In their book *Atlantis in America*,[78] Ivar Zapp and George Erikson address the mystery of the stone spheres scattered around Central America. Zapp, Estonian by origin, has taught at the University of Costa Rica, where he lives; Erikson is a Santa Barbara publisher and anthropologist. They believe that the stone spheres, which are up to two meters in diameter, were the tools of an ancient "navigational university," set out in patterns corresponding with the stars and indicating routes to distant sites. The authors bombard the reader with questions: Who made these spheres? Were they descendants of the Atlanteans? Did they and the Mayan astronomers interact with people of other great megalithic sites in Peru, England, or Egypt? Their answers are implicit in the idea of Atlanteans as survivors of the cometary impact that ended the Ice Age, who in time built the stargazing and seafaring civilizations of the Americas. These people were not limited geographically, but a good candidate for Plato's site is the Diquis Delta of Costa Rica, where many of the spheres are found.[79] *Atlantis in America* tries to cover all possible bases, calling on astroarchaeology and on the "New Archaeology" of Graham Hancock and others (see below, under "Everywhere"). Zapp and Erickson distrust the view of the past defined by scientific authority and Eurocentric attitudes. Like many contemporary Atlantologists, they conclude by moralizing and warn that if we fail to live in harmony with the cosmos, as did those peoples of the Golden Age, our civilization will go the way of Atlantis.[80]

VENEZUELA

When Rafael Requena (1879–1946) published *Vestigios de la Atlántida,* he had risen through a medical, diplomatic, and political career to become private secretary of the autocratic president of Venezuela, Juan Vicente Gómez. His book illustrates a collection of prehistoric artifacts and human bones, which, as the title implies, are seen as relics from a great continent of which Venezuela was once a part.[81] Many of them come from the "Cerritos del Valle de Tacriqua," mounds built by a prehistoric race different in character from any tribes known since the discovery of America, and of a more advanced civilization. Requena tentatively accepts Scott-Elliot's theory of races (see chapter 4) and reproduces his map of a large Atlantic island,[82] but there is nothing occult about his own work. As a medical doctor, he was particularly struck by the number of skulls with depressed foreheads and bulging at the back. Although such cranial deformation was later practiced worldwide, Requena did not believe that primitives could have done it and argues that it was natural.[83] In support of this, he points out that prehistoric American horses, too, have depressed foreheads.[84]

BOLIVIA

J. M. Allen,[85] a specialist in maps and their interpretation, who has worked with the RAF, based his search for Atlantis on Plato's description and dimensions of a rectangular plain, facing south and sheltered to the north by mountains. In *Atlantis: The Andes Solution* he finds this in the Altiplano (Bolivian Plateau), the largest high-altitude plain in the world, which stretches from Lake Titicaca to Lake Poopo. According to Allen, it not only supplies the geographical requirements but even contains a canal system, an ancient city on a lake, a lush soil, deposits of metals, and an alloy of copper and gold that could well be Plato's orichalcum.[86] But since the South American continent obviously did not sink into the sea, Allen has to blame local floods and volcanic eruptions for Atlantis's destruction. A lack of visible traces, especially on the supposed island capital, is one weakness of his theory. Another, depending on how much faith one puts in comparative etymology, is his explanation of the name Atlantis. Apparently "Andes" is a corruption of *antis,* the native name for copper, while *atl* means water.[87] Mix together the two words (or, on a figurative level, bring together copper and water), and there you have it: "atl-antis"!

ANTARCTICA

Charles Hapgood (1904–1982), a history professor who taught at Springfield College (Massachusetts) and Keene State College (New Hampshire), did not mention Atlantis in his best-known book, *Maps of the Ancient Sea Kings.*[88] Nor, as is sometimes said, did Albert Einstein validate that book and its theories. (The great man wrote a foreword to Hapgood's earlier work, *Earth's Shifting Crust.*) However, Hapgood's theory is a favorite of the New Archaeology. It implies that some prehistoric seagoing people was able to visit and map the coast of Antarctica at a time when it was yet unglaciated, and that their maps survived from copy to copy up to the era of Columbus. Hapgood's evidence is early modern world maps that show a southern polar continent, which was later omitted as sailors failed to reach it, and especially the map of 1517 compiled by the Turkish pirate (or admiral) Piri Reis.

The Reis map, like Plato's Atlantis, requires selective interpretation if it is to serve as evidence for a prehistoric culture. The portion that supposedly shows Antarctica must be taken as accurate, while the gross inaccuracies in mapping South America and the Caribbean islands cannot be allowed to impugn the credibility of the whole. As for how Antarctica acquired its covering of ice, Hapgood's earlier book had argued that the Earth's crust periodically slips around like a loose orange peel, while the inner bulk of it continues to rotate around the same axis. This puts different places at the poles, or, from another viewpoint, the poles migrate, and wherever they are, an ice cap is liable to build up, as it has done over Antarctica. Therefore the mapping in question must have been done before the last slippage, which in turn explains the catastrophes that destroyed that worldwide maritime civilization.

In Hapgood's later life two Canadian librarians, Rand and Rose Flem-Ath, corresponded with him and developed his theories further in their own writings. *When the Sky Fell*[89] works out the consequences of a crustal shift around 9600 BCE that would have moved the Antarctic continent from a comparatively temperate to a polar position. The sky would have seemed to "fall" because the elevations of the stars would have changed;

but the change would not be uniform. Some locations, such as North America, were wrenched from one zone to another, killing off their large mammals, while Africa remained relatively stable.[90] "Lesser Antarctica, the site of Atlantis," they wrote, "was destroyed not only by earthquakes and floods, but also by a dire winter that completely covered the achievements of a lost civilization."[91]

EVERYWHERE

Some Atlantologists have resisted the temptation to fit Plato's account to a specific location. Instead, they read it as testimony to some highly sophisticated culture that has left its traces on a continental, even a global scale.

Mary Settegast, an independent scholar with high academic credentials, determined in *Plato Prehistorian* not to take the easy route of the Minoan-Thera hypothesis, but to treat Plato's dates seriously and see what was going on then. She writes:

> The Thera hypothesis was formed before seafarers were discovered in the Late Paleolithic Aegean, and before the magnitude of the loss of Greek lands to the postglacial seas was fully known. The extent of the mid-to-late ninth millennium spread of arrowheads was not yet recognized; the date of Jericho's fortifications had not been moved back to the last half of the ninth millennium; and the depth and complexity of Magdalenian culture, whose location in time and space closely parallels that of the European holdings of Plato's Atlantic empire, was still to be demonstrated.[92]

In 16,000 BCE, at the height of the Ice Age, a pan-European and uniform culture tamed horses, painted caves, and carved figures out of mammoth ivory. What else they did can only be guessed, especially as much of their territory (including their ports) has been lost to the rise in sea levels. Settegast sees this as the "Golden Age" of Greek myth and reckons that it subsisted until the mid-eighth millennium BCE. Then occurred the wars, invasions, earthquakes, and floods recorded in Plato's Atlantis story, ushering in the new epoch of the Neolithic Revolution. From the Mediterranean to the Caspian Sea "extraordinarily advanced communities emerged, seemingly out of nowhere," complete with hybrid grains, rectangular architecture, pottery, and even metalwork.[93]

Plato Prehistorian is a complex book that defies further summary here. Its treatment of Plato moves the subject and its problems to a new level. Previous attempts to plant a flag (typically in one's native land) and declare that one has found Plato's Atlantis seem quite provincial by comparison. But Settegast's careful scholarship kept her from taking the next step toward a fully global concept of prehistoric civilization.

A new phase of Atlantology began in 1990 when John Anthony West persuaded Robert Schoch, a Boston University professor, to give a geologist's opinion of the weathering of the Sphinx of Giza.[94] West, an independent Egyptologist and defender of astrology, had long pondered a statement by R. A. Schwaller de Lubicz that the Sphinx showed the results of water erosion.[95] After several visits to the site, Schoch confirmed that the monument and its enclosure (which are both carved out of the native rock) had all the signs of exposure to centuries of torrential rain. But as everyone knows, the Sphinx is in the Sahara Desert, where heavy rains have not fallen for thousands of years. This verdict placed the Sphinx's construction in an epoch before Egyptian dynastic civilization and well before the accepted date for the Sphinx and the Giza pyramids of circa 2500 BCE. Schoch's findings did not trouble his fellow geologists, who think on a scale of millions of years and are unconcerned with Egyptian history; but they greatly perturbed the Egyptologists, especially when in 1993 the West-Schoch theory was the center of a high-profile television documentary.[96] High emotions were generated and are still swirling around as other geologists propose alternative explanations.

Worse yet for the guardians of orthodoxy, the English journalist Graham Hancock then entered the field. Hancock had a reputation for adventurous reporting from war and famine zones and had already written a bestseller on the search for the Ark of the Covenant in Ethiopia.

The theme of his *Fingerprints of the Gods* and *Heaven's Mirror*[97] is that there was indeed high culture in prehistoric times, and that it was not just continental, like Mary Settegast's, but worldwide. Its preoccupations were the stars and the destiny of the soul; its greatest talents, ocean navigation and moving large stones. Its legacy is the megalithic monuments of northwest Europe, Egypt, Mexico, Peru, Bolivia, India, Cambodia, and the Pacific islands. Much more might be found if we could properly explore the coastal shelves that were submerged after the end of the Ice Age. Hancock himself made a start at this with the diving explorations chronicled in his book *Underworld.*[98]

Hancock's work coincided at several points with that of Robert Bauval, a Belgian engineer who had grown up in Egypt.[99] Bauval's crucial intuition was that the three pyramids of Giza were laid out to replicate the configuration of the three stars of Orion's Belt, and that to make the replication accurate, one has to go back to the position of those stars circa 10,500 BCE. At that time, too, the Sphinx was properly aligned with the constellation of Leo, giving it a date anterior even to what Schoch was willing to allow. Although in Bauval's opinion the pyramids themselves were not built for another 8,000 years, they followed the ancient layout. This means that the worldwide culture tracked by Hancock somehow preserved its traditions from the prehistoric into the historical period, which in Plato's version is exactly what the Egyptian priest told Solon. It also requires a selective treatment of evidence. Paul LaViolette (see next section) points out that compared to the stars they are supposed to reflect, the pyramids err by 10 percent in their relative separations and by 32 percent in the angular deviation of the small pyramid from the line joining the larger ones.[100] Whether this discrepancy affects Bauval's Orion theory depends on the "tolerances" or margins of error that any engineering project involves. In this case (assuming no mysterious technology or extraterrestrial help) one must imaginatively reconstruct the processes of (1) the naked eye observation of moving stars, (2) projecting a hand-sized diagram over thousands of feet, and (3) much later, building the pyramids themselves; then calculate the cumulative tolerances of each stage, which may well suffice to explain the deviations.

Among those attracted by the New Archaeology was the omnivorous philosopher Colin Wilson. He summarized its findings and theories in the first of his three contributions to Atlantology, *From Atlantis to the Sphinx,*[101] but the theme of the book was the question that has inspired Wilson's whole career as a writer and thinker: what are the latent possibilities of the human being? In this particular case, why do we seem to have lost capabilities and sensitivities that prehistoric cultures possessed? Wilson, like Hancock, had a global approach to the problem of lost civilization. It was more a case of a recapturing a lost state of mind, even of soul, evidenced by the mysterious and awe-inspiring monuments scattered all over the globe.

Wilson's next step was to collaborate with Rand Flem-Ath, Hapgood's correspondent, on *The Atlantis Blueprint.*[102] Flem-Ath had been studying the location of sacred sites all over the world and had found an extraordinary number of them at points that made simple fractional divisions of the Earth's circumference, calculated not from the present poles but from the poles as they were (according to the Hapgood theory) before the crustal shift of 9600 BCE. This grid of strategically placed sites was the "blueprint" of the title. Wilson writes:

> We believe that the 'great catastrophe' took place about 9,600 BC, and that the North Pole then moved [from Hudson Bay] to its present position. Which implies, of course, that Atlantis (or whatever we choose to call this earlier civilisation) existed for some time before 9,600 BC. How long before? It must surely have been a long time, since the Atlanteans established more than sixty sacred sites all over the world.[103]

That was not all. Some of the sacred sites, such as Baalbek, turned out to be more closely aligned with an even earlier position of the North Pole, namely in the Yukon nearly 100,000 years ago. Also some of the placements, not explainable through the grid, turned out to divide the circumference of the globe through the Golden Section. With so many possible alignments relative to two or three poles and to the Great Pyramid, the reader may feel that it was too easy to find a rationale for almost any location.

To go along with the suggestion of civilization before the Magdalenian era (ca. 18,000–10,000 BP) and even before Cro-Magnon Man, *The Atlantis Blueprint* printed a letter from Charles Hapgood with the teasing statement: "Furthermore, in recent exciting discoveries I believe I have convincing evidence of a whole cycle of civilization in America and in Antarctica, suggesting advanced levels of science that may go back 100,000 years."[104] Two months later, Hapgood was hit by a car and died, so his evidence remained unpublished. But Wilson was on the track of it. He describes in his autobiography how, while writing *The Atlantis Blueprint,* he contacted an unnamed "retired New England academic" who said that it was he who had convinced Hapgood of the immense age of civilization. Wilson says: "When I asked him why he thought so, he mentioned two reasons. First: that the measurements of the earth prove that ancient man knew its exact size long before the Greeks. Second: that there is evidence that Neanderthal man was far more intelligent than we give him credit for."[105]

Because his co-author excluded this theory from *The Atlantis Blueprint,*[106] Wilson expounded it himself in *Atlantis and the Kingdom of the Neanderthals.*[107] Like its predecessors, the book is a lively summary of discoveries and writings, ranging in this case from the consciousness of plants to Goethe's color theory, from Rennes-le-Château to Hapgood's psychical researches. When eventually the Neanderthals come on stage, they are credited with a handful of anomalous artifacts that long predate *Homo sapiens* and with a "cosmological canon" involving precise knowledge of astronomical and geographic measurements. Wilson surmises that the Neanderthals may have realized one of the latent human potentials, a talent for calculation that only survives today in mathematical prodigies. But of the kingdom promised by the title, there is no sign.

Several of the authors in this section have strayed across the frontier that separates the rational from the occult. Colin Wilson is one of the most popular authors on the latter subject; John Anthony West has written a defense of astrology and leads tours to "sacred Egypt"; Graham Hancock now writes about experiences with entheogenic drugs; Robert Bauval, while perhaps not a believer, attaches his pyramid theory to concepts of astral immortality; Robert Schoch is now concerned with psychical research. The New Archaeology has a New Age aura about it. But the efforts, arguments, and theories that led to the works surveyed here do not rest on revealed, channeled, or traditional teachings. Their prime material is the monuments themselves; their prime intent, to understand why they are as they are. The only explanation that satisfies them is that prehistoric peoples experienced states of being incomprehensible through the materialist paradigm. The reasonable course, then, is to try a different paradigm.

ALLEGORICAL

Paul LaViolette, a systems science Ph.D. from Portland State University, based his theory of Atlantis on cosmogony and the role of the center of our galaxy. He argues that the naming of the zodiacal constellations contains clues to the exact location of this center, which is invisible even to telescopes, and that the chosen symbols imply an understanding of how the galactic center is continually spewing out newly created matter[108]—a controversial position, for LaViolette rejects the Big Bang theory of creation and the hypothesis that the galactic center is a black hole. This creative process periodically causes "superwaves" that impact the solar system, causing catastrophes recorded in myths from all around the world. LaViolette attributes the end of the last Ice Age to the arrival of such a superwave and assembles a large body of scientific data to support his theory. Although the process of deglaciation lasted several thousand years, the period around 12,700 BP (10,700 BCE) keeps coming up as significant, both in the data and in mythology. Among other events, it marks the unexplained extinction of large mammals in North America and the end of the "Age of Virgo" (see chapter 12). This is close to Bauval and Hancock's "First Time" of 10,500 BCE and to Firestone's date of cometary impact around 11,000 BCE.

As for Atlantis, LaViolette rejects the Atlantic, Thera, and Antarctic hypotheses and reads the Egyptian priest's story as a double allegory, one part of which Plato put into the *Timaeus* and the other into the *Critias*. The allegory in the *Critias* is "a highly sophisticated theory about the nature of subatomic matter and how it first came into being out of the primordial ether."[109] Unfortunately, it requires a knowledge of atomic physics to understand it, as well as an open mind about some of the basic presuppositions of that science. For instance, LaViolette revives the unfashionable concept of the ether and holds that at galactic centers, matter condenses out of some prematerial, etheric state. Like the New Archaeologists' speculations about prehistoric people's consciousness, this kind of thinking collides head-on with the materialist paradigm, from whose point of view it is all occult nonsense.

LaViolette's interpretation of the *Timaeus* is not so demanding. Plato's text states that after the defeat of the Titans, Poseidon received Atlantis as his only land territory. LaViolette continues:

It also states that the Atlantean civilization was spawned through Poseidon's union with Clito, a mortal maiden who lived within the earth, that is, through the union of the water and earth elements. Water becomes earth-like when it solidifies to form ice and it forms continent sized masses when it forms an ice sheet. One might then speculate that Atlantis is none other than the ice sheet that once covered North America.[110]

This cleverly satisfies Plato's location, size, and date of Atlantis. The Atlanteans' attack on Europe becomes an allegory for the "floods of glacial meltwater that the ice sheets periodically released from their surfaces. . . . Like Atlantis in the myth, the ice sheets eventually 'disappeared into the depths of the sea' as their meltwater coursed to the oceans and with their wasting, they left behind a shoal of mud and rock, or what some geologists call 'the drift'."[111] The date given to Solon of around 9600 BCE coincides with the warming at the end of the Younger Dryas period, when the glacier melting reached its peak. LaViolette does not speculate about who could invent such an allegory of events that took place 9,000 years before. He assumes that some prehistoric tradition of advanced thought, analogous to Hancock and Bauval's First Time, survived the millennia to resurface in dynastic Egypt.

No such assumptions are needed by two other allegorical readings of Plato's Atlantis story: those of John Michell and Ernest McClain. But even though they do not require advanced physics, they rest on the authors' elaborate mathematical or musical structures, to which no summary can do justice. Michell (1933–2009), an English philosopher and student of anomalous phenomena, interpreted Plato's numerical myths in *The Dimensions of Paradise*.[112] They are a part of Plato's writing that classical scholars have avoided, but which Michell believed to be the esoteric core of the philosopher's work, never fully explained because they came from a secret tradition (probably Pythagorean). In the case of Atlantis, Plato "believed no doubt that it was based on fact and that it came, as he said, from ancient Egyptian temple records. But the details of its dimensions and so on were clearly of his own devising. To existing traditions of the lost city he attached a mathematical allegory, designed to illustrate the crucial importance of number and true reckoning in all human affairs."[113] Plato's disciples were expected to take up the challenge by constructing the geometrical figures from his hints and calculating their numerical consequences. They had, after all, enrolled in an academy whose portal bore the motto *Let None Ignorant of Geometry Enter.*

One of Michell's lifelong concerns was the defense of traditional measures such as the mile, the foot, and the inch, with their duodecimal system and their links, via the sacred numbers, to cosmic measures (e.g., 5,040 miles as the combined radii of the earth and the moon[114]). He shared Plato's conviction that society can function harmoniously only if it respects the traditional canon of number. Michell finds Plato's lesson to this effect in the contrast between two imaginary city-states: Magnesia with its 5,040 inhabitants, described in the *Laws,* and Atlantis. Magnesia is the ideal city, like the New Jerusalem in the Book of Revelation, first conceived in circular form as a Platonic Idea, then brought down to earth as a square. Atlantis is its antithesis, the city that fell because it was "subtly incorrect, a close imitation but a travesty of the ideal, constructed from sacred numbers misapplied."[115] The misapplication in question was the use of the decimal system. Whereas Magnesia and the City of Revelation divide by 12s, everything in Atlantis divides by 5s and 10s, starting with the five pairs of Poseidon's descendants and going on with the 100 statues of nereids around the temple, the division of the plain into plots of 100 square stades, and so on. When the diligent Platonist actually works out the details, the figures do not add up, and the geometry is not exact. Consequently, as Michell says of the imaginary Atlanteans, "Their cumbersome number system and the ambiguities in their geometry and land measuring would have caused minor grievances which would grow ever more irritating as time went on. In the original formula and foundation plan of Atlantis lay the seeds of its eventual destruction."[116]

An utterly different reading of Plato's intentions inspired *The Pythagorean Plato* by the American musicologist Ernest McClain.[117] He treats the same numerical myths as Michell, but interprets them according to a musical scheme, derived from his earlier studies of sacred texts such as the Rig Veda and the Hebrew Bible. McClain finds that ancient peoples (or the intellectual elite among them) were obsessed by the problems of tuning. While practical musicians do this to the best of their ability, theorists want to quantify the intervals, and this produces endless difficulties and requires ever-increasing numerical matrices. (The *Well-Tempered Clavier* of J. S. Bach is the best-known monument to the problem.) "Atlantis," McClain writes, "was a sophisticated entertainment for Pythagoreans only—if my story is 'the likely one.' For the musically innocent, it is and must remain merely a Platonic fairy tale, incomprehensibly loaded with absolutely meaningless numerical detail."[118] To the Pythagorean, on the other hand, every number can be represented as a specific tone, and Plato's numbers in particular belong to an arcane dialog concerning perfect intonation. In the Atlantis myth, the generations descending from Poseidon imply progressively larger numbers for the definition of the octave (the larger ones allowing for finer divisions within it).[119] The Atlantean plain with its mountains and its network of canals is nothing but a fanciful image derived from a diagram that plots the powers of 3 along one axis (musically, intervals of a fifth; philosophically, the divine strain in the Atlanteans) and powers of 5 along another axis (musically, intervals of a major third; philosophically, the human strain). As one develops the diagram following Plato's numbers, the powers of 5 come to predominate, with consequences similar to those of which John Michell complained: the system gets so badly out of tune that a god has to intervene. And this leads to the famous ending of the *Critias*: "[Zeus] accordingly summoned all the gods to his own most glorious abode, which stands at the centre of the universe and looks out over the whole realm of change, and when they had assembled addressed them as follows."

McClain must be the only Atlantologist who accepts this as the intended end of the dialogue: "Plato's unfinished last sentence—a sentence that could never have been finished anyway, and addressed to an audience wholly familiar with his mathematical metaphors—deserves to be studied as the best punch line a musical comedy ever had."[120]

NOWHERE

After this parade, the most rational view of all might be that Plato's Atlantis never existed, either on Earth or in his own mind. This has long been the position of classical scholars, and it continues to generate books, though such a dampening attitude has little audience appeal. Two works of this genre seem to me outstanding, one from a scientific and the other from a literary point of view.

The first is by Zdeněk Kukal (born 1932), of the Central Geological Survey of Prague, who published in 1978 a book-length study of "Atlantis in the Light of Modern Research." Six years later, the academic journal *Earth-Science Reviews* devoted a special issue to a revised version in English.[121] Kukal was able to take advantage of advances in the earth sciences that followed the study of cores, plate tectonics, and paleomagnetism, and of publications in east European as well as Western languages. He was also a good writer, sympathetic to his subject, and never scathing about the theories of other Atlantologists even when refuting them.

Before embarking on a tour of proposed sites, Kukal treats the question of what could be left of an advanced civilization overcome by seawater 11,500 years ago. The answer is very little, due to chemical and biological degradation, and that extremely difficult to find under the sediment on the ocean floor. He dashes one hope after another. The Atlantic islands are not the remnants of large sunken islands; in geological terms they are young and grew up from the ocean floor as volcanic cones.[122] The Guanches, indigenous blue-eyed people of the Canary Islands, were not Atlanteans but Berbers, probably taken there as slaves by Arabs or even Carthaginians.[123] The freshwater diatoms found in the Atlantic sediments are not the result of ancient freshwater lakes but were blown there from Africa.[124] The Mediterranean was a desert, yes, but 6 million years ago.[125] Recent geological evidence is all against the possibility that a large meteorite struck the Atlantic or the Mediterranean around 11,500 BP.[126] During the same period, sea level was between 20 and 50 meters lower than today, but although this allowed broad areas in the Mediterranean to emerge and eventually be flooded, the process was gradual, not overnight.[127]

Despite his efficient demolition of these and other pillars of the Atlantologists, Kukal still wants something to be found that answers to Plato's myth. He writes:

> Atlantis, as described by Plato, has never been found by anyone anywhere, and it seems that it never will be. But it was the Mediterranean, with its ancient civilizations, its conflicts, and its tectonic activity, that inspired Plato. It is the Mediterranean, with its sunken harbors and cities, that can still reveal many surprises. Many parts of its floor remain to be explored. But even if we do not find Plato's Atlantis, we may well find a pseudo-Atlantis, some other

ancient civilization competing with the Phoenicians, the Cretans, or the Carthaginians, or, later, even with the Greeks and the Romans. We may even find the remains of some ancient monuments that were destroyed "*in a single day and night of misfortune.*"[128]

To those who deny any historical reality to the Atlantis story, there remains the fascination of how it has inspired philosophers, novelists, earnest seekers, and cranks. The science-fiction writer L. Sprague de Camp (1907–2000) reviewed this motley assembly in his *Lost Continents,*[129] with erudition and wit seldom equaled in the field. He covers the occultists and Theosophists, Donnelly and the post-Donnellians, the pseudoscientists like Hoerbiger and Velikovsky, and Atlantis fiction, on which he was an unrivaled expert. The main shortcoming is that a book written in 1954 cannot include later literature and films.[130]

De Camp was a complete skeptic but, like Kukal, a sympathetic one, with a novelist's appreciation of eccentrics and "bumptious amateurs." He writes of the Atlantis myth:

> Most of all it strikes a responsive chord by its sense of the melancholy loss of a beautiful thing, a happy perfection once possessed by mankind. Thus it appeals to that hope that most of us carry around in our unconscious, a hope so often raised and as often disappointed, for assurance that somewhere, some time, there can exist a land of peace and plenty, of beauty and justice, where we, poor creatures that we are, could be happy. In this sense Atlantis—whether we call it Panchaia, the Kingdom of God, Oceana, the Classless Society, or Utopia—will always be with us.[131]

This survey of the rational Atlantologists deserves a rational conclusion. The need to theorize and explain is a psychological trait that can lead, at the extreme, to a dissociation from reality and a humorless conviction of one's own special status. Atlantologists since Olaf Rudbeck must have finished their books with a serene smile and the certainty that they, and they alone, had put a stake through the heart of the matter. The fact that it now looks like a pincushion gives one pause. But every one of these authors has found something of value and contributed in some way to knowledge of the distant human past. Field researchers like Jürgen Spanuth and Eberhard Zangger may be wrong about Atlantis, but they have taught us a lot about the Bronze Age. Library addicts like Ignatius Donnelly have ransacked obscure sources and scientific journals that the ordinary reader would never find and shaped them into something readable. The New Archaeology draws attention to mysterious sites and arouses curiosities that the old archaeology cannot satisfy. All this is highly educational and entertaining, irrespective of any theories that may come trundling behind. As someone has pointed out, Plato's Atlantis story has turned out like the buried treasure in Aesop's fable "The Farmer and his Sons": there was no treasure buried in his vineyard, but in digging for it the sons so improved the soil that they raised a bumper crop.

TWO

The French Esoteric Tradition

———————— ✳ ————————

DELISLE DE SALES AND THE AGE OF THE EARTH

The later eighteenth century was a heady time for the French intellectual community. With the completion of Diderot's *Encyclopédie,* it seemed that a new universe was opened up for research and speculation. Science was no longer a slave to biblical authority, which Delisle de Sales (1741–1816) in his *Philosophie de la nature* (Philosophy of Nature, 1769) called "the most repugnant of philosophical systems."[1] Although that kind of sentiment got him jailed and his work publicly burned, there was no suppressing the impetus behind it. Like those other one-man encyclopedists, Antoine Court de Gébelin and Charles Dupuis, Delisle saw it as his task to recast the whole of knowledge in Enlightenment mode, but without falling into the trap of atheism.

While Court de Gébelin hung his universal history on the peg of language and Dupuis on that of sun worship, Delisle's interest was in the human being as a product of uncreated and eternal Nature. He writes: "It seems to me that the Supreme Being cannot create anything, just as he cannot annihilate anything, because it is absurd for nothingness to be the subject of his work or the result of his power. I think that matter has existed from all time; but its eternity, being successive, should not be confused with that of God which is not so."[2] However, this did not make the earth eternal. Delisle was not sure exactly how it had come into being, but one could calculate its age from astronomical data. Like several of our authors, he assumed that the earth's equator had originally coincided with the ecliptic, making the polar axis perpendicular to the plane of its orbit around the sun. Under those conditions there would have been no differentiation of seasons. Since the present angle of inclination is 23½°, and astronomers like Dortous de Mairan had ascertained that it was steadily diminishing, the earth must be at least 140,000 years old: already a shocking idea to most of Delisle's contemporaries. He even suggested that there might have been more than one such cycle of axial change, and that 100,000 cycles are no less probable than a single one.[3]

This leads Delisle to a meditation on human devolution and periodic catastrophe, both of which will be leitmotifs of our study.

It is probable that when our world began to be peopled by men, the ecliptic coincided with the equator; thus nature was at the height of its strength; our intelligence flourished on account of the excellence of our organs; and the men of those ages, far from being children in comparison to ourselves, were such that for all our enlightenment and pride, our fine men are nothing but children beside them.

I assume that the revolutions of the globe annihilated the greater part of the human race; the wretched survivors of this catastrophe would have felt all the more need to live in society; by gathering together they sought refuge from the menacing heavens, and there was no state of nature.[4]

FABRE D'OLIVET'S PHILOSOPHICAL HISTORY

Among those attracted by Delisle's philosophy of nature was the young Antoine Fabre d'Olivet (1767–1825), later to become one of the patriarchs of French occultism. Born to a well-to-do Protestant family, Fabre d'Olivet had been leading the life of a dilettante in drama, poetry, music, politics, and history. With the loss of his fortune after the French Revolution, he was reduced to literary hackwork. Delisle employed him to catalogue his library of 35,000 books,[5] then Fabre d'Olivet set out to reduce the sage's philosophy to something accessible to young ladies. The result was *Lettres à Sophie sur l'histoire* (Letters to Sophie on history, 1801), which was dedicated to Napoleon.

Sophie, imagined as the writer's sister, is first plunged into the mysteries of cosmogony. She learns of the primal element of fire and the twin forces, centrifugal and centripetal, that activate it.[6] She reads of how the sun emanated the earth, then, as our planet cooled, how it became covered with water. After the waters retreated, life was able to begin on the high mountains, though exactly how this happened, neither Delisle nor Fabre d'Olivet cared to explain. Humanity emerged first on the Caucasus and Atlas ranges, the latter being the original home of the Atlanteans.[7] As for Plato's Atlantis, says Fabre d'Olivet, no one agrees where it was. Some say Sweden (obviously thinking of Rudbeck); Bailly puts it in Spitzbergen and under the polar ice.[8] Court de Gébelin says that its remains are in the region of Sardinia and Corsica, and Fabre d'Olivet sensibly concludes: "Although that is not quite convincing, let's adopt it, rather than making up a new system."[9]

At this point of his career, Fabre d'Olivet seems to have shared Delisle's vague faith in a universe obedient to natural principles but designed by a noninterfering deity. This was to change quite suddenly between 1801 and 1805 as he underwent a psychological crisis, leading to a long period of retirement from public life. His biographer, Léon Cellier, has found hints that he received a visitation by a woman he had loved but who had died young, and that he practiced Mesmerism in the attempt to maintain contact with her spirit. Certainly Fabre d'Olivet's wife, whom he married shortly after this, acted as a mesmeric medium. Others have suggested that he had access to a secret tradition (see chapter 6), perhaps through Elias Boctor, an Egyptian colleague at the Ministry of War, where he now had an office job. Whatever the cause, he emerged from his retreat as an initiate and a theosopher, independent of any sect or master, and writing of metaphysical mysteries with absolute self-confidence. Fabre d'Olivet's subsequent work would address the esoteric wisdom latent in sacred writings such as the Golden Verses of Pythagoras, the Book of Genesis, and the newly translated Hindu scriptures, as well as speculative music and universal history. His work puts him among the most influential proponents of the *philosophia perennis,* the perennial philosophy that is as old as humanity and ever reborn in different guises.

Fabre d'Olivet's universal history is summed up accurately, if ungenerously, by Auguste Viatte, the historian of French illuminism.

He aspires to reconstruct the whole history of the world, not just that of Paradise; we drift off into improbable realms. On his own authority he invents a most extravagant succession of empires and dynasties, with just a few facts provided by Delisle de Sales or the oriental epics. He goes back to the age of fables, after an alteration in the axis of the earth had caused the ruin of Atlantis. At that time, the White race was vegetating around the North Pole; the Blacks were dominating Africa and oppressing part of the Yellow race; those of the Red race who had escaped from the catastrophe were living out of sight on the highest mountains of America. We will not go into detail about the quarrels between Boreans, Sudeens, and Atlanteans, but if the reader will turn to the "Philosophic History of the Human Race," he will find there the origins of religions, castes, the arts, and writing. He will also notice the Hindu coloring that Fabre d'Olivet gives to his hypotheses.[10]

The *Histoire philosophique du genre humain* (Philosophical history of the human race) is indeed an ambitious work, purporting to trace the influence of three metaphysical principles: Providence, whose aim is the perfection of all beings; Destiny, whose law is necessity and which links cause and effect in the natural world; and the Will of Man, which can interrupt and change Destiny and, if he chooses, align itself with Providence.

From the start, Fabre d'Olivet dismisses the literal reading of Genesis in favor of the "sacred writers of the Chinese, Hindus, Persians, Chaldeans, Egyptians, Greeks, Etruscans, and our ancestors the Celts . . . for all, without exception, attribute to the earth an antiquity incomparably greater than this cosmogony."[11] That antiquity allowed him to enlarge on the prehistoric evolution and encounters of the four races, distinguished by color, into which the anthropology of his time divided the human family. The first of these was the Yellow race. Fabre d'Olivet has little to say about it except that "a few hordes of wandering Tartars, ancient *débris* of the Yellow Race," remained on the banks of the Yellow River to form the basis for the later Chinese Empire.[12] In an earlier work he gives a hint of their past by mentioning that the Chinese language is the most ancient of all, and that its people were "separated from others by the result of a physical catastrophe which had happened to the globe."[13] That, however, cannot have been the catastrophe of Atlantis, for according to the *Histoire philosophique,* that affected the second, Red race. Fabre d'Olivet calls them the Austral (from Auster, the South Wind) because their homeland of Atlantis was in the south, and thus describes their fate.

> This first race . . . to which, perhaps, belonged the primitive name of Atlantean, had perished utterly in the midst of a terrible deluge, which, covering the earth, had ravaged it from one pole to the other and submerged the immense and magnificent island which this race had inhabited beyond the seas. At the moment when this island had disappeared with all the peoples which inhabited it, the Austral Race held the universal empire and dominated the Sudeen which was hardly beyond a state of barbarism, and was still in the childhood of social state. The deluge which annihilated it was so violent that it left only a confused memory in the minds of the Sudeens who survived there.[14]

Fabre d'Olivet adds that only the Egyptians, as testified by Solon in Plato's Atlantean texts, preserved a true account of this people and their vanished land.

After the fall of the Austral Race, it was the turn of the Sudeen or Black race. Their empire came to dominate Africa, Asia, and much of Europe, whereupon they too confusingly styled themselves "Atlanteans." The name meant "Masters of the Universe," for, as Fabre d'Olivet explains, "this well-known name is composed of two words *atta,* the master, the ancient, the father, and *lant* universal space."[15] The monuments of the Sudeens are to be seen in "the enormous constructions of Mahabalipuram, in the caverns of Ellora, the temples of Isthakar, the ramparts of the Caucasus, the pyramids of Memphis, [and] the excavations of Thebes in Egypt."[16]

Last came the Borean or White race, whose homeland (obediently following Bailly—see chapter 1) was the Arctic region. What most distinguished them, in Fabre d'Olivet's eyes, was their providential realization of two essential truths: the immortality of the soul, and the existence of God. With the confidence of an eyewitness, he describes the Boreans' descent from the North, driven by overpopulation, and their long rivalry with the Sudeens.[17] After centuries-long conflicts, the Sudeens were vanquished and confined to Africa, while the Boreans, now taking the name of Celts, occupied the whole of Europe.

The Celts, ruled by visionary priestesses called Voluspas, had contracted the bad habit of human sacrifice, and when a powerful Druid named Ram tried to abolish it, he was forced into exile. He and his companions went East, gathering forces and conquering as they went, and eventually reached India, then the seat of a decaying Atlantean (i.e., Sudeen) empire. Ram easily mastered the subcontinent and founded there the first Universal Empire of the Borean Race. The Greeks would later celebrate him as Dionysus; the Hindus as Rama, an avatar of Vishnu and the hero of the epic Ramayana. An even better-known monument to his achievement is the zodiac, whose twelve signs Fabre d'Olivet reads as a symbolic biography of Ram, beginning with his eponymous heraldic beast.

Fabre d'Olivet dates the founding of Ram's empire to about 6700 BCE and the beginning of its decline to 3200 BCE. Thanks to Ram's successor, Krishna, it survived until 2100 BCE.[18] Eventually India fell to the

Assyrian invaders, and its Supreme Pontiff was banished to the mountains of Tibet.[19] Humanity, having refused the ways of Providence, was left in the hands of Destiny until the fifteenth century BCE, when Providence sent it three extraordinary men: Orpheus among the Thracians, Moses among the Egyptians, and Fo-Hi, later called Buddha, among the Hindus.[20] Subsequent events, fascinating as they are, do not concern us here.

Fabre d'Olivet played fast and loose with the historical facts even as these were known in his own day. Until *Histoire philosophique* reaches historical times, it reads like fantasy fiction, with anecdotal scenes and characters unknown to history emerging to change the course of nations. Among other curiosities we learn that Ram's rise to power was due to his having cured an epidemic of elephantiasis through mistletoe. No less surprising is the cause of the "Schism of Irshou" that eventually brought down the Universal Empire: it was the discovery that the musical system was based on two principles, not one. This led stage by stage to rival cults worshiping the male and female principles.

Where did Fabre d'Olivet get his information? Partly from wide reading, not least in Delisle de Sales's library, and from a lively interest in current publications, especially those of the British school of Calcutta (publishers of *Asiatic Researches*). But the rest I can only suppose came from a vivid imagination, which he took, rightly or wrongly, to be a window into the actual past. Fabre d'Olivet's biographer, Léon Cellier, writes of how all his works mingled scholarship with fiction or even mild fraud, as in the case of the anthology of Troubadour poetry into which he slipped some poems of his own. After a long analysis of Fabre d'Olivet's deceits and psychology, Cellier sums up his character: "Two essential traits are a constant feature of this strange mind: the paradoxical alliance of a maniacal attention to detail with enthusiasm; and a prodigious erudition at the service of an unconfined imagination."[21]

SAINT-YVES D'ALVEYDRE'S SYNARCHIC HISTORY

After Fabre d'Olivet's death in 1825, his fantastic panorama of prehistory was shelved, along with his other works, by all but a few disciples. One of these, Virginie Faure, had known him in his final years when he was heading a mysterious quasi–Masonic order.[22] Decades later she settled on the Channel Island of Jersey, home to the French exiles who had opposed Napoleon III. Thither around 1865 came the young Joseph Alexandre Saint-Yves (1842–1909), recently demobilized and working as a private tutor. Through friendship with her grandson, he met the personable Madame Faure. Fluent in many languages, her memory undimmed, she opened to him her collection of books, and maybe even manuscripts, by her master.

The encounter was decisive. The reading of Fabre d'Olivet's historical work would orient Saint-Yves to esoteric studies and become the basis for his own central project, a universal history called *Mission des Juifs* (Mission of the Jews), which he published in 1884. In this as in other ways, Saint-Yves seems to have replayed Fabre d'Olivet's program with his own political and Christocentric agenda. The resemblance began with their chosen names. Just as Antoine Fabre dropped his Christian name and added his mother's surname of d'Olivet, with its suggestion of superior birth, J. A. Saint-Yves became on his title pages "Saint-Yves d'Alveydre." Both men wrote universal histories, esoteric expositions of the Book of Genesis, and treatises on speculative music. They were both competent musicians and composers and believed themselves to be poets and dramatists of stature. They were sure that sacred alphabets such as Hebrew and Sanskrit concealed esoteric wisdom. While neither of them traveled beyond Europe, India and its philosophy fascinated them. Both aspired to high political influence: Fabre d'Olivet claimed to have played a key role in the French Revolution and became convinced that Napoleon nurtured a personal vendetta against him, while Saint-Yves was a friend of Earl Lytton, the Viceroy of India, and through him addressed Queen Victoria. Both practiced magnetism and had a relationship with the departed spirit of a lover or wife. And incidentally, both relied on their wives for support, though

Saint-Yves' wife, a Russian aristocrat, was much richer than Madame d'Olivet, who ran a private girls' school.

Whereas Fabre d'Olivet used world history to demonstrate the workings of his three principles, Providence, Destiny, and Will, Saint-Yves used it to support his ideal political system that he called Synarchy—the opposite of Anarchy. Later uses of the term, and indeed Saint-Yves' own writings, make Synarchy a complicated and controversial matter, connected with conspiracy theory, accusations of fascism, globalization, and so on. In its simplest form, it represents government through the equilibrium of three separate powers, respectively controlling the Economy, Legislation (including the military), and Culture (including religion and education). It is international in scale and run by an esoterically minded elite.[23] In a way, Synarchy reaffirms the ideally cooperative but separate roles of the three "twice-born" castes of Hinduism: merchants (*vaishyas*), warriors and princes (*kshatriyas*), priests and teachers (*brahmins*), which we will have reason to revisit later.

Saint-Yves would boast: "I have drowned the eclecticism of Fabre d'Olivet in my universalist and rational Christianity."[24] The curious thing is that such a strong-minded and self-important figure should have accepted Fabre d'Olivet's version of prehistory wholesale, with every semblance of belief in it. This is what Saint-Yves did in the early chapters of *Mission des Juifs,* often quoting *Histoire philosophique* verbatim and in general paraphrasing it, without indicating his source. We meet again the four colored races, dominating the world in turn; the Celts and the exile of Ram the Druid; his conquests and Universal Empire in India, which, following Saint-Yves' agenda, becomes the first Synarchic government; the origin of the zodiac; the 3,500 years of peace until 3200 BCE, when the Schism of Irshou established the worship of the female principle; the coming of Krishna, Fo-Hi, and the Egyptian mysteries; the invasions of the Assyrians and the exodus of Abraham from their territory. With this last episode, Saint-Yves diverges from Fabre d'Olivet to pursue the restitution of Synarchy by Moses, its renovation by Jesus Christ, and its fortunes in historical periods.

Saint-Yves paid dearly for his unacknowledged borrowing, for when *Mission des Juifs* was reviewed, he was accused of plagiarism. His feeble defense was that since Fabre d'Olivet's work was regarded with disdain and ridicule, he did not want to attract a similar reaction.[25] But the incident, coinciding as it did with a scurrilous fictionalization of his career by a jilted lover,[26] put paid to his political ambitions.

I have written elsewhere about how Saint-Yves, having no interest in Atlantis as such, created his own lost land of Agarttha.[27] This supposedly exists underground somewhere in Asia, and its large, technologically advanced population is ruled by a Sovereign Pontiff who unites in himself the offices of high priest and king. Saint-Yves' account of Agarttha is deceptively called *Mission de l'Inde* (Mission of India). The book was already printed in 1886 when he decided to withdraw it, and all but two copies were destroyed. Consequently the Agartthian myth did not enter public consciousness until 1910, after the author's death, when his disciple Papus obtained a copy from Saint-Yves' stepson and arranged for its publication.

The source of Saint-Yves' knowledge of Agarttha, setting aside possible literary influences, was his own "astral traveling." He makes no secret of this in the book. What his motives were, both for writing and suppressing it, are hard to fathom unless we accept that in some altered state of consciousness he saw what he describes and transcribed it as faithfully as he could. He certainly did not have sufficient sense of humor to put the whole thing over as a practical joke. I do not know whether to feel sorrier for a person afflicted with such a "wild talent," or for those (see chapter 6) who believe on his authority in Agarttha, its underground railways, its necromantic practices, and its sinister "King of the World."

EDOUARD SCHURÉ'S *GREAT INITIATES*

The French occultists of the fin-de-siècle did not hesitate to follow Saint-Yves in adopting Fabre d'Olivet's prehistoric scenario. For example, Stanislas de Guaïta (1861–1897), in his introductory book on occult

science, *Au seuil du mystère* (On the threshold of the mystery, 1886), recommends *Mission des Juifs* for its updating of Fabre d'Olivet, then adds
his own authority to the same story of Ram, "who conquered a third of
the world, only to pacify it; then, this goal achieved, renounced the sword,
the crown, the standard of the Ram, . . . and, wearing the tiara of the universal Sovereign Pontiff, raised the oriflamme of the Lamb, hieroglyph of
sacerdotal authority."[28] Readers of Saint-Yves would recognize his characteristic vocabulary here.

Fabre d'Olivet's prehistory found its most effective proponent in
Edouard Schuré (1841–1929), author of the bestseller *Les grands initiés*
(The great initiates, 1889). Its chapters treat Rama, Krishna, Hermes,
Moses, Orpheus, Pythagoras, Plato, and Jesus. The big news, to the unini-
tiated, was that Jesus was not unique but one of a series of enlightened
beings, although, as Jesus was last in the line, Schuré considers his message
the most relevant to our times. To anyone familiar with the Renaissance
idea of the *prisca theologia* (the ancient theology common to Jews and
Gentiles), or the Islamic prophetic cycle that includes three of these initiates (Hermes, Moses, and Jesus), the only novelty is the inclusion of the
two Hindu avatars, Rama and Krishna.

In Schuré's explanation of the origin of races we hear hints of cosmogonic theories and a definite vote in favor of multiple human origins.

> The four races which cover the globe at the present time are the
> offspring of different earths and zones. Successive creations, slow
> elaborations of the earth in travail, the continents emerged from the
> seas at considerable intervals of time, which the ancient priests of
> India called interdiluvian cycles. Stretching over thousands of years,
> each continent gave birth to its own flora and fauna, crowned by a
> human race of different colour.[29]

Schuré follows Fabre d'Olivet's sequence of dominant races. Like the
other authors mentioned here, he found nothing to say about the Yellow
race, but began with the Red (Austral) race, which occupied Plato's

Atlantis, a "southern continent now sunk beneath the waves." He continues with the story of the White (Borean) race, the Celts, Druids, Ram, the zodiac, and so on, following Fabre d'Olivet, but with more picturesque detail that increases as the book proceeds.

If Schuré has a virtue from our point of view, it is in clarifying the status of ancient Egypt and its remains: "The first Egyptian civilization, almost as old as the very carcase of our continents, dates back to the ancient Red race. The colossal Sphinx of Gizeh, near the Great Pyramid, is its work."[30] Everything else in Egypt comes from much later, after the Black (Sudeen) race made its principal sanctuary in Upper Egypt. Later still, there was "a pacific mingling of the White and the Black races in the regions of Ethiopia and Upper Egypt, long before Aryan times."[31] It was at this point that the great initiate Hermes appeared and founded the Egyptian Mysteries.

Schuré never pretended to be a visionary or illuminate: he was a literary man with a passion for Wagner (whom he knew), and he tells the tales of his initiates as he might bring to life the adventures of Brunnhilde or Parsifal. His work suited the taste of the time, and among those who can bear its overwritten style, it has found readers ever since. Thanks to *The Great Initiates,* Fabre d'Olivet's scheme became firmly embedded in French popular occultism.

To the author himself, however, it was a passing phase. With the new century Schuré moved into the ambit of Rudolf Steiner (see chapter 4), of whom he wrote, "For the first time in my life, I was certain that I was in the presence of an Initiate. I had long lived with the initiates of antiquity, whose history and development I had had to depict. And now at last one of them stood before me on the physical plane."[32] Steiner and his wife arranged for performances of Schuré's *Sacred Drama of Eleusis,* and Schuré returned the compliment with his second work of universal history, *L'évolution divine du Sphinx au Christ* (Divine evolution from the Sphinx to Christ, 1912). In this he was as obedient to Steiner's vision of prehistory as he had previously been to Fabre d'Olivet's.

PAPUS AND THE CANCEROUS MOON

From Schuré the baton passed to Papus (pseudonym of Dr. Gérard Encausse, 1865–1916), who dominated the French occultist scene, driven by the ambition to join, then control, every secret society and order. At first, Papus was a keen member of the Theosophical Society, but after personal differences he became one of its worst enemies. In his much-reprinted *Traité élémentaire de science occulte* (Elementary treatise on occult science), Papus revealed the secret history of the earth in his own fashion. Again, each human race is the product of the evolution of a continent: the Eastern or Yellow race, of Asia; the Western or Red race, of America; the Southern or Black race, of Africa; and the Northern or White race, of Europe. Each in turn has dominated the earth.[33] The theme of the uninclined axis also appears, as Papus explains that if the equator and the ecliptic coincided, the earth would be in physical harmony. But instead, the poles oscillate periodically, occupying eight successive positions relative to the equator, and this brings about the rise and fall of continents, deluges, and geological catastrophes. The immediate cause of this is the moon.

At this point, Papus blended Fabre d'Olivet's prehistory with what he called the "high revelations" of Louis Michel (1816–1883), a peasant seer sometimes known by the name of his birthplace, Figanières.[34] According to these, the earth was originally compounded from four small planets in the course of disintegration, which, once joined together, became the four continents. A fifth fragment refused to become integrated with the others and was condemned through its own will to become a satellite. Remember, Papus says, that there are peoples whose names indicate that they did not know of the moon![35] (He does not tell us which they are.) Each continent, he continues, brought forth its own human race, and each has its own history of birth, maturity, and decline: they do not all march in step. The four races are different in style but equal in their access to the Divine.

Each of these races has made, *from its personal point of view,* an intellectual evolution crowned by a Science and a Tradition, and confirmed by an INVOLUTION OF DIVINITY in the said race. Moreover, each race has used particular procedures to raise itself from the instinctive state to that of divine illumination. Hence the apparent differences of the various traditions, beneath which one always finds a *unity* that only the initiate is able to grasp in all its integrity.[36]

Papus seems unsure of whether to recommend to his readers the most radical of Michel de Figanière's revelations. Before he starts on the history of the races, he asks rhetorically:

Have the Yellow, Red, Black, and White races completed their successive evolution on the same planet, or is each terrestrial continent just the crystallization of another planet; and have the remains of four of these planets formed the Earth? . . . Is the Moon one of those continents destined to form the Earth which willfully separated from the others, thus causing the terrestrial disharmony and becoming not a normal satellite, but a real cancer to the Earth?[37]

Ignoring the history of the Yellow race, Papus continues from the period when the Red race was dominant. Unlike Fabre d'Olivet, he identifies its achievements with those of the megalithic builders, for he says that remnants of its colonies are to be found in the Old World in Great Britain, in Brittany, Spain, Italy (the Etruscans having been of that race), and most of all in Egypt, "where the Red race founded the Atlantean colony which, after the great catastrophe, transmitted the high truths of initiation to the other races."[38] Papus then quotes or summarizes many pages from Fabre d'Olivet on the Borean Race, its Arctic origins, its rivalry with the Sudeens, the creation of a Druid college, Ram's career with its twelve stages symbolized by the zodiac, the coming of Moses, and so forth. Emulating Schuré, he tells of the other "great divine messengers" (a term borrowed from Michel de Figanières): Krishna, Orpheus, multiple Zoroasters and Buddhas, Lao-Tsu, Confucius, Son-Mou of Japan, Hermes Trismegistus, Esdras, Pythagoras, Numa. As the Christian era approached, there were the School of Alexandria (founded by Buddhists), the Essenes, Socrates, Plato, and Aristotle, "all of whom tried to reveal the great mystery that was in preparation." [39] This would be the incarnation of the Divine Word in Jesus Christ, to whom Papus, like Saint-Yves and many other French esotericists, accords an incomparably higher status.

PAUL LE COUR AND THE SACRED HEART

The French esoteric world has long had the name of Atlantis before its eyes, transfixed by Poseidon's trident on the cover of its longest-lived periodical. The review *Atlantis* was founded in 1927 and is still flourishing after more than 400 issues. It was the creation of Paul Le Cour (1871–1954), a well-educated civil servant and keen outdoorsman. [40] Over the years he was involved with psychical research, spiritualism, Theosophy, Earth mysteries, Platonism, astrology—in short, the whole panoply of *occultisme*, with a leaning toward its more serious and philosophical side.

Le Cour's mission became more focused in the 1920s, after he came into contact with a Christian esoteric group called the Hiéron du Val d'Or. Jean-Pierre Laurant, the authority on French esotericism, calls it "the crossroads of Catholicism, esotericism, the occult sciences, and an ultra-conservative nationalism." [41] This semisecret society had been founded in 1883 by Baron Alexis de Sarachaga (1840–1918), who built an extraordinary temple-museum in the town of Paray-le-Monial. Pier Luigi Zoccatelli, another authority on Christian esotericism, describes the Hiéron's four purposes as: (1) the demonstration of the origins of Christianity from the mythical Atlantis; (2) the reconstitution of a universal sacred tradition; (3) the preparation for the year 2000 of a political and social reign of Christ the King and the teaching of the sacred name of *Aor-Agni*—Light-Fire—as the key to all knowledge; (4) a secret purpose to fight against anti-Christian Freemasonry through the creation of a "Christian Freemasonry of the Great West." [42] (This alluded to the "Grand Orient," the militantly secular branch of French Freemasonry.)

Paul Le Cour was drawn into the whole mythology of Paray-le-Monial, which had begun in 1673 when St. Margaret Mary Alacoque had a vision of Jesus taking her heart into his. This led to a popular Catholic cult of the Sacred Heart, to papal approval, and eventually to such monuments as the Sacré Coeur basilica in Montmartre, Paris, built in a spirit of nationalist renewal after the Franco-Prussian War. Although Le Cour did not share the more extreme ideals of the Hiéron, he thought that it might have some initiatic connection with the Templars,[43] for whose Christian chivalry he had a great admiration. As his official biography says, "He realized little by little that through his research he was on the quest for the *Primordial Tradition,* the lost word revered by religions and initiatic societies, which originates from Atlantis considered as mother of Western civilization. The mythical king of the vanished continent was Poseidon, patron of knights, whose ideal qualities Le Cour extolled."[44]

In 1926, Le Cour founded the Société d'Études Atlantéennes (Society of Atlantean Studies) and published his first book: *À la recherche d'un monde perdu: L'Atlantide et ses traditions* (In search of a lost world: Atlantis and its traditions).[45] The title alluded to Proust's *À la recherche du temps perdu* (*Remembrance of Things Past*), whose penultimate volume had just appeared. The theme of Le Cour's book is that "through iconographic symbolism and the comprehension of the names of divinities and of places, one may hope to reconstitute the great and unique tradition coming from Atlantis."[46] One of the symbols in question is the serpent, which appears to signify the primordial light that Le Cour calls *Aour.* A second symbol is the heart, symbol of fire, *Agni.* These together made up the sacred name of Aor-Agni used in the Hiéron's devotions.

The discovery that Le Cour is most eager to share is that the serpent and the heart are carved into monuments of the megalithic period, such as the dolmens and standing stones of Brittany. As always with such discoveries, their worn state leaves much to the interpreter, and many an irregular concavity may take on the shape of a heart. The importance for

Le Cour was that these symbols appeared in monuments that he believed to be Atlantean in origin, thereby rooting the relatively modern revelations of Paray-le-Monial in the deep past.

As suggestive proof of a continuing underground tradition, Le Cour borrows from Brasseur de Bourbourg a German map of 1708 in the shape of a heart, in which the place of Atlantis is filled by a wound dripping blood. Even the presence of nine drops seems to him significant, for the number nine, he reminds us, has an important role in Kabbalah! Everywhere he goes, Le Cour sees or hears momentous coincidences, his will to believe granting him a generous margin of error and historical improbability. Here is a specimen of his linguistic method, employed in a gentle diatribe against the Theosophists and their excessive admiration of India:

> As for those who are currently seeking the sources of wisdom in India, they find towns there whose names come from our own West, like *Agra,* which is the name of a suburb of Eleusis where the Lesser Mysteries were celebrated; they will find Maya and Aor-Agni in the names of the chief divinities of the Rig-Veda: *Yama* and *Varouna,* and they might also connect the word Thibet with the word Thebes. All these names in fact belong to the sacred language of Atlantis; they are vestiges of that distant past when the Atlantean people stamped the mark of their profound knowledge onto place names, for the sake of generations far in the future. But if these researchers find in India the symbol of the serpent, they will not find the heart there, the key to the mysteries, at least not in the profound sense given it in the Western tradition.[47]

Perhaps it is this very looseness of interpretation that caused Le Cour, rather than pressing a personal agenda, to welcome writers of all sorts to his journal. *Atlantis* carried articles from members of the Académie Française, from scientists, and from all the more serious occultists of the day. A conspicuous exception was René Guénon, who had himself been involved with the Hiéron du Val d'Or but seldom mentions Le Cour without some snide remark. We will treat Guénon's views on Atlantis in chapter 6, and in chapter 12 return to Le Cour as apostle of the Age of Aquarius.

PANDORA'S BOX

For all the errors, distortions, and plain untruths that pepper *Le matin des magiciens* (*The Morning of the Magicians*) by Louis Pauwels and Jacques Bergier, it was an exhilarating read.[48] Where else in 1963 could one learn of Gurdjieff, Guénon, Charles Fort, Fulcanelli, Nazi occultism, the Hollow Earth, or the Baghdad Batteries? Its authors presented themselves as open-minded inquirers (Pauwels being a journalist, Bergier a physicist), but their work reeked of the occult.

Pauwels and Bergier's version of Atlantis owed nothing to the French esotericists mentioned above but grew out of their fascination with Hoerbiger's *Welteislehre* (*WEL*). As mentioned in chapter 1, this taught that the earth has captured four planetoids that have successively become its satellites, then crashed onto its surface. The present moon is its fourth. In France the *WEL* was promoted by Denis Saurat in *L'Atlantide et le règne des géants* (Atlantis and the reign of the giants, 1954) and *La religion des géants et la civilisation des insectes* (The religion of the giants and the civilization of insects, 1955). Saurat shared with Pauwels an acquaintance with Gurdjieff's movement, and his influence lurks behind *The Morning of the Magicians*.

In conformity with the *WEL*, Pauwels and Bergier explain that the periods of the four moons correspond with the four geological epochs. The first humans appeared in the Secondary Epoch "thanks to miraculous processes of mutation which happen more frequently as the cosmic rays become stronger." They were giants, and the few who survived the fall of the second moon nurtured the inferior humans of the Tertiary Epoch. Under the benevolent rule of these "gods," Tertiary humans lived in an earthly paradise for several million years. More than 900,000 BP, the third moon began its inexorable approach to earth, and its gravity caused the seas to rise. On the highest mountains, a worldwide maritime civilization flourished. The giants, for whom lifting huge stones was child's play, built five great megalithic cities: at Tiahuanaco in the Andes, in New Guinea, Mexico, Abyssinia, and Tibet.[49]

Apparently the tertiary moon took its time falling, for it was not until 150,000 BP that the catastrophe occurred.

> Gravitation ceased, the belt of oceans suddenly retracted and the waters receded. The mountain tops which had been great maritime centers, were turned into swamps and isolated. The air became rarefied, and temperatures fell. Atlantis perished, not by being engulfed in the ocean, but, on the contrary, because the waters left it high and dry. . . . Though the Atlantidean civilization had attained the highest possible degree of social and technical perfection, with a unified and well-established hierarchy, it vanished in an astonishingly short space of time, and almost without leaving a trace behind it.[50]

The dregs of humanity were left in the mud, with a moonless sky, but in time civilization revived in the Andes center and its four subsidiary cities. A lesser civilization arose on high plateaus in the North Atlantic, between 40° and 60° latitude, which was the Atlantis of Plato. About 12,000 BP the earth acquired its fourth moon (our present one) and again suffered catastrophic changes in sea levels. The moon's gravity sucked the water from the poles toward the equator, and this is what overwhelmed Plato's Atlantis in a single night. Once again, civilization had to be rebuilt, and once again its only certain prospect is destruction when the Quaternary moon eventually falls to Earth.[51]

Pauwels and Bergier did not necessarily believe the *WEL,* any more than the other theories that keep their readers open-mouthed. In fact, they held it responsible for the Nazis' vision of a Thousand-Year Reich culminating in a *Götterdämmerung* (twilight of the gods). However, the borderline is blurry between what one is supposed to accept from them as fact and what is merely suggestive fiction, and their scholarly apparatus is pitiful. The result was that careless writers have ever after pillaged *The Morning of the Magicians* for material, whose boundaries they in turn blur.

Pauwels and Bergier's project continued with *Planète,* a periodical in some ways akin to Le Cour's *Atlantis.* Both owed their success to a reading public bored to death with the one-dimensional world of politics and economics, and no less so with the chatter of Left Bank intellectuals like Jean-Paul Sartre. Both reviews disclosed a world of fantastic realities, revisionist histories, and theories that turned the received worldview on its head. But whereas Le Cour's contributors mostly shared a spiritual outlook if not an actual grounding in esoteric traditions, *Planète's* were more likely to be agnostics with an exaggerated faith in science. True, their concept of science burst the materialist paradigm, for they did not turn their backs on psychic phenomena or occult powers. Their revisionist history even hinged on accepting the reality of such powers, and on supposing that prehistoric civilizations had mastered them, probably with extraterrestrial assistance.

A successful rider of this wave was Robert Charroux (1909–1978), described on his book jackets as a sort of "Indiana Jones" figure.

Athletic champion, deep-sea diver since 1930, treasure hunter, globe-trotter, journalist, archaeologist, producer at the R.T.F. (=Le Club de l'Insolite), his curiosity has led Robert Charroux to explore the most varied regions of human history and activity, far removed from familiar paths and orthodox science. The study of Tradition and Prehistory, research trips to the lands of the most ancient civilizations, the discovery of millennia-old documents and messages— this soon made him suspect that a fantastic truth, unknown to most of mankind, could shed light on our beginnings. He then developed the hypothesis of a "parallel universe" more authentic than the one invented in classical times. Convinced that a vast mystery lies hidden from human knowledge, he strove to penetrate it, gathering the evidence, documentation, and proofs, creating a terminology for terrestrial anomalies, and wrote *Histoire inconnue des hommes depuis cent mille ans* [Unknown history of mankind over 100,000 years], published in 1963, followed by *Le livre des secrets trahis* [The book of secrets betrayed, 1964] and *Le livre des maîtres du monde* [The book of the masters of the world, 1967].[52]

Charroux's hypothesis of a parallel universe served him as a "scientific" excuse for anything too challenging to rationality. Starting from the speculations of physicists and mathematicians, he suggests that clairvoyance and precognition might be explained through interference of that universe with this one. So might the medieval accounts of visits to the Grail kingdom, which "suggest the survival of a scientific knowledge that has deteriorated through its long history, but which was originally very complex."[53]

This need for scientific explanation, or rather for technocratic fantasy, makes Charroux a firm believer in the extraterrestrial hypothesis. In the second book of his trilogy he sets out to convince us that humanoids from Venus visited the earth, settled in Hyperborea, bred with the autochthonous race, and created two principal civilizations. One was on Atlantis, just emerged from the ocean and stretching from North America as far as Tiahuanaco. The other was on the Pacific continent of Mu, which included the Gobi Desert and part of India. After a few thousand years the Venusians, revered as angels or gods by these two civilizations, had reconstituted the technology of their homeland, not least the use of nuclear energy.[54]

Everyone's view of the past risks being clouded by their present, and Charroux was writing soon after the Cuban missile crisis. What was narrowly avoided in October 1962 happened between his Atlanteans and the people of Mu, leading to mutual assured destruction: "The atomic bombs of Mu devastated Atlantis and the American continent, at the same time as the Atlantean reprisal brought death and destruction to Mu."[55]

A few years later, in his third volume, Charroux was more interested in the possibility of a natural cause for these early civilizations' fall, which he dates to about 10,000 BCE. Besides nuclear war, he suggests a collision or near-collision with a comet or meteorite shower, volcanic eruptions, or a brutal wakeup call from the extraterrestrials, sending an enormous space rocket to impact North America or Mongolia.[56] Whatever the cause, almost all humanity died in the consequent rain of fire and the deluge that swept all the land, up to an altitude of 2,000 meters. The survivors, very few in number, clustered on the high mountains and plateaus. In time, the new humanity emerged from five widely separated points: the Red race from the Rocky Mountains and the Andes, the Black race from Ethiopia, the Yellow race from the Himalayas, and the White race from the Iranian plateau. Of these, the Atlanteans and the children of Mu carried the heritage of the extraterrestrials with humans; the Blacks were autochthonous; and the Whites came from Hyperborea, where a small colony of "angels" may also have survived the deluge.[57]

Civilization suffered another setback around 3000 BCE, when a second, partial deluge occurred. Its cause was the planet Venus, formerly a comet. Following Velikovsky, Charroux assures us that there is no evidence in ancient sources that such a planet was known before this date, whereas a mass of testimony exists that can be interpreted as the comet's arrival and close approach to the earth before settling into its planetary orbit.[58]

The reader may have noticed the emphasis of French Atlantology on the variously colored races. According to Charroux, Adam and Eve were black,[59] and so were all their descendants until the coming of the light-skinned "Sons of God" in their spaceships. These, as we know from the Bible, desired the "Daughters of Men," and by interbreeding with the autochthonous race gave rise to the three hybrid races: Yellow, Red, and White. Among other observations that would scarcely pass today's censors, Charroux suggests that the Blacks will further their evolution through miscegenation with Whites, thus supplementing the efforts of the extraterrestrials to raise the general level of earthly humanity through hybridization.[60]

"Pandora's Box" is an apt description of the *Planète* project, for the glamor of lost knowledge is irresistible. These writers have done a service by opening it up, but since they lack any scholarly responsibility and any metaphysical grounding, what flies out is uncontrolled. To the average reader, one thing is as credible as another. Recognizing the profit to be made by exploiting such appetites, there is now an entire genre of occultist sensationalism masquerading as fact.

A mild version of this was propagated by the influential French branch of AMORC (Ancient and Mystical Order Rosae Crucis; see chapter 8 for more on the Rosicrucians.) Its French Grand Master and Supreme Legate Raymond Bernard (1923–2006) boasted innumerable other titles and dignities, as well as contacts in political circles. At the end of his book *Les maisons secrètes de la rose-croix* (The secret houses of the rose-cross) he gives a translation of Plato's Atlantean writings and a summary of Donnelly's book.[61] Then he discloses that he has special knowledge that he is only now ready to share.

True to the Rosicrucian myth of Unknown Superiors who go their way unnoticed by the world but occasionally appear to initiates, Bernard tells us that he met his master in a hotel in Brussels. This sage told him that it was not by chance that there was so much interest in Atlantis today. Then he revealed that some Atlanteans had escaped its destruction, and that their heirs still exist![62] Atlantis was absolutely monotheist, like Islam or Judaism, and held the sun to be the first divine manifestation. Egyptian beliefs were a degenerate remnant of it, adapted to include the Nile in its theology. Atlantis was very civilized; we have nothing comparable to its methods of transportation. It had colonies, to which it gave part of its secret wisdom. This was preserved in its supreme pyramid, reproduced in "different measure" by the Pyramid of Cheops and others. Soon its secrets will be discovered, to the great good of humanity, and will put an end to much polemic.[63]

Continuing, Bernard's master tells him that the Atlanteans knew nature's forces, especially the telluric currents, and applied them to agriculture. The pyramids served to maintain "geological harmony," while dolmens and menhirs, too, focalized the universal energy. All these sites were attached to the supreme pyramid, as only the sages knew how the energy system worked. The Atlanteans used it as we do electricity, without completely understanding it. But then they abused it, and finally made alterations in the supreme pyramid with catastrophic results: the Deluge. The Atlantean colonies were left to themselves without proper knowledge. Each developed its own school, rites, and myths, and created local secret societies with remnants of their knowledge. Even African secret societies have fragments of this, and so did the Druids.[64]

Bernard says that before this meeting he had read Andrew Tomas's book on the secrets of Atlantis. This would be *Les secrets de l'Atlantide,* published in Laffont's "Bibliothèque des grandes énigmes" (Library of the great enigmas), along with Robert Charroux's and Eric von Däniken's works.[65] Bernard adds in an aside that the book was dedicated to Roerich, who was Spencer Lewis's legate to Tibet. The great painter Nicolas Roerich (1874–1947) was no longer in a position to accept or decline Tomas's dedication. Nor could Roerich confirm or deny Bernard's implication that he had really worked for Harvey Spencer Lewis, the founder of AMORC.[66]

After this superficial grounding in the *Planète* school of Atlantology, Bernard now received the key to the mystery. The master explained to him that after the fall of Atlantis, the world entered a period of obscurity, as the sages refused to reconstitute the Atlantean empire. Instead, the whole world now has to become a New Atlantis, even if it takes thousands of years over it. The choice is offered: to usher in an era of extraordinary civilization, or to suffer the end not just of a continent, but of a world. This time of choice is approaching. To general stupefaction, Atlantis will reappear! The sages have had to leave humanity to grow up by itself, as demanded by the universal plan, but they have guided this evolution, gradually giving humanity the discoveries, science, and technology acquired by the Atlanteans.[67]

In Raymond Bernard's version of these familiar ideas, it is not the space gods but the Rosicrucians under one guise or another who have been steering the course of humanity. If so, I marvel at their naivety.

That the sages' idea of evolution is to give adolescent humanity the technological toys that can destroy a world suggests criminal folly on their part.

JEAN PHAURE: RETURN TO TRADITION

Paul Le Cour's admirer Jean Phaure, whose cyclical theories will figure largely toward the end of this book, agrees. He writes:

> To none of our new-style prophets does it occur that every gain in power over matter that is not the consequence of a properly disinterested spiritual progress is Satanic in nature, which is an elementary teaching of every authentic tradition. None of these propagandists obsessed by searching for the fantastic seems ever to have thought, even in passing, that the purpose of human life might be the search for Salvation, much less for Liberation.[68]

Jean Phaure appreciates the stirring up of the common mentality by Charroux and the *Planète* group, but as a Christian esotericist, he takes our spiritual nature as the primary reality, and material evolution or devolution as secondary. His own prehistory also begins in Hyperborea, as the cradle of our present humanity. Answering the obvious objections based on climate, he asks: "Might there have existed, on the scale of a small continent, a 'micro-climate' maintained through energy sources that are mysterious to us, because they were spiritual?"[69] Phaure is certain that Hyperborea was the primordial home of *Homo sapiens,* because all esoteric traditions testify to a "light from the North," and because paleontology, geology, and climatology all agree that the Arctic region once enjoyed a temperate climate. (He does not mention their timescale of millions of years vis-à-vis his of thousands.) He is less confident about the legendary continents of Lemuria and Mu, on which science fails to agree with the "occultists," of whom he seems to know only James Churchward (see chapter 8). He accepts that

Mu was a continent in the Pacific contemporary with Atlantis, and that it disappeared in the same cataclysm of the eleventh or twelfth millennium BCE.

Jean Phaure, like Charroux, distinguishes two separate deluges. One sent Atlantis to the seabed around 10,800 BCE. Another was in the fourth millennium BCE, remembered in the Greek legend of Deucalion and Pyrrha and in the biblical Noah.[70] Both authors believe that the earth's axis was once perpendicular to the ecliptic. Charroux writes: "About 10,000 years ago the North Pole was situated on Baffin Island, and the earth turned on an uninclined axis, causing equal climates at all seasons."[71] During the approach of Venus, "the Earth turned over completely, so that the South Pole came to the North, the North Pole to the South, and East and West changed places. This situation lasted for an undetermined time, perhaps only a few days."[72] Phaure writes that both tradition and science "speak not only of a time when the Earth, without seasons, turned on an axis perpendicular to this [ecliptic] plane, but also of sudden flips of the globe, the North Pole taking the place of the South and vice versa."[73]

Phaure also has a theory of the origin of races, but spiritual rather than material. The descendants of the primordial couple, newly clothed in physical bodies (the "coats of skin" of Genesis 3:21), misused these by mating with prehuman species already existing on Earth. We will see in the next chapter that this is a mainstay of Theosophical prehistory, though Phaure is not sympathetic to that movement. He interprets the Sons of God not as extraterrestrials but as *Homo sapiens,* and the Daughters of Men as perhaps Neanderthals. This miscegenation, he thinks, could explain the appearance of races with marked bodily differences. It also provides a rationale for Plato's statement that Atlantis declined when its inhabitants mixed their divine substance with mortal elements, until the latter prevailed. Instead of privileging one race over another, Phaure points out that we are all of mixed blood, but whether we are yellow, white, black, or red, we possess that fragment of the divine Spirit that makes us humans and not animals.[74]

After the great cataclysm of the eleventh millennium, Phaure says, the survivors strove to reconstruct the lost knowledge of the vanished continents. This accounts for the hiatus between the Mesolithic and Neolithic eras, and also for the similarity of megalithic structures all over the globe, without requiring a diffusionist explanation.[75] Phaure despises the extraterrestrial hypothesis as a strategy for eliminating God and the primordial tradition from prehistory. Certainly there are extra-terrestrial beings; perhaps some are "para-human" and may have communicated with us and continue to do so (here he mentions UFOs). Nevertheless, at our origin is the sacred and the divine: "This Primordial Revelation easily suffices to explain the original knowledge of mankind, just as the traditional science of qualified Time and Cyclology amply accounts for the successive birth and death of civilizations."[76] From that point of view, material progress is nothing but a compensation for the loss of spiritual powers that could act on matter without the necessity for tools. "As humanity moves further from its spiritual source, it 'solidifies' and 'materializes,' seeking in the mastery of technical powers the memory of its lost natural powers."[77]

This and many other passages in Phaure's work echo the teachings of René Guénon, whom no account of the French current of Atlantology can ignore. Here Guénon is held over for later discussion (see chapter 6) because of his relationship with other currents to which the intervening chapters are dedicated.

Three chapters in the present book are devoted to national Atlantologies: the French, German, and British. Although one cannot call them "schools," there are definite trends and peculiarities to each of them. The French, for all their interest in races, make no claims of their own racial superiority, as do the Germans. They do not favor medium-istic revelations, as the British have done. They make their pronouncements ex cathedra, keeping their sources to themselves, as though what they have to say about prehistory is obvious to any reasonable person. Reason does not exclude immaterial or even spiritual realities, but once these are accepted as part of the natural order of things, certain consequences follow. The same method is followed by writers as disparate in context and culture as Fabre d'Olivet and Robert Charroux. They address a public stultified by the received canon of belief (whether imposed by the church or by science) and tell them that things are not as commonly supposed; history is driven by unseen forces, and a proper view of the most ancient times reveals what these were, and are.

THREE

H. P. Blavatsky and the Early Theosophists

———————— ✳ ————————

NEOPLATONIC FORERUNNERS AND *ISIS UNVEILED*

Helena Petrovna Blavatsky (1831–1891) was the most influential contributor to occult Atlantology, as her contemporary Ignatius Donnelly (see chapter 1) was to the rational stream. In her early work *Isis Unveiled,* written during the years around the foundation of the Theosophical Society in New York (1875), Blavatsky was tentative on the subject and still indebted to flawed authorities such as Brasseur de Bourbourg and Augustus Le Plongeon (see chapter 8). After she had left America for India, an entirely new prospect of prehistory opened up. Its source was in letters signed by the Mahatmas Koot Hoomi and Morya which, together with a cryptic *Book of Dzyan,* furnished the basis for the much more extensive Atlantean and Lemurian lore contained in Blavatsky's second major work, *The Secret Doctrine* (1888). This chapter tells the story of how her information was obtained and released to the world.

First, however, we must trace a thin line of succession in the English-speaking world that leads from the era of Fabre d'Olivet up to that of the early Theosophists. Its originator was Thomas Taylor (1758–1835), the first translator of Plato and the Neoplatonists into English. Like the

French philosophes, Taylor had to defend Platonic chronology against the narrow, biblical view of history. When he came to translate the *Critias,* he wrote this stirring defense of his master (emphases and spelling as in the original).

That the authenticity of the following history should have been questioned by many of the moderns, is by no means surprising, if we consider that it is the history of an island and people that are asserted to have existed NINE THOUSAND years prior to Solon; as this contradicts the generally-received opinion respecting the antiquity of the world. However, as Plato expressly affirms, that it is a relation in *every respect true,* and, as Crantor, the first interpreter of Plato, asserts, "that the following history was said, by the Egyptian priests of his time, to be still preserved inscribed on pillars," it appears to me to be at least as well attested as any other narration in any antient historian. Indeed, he who proclaims that "truth is the source of every good both to Gods and men," and the whole of whose works consists in detecting error and exploring certainty, can never be supposed to have wilfully deceived mankind by publishing an extravagant romance as matter of fact, and with all the precision of historical detail.[1]

Taylor was a true pagan, committed to the philosophy, theology, and mystical practices of Neoplatonism. He had no doubt that Plato had transmitted, as accurately as possible, what the Egyptian priest told Solon; and, as a mathematician, the last thing Taylor was going to quarrel with was Plato's plainly stated number of 9,000 years.

Spurned by English classicists because he lacked academic credentials, Taylor found more open-minded readers in America. Among the most dedicated admirers of his work and example was Alexander Wilder (1823–1908), a physician and classical scholar. Wilder brought a strong Platonic influence into the early Theosophical Society and was mainly responsible for the essay "Before the Veil" that prefaces *Isis Unveiled.* It begins with an argument in favor of Plato as the best way of access to the "abstruse systems of old India" that were already Blavatsky's main interest. Plato's wisdom, after all, came from Egypt, and Egypt herself, as she wrote, "received her laws, her social institutions, her arts and her sciences, from pre-Vedic India."[2] With her natural inclination to synthesis, she set out to correlate Plato's Atlantis with the oriental sources known to her: both the published ones and a *Great Book* or *Secret Book* accessible only to initiates.

These sources told of a sacred place approximately in today's Gobi Desert that would play an important part in occult historiography. Blavatsky dates it before the Adamic race, that is, the race whose history the Bible encodes under the story of Adam and Eve. At that time,

> there was a vast inland sea, which extended over Middle Asia, north of the proud Himalayan range, and its western prolongation. An island, which for its unparalleled beauty had no rival in the world, was inhabited by the last remnant of the race which preceded ours. This race could live with equal ease in water, air, or fire, for it had an unlimited control over the elements. These were the "Sons of God;" not those who saw the daughters of men, but the real *Elohim*. . . . The hierophants of all the Sacerdotal Colleges were aware of the existence of this island. . . .[3]

There was no communication with the fair island by sea, but subterranean passages known only to the chiefs, communicated with it in all directions. Tradition points to many of the majestic ruins of India, Ellora, Elephanta, and the caverns of Ajunta (Chandor range), which belonged once to those colleges, and with which were connected such subterranean ways. Who can tell but the lost Atlantis—which is also mentioned in the *Secret Book,* but, again, under another name, pronounced in the sacred language—did not exist yet in those days? The great lost continent might have, perhaps, been situated south of Asia, extending from India to Tasmania? If the hypothesis now so much doubted, and positively denied by some learned authors who regard it as a joke of Plato's, is ever verified, then, perhaps, will the scientists believe that the description of the god-inhabited continent was not altogether fable. And they may then perceive that Plato's guarded hints and the fact of his attributing the narrative to Solon and the Egyptian priests, were but a prudent way of imparting the fact to the world and by cleverly combining truth and fiction, to disconnect himself from a story which the obligations imposed at initiation forbade him to divulge.[4]

Isis Unveiled is a formidable and sprawling tome, written in an impossibly erudite stream of consciousness. Blavatsky's colleague Henry Steele Olcott observed her writing it in a state of trance, as though taking dictation or copying from invisible books,[5] as she herself confirmed in a letter to her sister: "Whenever I am *told* to write, I sit down and obey, and then I can write easily upon almost anything—metaphysics, psychology, philosophy, ancient religions, zoology, natural sciences, or what not."[6] Although the early Theosophists helped her with it, especially since she had yet to master the English language, much of *Isis* might qualify as channeled material.

The next quotation contains a rich vein of material for our subject.

To continue the tradition, we have to add that the class of hierophants was divided into two distinct categories: those who were instructed by the "Sons of God," of the island, and who were initiated in the divine doctrine of pure revelation, and others who inhabited the lost Atlantis—if such must be its name—and who, being of another race, were born with a sight which embraced all hidden things, and was independent of both distance and material obstacle. In short, they were the *fourth* race of men mentioned in the *Popol-Vuh,* whose sight was unlimited and who knew all things at once. They were, perhaps, what we would now term "natural-born mediums," who neither struggled nor suffered to obtain their knowledge, nor did they acquire it at the price of any sacrifice. Therefore, while the former walked in the path of their divine instructors, and acquiring their knowledge by degrees, learned at the same time to discern the evil from the good, the born *adepts* of the Atlantis blindly followed the insinuations of the great and invisible "Dragon," the King *Thevetat* (the Serpent of *Genesis?*). Thevetat had neither learned nor acquired knowledge, but, to borrow an expression of Dr. Wilder in relation to the tempting Serpent, he was "a sort of Socrates who *knew* without being initiated." Thus, under the evil insinuations of their demon, Thevetat, the Atlantis-race became a nation of wicked *magicians*. In consequence of this, war was declared, the story of which would be too long to narrate; its substance may be found in the disfigured allegories of the race of Cain, the giants, and that of Noah and his righteous family. The conflict came to an end by the submersion of the Atlantis.[7]

Without any idea of what he was starting, Alexander Wilder contributed some remarks to the discussion: "The Pacific also shows signs of having been a populous island-empire of Malays or Javanese—if not a continent amid the North and South. We know that Lemuria in the Indian Ocean is a dream of scientists; and that the Sahara and the middle belt of Asia were perhaps once sea-beds."[8] Lemuria was the name proposed in 1864 by the English zoologist Philip Sclater for a hypothetical sunken land linking India with Madagascar. His reason was that lemurs, living or extinct, are found in both places; but the term, soon dropped by scientists, would enjoy a far different career.

These early passages anticipate themes of Blavatsky's later Atlantis lore, but in the 1870s her system was still at a formative stage. Just before *Isis Unveiled* went to press, she received a shipment of the complete works of Louis Jacolliot, in twenty-one volumes, and added a two-page footnote on the basis of her initial skimming of these. Jacolliot (1837–1890) was a French magistrate who worked many years in India and wrote on the borderline between anthropology and myth. Blavatsky was particularly taken with his statement that all the islands from Malacca to Polynesia "once formed two immense countries, inhabited by yellow men and black men, always at war; and that the gods, wearied with their quarrels, having charged Ocean to pacify them, the latter swallowed up the two continents." This tradition of a prehistoric civilization, she writes, "corroborates with the one we have given from the 'Records of the Secret Doctrine.' The war mentioned between the yellow and the black men, relates to a struggle between the 'sons of God' and the 'sons of giants,' or the inhabitants and magicians of the Atlantis."[9]

There are resonances here with Fabre d'Olivet's interracial conflicts and vanished southern (Austral) continent, but with Blavatsky a more occult type of prehistory was taking shape. Among points to note are the not-quite-materialized nature of the inhabitants of the sacred island, and the existence among ancient races of an intuitive, clairvoyant state of consciousness. Wilder thinks immediately of Socrates and his daimon; Blavatsky, a natural-born medium if ever there was one, is aware of the dangers of that condition. Whereas in Plato, the fall of Atlantis was due to a preponderance of the human over the divine element in the genetic makeup of the inhabitants, here it is a more dramatic battle of good versus evil magicians. Whereas Plato was obliged to suppress the truth, the whole theme of *Isis Unveiled,* starting with the title, was that something kept secret for ages would now be divulged.

THE MAHATMA LETTERS

Soon after Blavatsky and Olcott arrived in India in 1879, the Theosophical Society became a magnet both for educated Indians and for British colonial society. Among the latter were Alfred Percy Sinnett (1840–1921), editor of India's leading daily, *The Pioneer,* and Allan Octavian Hume, C.B. (1829–1912), a highly placed civil servant. They were enthralled by Blavatsky and the occult phenomena she produced, especially in the summer of 1880 when she stayed in Simla as guest of the Sinnetts. More alluring still was the information that she was acting on orders from certain masters or "Mahatmas" (great souls) who lived in Tibet. Sinnett, eager to demonstrate the reality of paranormal phenomena to his readers, suggested asking the Masters for an incontrovertible proof: a copy of the London *Times* should appear in Simla on the day of its publication, instead of arriving by sea a month later.

Sinnett's challenge produced, not the *Times,* but on October 15, 1880, the first of a series of letters from the Masters. The most communicative of these signed himself "Koot Hoomi Lal Singh," or plain "KH." The second was known as "Morya." Other masters made brief appearances, including a junior one called Djwal Khul (variously spelled). The resulting collection of "Mahatma Letters" remains, especially for those who have examined the originals in the British Library, one of the great enigmas of its time. Blavatsky and the writers asserted that the letters were not written by hand but "precipitated" or materialized through an occult process. Now that the letters are encapsulated for preservation, it is virtually impossible to tell what instrument was used to write them, but it does not resemble pen, pencil, or crayon. Many witnesses testified to the strange circumstances of their delivery. The letters would seemingly drop from the ceiling; one had to be dug out of a cushion; others appeared during train or sea journeys. Sometimes they would take the form of postscripts to an unrelated letter that arrived, sealed, in the mail. Some people saw them in the process of precipitation, the words forming on blank paper. Another question was who was responsible for their contents. Theosophical orthodoxy takes the letters and the Masters at face value. Blavatsky herself is the skeptics' choice, which implies an elaborate plan involving many co-conspirators, a system of delivery that would challenge any stage magician, and an epidemic of self-deception by otherwise intelligent people. In between is a range of more subtle possibilities, which, as often with paranormal phenomena, may not have been uniform in kind or unmixed with deception.

The mystery of the Mahatma Letters is important to our study, because it was they that first outlined the Theosophical system of prehistory, correlated it with the epochs of paleontology, and established the place of Atlantis in the scheme, thus superseding the disjointed information given in *Isis Unveiled.*

Sinnett and Hume were at first interested in the big questions: the existence of God (which the Masters, disconcertingly, denied), the problem of evil, the nature of the soul, spirit, and other elements of the human being, what happens to them after death, where the universe comes from, how humans arose, and so on. They soon got more than they had bargained for, in the shape of a tremendous system of Globes, Rounds, Root Races, and Sub-races that still has the average Theosophist flummoxed. Part of the problem is that the system is viewed variously from the perspectives of a cosmic observer, of the earth, of the human race, or of the individual. For our purposes, the second and third of these are the most relevant.

In a letter received by Sinnett in June 1882, Morya explained that while science believes there to have been four races successively inhabiting Europe, "there were not *four* but *five* races; and we are that fifth with remnants of the fourth."[10] The next month, Koot Hoomi wrote, "There are seven root-races, and seven sub-races or offshoots."[11] This and other tidbits prompted Sinnett to pose twenty-nine distinct questions, which Koot Hoomi answered at length in October.

To Sinnett's question about the fifth race, Koot Hoomi writes, "Yes; the fifth race—ours—began in Asia a million years ago."[12] In conformity with nineteenth-century notions of migrations and racial origins, he calls this race Aryan.[13] The race prior to that was the Atlantean, and for the one before that Koot Hoomi uses Sclater's term, Lemurian. He also uses the terms Eocene and Miocene. These had been coined in 1833 by Charles Lyell in his *Principles of Geology* as part of his division of the Tertiary (post-dinosaur) period. Although Lyell had no means of dating the periods, his "uniformitarian" view of geology required a time scale of millions of years for gradual Earth changes to occur. In conventional science, which now dates the Tertiary period to circa 65 million to 1.8 million years BP, there was and is no question of humans having existed then. Here are the essential passages from Koot Hoomi's letter:

In the Eocene Age—even in its "very first part"—the great cycle of the fourth Race men, the Atlanteans, had already reached its highest point, and the great continent, the father of nearly all the present continents, showed the first symptoms of sinking—a process that occupied it down to 11,446 years ago, when its last island, that, translating its vernacular name, we may call with propriety *Poseidonis,* went down with a crash. Bye the bye, *whoever* wrote the Review of Donnelly's *Atlantis* is right: Lemuria can no more be confounded with the Atlantic Continent than Europe with America. Both sunk and were drowned with their high civilizations and "gods," yet between the two catastrophes a short period of about 700,000 years elapsed; "Lemuria" flourishing and ending her career just at about that trifling lapse of time before the early part of the Eocene Age, since its race was the *third.*[14]

The sinking of Atlantis (the group of continents and isles) began during the Miocene period—as certain of *your* continents are now observed to be gradually sinking—and it culminated—*first,* in the final disappearance of the largest continent, an event coincident with the elevation of the Alps; and *second* with that of the last of the fair Islands mentioned by Plato.[15]

The great event—the triumph of our "sons of the *Fire Mist,*" the inhabitants of "Shamballah" (when yet an island in the Central Asian Sea) over the selfish but not entirely wicked *magicians* of Poseidonis occurred just 11,446 years ago. Read in this connection the incomplete and partially veiled tradition in *Isis,* Volume I, p. 588–94, and some things may become still plainer to you.[16]

From 1881 to 1883 Hume gave out extracts from the Masters' letters in the monthly journal *The Theosophist* under the title "Fragments of Occult Truth." These led to further questions and explanations, some of them by Blavatsky. At the beginning of 1883, A. P. Sinnett published a book-length collection of extracts from the letters with his own commentary, called *Esoteric Buddhism.* He explained that "esoteric science" is not merely about religious matters, but a comprehensive system that can also "search out and ascertain the manner in which the human race has evolved through aeons of time and series of planets." Not only can it discover the history of Atlantis and Lemuria:

> It goes back still further indeed, but the second and first races did not develop anything that could be called civilization, and of them therefore there is less to be said than of their successors. The third and fourth did—strange as it may seem to some modern readers to contemplate the notion of civilization on the earth several millions of years ago.
>
> Where are its traces? they will ask. . . . The answer lies in the regular routine of planetary life, which goes on *pari passu* with the life of its inhabitants. The periods of the great root races are divided from each other by great convulsions of Nature, and by great geological changes. Europe was not in existence as a continent at the time the fourth race flourished. The continent on which the fourth race lived was not in existence at the time the third race flourished, and neither of the continents, which were the great vortices of the civilizations of those two races, are in existence now. Seven great continental cataclysms occur during the occupation of the earth by the human life-wave for one round-period. Each race is cut off in this way at its appointed time, some survivors remaining in parts of the world, not the proper home of their race; but these, invariably in such cases, exhibiting a tendency to decay, and relapsing into barbarism with more or less rapidity.
>
> The proper home of the fourth race, which directly preceded our own, was that continent of which some memory has been preserved even in exoteric literature—the lost Atlantis.[17]

FRAGMENTS OF FORGOTTEN HISTORY

The explanation in Sinnett's *Esoteric Buddhism* of rounds, root races, and sub-races was anything but lucid, and others now joined him in the effort to clarify the matter. These were Mohini Mohun Chatterji

(1858–1926), an Indian Theosophist and attorney who traveled to England with Blavatsky in 1884 and testified on her behalf before the committee of the Psychical Research Society; and Mrs. Laura C. Holloway-Langford (or Langford Holloway, 1848–1930), an American Theosophist then staying in London. In a whirlwind of activity during the summer of 1884, they collaborated on a pseudonymous book, coyly calling themselves "The Eastern Chela" and "The Western Chela." Entitled *Man: Fragments of Forgotten History,* it was supposed to be an example of East-West collaboration and to supplement the Masters' and Blavatsky's information on the prehistory and nature of the human race.

A. P. Sinnett wrote that Laura Holloway "used to get vivid clairvoyant visions of the Masters, could pass on messages to me from K.H. and on one occasion he actually made use of her to speak to me in the first person."[18] Evidently this gave her a claim to independent authority in the matter of humanity's past.

The "forgotten history" begins in an ethereal, prehuman state. Its location recalls Bailly's Arctic origins and the French tradition of a shifting axis of the earth (see chapter 2): "The cradle of the first objective race of man in the present Ring was the North Pole, which at the time we are speaking of was almost on the ecliptic. Since that period the poles and the equator have changed places."[19] *Man* is full of curious details about human evolution, such as how and when humans began to eat food, rather than living on air; how humans relate to nature spirits and elementals, how the sexes separated, how pain and death entered into the picture, and how survivors of past root races are living on today. Apparently one feature of the seven root races was their successive development of the physical senses, in addition to "astral senses" that they already possessed. The first race developed sight; the second, touch; the third (Lemurian), hearing; the fourth (Atlantean), smell; and the fifth (Aryan), taste. That leaves two further senses to be developed by the sixth and seventh races of the present "ring" or round.[20]

Regarding the Atlanteans, "They knew how to navigate aërial vehicles with the help of the subtle agency which Bulwer-Lytton refers to under the name of *Vril*. Their houses, like those of the ancient Peruvians, were floored with gold. The weapons of destruction they constantly used were so far superior to those known to us as to be hardly conceivable."[21] Although the evil magicians of Atlantis were overthrown, we are not rid of them yet: "Ages after this event, which but robbed black magicians of predominance and not of existence, we find Atlantean black magicians at times interfering with the progress and development of students of the real occult science."[22]

Neither Blavatsky nor the Masters were pleased with the Two Chelas' effort. Here is Koot Hoomi, writing to Sinnett confidentially about Holloway, after she had returned to America but before the book was sent to press:

> Aroused some 18 months ago to spasmodic, hysterical curiosity by the perusal of your *Occult World*[23] and later on by that of *Esoteric Buddhism* to enthusiastic envy, she determined to "find out the truth" as she expressed it. She would either become a chela herself— first and foremost, *to write books,* thus eclipsing her "lay" rival, or upset the whole imposture in which she had no concern. She decided to go to Europe and seek you out. Her surexcited fancy, putting a mask on every stray spook, created the "Student" [the Master whom she believed to have appeared to her] and made him serve her purpose and desire. . . . Her thoughts were for a certain period guided, her clairvoyance made to serve a purpose. . . . Try to save "Man" by looking it over with Mohini, and by erasing from it the alleged inspirations and dictations by "Student."[24]

Man came out in 1885 without the desired corrections. Blavatsky wrote an apologetic statement for Theosophists who marked its contradictions vis-à-vis *Esoteric Buddhism*. She tried to release Mohini from blame and promised to set right the confusion over rounds, root races, and sub-races in her forthcoming book *The Secret Doctrine*.[25] She also sent Sinnett a long list of corrections intended for future editions (but never used). Here is one of them, its tone of tender exasperation quite different from Koot Hoomi's:

> You surely dream *dreams,* my gentle child. If you had Humanity of the second Round in your mind's eye when writing this—*passe encore*—but *on this Earth and in this Round!?* Why see what Master says in his letter to Mr. Sinnett. 1st Round man, an ethereal being, non-intelligent but *super-spiritual.* 2nd Round gigantic ethereal, growing more condensed in body a more PHYSICAL MAN. In the third Round—less gigantic, a more rational being, "more ape than *Deva*-man"—(still a HUMAN MAN). The Lord love you innocent sweety. . . go to confession dear, and learn from the *Padris* something of Chapter VI 2nd verse *in Genesis.* You *have* "Forgotten History."[26]

THE SECRET DOCTRINE: THE FIRST TWO ROOT RACES

It remained for Blavatsky to pick up the pieces and to retell the story in her own style. Her second major work, *The Secret Doctrine* (1888), treated the subject of "Anthropogenesis" or human origins with no less prolixity and erudition than *Isis,* but with better structure. The work takes the form of an immense commentary on the *Stanzas of Dzyan,* an archaic and otherwise unknown text that proceeds chronologically from the very beginnings of the universe. If the reader has difficulty with the concepts contained in the work, he or she is not alone. Blavatsky herself writes:

> Born and bred in European, matter-of-fact and presumably civilized, countries, she assimilated the foregoing with the utmost difficulty. But there are proofs of a certain character which become irrefutable and are undeniable in the long run, to every earnest and unprejudiced mind. For a series of years such were offered to her, and now she has the full certitude that our present globe and its human races must have been born, grown and developed in this, and in no other way.[27]

In *The Secret Doctrine,* as in *Isis Unveiled,* Blavatsky uses the twin opponents of Science and Religion as a sounding board for her esoteric doctrines. Science she respects, though she reminds us that it is in a perpetual state of revision and change, and that its methods are only a couple of centuries old. Its sticking point, which remains the same today as in the 1880s, is its refusal to consider anything beyond material reality. This disbars it, in her opinion, from ever penetrating the mysteries of human or cosmic origins. Religion she loathes, at least the exoteric Judeo-Christian kind that takes the Bible as literal truth and rejects every other faith. But the Bible, as she demonstrates, is a document written by initiates that conceals esoteric truths under its incredible fables. As such, it agrees with the esoteric doctrines of the East, of Egypt, and of pre-Christian Europe.

Blavatsky was well aware that her exposition of prehistory would have little chance of an impartial hearing. Materialistic science could not grant any role to nonphysical elements of man, whether these are called astral, ethereal, spirit, or soul. Nor could it allow a purpose to nature beyond the blind evolutionary impulses of Darwinism. Then there were her three radical claims: "(*a*) the appearance of man before that of other mammalia, and even before the ages of the huge reptiles; (*b*) periodical deluges and glacial periods owing to the karmic disturbance of the axis; and chiefly; (*c*) the birth of man from a Superior Being, or what Materialism would call a *supernatural* Being, though it is only super-*human*."[28]

The Theosophical system is evolutionary, but its concern is above all with the destiny of the "monads" (a term borrowed from Leibniz) that have traveled through eons of cosmic evolution before becoming the sort of humans we are. Part of this evolution was taken care of by nature, but its later phases needed something more.

> Thus physical nature, when left to herself in the creation of animal and man, is shown to have failed. She can produce the first two [mineral, vegetable] and the lower animal kingdoms, but when it comes to the turn of man spiritual, independent and intelligent powers are required for his creation, besides the "coats of skin" and the

"Breath of animal Life." The human Monads of preceding Rounds need something higher than purely physical materials to build their personalities with, under the penalty of remaining even below any "Frankenstein" animal.[29]

Nature (in man) must become a compound of Spirit and Matter before he becomes what he is; and the Spirit latent in Matter must be awakened to life and consciousness gradually. The Monad has to pass through its mineral, vegetable and animal forms, before the Light of the Logos is awakened in the animal man. Therefore, till then, the latter cannot be referred to as "MAN," but has to be regarded as a Monad imprisoned in ever changing forms.[30]

For humans to become more than animals, higher beings had to intervene. In *The Secret Doctrine* these are variously called Gods, Angels, Creators, Progenitors, Fathers, Pitris, Dhyanis, and so on, but their histories and fine distinctions cannot concern us here. It suffices to know that a certain group of them was responsible for the appearance of the first root race of the present life-wave or "round" on Earth. In some way they "projected" it out of their own essences,[31] producing images or "astral doubles" of themselves.[32] But being in such an immaterial condition, these protohumans had no consciousness, no will, and consequently no spiritual development. "The first Humanity therefore, was a pale copy of its Progenitors; too material, even in its ethereality, to be a hierarchy of Gods; too spiritual and pure to be MEN."[33] This is the first of the seven root races, which inhabited an "Imperishable Sacred Land" that has never disappeared, despite all the changes that have taken place on the earth's surface since then. Its connection with physical geography is necessarily tenuous, but there is some occult link with the North Pole.[34]

Having no bodies to speak of, the first root race "could not be injured, or destroyed by death. Being so ethereal and so little human in constitution, they could not be affected by any element—flood or fire."[35] Instead of dying, "its 'men' melted gradually away, becoming absorbed in the bodies of their own 'sweat-born' progeny, more solid than their own."[36]

These "sweat-born" beings, exhaled or exuded by their parents, were the second root race. Blavatsky calls this race the Hyperborean, because it inhabited "the land which stretched out its promontories southward and westward from the North Pole to receive the Second Race, and comprised the whole of what is now known as Northern Asia."[37] Being more materialized than the first root race (though still "ethereal" in comparison to ourselves), the second root race was affected by physical conditions on the globe.

> The ever-blooming lands of the Second Continent (Greenland, among others) were transformed, in order, from Edens with their eternal spring, into hyperborean Hades. This transformation was due to the displacement of the great waters of the globe, to oceans changing their beds; and the bulk of the Second Race perished in this first great throe of the evolution and consolidation of the Globe during the human period. Of such great cataclysms there have already been four. And we may expect a fifth for ourselves in due course of time.[38]

Although there is plenty of evidence, such as fossil flora and coal, that the Arctic region was once warm, to look there for remnants of the first two root races is futile. While the earth and its lower kingdoms were already well advanced in materialization, these races were simply "too ethereal and phantom-like in their constitution, organism, and *shape*, even to be called physical men," and consequently left no fossils.[39]

THE THIRD (LEMURIAN) ROOT RACE

One can see why so little is written about the first two races. They lacked all that makes for human interest from our point of view, such as personality, a foothold in the material world, and of course sex. All this changed with the third root race (Lemurian), whose occult history is the most dramatic of all.

The First Race having created the Second by "budding," as just explained, the Second Race gives birth to the Third—which itself is separated into three distinct divisions, consisting of men differently procreated. The first two of these are produced by an oviparous method, presumably unknown to modern Natural History. While the early sub-races of the Third Humanity procreated their species by a kind of exudation of moisture or vital fluid, the drops of which coalescing formed an oviform ball—or shall we say egg?—that served as an extraneous vehicle for the generation therein of a *foetus* and child, the mode of procreation by the latter races changed, in its results at all events. The little ones of the earlier races were entirely sexless— shapeless even for all one knows; but those of the later sub-races were born androgynous. It is in the Third Race that the separation of sexes occurred. From being previously a-sexual, Humanity became distinctly hermaphrodite or bi-sexual; and finally the man-bearing eggs began to give birth, gradually and almost imperceptibly in their evolutionary development, first, to Beings in which one sex predominated over the other, and, finally, to distinct men and women.[40]

In parallel with these surprising developments, other higher beings became involved in human evolution. A particular class of them, called Dhyanis or Sons of Wisdom, were destined to incarnate in human form, both for reasons of their own and to help bring infant humanity to consciousness. This took place during the Lemurian and Atlantean ages, in three main waves. (1) The first group of Dhyanis incarnated "immediately the men of the Third Race became physiologically and physically ready, *i.e.,* when they had separated into sexes," providing these "senseless monads" with an ego, conscious knowledge, and will. They became the "seed on earth for future adepts." (2) A second group, preferring its immaterial state and "intellectual freedom," hesitated to undergo incarnation until far later in the Lemurian age. When at last they did so, "they got bodies (physiologically) inferior to their astral models, because their *chhayas* had belonged to progenitors of an inferior degree in the seven classes." These became the ancestors of average humanity. (3) Some of the Sons of Wisdom deferred incarnation until the fourth, Atlantean root race. By that time, some of the protohumans, being mindless and consequently not responsible for their actions, had mated with females of an extinct apelike species and bred a hybrid race. (Apparently interspecies breeding was more feasible in those times; shortly afterward, the possibility was blocked.) The Dhyanis who had come late to the game had to incarnate in these human-animal bodies. In so doing, "they produced a terrible cause, the Karmic result of which weighs on them to this day. It was produced in themselves, and they became the carriers of that seed of iniquity for aeons to come, because the bodies they had to inform had become defiled through their own procrastination."[41]

Among the descendants of this hybrid race were the apes. So Blavatsky turned the tables on Darwin: instead of humans evolving from monkeys, it is the apes that are the unnatural result of human iniquity.

In the course of the Lemurian age, humans, besides evolving from "sweat-born" to "egg-born" to sexually differentiated, became sufficiently adept in the material world to start manipulating it: "The oldest remains of Cyclopean buildings were all the handiwork of the Lemurians of the last sub-races. . . . The first large cities, however, appeared on that region of the continent which is now known as the island of Madagascar. There were civilized people and savages in those days, as there are now."[42]

In Theosophical doctrine, every root race has its own continent. The following extracts give the location of Lemuria and of the fourth continent, Atlantis.

> It must be noted that Lemuria, which served as the cradle of the
> Third Root-Race, not only embraced a vast area in the Pacific and

Indian Oceans, but extended in the shape of a horse-shoe past Madagascar, round "South Africa" (then a mere fragment in process of formation), through the Atlantic up to Norway. . . . No more striking confirmation of our position could be given than the fact that the ELEVATED RIDGE in the Atlantic basin, 9,000 feet in height, which runs for some two or three thousand miles southwards from a point near the British Islands, first slopes towards South America, then *shifts almost at right angles* to proceed in a SOUTH-EASTERLY line *toward the African coast,* whence it runs on southward to Tristan d'Acunha. This ridge is a remnant of an Atlantic continent, and, could it be traced farther, would establish the reality of a submarine horse-shoe junction with a former continent in the Indian Ocean.[43]

Atlantis is often described by believers in Plato as a prolongation of Africa. An old continent is also suspected to have existed on the Eastern coast. Only Africa, as a continent, was never part and parcel of either Lemuria or Atlantis, as we have agreed to call the Third and Fourth Continents. . . . The area between Atlas and Madagascar [was] occupied by the waters till about the early period of Atlantis (after the disappearance of Lemuria), when Africa emerged from the bottom of the ocean, and Atlas was half-sunk.[44]

Thus the Fourth-Race Atlanteans were developed from a nucleus of Northern Lemurian Third Race Men, centred, roughly speaking, toward a point of land in what is now the mid-Atlantic Ocean. Their continent was formed by the coalescence of many islands and peninsulas which were upheaved in the ordinary course of time and *became ultimately the true home of the great Race known as the Atlanteans.*[45]

THE FOURTH (ATLANTEAN) ROOT RACE

Blavatsky tells us little about this great fourth root race except to extol their knowledge and science. This included "the knowledge of flying in air vehicles," the arts of meteorography and meteorology, the "most valuable science of the hidden virtues of precious and other stones, of chemistry, or rather alchemy, of mineralogy, geology, physics and astronomy."[46] What were the destructions of the Library of Alexandria, she asks, in comparison with that of the Atlantean Libraries, "wherein records are said to have been traced on the tanned skins of gigantic antediluvian monsters?"[47] The said monsters presented no threat to the Atlanteans, who, like many past races, were of giant stature (a topic to which Blavatsky dedicates many pages). The threat to their civilization came from within. Magic, she writes, "was practised in such ungodly ways by the Atlantean Sorcerers that it has since become necessary for the subsequent race to draw a thick veil over the practices which were used to obtain so-called magical effects on the psychic and on the physical planes."[48]

These Atlantean sorcerers fought a war with the "Initiates of the Sacred Island" that has already been mentioned as the refuge from Atlantis's destruction and the cradle of the fifth root race. T. Subba Row (1856–1890) gives some disconcerting information about its later consequences. Of all Blavatsky's associates, after the Masters it was Subba Row whom she most respected for his esoteric knowledge; in secular life, he was a pleader (advocate) at the Madras High Court. He writes, à propos elemental beings:

> There are all the powerful elemental gods and goddesses worshiped by the Atlanteans, and these still exist. They are most ferocious things, but they cannot be evoked easily. It is fortunate for us that they do not interfere more than they do.[49]

The following passage from *The Secret Doctrine* describes how the primordial wisdom was transmitted through the root races, and, by implication, to the authors of the *Book of Dzyan* and the spiritual ancestors of the Theosophical Masters:

Let us remember that the Atlanteans became the terrible sorcerers, now celebrated in so many of the oldest MSS. of India, only toward their fall, the submersion of their continent having been brought on by it. What is claimed is simply the fact that the wisdom imparted by the "Divine Ones"—born through the *Kriyasakti powers* of the Third Race before its Fall and Separation in to sexes—to the adepts of the early Fourth Race, has remained in all its pristine purity in a certain Brotherhood. The said School or Fraternity being closely connected with a certain island of an inland sea, believed in by both Hindus and Buddhists, but called "mythical" by geographers and Orientalists, the less one talks of it, the wiser he will be.[50]

Whether or not as the consequence of its misdeeds, every root race except the ethereal first suffered one or more cataclysms. Continents disappeared, new lands appeared, mountain chains rose: "The face of the Globe was completely changed each time; the *survival of the fittest* nations and races was secured through timely help; and the unfit ones—the failures—were disposed of by being swept off the Earth. Such sorting and shifting does not happen between sunset and sunrise, as one may think, but requires several thousands of years before the new house is set in order."[51] The immediate cause of these cataclysms was not outside agency, such as a comet, but changes in the inclination of the earth's axis—another topic to which Blavatsky repeatedly alludes, without properly explaining it.

As to the dating of these events, Blavatsky was aware that the most advanced scientists of her day allowed an age of the earth of up to 500 million years, calculated partly from measuring sediments and partly from how long the earth would have taken to cool after having been thrown off by the sun. She herself gives a figure of 300 million years for the mineral and vegetable development preceding physical man,[52] or 320 million years from the "first sedimentary deposits" until the present. She extends the example of Koot Hoomi in correlating the occult history of mankind with geological periods. Here is her summary of the scientists' estimates, which "harmonize with the statements of Esoteric Ethology in almost every particular," except that she considers the durations of the Tertiary and Quaternary periods to be somewhat too long:[53]

			Rough Approximations
	Laurentian		
Primordial	Cambrian	lasted	175,0000,000 years
	Silurian		
	Devonian		
Primary	Coal	"	103,040,000 years
	Permian		
	Triassic		
Secondary	Jurassic	"	36,800,000 years
	Cretaceous		
	Eocene		
Tertiary	Miocene	"	7,360,000 years
	Pliocene		(probably in excess)
Quaternary		"	1,600,000 years
			(probably in excess)

This serves as the matrix into which to fit the occult chronology of the rise and fall of Lemuria and Atlantis:

Lemuria is said to have perished about 700,000 years before the commencement of what is now called the Tertiary Age (the Eocene), and it is during this Deluge—an actual geological deluge this time—that Vaivasvata Manu is also shown as saving mankind (allegorically it is mankind, or a portion of it, the Fourth Race, which is saved); so also he saves the Fifth Race during the destruction of the last Atlanteans, the remnants that perished 850,000 years ago,* after which there was no great submersion until the day of Plato's Atlantis, or Poseidonis, known to the Egyptians only because it happened in such relatively recent times. . . . The cataclysm which destroyed the huge continent of which Australia is the largest relic, was due to a series of subterranean convulsions and the breaking asunder of the ocean floors. That which put an end to its successor—the fourth continent— was brought on by successive disturbances in the axial rotation. It began during the earliest tertiary periods, and, continuing for long ages, carried away successively the last vestige of Atlantis, with the exception, perhaps, of Ceylon and a small portion of what is now Africa.[54]

Blavatsky's work was not designed to simplify the picture of prehistory, but rather to convey its complexity. The races overlap in time; their continents bear little relation to any that we know, neither do the poles of the earth; they do not vanish "in a night and a day" but break up piecemeal. Their inhabitants are not uniform in culture, lifestyle, or consciousness. Nor is the simplistic division by color, favored by the French occultists, of much relevance: "There were brown, red, yellow, white and black Atlanteans; giants and dwarfs (as some African tribes comparatively are, even now)."[55]

As for Plato's Atlantis, it is little more than a postscript: "The civilization of the Atlanteans was greater than even that of the Egyptians. It is their degenerate descendants, the nation of Plato's Atlantis, who built the first Pyramids in the country, and that certainly before the advent of the 'Eastern Aethiopians,' as Herodotus calls the Egyptians."[56]

---

*This event, the destruction of the famous island of *Ruta* and the smaller one *Daitya*, which occurred 850,000 years ago in the later Pliocene times, must not be confounded with the submersion of the main continent of Atlantis during the Miocene period. Geologists cannot place the Miocene only so short a way back as 850,000 years; whatever they do, it is several million years ago that the main Atlantis perished.

But Plato himself gets more respect, for in Blavatsky's view he was an initiate who knew this whole history, but was only allowed to disclose it in hints: "Aiming more to instruct as a moralist than as a geographer and ethnologist or historian, the Greek philosopher merged the history of Atlantis, which covered several million years, into one event which he located on one comparatively small island . . . about the size of Ireland."[57]

FOUR

Later Theosophists

———————— ✳ ————————

A. P. SINNETT AND "MARY"

Just as the "Two Chelas" had offered their version of "man's forgotten history" when the ink of the Mahatma Letters was scarcely dry, so later Theosophists continued to improve on it according to their lights. A. P. Sinnett, to whom Koot Hoomi and Morya had addressed most of their letters, ceased to receive any after 1885, when Blavatksy settled in Germany to write *The Secret Doctrine*. But the socially and psychically ambitious Sinnett was not going to be dropped so easily. He immediately started holding "mesmeric sittings" with a woman he called "Mary," keeping them secret from Blavatsky and other Theosophists.[1] By 1888, these sessions were taking place almost daily, as Sinnett wrote in his unpublished autobiography, with "the Masters talking to me through her in most cases. In this way I gathered a great deal of miscellaneous occult information."[2] This included Sinnett's own past lives in Egypt and Rome, during which he discovered that he had been involved with the previous incarnations of his wife, of Mary the medium, and of his son's tutor, Charles Leadbeater.

In 1892 Sinnett revealed the existence of his new channel of communication to an elite group from his London Lodge, which began meeting for "special work in which the Master undertook to help us."[3] Some of the results of this work, presumably based on Mary's mediumship, were given out in lectures to the rest of the lodge and published in booklets. Such was a lecture that Sinnett gave on December 19, 1893, on "Stonehenge and the Pyramids." He explained that, helped "by psychometric power of a very high order," he had been able to build up a proper conception of Egyptian civilization that was quite unlike the gropings of the archaeologists. Egypt had been gradually settled by Atlantean adepts during the long period when the Atlantean continent was breaking up. The pyramids were built a little more than 200,000 years ago, primarily as temples or chambers of initiation and secondarily to protect from future Earth-changes "some tangible objects of great importance having to do with the occult mysteries."[4] Later the land sank, the sea rose, and the pyramids were submerged. After they reemerged, Egyptian civilization reached its golden age. Finally, the land was swept by an immense flood when the last of Atlantis sank, 11,500 years ago.

Sinnett's sources declared that Stonehenge, too, was the work of Atlantean adept immigrants. They had come to the British Isles and established a civilization there about 100,000 years ago. They made Stonehenge crude and unroofed "as a mute protest against the corrupt luxury of the perishing civilization they had left behind."[5] But their building method was not crude in the least. In this and other megalithic structures, "the adepts who directed their construction facilitated the process by the partial levitation of the stones used."[6] Clairvoyant observers, Sinnett assures us, have seen the process going on. Only much later was Stonehenge taken over by the Druids of the fifth root race and made the scene of bloody sacrifices.

WILLIAM SCOTT-ELLIOT AND HIS SOURCES

While Sinnett's lecture on the pyramids and Stonehenge was only heard or read by a small coterie, the next wave of Atlantean revelation was destined for widespread and lasting fame. Its vehicle was William Scott-Elliot (1849–1919), Tenth Laird of Arkleton. We know almost nothing about him, but one gets a sense of his milieu from the fact that his father held the record for attending the opening of the grouse-shooting season, and his son fell victim to a multiple murder plot hatched by the family butler.[7]

By some unknown but surely interesting route, this Scottish aristocrat had made his way into Sinnett's special research group, which only numbered about ten people.[8] By February 17, 1893, Scott-Elliot had assimilated enough Theosophical lore to address the London Lodge on "The Evolution of Humanity." On October 10 he married an Irish physician's daughter called Maude Boyle-Travers. Research by Daniel Caldwell and Michelle Graye has proved that Maude was none other than the "Mary" who had been serving A. P. Sinnett for years as a medium.[9]

On February 29, 1896, Scott-Elliot gave another paper at the London Lodge entitled "Atlantis—A Geographical, Historical, and Ethnological Sketch." It was published with a preface by Sinnett, who assures the reader, "Every fact stated in the present volume has been picked up bit by bit with watchful and attentive care, in the course of an investigation on which more than one qualified person has been engaged, in the intervals of other activity, for some years past. And to promote the success of their work they have been allowed access to some maps and other records physically preserved from the remote periods concerned."[10]

More than one qualified person? Who, other than "Mary," now Mrs. Scott-Elliot, was involved? The curtain rises on Charles Webster Leadbeater (1854–1934), who would become, with Annie Besant, the most prominent of the second-generation Theosophists. Before considering his contribution to Scott-Elliot's work, we need to sketch his career up to this point. Sinnett had admitted him to the Theosophical Society in 1883, albeit reluctantly, since Leadbeater was a Church of England priest. The next year he left the church, and, spurred by a letter from Koot Hoomi, joined Blavatsky on her voyage to India. There he received occult training from Koot Hoomi,[11] Djwal Khul, and the more tangible Subba Row.[12] A period of lonely and menial labor for the society followed, ending in 1889 when Sinnett summoned Leadbeater back to England to tutor his son Denny. After Blavatksy's death in 1891, he was taken up by the society's rising star, Annie Besant.

Leadbeater's occult training had not been for nothing. He could access knowledge about the etheric and astral planes, even ascending to Devachan, home of demigods. He knew the faculties of the human being that correspond to these planes, and had solved the enigmas of sleep, death, and rebirth. Already a member of Sinnett's special group, he now began one of his favorite activities: psychically reading the past lives of his friends and others of note. His method was very different from that of "Mary," who spoke from a mesmeric trance. As his biographer, Gregory Tillett, writes, "For these researches Leadbeater did not find it necessary to leave the physical body, and carried out his investigations whilst fully conscious and awake."[13] Apparently he was able, in normal social settings, to call up astral visions and describe them, just as the rest of us can make conversation based on our own visual memories. Annie Besant's biographer, Arthur Nethercot, adds that most of the sessions "were held after dinner in the drawing-room of Mr and Mrs Varley, but . . . some took place on Saturday or Sunday afternoons while they were all seated in a small park in Wormwood Scrubs, in the west of London."[14] In these unglamorous surroundings, Leadbeater recounted to Varley the tale of his sixteen previous lives.

Such researches yielded incidental information about the times and places in which the previous lives had occurred, and this led to a concentrated effort to discover more about the distant past. In August 1895, Besant, Leadbeater, and two others (Bertram Keightley and Curuppumullage Jinarajadasa) retreated for this purpose to Box Hill, Surrey. Leadbeater wrote to a friend that, in addition to discoveries about Devachan,

we also made further investigations into the different orders of atoms and molecules, the arrival of the first class pitris from the Moon, and the manners, customs, religion and history of some Lemurian and early Atlantean races, to say nothing of a few casual incarnation hints. During the latter we witnessed the first birth of Mahatma Morya on this earth, on arrival from the spiritual state following the Lunar

Chain, and found him again about a million years ago as one of the great dynasty of the Divine Rulers of the Golden Gate in Atlantis.[15]

These "manners, customs, religion and history" went to form the core of Scott-Elliot's *Story of Atlantis*. The small book had an attractive supplement of four folding maps printed in pink and green, showing the world (1) as it had been for many ages up to 1 million years ago, (2) after the catastrophe of 800,000 years ago, (3) after the catastrophe of 200,000 years ago, and (4) after the catastrophe of 80,000 years ago until the final submergence of Poseidonis in 9564 BCE. So the two Atlantean catastrophes of the Mahatma Letters and the three of *The Secret Doctrine* have now become four. Years later, Jinarajadasa wrote about how Leadbeater had obtained these maps. Apparently Koot Hoomi, among his many other responsibilities, was Keeper of the Records for the Museum of Records of the Great White Brotherhood. When Leadbeater gave his lecture on "The Astral Plane" to the London Lodge in November 1894, Koot Hoomi thought it so epoch-making that he asked if its manuscript might be donated to the museum. It was duly sent to him, vanishing in London and presumably appearing in Shigatse.[16] Jinarajadasa, who had compiled the actual manuscript from Leadbeater's notes and witnessed the phenomenon, explained:

> This Museum contains a careful selection of various objects of historical importance to the Masters and Their pupils in connection with their higher studies, and it is especially a record of the progress of humanity in various fields of activity. It contains, for instance, globes modelled to show the configuration of the Earth at various epochs of time; it was from these globes that Bishop Leadbeater drew the maps which were published in another transaction of the London Lodge, that on Atlantis by W. Scott-Elliot.[17]

These, then, were the "records physically preserved" mentioned in Sinnett's preface. I do not understand why Leadbeater entrusted all this valuable information to Scott-Elliot, first to reveal in his lecture, then to publish under his own name with Sinnett's preface.[18] Since one of the main points of the book is to argue and demonstrate the value of clairvoyance to archaeology, it may have been thought more convincing not coming from the clairvoyant himself.

The first part of *The Story of Atlantis* was probably by Scott-Elliot, as it summarizes the standard Theosophical teachings on the root races and supplies well-worn arguments of the Donnellian type, based on cross-Atlantic parallels. Then we learn the names of the seven sub-races of the Atlantean root race, which surely came from Leadbeater. Nos. 3–7 are named for later peoples descended from them, but the first and second are "the names by which they called themselves,"[19] which may explain why we have difficulty pronouncing them:

1. Rmoahal
2. Tlavatli
3. Toltec
4. First Turanian
5. Original Semite
6. Akkadian
7. Mongolian

These Atlantean sub-races seem to have uniformly loathed one another. They suffered constant wars and forced migrations, befitting their status as the lowest of the seven root races, the most sunk in materiality. One respite was a golden age of 100,000 years under the "divine dynasty" of the Toltecs.[20] After that came the sorcerers and their black arts, and the first breakup of the continent, 800,000 years ago.

Scott-Elliot seems to have drawn on Sinnett for his Egyptian material. He, too, relates that the first colonists came to Egypt about 210,000 years ago, and thereupon built just the two great pyramids of Giza, the third, presumably, coming later. The pyramids had a dual purpose, "partly to provide permanent Halls of Initiation, but also to act as treasure house and shrine for some great talisman of power during the submergence which the Initiates knew to be impending."[21] In Scott-Elliot's version, Egypt was a casualty of the Atlantean catastrophes, being first sunk beneath the seas 200,000 years ago; secondly 80,000 years ago, after which the great Temple of Karnak was built; and thirdly swept by a tidal wave when Plato's Atlantis went down. Not only were those pyramids ancient beyond modern imagining: Stonehenge with its "rude simplicity"[22] was built by a colony that landed in early Akkadian days, about 100,000 years ago. Nineteenth-century utopianism colors the part of the book dealing with Atlantean life. In its heyday, temple worship did not abet superstition but focused on the sun-disk as symbol of "the nameless and all-pervading essence of the Kosmos."[23] Women had rights and education equal to men; there were no slaves. Each child was psychically examined to determine its abilities and placed in the appropriate educational stream; not all needed to learn to read and write. The common people ate meat and even drank blood, but the high officials, being more spiritually advanced, were vegetarian. When strong liquor became a social problem, prohibition was enforced. All the land belonged to the emperor and was divided into collective farms that shared their bounty out fairly. The eugenic improvement of animals and crops, combined with manipulation of the weather, ensured plenty for everybody. Instead of money, the Atlanteans issued tokens that functioned as IOUs. They never issued these in excess of their capital, for their creditors could see through any deception by focusing their clairvoyant powers.

Of the technological achievements that Scott-Elliot describes, the Atlantean "air-boats" are the most intriguing.[24] At their highest development they were made of *an alloy* of two white-colored metals and one red one that was *even lighter than aluminum*. Their outside surface was *apparently seamless and perfectly smooth*, and they *shone in the dark* as if coated with luminous paint. They were *boat-shaped but invariably decked over,* with propelling and steering gear at both ends. Their motive power was *an etheric force* made in a generator and passed through adjustable tubes, which then operated like a modern jet. The course of flight was never straight, but *in long waves*. Do not the phrases I have italicized evoke a classic UFO? Or perhaps a preclassic one, for apparently its maximum speed was only 100 m.p.h., and its ceiling under 1,000 feet.

Maude Scott-Elliot had stopped acting as Sinnett's medium in 1898, as she became more worldly in her interests and "anxious to conceal her connection with Theosophy from her husband's relations."[25] Nonetheless, in 1904 William Scott-Elliot put his name to *The Lost Lemuria*,[26] a companion to the Atlantis book.[27] Unlike Atlantis, the existence of a Lemurian continent was acceptable to contemporary scientists, and Scott-Elliot quotes from Wallace, Haeckel, Blandford, and Hartlaub to prove it. Some scientists still entertained the possibility of a Tertiary Man, whose absence from the fossil record could now be explained by the not-quite-physical nature of the early third root race. As for occult sources, *The Secret Doctrine* had contained much more on Lemuria than on Atlantis, and this fills out Scott-Elliot's work. He describes how the Lemurians evolved from sexless giants into a sturdy Stone Age people, cultivating the wheat that their preceptors had brought from Venus, building cities on a cyclopean scale, and still endowed with the third eye of psychic vision. Then came the volcanic upheavals in which almost all of them perished, and the dawn, some five million years ago, of a new race on a new land. He also disclosed something of the sources for the maps that both books contained. Whereas for Atlantis, "there was a globe, a good bas-relief in terra-cotta, and a well-preserved map on parchment, or skin of some sort, to copy from," for the earlier continent "there was only a broken terra-cotta model and a very badly preserved and crumpled map."[28] Still, Leadbeater did his best and was able to produce two maps of Lemuria for the new work, as well as a florid description of a Lemurian hunter leading his pet dinosaur.

A CHILD'S STORY

The Theosophists' clairvoyant reading of the past was not entirely new. The Mesmerists had experimented with it, and among Spiritualists psychometry (holding an object and reading its past) was almost a parlor game. Children also took part; they were believed to be purer channels than adults, less apt to project their own ideas onto what they saw in magic mirrors or with the inner eye. Such was the case with an unnamed Theosophical family in the early 1900s, whose nine-year-old son Laurie was frequently visited and instructed by what he called "angels." He dictated what they told him to his mother, who showed the material to William Kingsland (1855–1936), an electrical engineer and long-time member of the Theosophical Society.[29] Kingsland was excited enough to edit it for publication by the society's own press as *A Child's Story of Atlantis.*[30]

Laurie's "angel" informant was called Jonathan Er-Whaler, "because he has to do with the greatest Fish of the sea." Jonathan had been a spiritual ruler on Atlantis, where he had known the previous incarnations of Laurie and his mother, Mr. Kingsland, and many other friends. He took Laurie in spirit down under the ocean to see what was left of the continent. Everything they saw there was petrified: houses, tables, chairs, and even a statue of the former Laurie himself. Laurie also learned of the hollows beneath the ocean floor.

> There is more Hollow than what is on top of the earth. There is a lot of Lava inside much of the Hollow. Suppose you had a great Orange with an inch-thick skin, and a yard inside after that—well, then, this World is something like that. There are all sorts of "Forces" inside the World as well as outside. . . . In tunnelling through the mountains for railways, men should watch and look for all these valuable and strange *Forces.*[31]

Laurie was able to view and describe his former life in Atlantis, its "churches" and their rites (very Anglican in flavor), and especially the ubiquitous airships. As he was a nine-year-old boy, this was his major interest, and it occupies much of the small book. As the ultimate wish fulfillment, the former Laurie has his own airship and pilots it from the age of five onward. The airships come in many forms, but are strictly of the Wright Brothers and zeppelin era: most of them have balloons and propellers, and they dock on high masts. Their motive power is "Scear-Force," which is "something between Electricity and Radium," but none in the least resembles Scott-Elliot's luminous vessels.

As to the method of these revelations, Kingsland explains, "Laurie does not at any time go into a trance. He is in full possession of his physical consciousness all the time."[32] There seems to have been no prompting or questioning: Laurie followed where Jonathan took him and told his mother what he saw. On comparing Laurie's diction, as quoted above, with William Kingsland's at the end of this paragraph, one concludes that the editing was minimal. As Kingsland admits, "Some of the things he describes are what he himself sees at the time he is describing them, and it is tolerably evident that in many instances—as is so often the case with 'clairvoyant' vision—there is a good deal of what we may call *personal colour,* that is to say, a good deal of admixture with normal brain impressions and mental images."[33]

Some chapters of *A Child's Story of Atlantis* make tiresome reading today, such as the list of competitors in an airship race, or the Atlantean romance of a present-day gentleman called "Mr. N," who won his fifteen-year-old bride by fighting all the other boys who wanted her, one by one. However, when it comes to the wedding, Laurie has an eye for costume and social mores worthy of Daisy Ashford.[34] Other cringeworthy episodes are the death and burial of Laurie's grandmother and the flood in which he himself perished at nine years of age. Potentially the best chapter, called "Secrets," was suppressed for the time being at Jonathan's wish, to which Kingsland submitted "however much we should like to share with our readers certain information of scientific value given therein."[35] This must be why the title page says "Book 1." These disclosures never saw the light of day, probably to Kingsland's chagrin.

The suppressed "Secrets" apart, nothing in *A Child's Story of Atlantis* exceeds the imaginative powers of a child raised in a Theosophical family. But for that very reason, this minor work casts a particular light, or should we say shadow, on the other channeled communications with which we have to deal. I do not think that Laurie was deliberately putting one over on his mother. The phenomenon of "invisible companions" is evidence enough that children from quite ordinary families can live partially in a world that is real to them alone. Some parents find this infuriating; others treat it as a harmless phase or even play along with it. Theosophists in 1908 might well have interpreted it as a breakthrough into higher consciousness. Laurie could only have been encouraged in his flights of active imagination by these adoring and admiring adults.

LEADBEATER AGAIN

For "adults," we should now read "disciples" as we return to Charles Leadbeater and examine his 500-page treatise on prehistory, *Man: Whence, How and Whither* (1913), nominally written with Annie Besant.[36] Some of it derived from sessions held in the 1890s by the authors and other unnamed Theosophists, other parts from "investigations" in the summer of 1910.[37] Much of it was prepublished piecemeal in *The Theosophist*. Their story is not substantially different from those of Blavatsky and her Masters, Sinnett, or Scott-Elliot, but it gives a sense of the great evolutionary adventure that lies both behind and before the human race. Half of the book deals with the post-Atlantean period: first with the current fifth root race, then, skipping to the future, with a vision of the coming sixth root race. This was by Leadbeater alone. It deserves a place in any survey of utopian or futuristic literature but cannot delay us here.

Man: Whence, How and Whither is quite similar in concept to Fabre d'Olivet's "Philosophical History of the Human Race." It mixes narrative in the style of a history book with scenes in which the writer exercises his power of imagination (however we understand that term). Here is one such scene, describing creatures that lived at a time while the earth's surface was still hot enough to melt copper:

> The pudding-bag creatures did not seem to mind the heat, but
> floated about indifferently, reminding one in their shape of wounded

soldiers who had lost their legs and had had their clothes sewn round the trunk; a blow made an indentation, which slowly filled up again, like the flesh of a person suffering from dropsy; the fore part of the thing had a kind of sucking mouth, through which it drew in food, and it would fasten on another and draw it in, as though sucking an egg through a hole, whereupon the sucked one grew flabby and died; a struggle was noticed in which each had fixed its mouth on the other, and sucked away diligently. They had a kind of flap-hand, like the flap of a seal, and they made a cheerful kind of chirruping trumpeting noise, expressing pleasure—pleasure being a sort of general sense of *bien-être,* and pain a massive discomfort, nothing acute, only faint likes and dislikes. The skin was sometimes serrated, giving shades of colour. Later on, they became a little less shapeless and more human, and crawled on the ground like caterpillars. Later still, near the North Pole, on the cap of land there, these creatures were developing hands and feet, though unable to stand up, and more intelligence was noticeable. A Lord of the Moon—an Arhat who had attained on globe F of the Moon Chain—was observed, who had magnetised an island and shepherded on to it a flock of these creatures, reminding one of sea-cows or porpoises, though with no formed heads; they were taught to browse, instead of sucking each other, and when they did eat each other they chose some parts in preference to others, as though developing taste.[38]

One imagines Leadbeater dictating this from an easy chair, his magnetic blue eyes fixed on the middle distance, while Annie Besant eagerly looks on and contributes her occasional mite, and a disciple scribbles down every word.[39] Freudian undertones apart, they must have been able to laugh at this kind of thing without doubting its veracity. Leadbeater regularly adopts an archly humorous tone when dealing with disgusting habits, ugly people, or lowly human types.

The Lemurian root race, as Blavatsky had explained, was the evolutionary turning point when higher beings incarnated themselves as the human egos. This took place about six-and-a-half million years ago. The astrological conditions were just right, the earth in the optimum magnetic state:

> Then, with the mighty roar of swift descent from incalculable heights, surrounded by blazing masses of fire which filled the sky with shooting tongues of flame, flashed through the aerial spaces the chariot of the Sons of the Fire, the Lords of the Flame from Venus; it halted, hovering over the 'White Island,' which lay smiling in the bosom of the Gobi Sea; green was it, and radiant with masses of fragrant many-coloured blossoms.[40]

So the "Chariots of the Gods" did not begin with Eric von Däniken or Zecharia Sitchin! They are already here: the Mother Ship descends, and out steps Sanaṭ Kumāra, the new Ruler of Earth, with his thirty helpers. Some Theosophists would consider this grossly materialistic; likewise the process by which the Manu, founder and presiding director of the Atlantean root race, bred the latter from Lemurian stock. This, too, anticipates the later popularity of the idea that *Homo sapiens* is the result of genetic interference by some higher or more advanced entity. (Note the imitation of Christian writers in capitalizing pronouns.)

> Subba Rao distinguished the Lemurians as blue-black, the Atlanteans as red-yellow, and the Aryans as brown-white. We find the fourth Race Manu eliminating the blue from the colour of His people, passing through purple into the red of the Rmoahal sub-race, and then, by mixing in the blue-white of the seventh Lemurian sub-race, He obtained the first sub-race which seemed to be fully human, and that we could imagine as living among ourselves.[41]

This matter of breeding a better race should be seen in a context of Leadbeater's preoccupation with past lives. He was engaged, at this period, on a massive project of tracing the former incarnations of all the prominent Theosophists.[42] Central to this was his recent discovery of Jiddu Krishnamurti (1895–1986), an Indian boy whom Leadbeater and Besant were now preparing to become the "World Teacher." As other occultists might cast a horoscope, Leadbeater had been investigating the past lives of the boy he called "Alcyone," every one of them crucial to the grand design. In the process, he came across the past lives of a "Clan" that had been involved with Alcyone ever since they were monkeylike beings on the moon.[43] They included Sirius (currently incarnated as Leadbeater himself), Herakles (Besant), Ulysses (Olcott), Mars (Morya), Mercury (Koot Hoomi), Vajra (Blavatsky), and Siva (Subba Row). Others were not currently incarnated, such as Corona, who had been Julius Caesar.[44] Many Theosophists clamored more or less loudly to be included and were gathered into a gigantic genealogical table, kept in ledger form by Leadbeater's assistants.[45] The series of incarnations showed these pioneers going through their own evolution from subhumans to worldly and spiritual leaders of the race. In a way, the whole project was an alternative to Darwinian evolutionary theory, not so much under intelligent design as under inexorable cyclical law, in which all beings played their appropriate roles.

Here is an episode from the latter days of Atlantis, around 100,000 BCE, that is interesting for several reasons. First, it assumes the dualistic commonplaces of white and dark, good and evil, solar and chthonic, that put it somewhere between *The Magic Flute* and *The Boy's Own Paper*. Second, it shows the satyrs of mythology as actual beings, an idea that will recur with Edgar Cayce in chapter 9. Third is the implicit disavowal of the literary cult of the Great God Pan.[46] During the decades around 1900, Pan stood for paganism, sexual (especially homosexual) license, and a general rejection of Victorian values.

> Corona was then the White Emperor at the City of the Golden Gates; Mars was a general under him, and Herakles was the wife of Mars. A great rebellion was being plotted, and a man of strange and evil knowledge—a "Lord of the Dark Face," leagued with the dark

Earth-Spirits who form the "Kingdom of Pan," the semi-human, semi-animal creatures who are the originals of the Greek satyrs—was gradually gathering round himself a huge army which followed him as Emperor, the Emperor of the Midnight Sun, the Dark Emperor, set over against the White. The worship he established, with himself as central idol—huge images of himself being placed in the temples—was sensual and riotous, holding men through the gratification of their animal passions. Against the White Cave of Initiation in the City of the Golden Gates was set up the Dark Cave in which the mysteries of Pan, the Earth-God, were celebrated. All was working up toward another great catastrophe.[47]

Leadbeater revels in descriptions of the hand-to-hand combats that accompanied the wars between Atlantean factions, in which members of the Clan often perished heroically and their enemies shamefully. The catastrophe in question is the one of 75,025 BCE, in which the islands of Ruṭa and Ḍaitya (note the pseudo-Sanskrit diacritics!) were destroyed by gas explosions, floods, and earthquakes. Here a correction to *The Secret Doctrine* becomes necessary, for this occurred not long after the Manu of the fifth root race had led his people out of Atlantis in 79,997 BCE.[48] (Blavatsky, following Koot Hoomi, had written that the fifth root race began 1 million years ago.) They sailed over the Sahara Sea to Egypt, then trudged on foot to a high plateau in Arabia. As the millennia passed, their numbers grew into several millions and their religion became oppressively orthodox. This necessitated a second exodus of 700 people who were all the Manu's own descendants, for he kept reincarnating to improve the stock with his own genetic input. As Leadbeater puts it, "As bodies died, He packed the egos into new and improved ones."[49] Through this means, and a general survival of the fittest through the privations that followed, the Manu bred the fifth root race.

The home of the race, as we know from Blavatsky, was the sea occupying the present Gobi Desert, and their great city was built beside it. The White Island was not far offshore, joined to the city by a cantilever bridge.

Leadbeater gives to this city, or perhaps to the general region, the traditional Buddhist name of Shambhala, adding, in a footnote, "Shamballa is still the Imperishable Sacred Land, where dwell the four Kumāras, and where gather, every seven years, Initiates of all nations."[50]

Finally come the familiar events that the Egyptians recounted to Solon, and Plato to us. The Emperor of Poseidonis (the rump state that was all remaining of Atlantis) decided to bolster his empire by invading the Mediterranean, and after conquering the western lands was repulsed by the plucky Pelasgians. (Leadbeater draws a patriotic parallel with the fate of the Spanish Armada in 1588, routed by the more agile English vessels.)[51] Then came the final catastrophe of 9564 BCE. Poseidonis collapsed, and dry lands emerged from the Sahara and Gobi Seas. The Manu, as always foreseeing the future, had already emptied the Central Asian Kingdom of its inhabitants, leading the elect into India. To keep their Aryan blood pure and unmixed with that of the indigenous peoples, he instituted the caste system.[52] With that, Leadbeater's tale joins seamlessly with the traditional history of the subcontinent, which seems to have returned the compliment. No less a figure than Ramana Maharshi stated that the lost continent of Lemuria had once stretched all the way across the Indian Ocean, embracing Egypt, Abyssinia, and south India in its confines, implicitly attributing his own Dravidian roots to it.[53]

RUDOLF STEINER AND THEOSOPHY

Rudolf Steiner (1861–1925), the founder of the Anthroposophical movement, never knew Blavatsky or the first generation of Theosophists, nor was he originally drawn to them. As a young man he had experienced the rich mixture of avant-garde art, Wagnerism, spiritualism, psychical research, and Theosophy that swirled around in Vienna; in 1888 he read Sinnett's *Esoteric Buddhism* in German and found its materialistic outlook repellent. A dozen years later, now in Berlin and a recognized figure in the intellectual world, he consented to lecture at a Theosophical library.

Steiner seldom did anything by halves. During the two winters of 1900–1902 he gave fifty-two lectures that covered the history of mysticism, its links to German philosophy, and most especially "Christianity as a Fact of Mystical Experience." Although the library's patrons were Theosophists, Steiner insisted that his lectures were drawn exclusively from his own experiences in the spiritual world,[54] and this would remain his position throughout his life.

One of the lectures was attended by Steiner's future wife, Marie von Sivers. She was an actress with a sophisticated cosmopolitan background who knew Edouard Schuré (see chapter 3) and had translated his work. She was also a keen Theosophist and soon drew Steiner into the movement. With his charisma, Steiner did not need to rise through the ranks. A German section was founded with him as its general secretary, and he attended the London congress in July 1902, lodging with Blavatsky's old friend Bertram Keightley and meeting Annie Besant, Sinnett, G. R. S. Mead, and other worthies. On Steiner's return to Germany he took over the entire central European branch and started his own journal, first called *Lucifer** (just like Blavatsky's London journal), then *Lucifer-Gnosis*.

Even so, Steiner asserted his independence from prevailing trends in the Theosophical Society. He rejected the cult of the Mahatmas, any hint of spiritualism or mediumship, and any engagement with oriental philosophy. Instead he brought along a whole subcontinent of German thought that had been vital to his own intellectual formation. One detail says it all: when Steiner organized the Theosophical Congress in Munich in 1907, he decorated the hall not with portraits of the Masters but with busts of the German idealist philosophers Fichte, Schelling, and Hegel.[55] Most of all, his cosmology was centered on Christ, and in a very different way from the "esoteric Christianity" of Besant and Leadbeater, which was largely a matter of reading Theosophical ideas

---

*This provocative title, associated in the public mind with evil, honored the original meaning of *lucifer* as "light-bearer."

into Christian myths and symbols. Rather as Saint-Yves d'Alveydre took Fabre d'Olivet's work and Christianized it (see chapter 2), Steiner recast Theosophy in a Christocentric mold; and that might serve as a pocket definition of Anthroposophy.

Steiner lost little time in establishing his Theosophical authority for the German-speaking audience. In 1904 he published *Theosophie*,[56] a book that might have been taken for the canonical document of the movement, but which expounds a peculiarly Steinerian system of human consciousness and the process of reincarnation. In the same year, *Lucifer-Gnosis* carried two important series of articles, on "How One Obtains Knowledge of the Higher Worlds,"[57] and "From the Akashic Records: Our Atlantean Ancestors."[58] Material on Lemuria followed and was included in *The Submerged Continents of Atlantis and Lemuria,* a book first published by Steiner's English admirers.[59] Like Scott-Elliot and Leadbeater before him, Steiner began by defending supersensible knowledge as a supplement and corrective to the material sciences of the past.

> These present essays will also show that at a certain high level of his cognitive power, man can penetrate to the eternal origins of the things which vanish with time. . . . The one who has acquired the ability to perceive in the spiritual world comes to know past events in their eternal character. The events do not stand before him like the dead testimony of history, but appear in full *life.* In a certain sense, what has happened takes place before him.[60]

Steiner does allow that this kind of spiritual perception is fallible, but says that it is much more dependable than sense perception, and that "what various initiates can relate about history and prehistory will be in *essential* agreement." He refers the reader approvingly to Scott-Elliot's *Story of Atlantis,* with its information about the civilization that existed for a million years on the floor of the Atlantic Ocean. Steiner's stated intention is to supplement Scott-Elliot's information, and especially to tell more about the spiritual character of the Atlanteans.[61]

Scott-Elliot's book had been published in German the year before (1903), and his companion work *Lost Lemuria* in 1905. The specialist on Anthroposophy Helmut Zander surmises that Steiner's Lemurian information, which began to emerge in October 1904, was gleaned instead from Blavatsky and Sinnett.[62] This raises the question of exactly what were Steiner's sources. "*Today*," he writes in the same preface, "I am still obliged to remain silent about the sources of the information given here. One who knows anything at all about such sources will understand why this has to be so. But events can occur that will make a breaking of this silence possible very soon."[63]

Why the mystification? Steiner had already described how a person can penetrate to a direct perception of the past; he had defended the veracity of what is thus seen; and he had promised to tell more than the English Theosophists had to offer. No reader could possibly expect the source to be other than himself, otherwise why should one believe a word of it? But then, why should he mention Scott-Elliot at all? If we hold Steiner to his own principles, it must have been because initiates are in "essential agreement" about the past. Therefore any agreement between Steiner and the Theosophists would have been due to the fact that they both "saw" the same things. This implies a massive compliment to the Theosophists, and more especially to Charles Leadbeater, who as we know was the source of most of the material in question.

Steiner was not ungenerous with such compliments. In 1907, in an important statement to Schuré, he admitted that "true initiates" stood at the Theosophical Society's cradle.[64] Even after his resignation, whenever he spoke on the anniversaries of Madame Blavatsky's death (May 8, 1891) he did not fail to "evoke feelings of admiration, veneration, and gratitude"[65] toward her. He conceded that "*The Secret Doctrine* contains the greatest revelations of this order that humanity was able to receive at the time," and that in the Mahatma Letters "we may find some of the greatest wisdom given to humankind."[66] But he could not stand Leadbeater.

From the start of his involvement with the Theosophical Society, Steiner had made it plain to Annie Besant that the society's general attitude to Christianity was not his own, and they agreed to differ on the subject. This worked for almost a decade, while Steiner went his own way in almost total independence from the parent society. But the scandals surrounding Leadbeater, and Besant's reinstatement of him against many Theosophists' objections, sorely tried Steiner's puritanical principles. In 1911, when Besant and Leadbeater founded the Order of the Star in the East to prepare the world for the return of Christ-Maitreya in the form of Krishnamurti, it was the last straw. Steiner called on Besant to resign; she responded by withdrawing his charter for the German branch; and he founded the Anthroposophical Society.

Once freed from obligatory courtesy, Steiner was more outspoken about the Theosophists' methods and materials. He took up the allegation of a Christian esotericist, C. G. Harrison (see chapter 12), that Blavatsky had been subjected to "occult imprisonment" for teaching false doctrines.[67] He dismissed Sinnett's *The Occult World* and *Esoteric Buddhism* as having been produced by "precipitation" by the spirit of John King, a pirate well known to Spiritualist séances.[68] He claimed that the Theosophists' information on the world of Atlantis had been obtained through putting a person into a mediumistic state, and that all their communications from the spiritual world, including those in Scott-Elliot's book, came in that way. As for Steiner's own path, he insisted that it was entirely different from anything the society had known: it was "to reject all earlier ways of investigation and, admittedly by means of supersensible perception, to investigate by making use only of what can be revealed to the one who is *himself* the investigator."[69]

Here Steiner was mistaken. He may have heard about Sinnett's séances with Maude Scott-Elliot (see chapter 4), but he seems to have known very little about Leadbeater, whose reading of the Akashic Records was not mediumistic at all but done in full consciousness, as we assume Steiner's to have been. The two cases are closely parallel, even to the point that Steiner, in his last year, spun out long chains of reincarnations,[70] just as Leadbeater had done with the lives of Alcyone and his Clan. Moreover, Steiner's story of the past concurs with the Theosophical one in most of its fundamental principles. It includes the progressive materialization of the human body; the seven root races, and, after the first two (Polarian and Hyperborean), seven sub-races in each; the separation of the sexes during the Lemurian root race; the role of the Manu, assisted by other divine messengers, in managing the development of the Aryan root race and gradually entrusting it to human initiates.[71] Steiner hints at the dark arts of the Atlantean sorcerers but coyly breaks off, saying in a footnote, "*For the present* it is not permitted to make public communications about the origin of this knowledge and *these* arts. A passage from the Akasha Chronicle must therefore be omitted here."[72] As though any well-read Theosophist didn't already know about them!

Building on this foundation, Steiner goes beyond the Theosophists in several respects. This is not the place to elaborate on their concept of "Rounds," which first came up in the Mahatma Letters: it is sufficient to know that our present Manvantara (large-scale time cycle), with its seven root races, is the fourth of seven such cycles, the other six taking place on other planets. Blavatsky said very little about these, but Steiner discourses freely about the evolution of protohumans on Saturn, the sun, and the moon,[73] and even the developments that will take place far in the future on Jupiter, Venus, and Vulcan.[74] Moving to our own round on Earth, we learn some surprising things about the Polarian and Hyperborean epochs. As the cycle began, there was no material separation between sun, Earth, and moon. During the Polarian epoch, the sun was "extruded from the earth," taking with it the more subtle elements, and during the Hyperborean, the moon was extruded, taking the coarsest ones.[75] Human beings were present throughout the whole process, their form and consciousness changing along with the cosmic process.

If any astronomers or physicists should object to the above, they should know that in Steiner's cosmology there is a continuum that runs from the spiritual world to the astral, from there to the etheric, and from that to the gaseous, fluid, and solid states of matter. Human life is viable in any of these states, and in earlier times, it took place entirely in the former ones. The same applies to the earth, which has gradually solidified during the present Manvantara. Before the separation of the sexes, the human body was a soft, malleable mass, controlled not by muscle but by the will. The future cartilages and bones were latent in the etheric body, but not present physically. Humans had the senses of hearing and of hot and cold, but sight came later.[76] Parts of the earth were still not solidified, and that is where human and similar animals lived. Other animals that had already developed sexual differentiation and senses, such as the reptiles, lived in the more solid parts, but having solidified too soon, their evolution stopped there.[77]

It is hardly surprising that Steiner's Lemurians related to nature, and to the laws of physics, in a way very different from our own. They had an intuitive understanding of natural forces and could control the weather, the growth of plants, and even the evolution of animal into human forms, just by applying the will. They used this power to remodel the hills, and in later periods built cities in stone,[78] but what they perceived was blurred to their dawning sight, because the atmosphere was filled with mist and the sun never shone through the clouds. Gradually the Lemurian body formed cartilages, and then, with the Atlantean period, a bony skeleton appeared. But there was still a lot of leeway for the force of will. An early Atlantean could break an iron rail or stop a cannonball, had such things existed, through psychic force alone. His physical form also adjusted to his will and soul quality, so that the more intelligent beings became smaller and neater in stature, the stupider ones giants.[79] Later in Atlantis, the perversion of magical powers led to the creation of grotesque human monsters, but these were not able to survive into the next epoch.

Under the supervision of higher beings, the Atlanteans developed from the elite of the Lemurian race, saved from the cataclysm that destroyed the southern continent. At first they passed much of their lives in the spiritual world, with spiritual beings for companions. They would spend the night busily there, then at daybreak would return to their bodies to rest, like snails into their shells.[80] As the seven sub-races succeeded each other, their consciousness and habits changed to become steadily more like our own. Stated very briefly, the Rmoahals developed a memory of vivid sense impressions and feelings and began to use language. The Tlvatlis began to form groups and acquire a sense of self, from which came the awareness and worship of their ancestors. The Toltecs had larger communities, led by initiate kings, that helped create common memories, and these in turn made for harmonious group relations. The Turanians began to misuse the newly gained powers for selfish ends. The Original Semites developed logical thinking and the presence of an inner voice. The Akkadians took the development of thinking further, replacing the natural harmony of the Toltecs with constrictive laws. Finally the seventh sub-race, the Mongols, preferred to trust in the life force rather than in thinking, and to reverence everything that was old rather than new. As Steiner remarks, their descendants still have this characteristic.[81]

Steiner does not say at what stage the Atlanteans took to the air, but when they did, their airships were powered by harnessing the energy in growing things. To this end, they stocked great quantities of seeds in the sheds where these contraptions were kept and somehow extracted motive power from them. Their airships could only float a short distance above the ground and would not work at all today, because in those days the air was thicker, the water thinner.[82] The power of growth and reproduction, which Steiner also does not explain, was what the Atlanteans now abused, turning it to selfish ends; initiates were as guilty of this as anyone. Because this power is intimately linked to air and water, meddling with it had repercussions in the environment, first as storms and eventually as the cataclysm with which we are familiar.[83]

Before the final fall, however, the Manu, who was a divine being in charge of human development, had gathered the core of the future fifth root race.[84] He and his kind had already reached the human state in previous cycles; they could take on human form, or not, as it suited their purposes. Now they deliberately chose people from the fifth sub-race who were poor in clairvoyant and magical powers, but more developed in the novel faculty of thinking. The divine being called by Steiner "the great initiate of the Sun Oracle" led these pioneers to a place in central Asia (elsewhere he mentions the Gobi Desert) where they could be isolated from other human groups and work intensively on their evolution. They needed to put their Atlantean psychic powers behind them and learn to think. This is the primary task of the Aryan root race, but it should be devoted to higher rather than selfish purposes.[85]

Once Steiner's reading of the Akashic Records reaches the fifth root race, his revelations revolve around the occult Christology that had been his central concern ever since his early vision of what he called the "Mystery of Golgotha." Our interest is in his prehistory, and in how it fits into the broader context of this study. In the end, it seems to be a variation on the Theosophists' themes. Steiner's Atlanteans and Lemurians differ from Leadbeater's, but much less than the two occultists differed in character and style. Steiner is less a master of the bizarre detail; there is very little sense of humor in him, but more psychological insight. Consequently, all the questions that may trouble us about Leadbeater's methods, sources, motivation, and ethics apply to Steiner, too. Both seers claimed to be reading the Akashic Records, but as it turned out, Leadbeater's reading confirmed that of Blavatsky and the Mahatmas, and Steiner's confirmed all of them.

As for later influence, Steiner's death at sixty-four and the rise of the Nazi party deprived Anthroposophy of the role he had had in mind for it. For example, he had a political theory called the "Threefold Commonwealth," much resembling Saint-Yves d'Alveydre's Synarchy. His ambitions were not slight. In one of the lectures drawn on for the above digest, titled "Rosicrucian Esotericism," he likens the pioneers of the Aryan root race to the early Christians huddling in the Roman catacombs, then to the Anthroposophists, equally despised by their contemporaries but by implication as momentous in their future influence. Nowadays his followers are more ignored than despised, and Steiner's prehistory belongs to those aspects of his teaching that they prefer to play down. If Anthroposophy has an influence on society today, it is through its educational system, practiced worldwide in the Waldorf Schools, and to a lesser extent in alternative medicine and agriculture (e.g., Weleda products; biodynamic farming). Many people who make use of these schools and products are not Anthroposophists, and talk of Lemurians or the extrusion of the moon might not bolster their confidence.

Rudolf Steiner is a phenomenon: a man of seemingly superhuman knowledge, abilities, and energy who poured out a torrent of information that would take a lifetime to encompass. Besides his many books, he gave almost daily lectures that were taken down in shorthand. Many of them were published later, unrevised, but they are perfectly cogent, and the resulting system is consistent through and through. He had the perfect answer to critics: that what he was practicing was spiritual *science,* and if they took the trouble to work at it, they would achieve similar results and confirm his findings with their own. In contrast, our next Theosophical offshoot never claimed to have seen anything herself, yet when it came to prehistory, she too held firmly to the party line.

ALICE BAILEY AND "THE TIBETAN"

In November 1919, Alice A. Bailey (1880–1949) was snatching a moment of peace and solitude when she heard a disembodied voice: "There are some books which it is desired should be written for the public. You can write them. Will you do so?" it said. "Certainly not," she replied. "I'm not a darned psychic and I don't want to be drawn into anything like that."[86]

She had reason to be wary. Born to a prosperous Scottish family, she had descended via missionary work in India to become the battered wife of a clergyman, thence to working in a sardine factory to support her three daughters. A period spent at the Theosophical community in Krotona, Hollywood, had given her an appreciation of its principles and of *The Secret Doctrine,* but also disillusionment with the competitive and bickering atmosphere; it also brought her Foster Bailey, her second husband.

After this mysterious summons was repeated, she decided to give it a try. The process of dictation by a being who called himself "The Tibetan" scared her, and she again backed out, but was encouraged to contact Koot Hoomi to discuss her doubts. This she did, "following the very definite technique He had taught me," and was reassured that the plan came from him: she had nothing to fear by acting as the Tibetan's "amanuensis and secretary."[87] The result was the first chapters of *Initiation, Human and Solar.*

The communicator (whom Carl Jung allegedly took to be Alice Bailey's higher self[88]) identified himself privately as the Master Djwal Khul, a junior member of the group to which Koot Hoomi and Morya belonged and who figures frequently in their letters. Bailey, still a member of the Theosophical Society, submitted her material to the Indian headquarters for publication in *The Theosophist*.[89] But with Besant and Leadbeater's clairvoyant activities in full swing, the society did not approve of individuals claiming their own contacts with the Masters. The Baileys started their own publishing company, at first following the examples of Blavatsky and Steiner in styling it "Lucifer." In 1922 it issued *Initiation*[90] along with two other books.[91]

Bailey thereafter followed her own path, independently of the Theosophists but with a basic commonality of doctrine and outlook. Through her, Djwal Khul poured forth a whole shelf of books on cosmic evolution, the hierarchy of masters and initiations, the subtle worlds and the ways of working with them, esoteric Christianity, astrology, and the political problems of the twentieth century. To a nonenthusiast, his writing is turgid and textbook-like, lacking the color that Blavatsky or Leadbeater could lend to their equally pretentious works. *Initiation, Human and Solar* is a fresh approach to familiar Theosophical themes, notably the hierarchy of beings supervising evolution and their relationship to the individual. Leadbeater, too, had become interested in these matters and in the "seven rays" on which Blavatsky had briefly touched. Gregory Tillett points out that although Bailey's material was unacceptable to official Theosophy, Leadbeater never criticized her and held her early books in high regard. His own book *The Masters and the Path* (1925) is so similar in substance to Bailey's *Initiation* that Tillett writes, "One wonders which came first."[92] The two of them together are at the root of all the later channeled material and lore concerning "ascended masters."

Bailey's hierarchy seems like a parody of corporate bureaucracy—or of the Masters' purported creation, the United Nations. At the head of affairs is Sanat Kumāra, the Lord of the World, with three advisers who, like himself, were perfected in an earlier solar system. Beneath them are officers responsible for adjusting karma from the global down to the individual level, and for the care and tabulation of the Akashic Records. Then come three departmental heads: the Manu, the Christ, and the Maha Chohan, with familiar Theosophical masters like Koot Hoomi and Morya attached to one or the other of them. The hierarchy itself is in perpetual evolution: its members pass through a series of initiations and get promoted, leaving behind vacancies that are filled by newcomers. It holds regular meetings in the council chamber of the Lord of the World and apportions jobs to each member according to his (and it is always "his") specialization. There they pass resolutions that decide the degree and manner of their intervention in human affairs.

The hierarchy's center is Shamballa, called in ancient books the "White Island" and located in the Gobi Desert. It exists in etheric matter and is perceptible only through the corresponding vision. (This, incidentally, accords with Tibetan Buddhist teachings on the subject.[93]) There the Lord of the World resides and receives daily reports from the three departmental heads. The first of these is the Manu of the fifth root race, who lives in Shigatse. We may remember him described by Leadbeater as manipulating the racial stock like an artist blending colors, with a generous input from his own DNA. Bailey gives his job description in more sober style:

> Largely concerned with planetary politics, and with the founding direction, and dissolution of racial types and forms . . . to Him is given the work of setting the race type, of segregating the groups out of which races will develop, of manipulating the forces which move the earth's crust, of raising and lowering continents, of directing the minds of statesmen everywhere so that racial government will proceed as desired, and conditions be brought about which will produce those needed for the fostering of any particular type.[94]

The second departmental head is the Christ, otherwise called the World Teacher and identified with the Buddhists' Maitreya and the Muslims' Mahdi. Leadbeater and Bailey have a great deal to say about this figure, but he is not relevant to our theme, having only come to Earth in 600 BCE. The third head is the Maha Chohan who arrived during the second sub-race of the Atlantean root race. From Bailey we learn that he was responsible for the changes that took place halfway through that root race, at which other Theosophists have hinted. First, she says that the Maha Chohan arranged at that time for many of the present more advanced humans to come into incarnation.[95] Second, the hierarchy decided that the time was ripe to open its door to admit humans, so that its ranks could be filled by those suitably qualified. At the same time the border between humans and animals was closed, so that animals will have to wait for another great cycle to move up to the human state.[96] But the most interesting thing is that to further human progress, "The problem of good or evil, light or darkness, right or wrong, was enunciated solely for the benefit of humanity, and to enable men to cast off the fetters which imprisoned spirit, and thus achieve spiritual freedom."[97] This problem does not exist either for higher or lower beings, but in Atlantis it led to the famous struggle between the forces of light and the forces of darkness. Bailey's informant adds, referring to the recent First World War, that on every side were found "those who fought for an ideal as they saw it, for the highest that they knew, and those who fought for material and selfish advantage. In the struggle of these influential idealists or materialists many were swept in who fought blindly and ignorantly, being thus overwhelmed with racial karma and disaster."[98] Like the choice of the title "Lucifer," this was a declaration of independence from Christian and every other orthodoxy that believes in an evil principle. It was also a challenge to those who looked on the war—or any war—in terms of absolute good versus absolute evil.

Later, after the Second World War, Bailey would return to the theme of Shamballa and its role in world affairs. Writing not long before her death in 1949, she announced that Shamballa was now intervening for only the third time in human history. The first time had been in Lemuria, when humans became individualized (presumably at the "separation of the sexes"); the second, during the great struggle in Atlantis between the "Lords of Light and the Lords of Material Expression." And now for a third time it was producing radical changes in the consciousness of the race, "which will completely alter man's attitude to life and his grasp of the spiritual, esoteric and subjective essentials of living."[99] However, the process had far to go because even now, "the masses of people are today Atlantean in their consciousness and are only slowly emerging into the Aryan point of view."[100]

Alice Bailey had much in common with Besant and Leadbeater, especially the respects in which their teaching and style diverged from those of Blavatsky and her Mahatmas. These included a devotional tone unknown in early Theosophy, especially regarding the Masters. Blavatsky had left Theosophists free to believe in them, or not; now they were shown to have been central to the whole cosmic enterprise and personally responsible for matters like the influx of human incarnations and Earth changes, which *The Secret Doctrine* left to nature's harmonious regulation.[101] Emotions were stirred up by expectation of the coming World Teacher, whether he was supposed to take over Krishnamurti, or return to Earth in his own form, as Bailey gave to believe. Discipleship was presented in terms of initiations to be passed like school examinations. Finally there was the unspoken assumption that Blavatsky's work had been superseded by the dicta of the new chosen ones.

While Leadbeater and Besant's Theosophy suffered a severe loss of membership and prestige after Krishnamurti's resignation in 1929, Bailey's movement was on the upswing, untouched by scandal or ridicule. After the war her books were faithfully kept in print by the Lucis Trust, their indigo covers conspicuous in every occult bookstore during the 1960s. Though the six volumes of *A Treatise on Cosmic Fire* may have found few buyers and fewer readers, the energetic "Group of World Servers" promoting Bailey's work ensured a new lease on life for many Theosophical concepts. As Wouter Hanegraaff writes, "Bailey's influence on the New Age movement, especially in its early phases, is pervasive; it is she who is also generally credited with having introduced the term 'New Age'."[102]

FIVE

Germanic Atlantology

————————— ✳ —————————

THE GERMANIC STRAIN of Atlantology brings us to the most sensitive point of our study. If the reader does not already know it, this chapter will make it plain that the Ariosophists, an obscure group of romantic nationalists, were a breeding ground for the racial doctrines of National Socialism. Whether the individual Ariosophists would have applauded the Nazis' policies is another question; in most cases it seems unlikely. Another question that has been raised is the responsibility of Theosophy and of Blavatsky herself, since Ariosophic racial theory arose in part from their doctrine of root races. The historian of religions James Santucci, after scrutinizing the doctrine as it appears both in Blavatsky's work and in the Mahatma Letters (see chapter 3), concludes that their concept of race did not concern the genetic classification of living people, but stages of universal human evolution. He writes: "To place this teaching in the context of the nineteenth century, Blavatsky probably employed the label 'race' only because of its scientific connotations, a term that would fit well into the notion of discrete evolutionary stages of humanity."[1]

Not so the Ariosophists, despite the alacrity with which they adapted Theosophical prehistory and handed it on to their readers as established truth. The rarity of Ariosophical writings outside German libraries, and even within them, makes study difficult, and I am indebted to Nicholas

Goodrick-Clarke's groundbreaking book, *The Occult Roots of Nazism,* which still serves as the main portal for understanding them.[2] The selection that follows shows some of the main trends.

LANZ-LIEBENFELS AND THE SODOMITE APELINGS

Jörg Lanz-Liebenfels (sometimes called "von Liebenfels," 1874–1954) may have received the seed of his "theozoology" from Theosophy, but its grotesque flowering was all his own. His theory, first published in 1904, was that the white race was originally endowed with godlike qualities, including sense organs that gave them a form of clairvoyance. Lanz describes it thus, equating these early humans with what were later worshiped as gods: "What we laboriously and indirectly see with the scientific eye was seen by the ancients using another kind of sight. Because of this they have an amazing knowledge of pre-history. The divine electricity transferred it into them! The gods were not only living electrical receiving stations, however, they were also electrical power- and broadcasting stations."[3] As long as the divine nature was alive in them, this fortunate folk enjoyed "indescribable happiness," dwelling, among other places, on Atlantis. This was a large body of land in the Atlantic Ocean that scientists (says Lanz) have proved to be the place of origin of the tall, white race that populated Europe and built giant stone structures.[4]

So far, we recognize a commonplace blend of Plato with contemporary Atlantology. It would not have needed Rudolf Steiner or Blavatsky to give Lanz the idea that the Atlanteans were clairvoyant. He knew the Greco-Roman classics and the scriptures, both biblical and apocryphal, and there was material aplenty there. Also, as we may suspect from the above quotation, he was interested in science and had his own ideas about electricity. Elsewhere in the same book he proposes a method of telegraphic transmission using "cold chemical rays"[5] that to readers of the 1900s probably sounded no less impressive and incomprehensible than Einstein's theory of relativity.

Furthermore, this ex-Cistercian monk and "New Templar" seems to have had a singularly materialistic philosophy in which everything spiritual comes down to ESP, and that comes down to electricity of one sort or another. Jesus was an "electrical entity," but the demons that opposed him also possessed these powers.[6] If asked to define divinity, Lanz writes:

> I understand [by it] the living beings of the ultraviolet and ultrared forces and worlds. In former times they were embodied and moved about in complete purity. Today they live on in human beings. The gods slumber in bestialized human bodies, but the day is coming when they will rise up again. We were electric, we will be electric, to be electric and to be divine is the same thing![7]

To return to Lanz's happy ancients, we learn that other, similarly gifted creatures were coeval with them. Some of these had two legs and wings, like the fossils of flying reptiles; they are remembered in legends of angels and devils. Others were more apelike. Dwarves, too, were much more common in those days. Scientists may deny that species of the dinosaur age could have survived into human times, but Lanz explains that in places like the Near East, where the earth's surface has remained unchanged since the Secondary and Tertiary Ages, "a gradual and gentle evolution occurred, where closely related older and younger forms cross-bred with each other and the whole animal world was able to maintain its archaic structure for a long time."[8] This is ripe stuff for science fiction; the two instances just mentioned being the themes behind Arthur C. Clarke's *Childhood's End* and Conan Doyle's *The Lost World*.

If we recall what Genesis and the Book of Enoch have to say about the Sons of God and the Daughters of Men (see chapter 3), we can predict the next step in Lanz's prehistory: the pure race started to interbreed with the nonhuman species. Plato bowdlerized it in the *Critias* as the waning of the divine element in the Atlanteans as it became mixed with the mortal element. For Lanz, as for Blavatsky, the two elements were not divine and human, but human and bestial.

Most occult Atlantologists, if they reach this point, leave it to the imagination, but for Lanz things were to get much worse. He had come to believe that these apelike creatures had persisted into biblical and classical times, when they were used as sexual partners by both men and women. In fact, they were very much in demand and fetched a high price among the decadent, leisured classes of Israel, Assyria, and Persia. Lanz then goes to work on the Bible to show how its compilers shared his obsession, and all the more so since they were living in the thick of it. All one needs to know are the code words. In the few dozen pages of *Theozoology,* we are warned to look out for any biblical mention of foreigners, earth, stone, wood, tower, city, house, fish, dragon, bread, water, flax, vessel, and gold. None of these words mean what they say; they are all euphemisms for the subhuman sex slaves, the "Sodomite hobgoblins," against whom the Hebrew prophets and Jesus himself railed. Lanz interprets Jesus's own temptations as being of intercourse with them, and his crucifixion as an attempted rape. So widespread was this practice that most people alive today are the degenerate result of this bestial copulation.

But not quite all of us. The Aryans, and especially some Germans, have more of the true human element in their genes. To Lanz, the consequence was plain. Cattle breeders know how to go about it, and we must do the same. The human race must be purified by a rigid eugenic program that will, in time, breed out the animal element, though we will still need some subhuman creatures as slaves.[9] For a start, he recommends cutting the babble about Christian brotherly love and focusing our charity more selectively. "Those who should be supported are strictly the old, and those of good Germanic descent, and for Jews, those of true Israeli descent."[10] Like other prophets urging a spiritual renewal to reverse the decline of the West, Lanz issues a clarion call to his countrymen to purge themselves of their ape-nature.

> Only today, now that almost the whole world has succumbed to ape-nature—right up to the Germanic countries which have not been fully spared either—does the truth begin to dawn on us, that we

are lacking the divine humanity in a general flood of ape-men. But it will not be long before a new priestly race will rise up in the land of the electron and the Holy Graal, which will play new songs on new harps, and as before, on the first feast of Pentecost, when the spirit descended in tongues of radiation on the apostles (Acts 2.3), so will the electrical swans of the gods come once more to the great Pentecost of mankind. Great princes, strong warriors, God-inspired priests, singers with eloquent tongues, and bright-eyed cosmologists will rise up out of Germany's ever-holy soil of the gods—put the Sodomite apelings in chains, establish anew the Church of the Holy Spirit, of the Holy Graal, and make the Earth into an "Island of the Blessed."[11]

Lanz's theories were first published without mentioning Theosophy, as though they were entirely his own deductions from classical and biblical sources. This makes it all the more surprising that in *Die Theosophie und die assyrischen 'Menschentiere'* (Theosophy and the Assyrian "Manbeasts," 1907) he showed how well Blavatsky's *Secret Doctrine* and other Theosophical works corroborated his own theories.[12] He even included one of Scott-Elliot's maps of Lemuria and correlated the five root races, as Scott-Elliot had done, with recent scientific chronology. Of course his prize exhibit was the "sin of the mindless," which corresponded in his system to the first miscegenation of humans with animals.

One might expect a work as eccentric as *Theozoologie* to garner few compliments. Quite the contrary: soon after its appearance the book and its author were highly commended by the father-figure of the Ariosophists.[13]

GUIDO VON LIST, FATHER OF ARIOSOPHY

Guido von List (1848–1919) was considerably older than Lanz, but he had a whole career behind him as a Viennese littérateur before entering the occult field. His main genre had been fiction of a romantic nationalist type, and one of his methods was to visit ancient sites and imagine what life was like in their glory days. His career was interrupted in 1902 by an operation for cataract that left him blind for nearly a year. The traumatic but transformational experience confirmed his belief in his own inherited gift for clairvoyance. As Goodrick-Clarke writes, "List's vision of the prehistoric past owed little to empirical methods of historical research. His surmises depended rather upon the clairvoyant illumination that certain places induced in his mind."[14] List's reimagination of ancient Germanic religion and culture now led to theories about an esoteric language of runes and symbols, and thence to a *prisca theologia* (primordial theology) that became the foundation of Ariosophy.

A theology needs a myth of origins, and for List this lay ready to hand in the Arctic-Aryan theory, combined with the Theosophical system of root races. In his book on cosmic and human law, *Die Rita der Ario-Germanen* (The law of the Aryo-Germans), written in 1907,[15] List writes that the Aryans came from the Northwest and spread to Europe, part of Asia, North Africa, and India. The contents of their sacred book, the Edda, dates from long before the last Ice Age, or even the next to last, and probably from before the last one or two great floods. (Elsewhere List dates their laws to the Miocene era, millions of years ago.[16]) Its real place of origin cannot have been Iceland or Scandinavia, whose landscape the Edda does not depict, but further north, in the land of Apollo where it was said that the sun did not set. Probably consequent on a shift in the earth's axis, the north polar lands faced the sun and had eternal day; we know that there were tropical fauna and flora there. With a further change in the axis came the dreadful *Fimbulwinter,* (the dire winter of Nordic legend), then floods and changes in the disposition of land and sea. The Aryans migrated south in all directions, bringing their wisdom and their Rita or laws to their new homes. For a long time they lived in "autochthonous" isolation, and only after their population increased did they meet other Aryan waves and form a single people. They named all localities after reminiscences of their polar home.[17]

This much is a variant of the Arctic origins theory of Bailly and Fabre d'Olivet (see chapter 2). The following quotation has a far different pedigree. It comes in a discussion of cosmic forces and their applicability to the aeronautical problem of the early twentieth century, namely the inability of aircraft to carry heavy loads: "The air-vehicles mentioned in the well-known catastrophe of Atlantis, the erection of the amazing cyclopean constructions that baffle us with their piles of monstrous stones, which would mock at our modern lifting devices, and many other mysteries of prehistoric technology, are to be explained by laws not only known to, but put to use by the 'ancient sages,' like so much else that we have lost."[18] We know that List read the Theosophist G. R. S. Mead;[19] this sounds as though he read Scott-Elliot as well (see chapter 4), who had already been translated into German.

A shorter work of 1909 or 1910, *Die Religion der Ario-Germanen* (The religion of the Aryo-Germans), is Theosophical through and through. Here List acknowledges Blavatsky in passing, but presents her notions more as his own ex cathedra statements. In short order he expounds such basic Theosophical themes as the future reconciliation of science and religion;[20] a universal, impersonal hidden god as distinct from the First Logos, and an emanational cosmogony;[21] the universality of consciousness, even of the atom;[22] the sevenfold vibratory law governing everything;[23] the creation of mankind by lunar ancestors;[24] the seven root races, with the earliest ones androgynous, the fourth being the scene of the separation of the sexes before its destruction in the Flood, and the Aryan as the fifth;[25] the sevenfold constitution of the human entity;[26] Karma (called *Garma*), reincarnation, and universal progress to higher states;[27] the experiences between death and rebirth (a favorite theme of Steiner's);[28] humans not evolved from animals, but some animals descended from humans through unnatural hybridization;[29] the presence of the divine within the self, and consequent lack of need for priests or saviors;[30] the human potential for freedom from the wheel of rebirth and for eventual divinization;[31] and the Four Yugas, the Kali Yuga lasting 432,000 years.[32]

Whereas Blavatsky's Aryan root race was raised in central Asia, List, obedient to the other constant in Germanic prehistory, has it coming from the land around the North Pole.[33] Moreover, when he mentions the human-animal hybrids, List cites the works of Lanz discussed above, telling the reader that more details will be found in those "pioneering works."

In his next work, a large-scale, illustrated study of symbolism, List corrected an error about when the separation of the sexes occurred, to bring it into accord with Blavatsky's system. In *Religion* he had written, "The Third Race of humans was still androgynous, and . . . only with the Fourth Race were the male and female genders split." In *Die Bilderschrift der Ario-Germanen* (The picture writing of the Aryo-Germans, 1910), he writes: "With the Third Race the distinction between male and female began."[34]

POSTWAR RECONSTRUCTION I

After the First World War, Germany was in need of myths that would excuse its defeat and give its people hope for the future. Ariosophy lay readily to hand with its enticing myth of a Nordic-Aryan-Atlantean origin for the German folk, their rational yet spiritual worldview, and their exile compelled by natural forces beyond their control. The recent war had proved how the inferior races, with whom the Aryans unwisely interbred, had become their enemies both from within, by polluting their blood, and from without. Lanz's proposal for eugenic purification, which in 1904 may have seemed almost parodic, now became a recipe for postwar reconstruction.

Already in 1920, Otto Hauser published an epic poem that he had been writing in Vienna during the war, called *Atlantis: Der Untergang einer Welt* (Atlantis: the fall of a world). The narrator, sole survivor of Atlantis, recounts Lanz-Liebenfels's theme of blond humans mating with apes as the reason for the fall. Two years later, the Theosophist Max Duphorn published a similarly titled *Atlantis: Eine untergegangene Welt* (Atlantis, a fallen world). I rely on Franz Wegener for a summary of these two works. Wegener writes that Duphorn uses as sources Blavatsky, Scott-Elliot, Karl Georg Zschaetzsch, and List, then predicts, on the authority of two Harvard professors, that a great island will rise in the western Atlantic Ocean. This will reroute the Gulf Stream, changing the climate of Germany to one like the Riviera. Of course the rising of one land must be balanced by the sinking of another, so most of England, parts of northern France, Belgium, and Holland will all disappear. But this is merely the prelude: the real deluge will arrive in 1,300 years' time. Duphorn moralizes that such changes, rooting out much that is sickly and evil, open up new paths to higher development; so the German folk should look forward with confidence to the future.[35]

Karl Georg Zschaetzsch, just mentioned, had already published *Die Herkunft und Geschichte des arischen Stammes* (The origin and history of the Aryan tribe). He uses a familiar method of picking suitable passages from South American mythologies, the Edda, and the Bible to show that the Aryans originally came from Thule, the mythic land in the far North.[36] Zschaetzsch followed this in 1922 with *Atlantis, die Urheimat der Arier* (Atlantis, the original home of the Aryans), adding a large dose of Plato to the mix and constructing the following scenario. The original Aryans, identified from the first sentence as blond-haired and blue-eyed, flourished on the Atlantic island from at least 29,500 years ago.[37] They inhabited a fertile plain in the southern part, the north being a heavily forested, volcanic zone. At an unspecified date, a close encounter with a comet caused a conflagration (*Sintbrand*) affecting the southern plain, in which all but three of the Aryans perished.[38] The survivors were an old man, a boy, and a young woman. The world's mythologies commemorate this trio under various guises, such as sun, Mars, and Venus, or, in the Book of Genesis, as God, Adam, and Eve.[39] Zschaetzsch pictures their adventures and way of life as though things must have happened "just so."

In time, their descendants mixed with survivors from other races, gave up their vegetarian habits (a constant of Aryan-Atlantean lore), and multiplied. Eventually they had to sail in search of other lands, bringing the gifts of civilization to the inhabitants who had lived till then in a subhuman condition. This is testified, with one accord, by the legends of Mesopotamia, East Asia, Africa, Australia, and America.[40]

As the centuries passed, Atlantis lost its pure Aryan population, and on the eve of the deluge, so American tradition says, was home to sixty-four million inhabitants drawn from every other race on Earth[41] (a number that betrays Zschaetzsch's reliance on Le Plongeon; see chapter 8). Zschaetzsch has no utopian illusions about their life. They lived under a theocracy, which began to crumble only after the return of the defeated Atlantean fleet. This, as Plato recounts, had been sent to conquer the Mediterranean lands and been repulsed by the Athenians. Here Zschaetzsch finds passages in the Edda and the Book of Revelation that he is sure refer to a rebellion against the priesthood, with the rebels characterized as the Fenris Wolf and the Beast. Such texts, he says, record events far separate in time that have been melded together. For example, the catastrophe called in the Edda *ragnarök* combines the fall of the last Aryan rule over Atlantis, around 3,500 years after the conflagration, with the wars just before the final deluge in 9600 BCE.[42]

For the cause of the deluge, Zschaetzsch considers the possibility of continental drift, recently proposed by Alfred Wegener but not widely accepted for a long time to come. If the American and European continents suddenly moved further apart, it would have stretched the surface of an Atlantic island so thin that the hot, fluid mass on which it rested could have burst upward.[43] In any case, after the catastrophe the Aryan race survived in its purest form in northwest Europe, and continued there into historical times. Wherever its blood has been mixed with that of other races, it has been to their evolutionary advantage, but not its own. It is not in the interests of humanity for a tribe of this quality to become extinct.[44] The solution is to find a region where those of pure Aryan descent can assemble and reconstitute their kind.

Where could this be? Zschaetzsch favors the region that used to be German East Africa, in the highlands of Rwanda and around Lake Tanganyika. Only young people would be allowed to settle there, and measures would be taken to prevent any miscegenation with the local Negroes. As for the difference in climate from northern Europe, Zschaetzsch reminds us that the Aryans originally came from a warm land, and could in time readjust to it, especially if they began on the highlands and gradually descended as they multiplied.[45]

I suppose that this proposal was intended as a sop to national pride, wounded by the confiscation in 1919 of Germany's African colony. It also sounds like a rejoinder to the Balfour Declaration of 1917, which expressed the intention of giving the Jews a homeland in Palestine. Curiously, it anticipated the "Madagascar Plan" later favored by some in the Nazi party, which was to relocate the Jews of Europe to that island.

Although Zschaetzsch does not mention the Theosophists, nor ascribe any occult powers to his Aryans, I include him here to show how Ariosophy adapted to the postwar mentality. The same applies to a third book of 1922, Hermann Wieland's *Atlantis, Edda und Bibel* (Atlantis, Edda and Bible). This is subtitled "Discovery of the secret of the Holy Scriptures, of the German folk's rescue from distress and death."[46] In 1925 it was enlarged with the more alluring subtitle, "200,000 years of Germanic world-culture and the secret of the Holy Scriptures."[47] Wieland identifies the poles as the place where humans first appeared in the Secondary or Tertiary Epoch, at least a million years ago. The reason is simple: the poles were the first parts of the earth to cool, hence the first places where life appeared. The Arctic region, where a temperate vegetation flourished, was home to the Aryans, a blond, blue-eyed, brachycephalic race. They lived there until a regularly recurring alteration of the earth's axis brought on an ice age, then were forced to migrate southward.[48]

Leaving their polar homeland, the Aryans settled on the island-continent of Atlantis, setting up a twelvefold nation that would later become the model for the zodiac and the divisions of time by hours and months. They were forbidden to kill animals and lived whenever possible as vegetarians, unlike the lower races who already inhabited the land and were little better than beasts themselves.[49] The Edda and both Testaments of the Bible are really chronicles of the Aryans' history. This is evident enough in the Edda, but the Bible has to be stripped of the Judeo-Christian overlay; then it will be found in perfect accord with the Edda and other ancient texts.

Wieland is not so extreme as Lanz, whose work he credits without mentioning the sexual material. He was simply convinced that racial purity and its opposite, miscegenation, were the most important factors in human history. Consequently, whenever the Bible speaks of beasts, it refers to lower races, as do all the laws of Moses and injunctions of Jesus.[50] The Book of Revelation really chronicles the oppression of the Atlantean Aryans by the races that had become so much more numerous than they, forcing them, for example, to worship their depraved idols. The plagues and destruction that follow were really caused by the earth's encounter with a comet. (In the later edition of his book, Wieland introduces the Hoerbiger theory.[51]) The vision of the New Jerusalem, like the Promised Land of Exodus, stands for the future reconstitution of the Aryans.

Wieland traces the German people through recorded history, presenting them as victims of incessant attempts to crush them. He devours the whole menu of conspiracy theory, blaming the Jews, the Jesuits, the Freemasons, the Illuminati of Bavaria, and popery and Catholicism in general for malice toward his folk.[52] The defeat of 1918 was a recapitulation of Atlantis, and for the same reason: in both places there were great cities full of racially mixed people, strengthened by their dose of Aryan blood.[53] (Wieland seems to forget that the fall of Atlantis was caused by a comet.) All this makes disagreeable reading. Yet from time to time, in all this literature, one is arrested by a passage, which deserves a better context, and remembers that Germany was also the land of Kant, Beethoven, and Goethe.

> The Aryans were filled with the feeling and awareness that an eternal, unnamable power links everything that happens in the world; it is active in every creature and has a fatherly care for all. This creative energy is called "God" by Jesus Sirach (Ch. 43),[54] the "All-Father" in the Aryan-Germanic version, and "Father in Heaven" in Christ's teaching. This original monistic-pantheistic religion is in no contradiction to science, but in accord with it. It does not divide faith from knowledge, but reconciles them, following Goethe in quiet reverence for the inscrutable. It suffers no dogmas, requires no external observance, no mediator between God and man, and no priestly

hierarchy. Each, like Christ, is his own priest, and responsible for his actions to God alone.[55]

Another admirer of the Edda was Rudolf John Gorsleben (1883–1930), who had been working for twenty years on his own universal theory of the primordial language, script, and beliefs of the Aryan race before completing *Hoch-Zeit der Menschheit* (Zenith of mankind, 1930) just before his death.[56] This author was a member of the famous club of racist nationalists, the Thule-Gesellschaft, named for the legendary land. Gorsleben's 700-page work is predictably polemical, opening with a clarion call to every German not just to study and admire the Greeks, but to

seek the land from which the Greeks arose in the Aryan North, in the land of Apollo, of the god Pol, of the Hyperborean near the Pole. This is his homeland, too, and the cradle of the Aryan race. Should not our schools and universities teach how to grasp and understand true Greekness on basis of our inner kinship, through studying our common Aryan-Nordic past, our old Germanic language, our ancient religion, which even today is our ancestral faith? Is not the Edda at least as good for this as Homer?[57]

Gorsleben is not the kind of author who troubles his readers with footnotes, bibliographies, the citation of sources, or an index. Everything comes from his undoubtedly erudite mind as fact, from the solution of theological problems downward. What is man's role on Earth? he asks, and answers: Man is God's consciousness and the vessel of the divine on Earth. He has not evolved from animals, but was already divine in his primordial form, with the consciousness of God within him. The Fall of Man came through miscegenation with animals; he lost his divine consciousness, and from the mixture came the lower races.[58] Elsewhere Gorsleben assures us of the truth of reincarnation: all the great ancient writings, and the great men and women of the past, were convinced that we are spiritually eternal beings who make many brief descents into corporeality.[59]

For all his seeming authority, Gorsleben's account of prehistory is disjointed and confusing because he tries to blend the Theosophical system of root races with current notions of Aryan origins and with Bailly's Arctic Atlantis (see chapter 1). He assumes that all life, including human, began at the North Pole, which once had an almost tropical climate. Due to the gradual cooling of the region, the inhabitants were driven southward and created on Atlantis a post-polar Paradise.[60] The Atlanteans' chief quality was technical skill, but unlike our own purely material technology, theirs made much use of magical powers. We are not told exactly what these were, but Gorsleben evidently had a strong belief in nonphysical energies and finer states of matter. He deplores the way in which modern science dismisses all such ideas as superstitious and suggests that the runes, which are his overriding interest, may have symbolized various energy paths on which all organic growth depends.[61]

As for the doctrine of root races, Gorsleben says that the first and second races vanished long ago through Earth changes, and that today's non-Aryan humanity stems from the third and fourth races. From the fourth root race of Atlantis, four cultural streams issued in the cardinal directions. The northern one came to northwest Europe, especially to an area now submerged beneath the North Sea, and thence proceeded across middle Europe to northern Asia. The eastern one began in Spain and North Africa, encircled the Mediterranean, and proceeded through south Asia to the Far East and even to Easter Island. The southern stream came from the south Atlantic island and arrived in West Africa, and the western one went to both Americas. The last island of Atlantis was destroyed around 9000 BCE.[62]

Gorsleben's real interest is naturally in the fifth, Aryan root race. He writes that it was developed under divine guidance and enjoyed many thousands of years of peace, remembered in legend as the Golden Age.[63] After the fall of the Aryans' homeland (whether Arctic or Atlantic is unclear), they lived in the Celtic and Germanic lands of middle and northwestern Europe.[64] From this point onward he is on his home ground and can proceed with the task of tracing all symbols and alphabets to the runes, and these to a prehistoric but literate people. Then he can imagine the "golden links of a spiritual chain" that runs from those times to his own. His list runs thus: Heliand, Widukind, the Templars, the Albigenses, Ekkehart, Walter von der Vogelweide, Luther, Wycliff, the Huguenots, Goethe, and Nietzsche.[65] Lacking any historical or logical linkage, its only principle seems to be a sentimental preference for anyone opposed to the Catholic Church.

Gorsleben may have been unnerved by the appearance, just as his book neared completion, of an even more ambitious one by Herman Wirth, which we will treat in the next section. Although Gorsleben praised it, his choice of title sounds like a deliberate upstaging of Wirth's book on the "ascent of mankind" with his own, on its "zenith." Gorsleben assures the reader that he was entirely independent of Wirth, and that the presence of many common conclusions can only make them more plausible.[66] He adds that Wirth's explanation of the runes as derived from the course of the year ignores their secret and magical meaning, allowing that this might make Wirth more acceptable in conventionally learned circles. With that rueful thought, Gorsleben died, not even seeing his book in print.

In selecting Gorsleben's passages on Atlantis, I necessarily neglect the bulk of his book and his runic ruminations, on which I am not qualified to pass judgment. I do however notice how closely his metaphysical principles accord with those of Theosophy, and perhaps even more with Anthroposophy. He acknowledges the innate divinity of the human being, its immaterial states and subtle forms of perception; he is certain that former races were aware of these and wielded powers we would call magical; he wishes for a science no longer limited to the material world— in effect, for a "spiritual science." Yet the whole book stands under the sign of racial superiority and the need for purification of the Aryans, hence the Germans, from the pollution of lower races. It illustrates the fact that one can share someone's metaphysics without in the least sharing their ethics (and vice versa).

After the National Socialists' election victory of 1933, these ideas about racial origins and identities took on a new and fateful meaning.

Ariosophy aside, many of the new men, from Adolf Hitler downward, belonged to a centuries-old tradition of Jew-hating Christians. Any philosophy that granted significance to racial origins was grist to their mill. This opened up career opportunities for ideologists and constructors of worldviews, but always with the risk of entanglement in party rivalries. Here we shall look at the rise and fall of one such, Herman Wirth, and more briefly at two others who introduced the now familiar mix of Theosophy and Nordic origins into the party's ideological heart.

HERMAN WIRTH AND *THE ASCENT OF MANKIND*

Herman Felix Wirth Roeper Bosch (1885–1981), to give him his full name, was neither Theosophist, Anthroposophist, nor Ariosophist. He would have considered his place to be our first chapter, but was he a rationalist? The reader must judge. Wirth was born in Utrecht, Netherlands, of a German father and a Dutch mother. His approach to Atlantology was unconventional, and, as it turned out, disastrous, because it clashed with the official ideology of the Third Reich. Yet to the end of his long life he held to the serene conviction of his own rightness.[67]

Wirth began his professional life as a musicologist, writing a dissertation on Dutch folksong and giving concerts of early music,[68] but he had many other interests and talents. His first post, in 1909, was at the University of Berlin as Reader in Netherlandish Language and Literature. During World War I he threw himself into activism on behalf of freedom for Flanders and solidarity of the "Duitch" with the "Deutsch." This earned him a promise from the Kaiser that after Germany won the war, he would become professor of musicology at the Brussels Conservatory. As things turned out, Wirth found himself in 1919 teaching in a high school in the remote region of Friesland.

On the bleak shores of the North Sea, where Pastor Spanuth would also hatch his Atlantean theories (see chapter 1), Wirth's antiquarian attention was drawn to the peculiar symbols carved on farmhouses that went back to the sixteenth century. The more he collected and compared these examples of folk art, the more convinced he became that the old Frisian carpenters had preserved the symbols of an incredibly ancient culture.

Gradually he assembled an unrivaled "paper museum" of early and prehistoric inscriptions and pictographs found on rock, bone, and wood throughout the Northern Hemisphere. Certain themes like the swan, the wheel, and the oared boat recurred in widely separated times and places. Wirth came to see them not as mere "pictograms" but as "ideograms," that is, as carrying specific, symbolic meaning. In time he was able to reconstruct a theological system and an astronomically based cosmology, containing internal evidence of being at least 10,000 years old. With this came the realization that a common culture had once encircled the entire North Atlantic region, and that it was responsible for the invention of writing. Before that, Wirth concluded, there must have been an even earlier culture within the Arctic Circle itself. Without any help from Bailly, Tilak, Steiner, or the Theosophists, he had hit on the myth of Hyperborean origins and was ready to write the book of the century, *Der Aufgang der Menschheit* (The ascent of mankind).

Besides the evidence of the ideograms, scientific confirmation came from the recent work of Alfred Wegener and Wladimir Köppen, pioneers of the theory of continental drift or plate tectonics, in which Wirth was another early believer. The crucial points were: (1) the location of the North Pole is not stable, but has wandered as much as 30° from its present position; (2) the movement of continental plates and the wandering of the poles cause the rising and sinking of lands; (3) Europe, Greenland, and North America once formed a single landmass that broke up in the Quaternary Era.[69] These are the reasons that the former Arctic continent changed climate and became uninhabitable, forcing its indigenous inhabitants to migrate south. Wirth's Atlantis was therefore not a separate geographic entity, but part of the former Arctic continent, "of which only Greenland, Spitzbergen and Franz-Joseph Land remain as fragments . . . these are distinct from the other Atlantic islands, which were created later through volcanic outbreaks out of the wreckage of the sunken Atlantic continent."[70]

Turning from geology to anthropology, Wirth favors an early date for the separation of humans from apes as part of the evolution of mammals in the Tertiary Era (here meaning the last 10 million years) and a correspondingly early differentiation of races. Based on the analysis of blood groups, which was the most advanced technology of his time, he posits two original groups. One was the light Nordic race, in its Arctic home; the other was the original black race, which originated in Gondwanaland, a now vanished continent that covered the Indian Ocean. (This had come to replace Lemuria in the schemes of geologists.) After the pole shift and the consequent ice age, the Arctic-Nordic race migrated southward, and the two original races began to mingle and produce variations. Wirth mentions the Asiatic race as a "mixovariation" containing elements of both original groups, and the Atlantic-Nordic as an "idiovariation" within the Arctic-Nordic.

As for the first evidence of Europeans, the Aurignacians seem to have been a black race, to judge from the peppercorn hair and steatopygy of their "Venus" figurines.[71] Nor were the famous Cro-Magnons, appearing about 30,000 years ago, the ancestors of the white race, because it takes much longer for racial characteristics to become fixed. The Cro-Magnons descended from a mixture of Nordics with Eskimos, thanks to intrepid sailors who were navigating the northern seas at least 50,000 years before conventional prehistory allows. It was this sea-people that brought culture, writing, law, religion, agriculture, and art to all the less-developed races. They colonized northern and northwest Europe, leaving megalithic relics such as Stonehenge and the dolmens. The latter were constructed for open-air burials, hence the paucity of human remains. As for Plato's Atlantis, Wirth allows that there was a landmass in the North Atlantic that sank around 11,000 years ago, its Stone Age structures and practices corresponding to Plato's account, though embroidered in the telling.

This summary does scant justice to the scale or style of Wirth's book. Here is Julius Evola, reeling from the experience of reading *Der Aufgang der Menschheit* shortly after its publication in 1928:

One can reject certain principles a priori, such as the very hypothesis of "sacred series" and of variations in them determined during various periods by the precession of the equinoxes. But if one does not do so, it is like finding oneself inside an enchanted castle: one can refuse to enter, but once the threshold is passed, it is difficult to get out again. One moves from signs to phonemes, from phonemes to symbols, from symbols to phonemes and signs, by way of idols, conjurations, calendrical notations, names of gods and demons, ornaments, rites and ritual objects, inscriptions, masks, prehistoric designs on rocks or in caves, funerary ornaments and finds of every sort, supplemented by specimens gathered in situ during years of research by Wirth himself—the author gives us no respite. And even if it is all reduced to a "myth," one still has to recognize the potency and extent of the synthesis behind it. It is hard to find its equal in these fields, monopolized as they are by an arid and pedantic erudition.[72]

As mentioned, Wirth felt that the ideograms had given him the key to the theology and religion of the Arctic-Nordic race. They perceived the great moral law of the universe as the eternal return, the perpetual coming into being and passing away. The annual journey of the sun, especially in the Arctic region, where it rose and set only once a year, represented for them the Son of the immutable God and the revelation of that God in time and space. Everywhere, among the Native Americans as much as in the Old World, Wirth found the concept of God the Father as a sexless and impersonal being, distinct from his Son, who brings light to the land, dies, and is reborn. Third of this pagan trinity was the All-Mother Earth, to whose bosom the Son/sun goes each winter, and from whom he is reborn at the solstice.

As the Nordic race left the Arctic and mingled with foreigners, its tradition withered away. From the animistic beliefs of spiritually inferior peoples came cults of demons and ghosts, anthropomorphism, and a whole pantheon of gods. But there have been periodic efforts to retrieve and reconstitute the Atlantic-Nordic spiritual heritage. They include Zoroastrianism, Aryan-Indian Brahmanism, the Samkya school, Buddhism, Greek philosophy, the Galilean's reform of faith, Roman Christianity, the Nordic Reformation of the sixteenth century, and the development of Western epistemology, right up to the natural philosophy of the present day.

Wirth's solitary path thus brought him round to a version of the *prisca theologia* and *philosophia perennis*: the primordial theology and the perennial philosophy. The Theosophists had taught this all along, but with an occultist baggage that he could not abide. Traditionalists like Coomaraswamy and Guénon (see chapter 6) were teaching it in these very years. But Wirth's spiritual genealogy, unlike theirs, excluded the religions of temple, church, and mosque, as well as all revealed scripture, all ritual, and anything redolent of a sentimental or person-to-person relationship with God. Nor had he any truck with the esoteric-exoteric division. There was only the authentic *Ur-Religion* based on the lived experience of a spiritually sensitive race, and then there was all the pernicious nonsense that later ages superimposed upon it.

Up to a point, Wirth's work was in harmony with the *völkisch* currents of his day, the sort that inspired the *Wandervogel* youth movement in which he had been a leader. He conceived of the Arctic-Nordics as a spiritual and pacific race that took its direction mainly from its wise "mothers" and accorded women commensurate rights. The tragedy was that it had been driven by climatic changes from its Arctic cradle. Looking back in 1960, he wrote:

> Our whole historical outlook is limited to the period of rupture that is the Eurasian migration epoch, the age of male rights and male domination. We stand today within the unmitigated collapse of this epoch, on the edge of the abyss of utter destruction of humanity, life, and earth. Yet the West is still trying, with all the "restorative means" of the Mosaic-Christian ideology, to maintain the fictions of this failed androcentric belief system. This male world of the period of rupture, the organized world of State, Church, and God, is no

longer organic, ever since the "Mothers" were driven out. For that severed the organic connection between "heaven and earth," cosmos and mankind, which is what the "world" used to be.[73]

While Wirth presented his findings as scholarship, there is no doubt that the Ur-Religion was his religion, and that this faith far outweighed his pretended scientific method. He was a true believer in his imaginary tradition, hence his presence here, rather than in chapter 1. Moreover, his biographer and bibliographer, Eberhard Baumann, was convinced that Wirth possessed some higher state of consciousness, such as was the universal possession of the ancient race. Baumann adds a comment about Frau Wirth's contribution to the great project, which although it surely did not take the form of "mesmeric trance," has something mysterious about it. He writes:

Wirth was sometimes able to observe higher consciousness "in action." A few years ago it was important for us, on beginning our study, to read his dedication in *Aufgang der Menschheit*: "Margarete Wirth-Schmitt. To her, who *gave* me this book (my italics, E.B.), the noble seeress of our spiritual heritage . . . it is returned in deep and grateful love." So inner perceptions poured out from the very lively consciousness of his wife, which he was then only able to acknowledge as "ancestrally remembered" (*erb-erinnert*). We do not know today to what extent Frau Wirth determined the contents and message of her husband's research.[74]

THE FALL OF HERMAN WIRTH

For a few years, Wirth reaped the rewards of his labors. In 1933 he received a professorship in Berlin and the commission to found an open-air museum of the old German religion. In the same year he took the fateful step of publishing an edition of the *Ura-Linda-Chronik*. (We have already mentioned the book in the context of Wirth's half-hearted supporter Albert Herrmann; see chapter 1.) Usually spelled *Oera Linda,* this was a manuscript that had first come to light in 1867, purporting to be a chronicle compiled over millennia and preserved in a Frisian family, the Over de Lindens. Wirth had already written about it ten years before;[75] now he enhanced his translation with commentaries and illustrations in the spirit of his *Aufgang.* He found the *Oera Linda Book* marvelously in tune with his idea of a Nordic Atlantic culture, maintaining the traditions of the earlier Arctic one.

The first portions of the *Oera Linda Book* were supposedly penned by a survivor of the flood that destroyed Atland, the Frisian's paradisal homeland, in the year 2194 BCE. Here are the relevant passages from William Sandbach's 1876 translation:

Before the bad time came our country was the most beautiful in the world. The sun rose higher, and there was seldom frost. . . . The years were not counted, for one was as happy as another.

On one side we were bounded by Wr-alda's Sea, on which no one but us might or could sail; on the other side we were hedged in by the broad Twiskland (Tusschenland, Duitschland), through which the Finda people dared not come on account of the thick forests and the wild beasts.

Eastward our boundary went to the extremity of the East Sea, and westward to the Mediterranean.[76]

Unfortunately, no map was provided to clarify this peculiar geography. Then came the catastrophe.

During the whole summer the sun had been hid behind the clouds, as if unwilling to look upon the earth. There was perpetual calm, and the damp mist hung like a wet sail over the houses and the marshes. The air was heavy and oppressive, and in men's hearts was neither joy nor cheerfulness. In the midst of this stillness the earth began to tremble as if she was dying. The mountains opened to vomit forth fire and flames. Some sank into the bosom of the earth, and in other places mountains rose out of the plain. Aldland, called by the seafaring people, Atland, disappeared, and the wild waves rose so high over hill and dale that everything was buried in the sea. Many people were swallowed up by the earth, and others who had escaped the fire perished in the water.[77]

Later members of the Over de Linden family, we are assured, dutifully copied this document. They added their memoirs of the Frisians' migrations, their encounters and battles with other tribes, and especially their customs and laws. The last contribution is dated "in the 3449th year after Atland's sinking, that is, 1256 in the Christian reckoning." The book was written in a unique "runic" alphabet based on the sixfold division of the circle, which Wirth immediately recognized as one of the primal solar symbols of his Arctic-Atlantic race. Since the manuscript was on nineteenth-century paper, he had to admit that the copying had continued, and that a "humanist" had had a hand in improving the original text. But still, he maintained, the core of it was authentic.

Wirth's *Ura-Linda-Chronik* was beautifully produced, as *Der Aufgang der Menschheit* had been, by the Jena publisher Eugen Diederich. If its erudite apparatus was not clear to everyone, its message was: this was the true history of the German *Volk*. To judge from Baumann's bibliography, every newspaper in the land reviewed it, and they continued to report on the controversy that exploded as soon as the academic world got hold of it. Experts in history, philology, religion, and philosophy proclaimed almost unanimously that the *Oera Linda Book* was a nineteenth-century forgery. In fact, Dutch historians had realized that decades ago and had paid little further attention to it. Wirth was perhaps blind to this because he had already projected ideals such as universal literacy, democratic government, women's rights, a hatred of priestcraft, and a deistic theology back onto his Arctic folk.

Emotions were naturally strong on both sides, and to air them, a sort of academic duel was staged in the New Hall of Berlin University on May 4, 1934, with the theme "The Value of the *Ura-Linda-Chronik* as History and Source." On the opposition bench was the Germanist Heinrich Hübner, who afterward issued a devastating pamphlet proving to any disinterested observer that the *Oera Linda Book* was written in modern times and in an entirely modern spirit. Few today would disagree with him that the book is an allegory of the principles of the Enlightenment, couched in a mixture of romantic and biblical style. Hübner even had the good luck to find a Dutch folk calendar of 1850 that dated itself "4043 years after the Flood," thus corroborating the date given for Atland's destruction and confirming its biblical source. He also used the occasion for some political one-upmanship.

Even worse is the book's lack of instinct for a correct worldview. Wirth purports to reveal the ancient Germanic spirit to our folk, and presents it with a book whose liberalistic origin is simply not in doubt. One may find it tragic that Herman Wirth, who refers so enthusiastically to the inherited memory that stirs in him, should fall into such an error. But when this error is introduced to a folk that needs to be educated away from liberalism into a heroic way of life, then personal tragedy becomes public peril. If anyone accepts the *Ura-Linda-Chronik* as a true and credible "revelation," as an "ancestral heritage" [*Ahnenerbe*], then it is preaching to them the complete opposite of what must be preached today. The *Ura-Linda-Chronik* is not only democratic, anti-Führer, and pacifistic in its basic attitude, it is a complete fabrication without taste or muscle, wishy-washy and sometimes tear-jerkingly sentimental.[78]

The debate over the *Oera Linda Book* degenerated into a squalid name-calling in which each side accused the other of not being Nazi enough, and Wirth gave as good as he got.[79] He still had patronage in high places, and in June 1935 Heinrich Himmler appointed him president of the Ahnenerbe ("ancestral heritage") research bureau. He led an expedition to study rock art in Scandinavia, but his career did not last long after that. Political and military realities were prevailing in the minds of Germany's leaders over the romantic fantasies about prehistory that they may have indulged in the 1920s. It was more important to keep the churches compliant than to challenge Christianity on the grounds of some Ur-Religion. Nor did the view of material and technological progress as signifying spiritual decline suit a nation preparing for total war. Consequently Wirth was seen for what he was: an obsessive scholar, out of touch with political reality. In January 1937 he was dismissed from the Ahnenerbe and from his Berlin chair and forbidden to publish. In a way this was his salvation, for the Ahnenerbe afterward supported experiments on human subjects that earned it universal infamy, and Wirth was not implicated in these. However, after Germany's defeat, his former connection ruled out any sympathy for him and his work. He was interned from 1945 to 1947, and after his release lived virtually as a nonperson, his work expunged from the historical and scholarly record.

ALFRED ROSENBERG'S *MYTH OF THE TWENTIETH CENTURY*

One who might have rejoiced at Wirth's discomfiture was Alfred Rosenberg (1893–1946), except that it presaged his own. Among the heavyweights of the Nazi Party, Rosenberg cuts a rather feeble figure. He aspired to be the party's philosopher, and to prove it by writing *Der Mythos des 20. Jahrhunderts* (The myth of the twentieth century), perhaps the dullest book that ever sold a million copies. If people read any of it, though, it would have been the first chapter, which puts the Arctic-Atlantis theory in a nutshell and shows how deeply the theory had penetrated the German mythological imagination. Like Wirth, Rosenberg calls on recent scientific research to show that there was once dry land between Greenland and Iceland; that sea levels were formerly more than a hundred meters lower than today; and that the North Pole has wandered, so that the Arctic may have had a much warmer climate. Hedging his bets, Rosenberg writes:

All this makes the ancient legend of Atlantis appear today in a new light. It seems we cannot exclude the possibility that where the waves of the Atlantic Ocean crash and gigantic icebergs loom, a flourishing land once rose above the deep, on which a creative race raised a great, wide-ranging culture and sent its children out into the world as seafarers and warriors; but even if this Atlantis hypothesis should prove untenable, a northern prehistoric culture center must be accepted.[80]

He goes on to mention some salient points of the Arctic-Atlantic theory: the cosmic experience of the sun, which divided the year into two halves; the southward migrations and the coming of the swan and dragon boats to the Mediterranean; the memories of the Artic homeland preserved in Persian and Indian mythology; the mixing with the indigenous races of the South, and the incongruous presence even today of blond-haired, blue-eyed North Africans. Once the Nordic race reaches India, the whole nineteenth-century Aryan myth of racial and religious diffusion is at Rosenberg's disposal.

Wirth's work had served its purpose as a dramatic curtain-raiser, and while Rosenberg did acknowledge its impact on prehistory, neither he nor any other committed Nazi could go along with its subversive feminism. The tough, mystical, freedom-loving Aryans of the *Mythos des 20. Jahrhunderts,* as Rosenberg pictured them, inevitably collided with Wirth's "chthonic, matriarchally inclined racial groups," and at that point the author inserts an unfriendly footnote:

It is completely misleading when Herman Wirth, in *Aufgang der Menschheit,* attempts to present mother-right as the original Nordic-Atlantic way of life, while also recognizing the solar myth as a Nordic possession. Matriarchy is always connected with chthonic religious beliefs, Patriarchy always with the solar myth. The high valuation of women among the Nordic people is directly based on the *masculine* structure of being. The feminine in the pre-Christian Near East always went along with prostitution and sexual collectivity. The evidence that Wirth adduces is thus worse than scanty.[81]

Rosenberg had always been one of the Nazi party's main ideologues. Not only virulently anti-Jewish, he was also anti-Christian, and he hoped that the Reich would eventually sever its connections with the churches and adopt some sort of mystic paganism. (This is what Lewis Spence interpreted as Satanism—see chapter 8.) In 1934 he received the high-sounding title of Delegate of the Führer for the Supervision of the Entire Spiritual and Ideological Teaching and Education of the NSDAP,[82] which was probably one of the reasons that his enemy Himmler hastened to form his own and better funded Ahnenerbe. As Reich Minister for the Occupied Eastern Territories (1941), Rosenberg's authority was again sidelined. This did not spare him from conviction and execution at Nuremberg because of the war crimes perpetrated in the territories under his jurisdiction.

KARL MARIA WILIGUT'S ANCESTRAL TRADITIONS

Himmler did not rely on the Ahnenerbe alone to feed his appetite for mythic history. In 1933 a curious character had come to his notice: Colonel Karl Maria Wiligut (1866–1946).[83] Wiligut was an Austrian, a decorated war hero, and an associate of Lanz-Liebenfels's New Templar Order. His career might be thought to have finished in 1924, when his wife had him committed to a mental hospital. However, on his release in 1927 he reentered völkisch and New Templar circles and started teaching them his stock of runic lore. In 1933 he met Himmler, who connived to suppress Wiligut's embarrassing past, making him an SS brigadier and head of the Department for Pre- and Early History in the Race and Settlement Office.[84] In spring 1935, just a month or two before putting Herman Wirth in charge of the Ahnenerbe, Himmler installed Wiligut in a Berlin villa as a member of his personal staff. There are rumors that he acted as a "medium" for Himmler, but this is improbable in the sense of someone entranced or possessed. Wiligut was more likely a medium for the ancient German tradition, which he claimed had been handed down from father to son in the Wiligut family from time immemorial. On the strength of this authority, which evidently made a great impression on Himmler, Wiligut wrote gnomic texts about the runes, astrology, and ancient Germanic theology and designed many of the symbolic trappings of the Schutzstaffel. These included rituals, especially ones to do with the selective breeding program (marriage, naming of infants, and so forth), and objects inscribed with runes, like the SS death's head ring. He also helped plan the transformation of the seventeenth-century castle at Wewelsburg into a ceremonial and initiatic center for the SS elite. The renovation used forced labor from a nearby concentration camp, and postwar adaptation as a youth hostel has not exorcised all the evil memories of the place.[85] Tourists still wonder at the two great circular halls, one of them with the twelve-fold runic symbol of the zodiac inlaid in the marble floor.[86]

Stephen E. Flowers, an acknowledged authority on runic traditions, rightly observes that besides influences on Wiligut from Guido von List and Lanz-Liebenfels, "the esoteric history provided by Blavatsky's Theosophy gave him the broad outlines of his own Germano-centric version of the prehistory of man. As early as 1908, in his 'Nine Commandments of Gôt,' he mentions the 'seven epochs of human history,' which echo the seven 'root races' of Theosophy."[87] These commandments, which survive in a later typescript signed by Wiligut and marked as read by Heinrich Himmler, are said to stem from oral tradition and to have been written down for the first time since the year 1200.[88] Much later, Wiligut wrote a fuller exposition for his patron, entitled "Description of the Evolution of Humanity from the Secret Tradition of our Asa-Uana-Clan of Uiligotis."[89]

The reputed source of this mythological document that Wiligut called the "*Irminsaga*" was seven oaken tablets in ancient Aryan linear script supplemented by images, preserved in the Wiligut family. In 1848 they were destroyed in a fire caused by Hungarian rebels, and their content had to be reconstructed through oral tradition. The saga describes four former epochs of humanity and the current fifth one, the description of the latter taken down almost verbatim from "the retired military officer K. Wiligut who died in his 89th year (1883)." Here are some of the characteristics and events attributed to the five epochs:

First epoch: "Aithar-beings," propagating through concentration of the will, are in constant struggle with water-beings.

Second epoch: Air- and water-beings solidify themselves into bisexual beings who live on earth and water, and can also fly.

Third epoch: The remnants of the second epoch struggle and mate with beings from "heaven" and complete the transition to sexual division. They have a third eye in the forehead. Some mate with animals and generate satyrs, fauns, centaurs, and bull-men, who are in constant struggle with humans.

Fourth epoch: Three races, red, black, and albino, all fight against the beast-men. The third eye disappears. They foresee the coming catastrophe and build giant caves as refuges.

Fifth epoch: To the few survivors of the fourth race come human beings from the moon and mate with them, having no women of their own. The wise organize clans. Asgard is established, but because the earth shifts, the Asa-Uanas have to migrate to "Attallant." The sixth and seventh humanities are yet to come.

This is so obviously a garbled version of Blavatsky's first five root races that one wonders how Wiligut could pass it off as his own family's secret tradition. It does have two conspicuous differences, though. First, there is no overall evolutionary plan under divine guidance, but an endless return of interracial strife and new beginnings. Secondly, the catastrophe that ends each epoch is caused by a moon or other cosmic body slamming into the earth, starting an ice age and forcing human development to start virtually from scratch. Equally obviously, the crashing moons came out of Hans Hoerbiger's *Welteislehre,* of which Himmler was a devotee (see chapter 1).

PERYT SHOU, THE OUTSIDER

We have to make a chronological leap backward to do justice to an eso-tericist whose career spans both world wars.[90] He was born in Pomerania as Albert Christian Georg Schultz (1873–1953), but he wrote under the name of a previous incarnation as a priest in ancient Egypt: Peryt Shou. After a scientific training and a period of creative work, Schultz gravitated to Theosophical and Ariosophical circles. He began to publish around 1909 on such topics as Indian fakirs, sexual mysteries in religion, and "psychic breathing." Unlike many esotericists, he actually gave practical instruction. Here is a summary of his teaching by Manfred Lenz, one of the very few researchers to have concerned themselves with him:

> Peryt Shou taught that man is in resonance with certain cosmic fields of consciousness and vibration, or can become so through certain "Logos-practices," so as to experience an "etherization" of his body and thereby an elevation of soul and spirit. In his writings, Peryt Shou gives many instructions and explanations for the "unfolding" of man into a corresponding "antenna-cross," which serves as receiver for cosmic rays and vibrations. Once one is tuned in, the "captured waves" generally lead quickly to a peculiar "current" whose surge is usually felt as a pleasant shudder.[91]

Peryt Shou wrote two short books on Atlantis, one before and one after the First World War. They take for granted the existence of a high civilization, which fell through its own fault, but are less concerned with history than with the Atlanteans' states of consciousness. Peryt Shou reads Plato's account as pregnant with esoteric symbolism and, alone among Atlantologists, fastens on the list of Atlantean kings. He analyzes these ten names into their phonetic contents and tabulates their correspondences with star names, the Egyptian decans (30° sections of the zodiac), the Sephiroth of the Kabbalah, the antediluvian patriarchs named in Genesis, and the multiples and divisions of the "mother number" 432.[92] This was not just an intellectual game, but part of Peryt Shou's practical teaching. He enjoins meditation on the "word essences" of the names to develop a subtle sense for their "energetic core." His purpose, in short, is to revive in modern humans the spiritual capacities that were lost with the fall of Atlantis.[93] Here is his summary of the situation:

> The two pillars [of Hercules, in the Atlantis myth] are the "electrical" secret of man, the twin poles of a fundamental energy. Where it arises and unfolds within him, as if with a lightning flash it illuminates new worlds. In the natural man it slumbers; it develops as he climbs to the spiritual zones of the World Soul. The secret of this double energy was not hidden to the Ancients, but they misused it. Thus it became their fate. And here we behold the moral catastrophe of the Atlanteans. They were in possession of higher knowledge, of a science through which they wielded great power over the natural forces. But this science served for their fall, for it served lower, blind, *egotistical purposes*. And thus they were destroyed through that which they most treasured.[94]

Apart from a few priestly castes, the vast majority of those who emerged after the Atlantean catastrophe lacked the clairvoyant faculty. Consequently we cannot put ourselves in the position of the Atlanteans when they looked up at the stars and entered into telepathic communication with higher beings.[95] But we still have the potential for it, because mankind is *"the echo of a world-order established from eternity"* (original emphasis). Man himself is the "consciousness of the universe, for into him there stream, from a great source (in Orion) of rhythmically gradated vibrations of the astral light, *intelligible values,* i.e., 'noumena,' concepts."[96]

Although it does not have to do directly with Atlantis, what follows anticipates today's interest in cosmogenesis and the constellation of Orion:

Modern astronomy, too, sees at this location [the constellation of the Salamander] the forking of the Milky Way, near the Swan, *the center of our cosmic system.* Out of it go clouds of a dark, ultraviolet light-matter, which accumulates most densely around the center of Orion, which corresponds to it. And here we see a remarkable cosmic drama. A dark, deep black primordial material floods into the so-called "Lion's Mouth" of the *great Orion nebula* in a white luminous cloud of cosmic dust. Two polar forms of primordial matter mingle and copulate in *elemental energy development.*[97]

After the First World War, Peryt Shou joined in the search for esoteric meaning in Nordic and Germanic mythology and wrote on "The Edda as Key to the Coming Age." He also seems to have accepted Lanz's concept of a degraded human type brought into being by some ancient misdeed.[98] On a completely different front, he took notice of the American "New Thought" movement and adapted its ideas for self-improvement to his own more subtle program. During the 1920s he visited the ancient sites of Rome and Egypt, both of which contributed to his broad spiritual synthesis. If he is rightly numbered among the Ariosophists, he was by far the most benign of them. His sympathy for ancient German religion did not make him hostile to Christianity, nor did he have any belief in racial superiority. In his view, all human races needed to be brought to their full spiritual development.[99]

In 1930, Peryt Shou's second book on Atlantis appeared, with even more correspondence tables, magic words, and dense passages on comparative philology. It frequently cites Herman Wirth's *Aufgang der Menschheit,* which helped Peryt Shou to focus his concept of an archaic religion based on direct spiritual experience. He also mentions the coming Age of Aquarius. There is little on Atlantis except as the implied home of the Ur-Religion, but the physical cause of its destruction, now, "can hardly be otherwise explained than through the fall of the Tertiary Moon"[100]—the Hoerbiger theory. Aleister Crowley, whom Schultz had met in Berlin,[101] makes a cameo appearance as "the English philosopher

'Therion'." Peryt Shou calls Crowley's Law of Thelema the "great law of destiny of the Atlanteans, which in fact is returning today."[102] By this time he was preoccupied with Communist Russia and its karmic destiny, but his basic message remained the same. We should remember it when we come to the New Age (see chapter 10), for there is indeed nothing new there.

> The primordial religion taught that man himself creates his destiny, for man was divine from the beginning.
>
> It lies in the essence of divine being that man forms himself, creates himself, for he possesses the divine guardian, the angel in his breast, who watches lest he thereby violate the divine law. If he violates it, he himself must atone for it. In the course of his development, man grew ever further from this primordial religion. He believed that the Godhead was there to care for him, and so he should entrust everything to it.
>
> But this God really dwelt in him, as God dwells in everything. God gave man his *higher self,* which is divine in nature, self-created and self-determining.
>
> Through the Fall, man lost the right to free self-determination. He had to lean on God for everything and thereby forgot that God burned with its holiest rays in his own breast. Today, *in greatest agony,* the free man again gives birth to his free primordial faith.[103]

The apolitical Schultz seems to have evaded the Nazis' persecution of occultists, perhaps through knowing people like Wiligut, by keeping a low profile, and virtually ceasing to publish. The diary leaves of one of his New Templar friends gives us a rare snapshot of his attitude as the Second World War neared its close.

> Dresden, 22.4.1944. We spoke about . . . the Jewish question. Peryt Shou: That damages our karma, to which he attributes the fate of Berlin. My description of the Eastern situation in a dream . . . let

him believe in a coming age in which gods come to earth again. That it already happened, and is not fairytales or legends, as generally assumed—he believes that—Creatures who came here from other planets.[104]

The jottings are prophetic of the direction that Atlantology would take over the next decade, with UFOs, space gods, contactees, and the alien intervention theory of human evolution. But these were phenomena of the New World, enjoying the freedom and moral complacency of the victors. Things were, and are, very different in the German-speaking world.

POSTWAR RECONSTRUCTION II

The postwar revelations of Nazi atrocities beggared rational explanation, and as Europe struggled back onto its feet, the Goddess Reason was the deity of choice. The Germans, so it was explained, had been possessed by "the Irrational," and to avoid a repetition it was necessary to purge the human mind of this virus. Never were esotericism, occultism, and Theosophy in lower esteem than in the period from 1945 until the sixties, and the excesses of that decade did little to endear them to the intelligentsia. To this day, it is easy to gain a hearing in academia or the media by associating such "irrational" movements with political extremism.

One example is the recent study of German Atlantology by Franz Wegener, to which I willingly admit my debt. In a part-Freudian, part-structuralist peroration Wegener demonstrates that the Atlantis myth is a "parasitical, semiological system with the meaning of Death."[105] So anyone who accepts it is suspect. The Berlin writer and filmmaker Rüdiger Sünner takes a more measured approach in his study of Nazi and post-Nazi mythology, *Schwarze Sonne* (Black sun). After quoting a passage from one of Lanz's associates on the sacred places of ancient Germany, Sünner comments:

In England, Ireland, Scandinavia or Brittany it would be entirely normal to speculate in this [lofty and enthusiastic] tone on the religion of one's ancestors. But for the German public this terrain lies under a taboo, thanks to the Nazis' overblown rhetoric and its connection with racist ideology. Only scholars and dubious cultists concern themselves with it, in more or less closed circles. One symptom of this is that travel guides maintain an almost embarrassed silence about our often impressive megalithic sites, so that it takes a detective's nose to discover many of them.[106]

I know nothing of these closed circles. However, every Whitsunday weekend since 1967 a group has been meeting quite openly at Horn, near Detmold in northwestern Germany. Horn's claim to fame is its proximity to the Externsteine, an awe-inspiring cluster of natural rock towers in a clearing of the Teutoburg Forest. Once a pagan place of worship, then Christianized, they were rediscovered by the völkisch movement and made much of by the Nazis. They are now on the way to becoming a normal attraction for tourists, prehistory buffs, and New Agers: a sort of German Stonehenge. Like that monument, they inspire scholars, amateurs, and cranks.

The group in question is called "Forschungskreis Externsteine" (Externsteine research circle).[107] It was founded by Walther Machalett (1901–1982), a village schoolmaster with a passion for mythology, history, and the landscape. As a youth he loved to visit old castles, and one morning, camping by the ruined Henneburg near his native Gotha, he had an experience worthy of Novalis or Blake.

Every tree, every twig, every bit of wall, every stone block in the courtyard, every one of my friends looked strange! All the outlines of the things around me were quivering and radiating! And the same was true of myself: my fingertips, my hands, my arms and legs were clothed in a bright light, like a solar flare. . . . Birds flying overhead had this sheath floating around them. Every dry blade of grass had it, every telegraph post . . . every church spire, house roof, chimney, every car, whether stationary or moving, every horse and cow in the meadow, every chicken, every person we met![108]

Machalett's biographer Heino Gehrts remarks, "Such experiences are often much more significant indications of a person's path and destiny than teachers and textbooks." By all accounts, Machalett himself was an inspiring teacher, and a comfort to his comrades, too, during the three postwar years he spent interned in Buchenwald. In the long evenings, lacking artificial light, he would entertain them with endless sagas, fairytales, and stories from German history. Toward the end of his life, he returned to the experience of his youth with a book of photographs called *Sichtbare Strahlen* (Visible rays),[109] in which he had succeeded in capturing on film the light-forms emanating from highly charged or sacred spots.

The men and women who came to speak at Machalett's annual conferences were the German equivalent of the British Avalonians, whom we will meet in chapter 7, but with the task of exorcising the perverse use to which Germanic mythology had been bent by the Ariosophists and Nazis. Few of them were academics, but many followed the honorable German tradition of independent scholarship by lawyers, high school teachers, and retired businessmen. A number of them had been Anthroposophists until Steiner's movement was banned, but they seem to have preferred the Machalett circle as less doctrinaire and Christocentric. Although occultism as such was not on the agenda, those who shared Machalett's psychic sensitivity felt free to speak of it before this sympathetic company. Their contributions ranged widely. Besides the core study of local history, both before and after Christianization, they touched on the subtle forces of nature; the interface of modern science with ancient knowledge; archaeoastronomy; pendulums and dowsing; ley lines and alignments in the prehistoric landscape; the pivotal Battle of the Teutoburg Forest (9 CE), in which three Roman legions were slaughtered; Stone Age technology; and, as a particular specialty, the theory of *Groß-Skulpturen:* rock formations turned into sculptures on a gigantic scale.[110]

Long before the founding of the Externsteine circle, Machalett had been working on his magnum opus: *Die Externsteine. Das Zentrum des Abendlandes. Die Geschichte der weißen Rasse* (The Externsteine. The center of the West. The history of the white race). The six volumes of about 400 pages each are entitled: I, *Atlantis;* II, *Externsteine;* III, *Cheopspyramide;* IV, *Salvage;* V, *Lichtenstein;* VI, *Annalen.*[111]

The writing of a "history of the white race" had different implications for Machalett's generation from those it carries in today's multiracial culture. While he says that equally thorough histories of the other races should be undertaken,[112] the most urgent need was the healing of the European family that had been at war, to a greater or lesser degree, from 1914 until 1945. He writes:

> Let the Western peoples today call themselves what they will—Germans, French, Italians, Russians, Poles, Greeks, Norwegians—they are and will remain members of a single people, just members of the White race.
>
> With this way of thinking we will save ourselves from the recurrent surge of national hatred, which for so long has brought in its wake blood and misery, terror and destruction, the annihilation of cultural values and of human beings.[113]

In pursuit of this ideal, Machalett set himself four interlinked objectives, which I understand as follows: (1) to expound his own theory of Atlantis as a high civilization and the original home of the white race; (2) to gather in translation all the ancient histories, annals, and myths concerning the Flood and the prehistoric period; (3) to catalog all prehistoric sites, megaliths, alignments, caves, and sacred places that derived from Atlantean civilization; (4) to develop his theory of prehistoric Earth measurement and surveying.

This ambitious program rested on twin dogmas: that Plato's account was true, and that Hoerbiger was right, at least about the moon.[114] Putting these together, Machalett deduced that it was the capture of the Quaternary

Moon that sucked the oceans to the equator and brought Atlantis to a watery end. In the fourth volume, *Salvage,* he provides a thumbnail sketch of what the Atlanteans did when that moon appeared in the sky:

> Realization of the cosmic danger.
>
> Remembrance of former and similar catastrophes [i.e., the capture and fall of the three prior moons].
>
> Building of moon observatories.
>
> Preparation of safe areas.
>
> Occupation of areas needed for refuge.
>
> Exodus of the privileged and selected ones.
>
> Confinement of those remaining in safe areas.
>
> General flight at the height of the catastrophe.
>
> Submergence of the Atlantean continent.
>
> Tentative feelers put out by the survivors from the underground shelters, after the subsidence of the flood.
>
> Beginning of rebuilding of the sunken cultures and cults.
>
> Mixing of the survivors with one another, forming new peoples and tribes.
>
> Attempts to return to the original home . . .
>
> Creation and building of a new culture worldwide . . .[115]

The reader may wonder what the Externsteine had to do with this, and why they should be called the "center of the West." Machalett's theory can best be expressed as a series of coincidences:

+ The coordinates of the Externsteine are latitude 51°52' North, longitude 8°55' East. (The longitude is based simply on the human convention of the Greenwich Meridian, but the latitude is a fact of nature.)

+ The angle of elevation of the sides of the Great Pyramid is 51°51'. This is mathematically determined by the builders' desire to express the value π in the ratio of perimeter to height.

+ The Great Pyramid's coordinates are 29°58' North, 31°9' East.
+ A line drawn on the earth's surface from the Great Pyramid north-west to the Externsteine makes an angle of 51°51' with the 30° line of latitude.
+ An isosceles triangle with its base as the 30° line of latitude and two of its points at the Great Pyramid and the Externsteine produces a third point at the island of Salvage (Portuguese: Selvagens), at latitude 30°5' North, 15°55' West.
+ Thus a triangle drawn between the three points Externsteine, Great Pyramid, Salvage reproduces the geometry of the Great Pyramid, placing its summit at the latitude corresponding to the angle of elevation.
+ A circle with center at the Externsteine and circumference passing through the Great Pyramid and Salvage encloses North Africa, the Mediterranean, Asia Minor, and all of Europe as far as the Urals, and touches Greenland. This is the historical ambit of the white race, its legends, and its prehistoric remains.

Are these just coincidences, or do they mean something? The reader must decide. To Machalett, they were proof of Atlantean geodesy and astronomical observation on a continental scale, all of it motivated by the need to calculate the course of the approaching moon. Hoerbiger's theory serves him as key to every prehistoric mystery, such as the purpose of stone circles, dolmens, and other megalithic constructs: they were all observatories. It accounts for the migrations from the once-inhabited far north, whose climate became insupportable as the air was drawn equatorward. Religion changed, too, from the Atlantean solar cult to a dismal lunar cult, aimed at pacifying the moon god through sacrifice. Even the Atlanteans' invasion of the Mediterranean, chronicled by Plato, falls into place: it was to secure safe areas on higher ground than their low-lying island.[116]

John Michell, whose interests accord with Machalett's at many points, has shown in his study of geographic and cultic centers that every people imagines itself to be at the hub of the universe.[117] Early civilizations fixed their centers by surveying the limits of their land, whether on a large scale like the British Isles, or on as small a scale as the Isle of Man. The center became the sacred omphalos, the seat of spiritual authority, and the point of reference for the political divisions of the land, which, as Michell also shows, was generally into twelve sectors.[118] From a mythic point of view, one can see Machalett's grand project as the re-creation of such a center.

The annual meetings of the Externsteine circle are to all appearances a conference, but there is a ritual aspect to them. They begin on Ascension Day (Thursday evening) with an elevating musical performance and end on Whitsunday with a tour of some interesting local sites. In the Christian tradition, Whitsunday (Pentecost) commemorates the descent of the Holy Spirit upon the twelve apostles: an event that non-Christians can interpret, too, in their way. The Externsteine circle celebrates the genius loci—the "spirit of place" honored by all traditional peoples. It meets in the shadow of one of nature's wonders and honors it with a free exchange of ideas between men and women, experts and amateurs, engineers and "spiritual scientists." As an effort at postwar reconstruction and the healing of the German psyche, it is as different as can be from the grim program of the Aryan supremacists. The rightness or wrongness of Walther Machalett's own theories seems a small matter in comparison to that.

SIX

Two Traditionalists

———————— ✳ ————————

RENÉ GUÉNON'S EARLY INVESTIGATIONS

This chapter is about the contributions to Atlantology of René Guénon (1886–1951) and Julius Evola (1898–1974), representatives of the twentieth-century Traditionalist current that also included Ananda Coomaraswamy, Marco Pallis, Frithjof Schuon, Titus Burckhardt, and Seyyed Hossein Nasr. What distinguishes the Traditionalists' approach to Atlantis from that of the "rationalists" is the metaphysical dimension that informs all their thinking and their reverence for sacred over profane authority.

Given these principles, the Traditionalists' approach to the past, as to everything else, contrasts starkly with modernist orthodoxy. One of their virtues is that they turn received notions upside down, but not in the nihilistic way of postmodernism, which, if they had lived to see it, would have elicited their deepest scorn. In one of his chief doctrinal works, *The Symbolism of the Cross,* Guénon states that historical facts conform to the principle of correspondence, "and thereby, in their own mode, translate higher realities, of which they are, so to speak, a human expression. We would add that from our point of view (which obviously is quite different from that of the profane historians), it is this that gives to these facts the greater part of their significance."[1] Julius Evola, prefacing his *Revolt Against the Modern World,* writes that in traditional studies "all materials having a 'historical' and 'scientific' value are the ones that matter the least; conversely, all the mythical, legendary, and epic elements denied historical truth and demonstrative value acquire here a superior validity and become the source for a more real and certain knowledge."[2] This attitude made them natural adherents of the Atlantis myth.

Guénon was raised in a Catholic bourgeois family in provincial France. Disappointed in his hopes for an academic career in philosophy, he spent his life as an independent scholar and authority on every aspect of Tradition. He first came to notice in the Parisian occultist milieu, dominated by Papus and haunted by the prestigious figure of Saint-Yves d'Alveydre (see chapter 2). It was a melting pot where Gnostic bishops and doctors of Hermetism hustled for attention among Theosophists, Martinists, and Freemasons. As he joined every available order, Guénon's intellectual stature soon asserted itself. During a séance of automatic writing held by a group of Martinists in 1908, the spirit of Jacques de Molay, last Grand Master of the Templars, demanded that the Order of the Temple be revived, with the twenty-one-year-old Guénon as its head.

The "Ordre du Temple Renové" was duly founded and went to work immediately, holding séances in which a multitude of questions were put to the spirits, or whatever was communicating.[3] Far from being interested in the Templars, many of the questions had to do with the "Archéomètre," the great synthetic system of Saint-Yves' latter years that was then coming to light. For instance, the spirits were asked about the symbolism of letters and numbers, the correspondences of colors and musical notes, the identity of Hebraic and Hindu traditions, and the primordial language of Vattan or Watan. Other questions were about topics that Guénon would later take for his articles or even whole books, such as the symbolism of cross, helix, swastika, cubic stone, and serpent; the multiple states of being, the distinction between Being and Nonbeing, the principles of infinitesimal calculus; and so on into rarefied realms of "metaphysics," Guénon's name for the field of study in which all esoteric traditions converge.

One of these séances was devoted to questions about former races and periods of prehistory, and it seems to be the answers that were recorded. Although the information on cosmic cycles belongs later in this book (see chapters 11–12), I give the transcript in its entirety, so that the whole scheme can be appreciated:

+ The Great Year (period of the precession of the equinoxes) = 25,765 years. Half (12,882) = length of the evolution of one earthly human race. Manvantara = 432,000 years.

+ Total duration of earthly humanity: 12,882 × 7 = about 90,000 years.

+ The cycle of 12,882 is divided into 7 sub-cycles of 1840 years, and these divided into 3 periods of 613 years.

   Thus there are 21 periods for the entire duration of one race, plus a period of transition of 78 years (but this does not count for the total duration of humanity, because the last period of one race coincides with the first period of another).

+ The deluge takes place at the end of the 22nd period.

+ The Earth is not the only physical planet where human beings are living.

   A. The origin of the White race, and consequently of the first appearance of man on the earth should be set at 62,500 years before our era [= BCE]. The end of this race dates from 49,618 before our era (race B).

   B. The Yellow race: the first men of this race came from the air (planet Venus), hence: "sons of Heaven," writing from the top downwards. Inhabited the Pacific continent, of which only Polynesia remains. Tradition later reconstituted by Fo-Hi. End of this race in 36,735 before our era.

   C. Black race. Lemuria. Drawn out of fire. Writing from below upwards. Deluge in 23,835 before our era. Extension in Africa, south of Asia, Pacific, Europe, whence many survivors.

   D. White [Red?] race, Atlantis (between Africa and America). Language Watan: America, north Africa, Europe, Egypt, India.

Deluge in 10,370 before our era. Remains: Antilles, Canaries, Azores, Cape Verde Isles. Tradition maintained in its purity by the Egyptians, mingled with the black tradition in India and Chaldea, with the white tradition in Europe.

E. Fifth race = white + red + black. Ends in 1912 of our era (22nd period from 1912–1990).

F. Fusion of the yellow race with the fifth race should give the sixth. Disappearance of America (in any case, of most of South America) and Japan. Invasion of yellow race peoples into Europe and America ending 14,794.

G. Fusion of the sixth with the remains of the black race will give the seventh race which will last until 27,677.[4]

This looks like a compromise between the French occultist tradition, with its distinction of four races by color, and the sevenfold divisions of Theosophy. It seems, forgivably, to confuse the root races with the sub-races, placing the Lemurian and Atlantean (root) races as the third and fourth, but within a timescale more suitable for seven sub-races, with "our era" correctly placed as the fifth of them. Admittedly Guénon was not responsible for any of this, at least not in rational terms. But if the material obtained by such methods is affected by the thoughts and preoccupations of the participants, then it might have reflected his interest in this kind of synthesis. From his later works (see chapter 11) one can deduce how much of it he retained, and what he discarded.

THE POLAR MOUNTAIN AND THE UNDERGROUND KINGDOM

After the World War, Guénon's Traditionalism declared itself with books on Hinduism and Vedanta, and two polemical works, one against Spiritualism, the other against Theosophy. He returned to the subject of prehistoric continents, races, and traditions in *Le Roi du monde* (The king of the world), a study of spiritual centers first published in 1924.[5] He writes there of Mount Meru, the celestial mountain of Hindu mythology, and identifies it with the North Pole.[6] The Atlanteans, he says, called it *Tula,* the Greeks and Latins *Thule.* It represents "the first and supreme center for the whole of the current *Manvantara* . . . and its situation at the origin was literally polar."[7] It is also called the White Island, the Home of the Blessed, and the Land of the Living.[8] Seven continents have emerged successively from it, "such that each one is the terrestrial world envisaged in the corresponding period."[9] The seven continents form a lotus with Meru at the center, and although Meru appears to have had a different location for each one of them, the mountain or pole itself is unchanging: it is the orientation of the terrestrial world that changes in relation to the pole.[10]

The Theosophists treated in chapters 3 and 4 had similar ideas on the successive emergence of continents and the consequent changes in the map of the world. The parallels are not surprising, considering that both they and Guénon were drawing on Hindu mythology. For instance, Blavatsky states outright in *The Secret Doctrine,* "Mount Meru, which is the North Pole, is said to have seven gold and seven silver steps leading to it."[11] She writes of the Imperishable Sacred Land, home of her first root race, "whose destiny it is to last from the beginning to the end of the Manvantara" and on which "the Pole-Star has its watchful eye."[12] Theosophy also has a White Island, though this was not polar but in the former Gobi Sea; it was and remains the spiritual center of the fifth root race, and is equated to Shambhala, the immaterial center of the Tibetan Kalachakra tradition. According to Alice Bailey, it is at "Shamballa" that the Lord of the World resides. He sounds much like the King of the World of Guénon's title, who rules an initiatic center hidden somewhere in the trans-Himalayan region.

On this topic Guénon diverged sharply both from Theosophy and from Hindu and Buddhist tradition. First, there is a large chronological difference. Whereas the Theosophists' Gobi center was founded during the later Atlantean era, around 70,000 BCE, in Guénon's version the supreme center was transferred to Asia at the start of the Kali Yuga (fourth and worst age of the Hindu system), whose traditional date is 3102 BCE.[13]

More significantly, there is a geographical difference, for Guénon's King of the World does not rule Shambhala (which is not mentioned), but the underground kingdom of Agarttha. For all the mystification surrounding this matter, the fact is that Agarttha has no basis in tradition but derives from the "astral travels" of Saint-Yves d'Alveydre (see chapter 2). So the first principles of Guénon's *Roi du monde* were firmly rooted in French occultism, a circumstance that has troubled more than one of Guénon's admirers.

It is all the more surprising that, having once mentioned it, Guénon set aside the traditional doctrine that the supreme spiritual center for this Manvantara persists unchanged through all the vicissitudes of the seven continents, in favor of Saint-Yves' subterranean kingdom with its sinister necromantic monarch. In a study already cited,[14] Marco Baistrocchi argues that Guénon deliberately promoted Agarttha as a parody of Shambhala, to turn the spiritual elites of Europe away from Theosophy and Buddhism. In fact, many Traditionalists have followed Guénon's example by becoming Muslims. At the same time, the Dalai Lama has been performing the Kalachakra Initiation, which is in some sense a gateway to Shambhala, with increasing frequency. Large numbers of Westerners are being initiated, even without the preparation that is traditionally required, presumably with some future end in view.

JULIUS EVOLA AND PAGAN IMPERIALISM

Evola's intellectual journey resembles Guénon's in some ways, while in others it could not have been more different. Guénon, as mentioned, had first published his *Roi du monde* theories in 1924 in a short-lived Italian esoteric journal, *Atanòr,* which was edited by Arturo Reghini (1878–1946). This Pythagorean mathematician, pagan, and Freemason was at the time a friend and close collaborator with Evola. For a while they saw the Fascist regime as a potential ally in the creation of a new Italy, free from communism on the one hand, and from the Catholic Church on the other. Reghini wrote hopefully of a "pagan imperialism" that would restore the spiritual authority of ancient Rome, and Evola took this up enthusiastically. The result was his book *Imperialismo pagano* (Pagan imperialism), written in 1926. Here he exhorted his countrymen in strident terms to disburden themselves of Christianity and return to a "Mediterranean Tradition," which he defined thus:

> It is not a myth. It is an archaic reality that even the profane historical sciences are now beginning to suspect. The epic and magical tradition of a positive, active civilization, strong in wisdom and strong in knowledge, it marked the elites of the Egypto-Chaldaic civilization, the paleo-Greek civilization, the Etruscan civilization, and others more mysterious whose echoes are heard in Syria, in Mycenae, in the Balearic Islands. The very spirit of paganism, it was then carried by the Mysteries of the Mediterranean basin until *Mithra* took his stand against the Judeo-Christian tide: Mithra, the "Conqueror of the Sun," the "Bull-slayer," the symbol of those who, regenerated in the "Strong strength of strengths," are beyond good and evil, beyond "need," beyond desire, beyond "passion."[15]

The fate of the book and of Evola's relations with the Fascist regime is a long story that cannot delay us here. The next step for Reghini and Evola was to gather a group of esotericists with an interest in Traditionalist studies and practical magic, called the Gruppo di Ur. In January 1927 they began publishing the members' contributions, all under pseudonyms, in a monthly journal of that name.[16]

Evola, still in his twenties, was a keen, self-taught student of Western and Eastern thought, as well as a trained engineer, a World War I veteran, a Dadaist poet and painter, and the creator of a philosophy of the "Absolute Individual." He was also fluent in German, and when Herman Wirth's *Der Aufgang der Menschheit* arrived on his desk in 1928, he introduced it in an article titled "The Hyperborean Tradition" that contains his later theories in embryo.[17]

Evola eagerly embraced the idea of human origins in the Arctic or polar region, once made habitable by a differently positioned axis of the earth. As researchers like Jean-Sylvian Bailly and Bal Gangadhar Tilak had already shown, world mythology gave every reason to believe that at least a part of the human race had come from there. Secondarily, there was the Donnellian material with its arguments for a vanished Atlantic land. But Evola warns his readers not to share Wirth's "Arctic Atlantis" confusion.

One must distinguish between the Hyperborean seat and the Atlantean seat, just as between Hyperborean tradition and Atlantean tradition. Once the Hyperborean cycle ended, it seems that a spiritual and traditional center was founded in Atlantis that reproduced, for a certain cycle, the Boreal one, appropriating many of its symbols since it was a kind of image of it. The two seats should not be confused. The Atlantean one was already secondary and particular in character, and many traditional centers were set up in the Eurasian continent independently of it, as direct offsprings of Hyperborea.[18]

Evola found much of Wirth's theory congenial, though deficient in the spiritual dimension and too much biased toward matriarchy and feminine values. It spurred him on to develop a vision of the past better suited to his own psychology. In this version the superior and primordial heritage is the Hyperborean one, oriented North-South in memory of its origins, with its particular spirituality "that has an Olympian character, as it were, of calm, immutable sovereignty and intangible transcendence, free from passion and becoming, as in the Apollonian symbol of the pure light and celestial heights."[19] In contrast to it is the Atlantean heritage with its East-West direction, whose symbolic world is feminine and maternal, lunar and telluric, and whose spirituality hinges on death and resurrection. One can hardly miss the projection into the mythic past of Evola's own exalted image of pagan Rome and his contempt for Christianity.

GUÉNON, EVOLA, AND WIRTH

Guénon did not read German, but was a regular, if diffident, reader of *Ur* and its successor *Krur*.[20] In May 1929 he published an article in *Le Voile d'Isis* (The Veil of Isis), the journal founded by Papus that Guénon had now come to dominate. Its apparent subject was thunderstones, the name given to prehistoric flint ax-heads in the belief that they were generated by thunder and lightning. Their symbolism, he writes, "is Hyperborean in origin, i.e. it connects with the most ancient of present mankind's traditions, the one that is truly the primitive tradition for the present Manvantara." Then he adds in a footnote the same caution as Evola:

> We should mention in this context that nowadays, through a strange confusion, some are talking about "Hyperborean Atlantis." Hyperborea and Atlantis are two distinct regions, just as North and West are two different cardinal points, and as points of departure for traditions, the former is far anterior to the latter.[21]

The footnote continues with a long-winded protest against those who have attributed this confusion to Guénon himself: of course he has done nothing of the sort and can't imagine how they got such an absurd idea! In the October 1929 issue of *Le Voile d'Isis,* readers discovered the guilty party: it was Paul Le Cour (see chapter 2), whom Guénon now accused of misreading the relevant passages in *Le Roi du monde*. This article on "Atlantis and Hyperborea" mentions Herman Wirth as an author of the said confusion, but it offers few facts about the vanished worlds and serves mainly to humiliate Le Cour.[22]

Evola's next contribution to the subject appeared in *Krur* (the successor to *Ur* after his break with Reghini) in July 1930, as "The Symbolism of the Year." It explained Herman Wirth's theories of the symbols with which his "Arctic-Atlantic" race had represented the sun and the course of the year and illustrated some of them. Evola's objection typifies the Traditionalist reversal of received values:

We have to take issue with the "naturalistic" interpretation [of the change in symbolism between northern and southern climates]. In primordial times, natural phenomena were never "worshiped" or treated religiously in that way, even when aspects of them were valid as revelations of the supernatural. The essence of religion at the origins was not a superstitious divination of natural phenomena, as [Wirth's] interpretation of modern data suggests, but the reverse: the natural phenomena received their value, in antiquity, from making perceptible and symbolizing divine essences. Only in this way did they appear absolutely real.[23]

THE PRIMORDIAL TRADITION AND ITS DECLINE

In the summer of 1931, Guénon came out with his long-awaited definitive statement about Hyperborea and Atlantis. He now stated outright that the primordial tradition originated from the Hyperborean or Arctic region at the beginning of our Manvantara, and that the secondary and derivative tradition of Atlantis appeared later on its own continent.[24] The Atlantean tradition belonged to one of the last divisions of the current cycle of terrestrial humanity, hence is comparatively recent and certainly in the second half of the present Manvantara. In chapter 11 we will see exactly how he dated it.

Guénon finds several allusions to Atlantis in the Book of Genesis, including "the fact that the literal meaning of Adam's name is 'red,' the Atlantean tradition having been precisely that of the Red race; and it also seems that the biblical Flood corresponds directly to the cataclysm in which Atlantis disappeared."[25] This leads him to suspect that "the Atlantean cycle was taken as its basis by the Hebrew tradition, and its transmission took place either by the intermediary of the Egyptians, which at least has nothing improbable about it, or by some other means."[26] At the same time, another current came directly from the seat of the primordial tradition in the North. The meeting point of these two currents (a theme to which Guénon often returned) might be sought in the Celtic region or in Chaldea. While warning us not to trust the conclusions of "profane archaeologists," Guénon adds that many vestiges of the forgotten past are now emerging from the earth, and that this may herald the end of the Manvantara, when everything must come together to prepare for the next cycle.[27]

When Evola came to revise *Imperialismo pagano* for a German edition (published 1933), he dropped the great Mediterranean tradition in favor of a "Nordic and primordial" tradition. He even called ancient Rome the last great creation of the Nordic spirit.[28] Although this revision was clearly strategic, not to say toadying, it reflected a genuine change of attitude. Evola was by then busy with the work for which he is most remembered, *Rivolta contra il mondo moderno* (Revolt against the modern world). Here he was able to rival Guénon with a display of Traditionalist erudition and polemic, taking on the task of explaining the whole course of the Manvantara.

Like all Traditionalists, Evola believed that humanity is not the result of the "ascent of man" from mammals, but of a separate origin better called a "descent." The Hyperborean phase was the "first age," "golden age," "age of the gods," or "primordial age," and the summit from which humanity has degenerated, following inexorable cyclical law. Evola does not try to date this primordial age, but its location is not in doubt: our cycle began in the extreme North, in the present Arctic Ocean,[29] and the Hyperborean civilization was destroyed in a catastrophe, probably due to a change in the inclination of the earth's axis.

The Hyperborean age was thus closed, and the second great age, the Atlantean, began. This entailed two separate migrations of the "Boreal" race that had inhabited the Arctic region, widely separated in both time and space.

> Groups of Hyperboreans carrying the same spirit, the same blood, and the same body of symbols, signs, and languages first reached North America and the northern regions of the Eurasian continent.

Supposedly, tens of thousands of years later a second great migratory wave ventured as far as Central America, reaching a land situated in the Atlantic region that is now lost, thereby establishing a new center modeled after the polar regions. This land may have been that Atlantis described by Plato and Diodorus.[30]

Working a well-known vein of Atlantology, Evola suggests that the second emigration gave rise to myths of wise rulers arriving from across the sea: Irish legends of the Tuatha de Danann coming from the West, and the Mexican legends of Quetzalcoatl coming from the East. The same emigration may also have been responsible for the appearance of the Cro-Magnons, the superior human type who appeared in western Europe at the end of the Ice Age without visible forbears, their culture fully formed.

As the Hyperboreans spread to the south, some groups interbred with peoples already living there

> with the aboriginal Southern races, with proto-Mongoloid and Negroid races, and with other races that probably represented the degenerated residues of the inhabitants of a second prehistoric continent, now lost, which was located in the South, and which some designated as Lemuria. [Also] the red-skinned race of the last inhabitants of Atlantis (according to Plato's mythical account, those who forfeited their pristine "divine" nature because of repeated unions with the human race); these people should be regarded as the original ethnic stock of several newer civilizations established by the migratory waves from west to east (the red race of Cretan-Aegeans, Eteicretes, Pelasgians, Lycians, Egyptians, Kefti, etc.), and of the American civilizations.[31]

The picture of the Boreal race descending from the Pole and meeting the Sudeen and Austral races is pure Fabre d'Olivet, whom Evola later credited with being the first person in modern times to assert the northern origin of the white race. He added that this was "less a scientific hypothesis than the exposition of a traditional teaching, still preserved in very restricted circles with which he was in touch."[32] As for Lemuria, Evola says next to nothing about it, because that continent "is connected to a cycle so ancient that it cannot be adequately considered in this context."[33] That said, we can summarize his version of prehistory as follows:

First land and first race: Lemuria, belonging to the previous cycle and situated in the South, from which some Negroid peoples descend.

Second land and second race: Hyperborea, corresponding to the Golden Age of the present cycle, situated in the North, whence Cro-Magnons and the Aryan race descended.

Third land: Atlantis, corresponding to the Silver and Bronze Ages, situated in the West; the place where the races met and mingled.

The historical period follows, corresponding to the Iron Age. Remnants of all races and their mixtures are present.

To anyone familiar with the order of root races in Theosophy and Anthroposophy, it seems strange to put Lemuria (supposedly the third) before Hyperborea (the second). But Evola's Manvantara, like Guénon's, was shorter than the Theosophists' by an order of magnitude, being no more than a few tens of thousands of years. His blend of Fabre d'Olivet, Tilak, and Wirth with some Theosophical terms perfectly satisfied the racial mythology that he was developing at this period.[34] The southern lands and their Lemurian inhabitants were consigned to the oblivion of a previous cycle. Hyperborea could then occupy the Golden Age of the current cycle, passing without interruption to Atlantis and thence to his own age. This provided Aryan humanity with the potential of a link with its Arctic ancestors, and one that, in suitably Olympian types, could bring about a rebirth of Hyperborean spirituality. For all his ups and downs, that remained Evola's lodestar.

PRIESTS VERSUS WARRIORS

Evola held Guénon, twelve years his senior, in high regard. In later life he is reported as saying, "René Guénon . . . he was my master. I simply continued his work by transposing it to action."[35] The encounter with Guénon's writings (they never met in person) had kindled in his ready mind the idea of the integral Tradition and given him a focal point for his life's work. However, there were many obstacles to a reciprocal admiration on Guénon's part, such as Evola's Germanophilia, his concept of magic, his love of Rome and classical civilization, and his privileging of the Kshatriya (royal and warrior) caste above the Brahmin (priestly) caste.

This difference shows up in their respective attitudes to the Hindu legend of the "Revolt of the Kshatriyas." Guénon interpreted this not as a single historical event but as the perennial revolt of temporal power against spiritual authority, which "may have had its beginnings either in Atlantis itself, or at least among the heirs of its tradition."[36] He devoted a whole book (*Spiritual Authority and Temporal Power*) to its consequences. These were part and parcel of his devolutionary outlook, for the revolt began the process by which power descended through the castes. Taken from the initiate-priests of the primordial tradition (called Brahmins in Hindu tradition) by the kings and warriors loyal to them (Kshatriyas), it later passed to the merchants (Vaishyas), and finally to the masses of modern democracy (Sudras).

While sharing this broad view, Evola had scant respect for any priestly caste. Like Wirth's Arctic-Atlanteans, his Hyperboreans did not need priests: they already had transcendent awareness, living in a world where (as quoted above) "natural phenomena received their value . . . from making perceptible and symbolizing divine essences." And although with human devolution, such perception had generally faded, it was perennially available to the superior individual. To this end, Evola devoted a book (*The Doctrine of Awakening*) to interpreting Buddhism as a Kshatriya-based movement, revolting against the corrupt priesthood of its day.

Guénon returned to the theme of Atlantis in his late work, *The Reign of Quantity and the Signs of the Times*. He does not mention it by name, but alludes to it while explaining the workings of the "counter-tradition" and "counter-initiation" that is in perennial opposition to Tradition. Apparently the counter-initiation originates from "the unique source to which all initiation is attached," but "by a degeneration carried to its extreme limit." One of its ploys is to fasten onto dead traditions abandoned by the spirit, using their residues for its own purposes.

> This leads logically to the thought that this extreme degeneration must go a very long way back into the past; and, however obscure the question of its origins may be, there is some plausibility in the idea that it may be connected with the perversion of one of the ancient civilizations belonging to one or another of the continents that have disappeared in cataclysms occurring in the course of the present *Manvantara*.[37]

Guénon, who not coincidentally passed his later life in Cairo, warned that archaeologists who open ancient tombs are risking letting such residues out into the world, with potentially dangerous results.[38] All this recalls the Theosophists' tales of the light and dark magicians of Atlantis and Subba Row's sinister words about the powerful elemental gods and goddesses worshiped by the Atlanteans, which still exist (see chapters 3–4).

Finally, as a word of caution to the rationalists, Guénon warns that there are two or three "time barriers" beyond which it is extremely difficult to obtain any accurate knowledge.[39] The first of these is around the sixth century BCE, before which chronologies become hazy. The second is around the beginning of the Kali Yuga, which he calls the limit for things so far made known by archaeology. The third barrier corresponds to the last great terrestrial cataclysm, that of the disappearance of Atlantis, and it is quite useless to try to go back any further.

SEVEN

The Britons

———————— ✳ ————————

IN EVERY NATION in which occult interests have flourished, those interests have had their own flavors and biases. Britain has a reputation as a place where eccentrics are tolerated, even admired, and as such it has already been a fertile field for our study. One purpose of the selections in this chapter is to illustrate the variety of methods by which occult information arrives. We have instances of a self-trained trance medium (Dion Fortune, Margaret Lumley Brown); dictation by an inner voice (H. C. Randall-Stevens); vision of the past induced by meditating at an ancient site (Paul Brunton); open-eyed vision on site by a medium (Olive Pixley) whose report is written down by another (F. C. Tyler, Foster Forbes); the study of manuscripts made available during initiation into an arcane order (Lewis Spence); a discarnate entity who takes the subject on a tour of Atlantis (Daphne Vigers); the appearance of a well-known nineteenth-century control (Mandasoran); another medium (Anthony Neate) who acts as mouthpiece for his controlling entity; a person who has a single flash of inspired vision (Katharine Maltwood) from which she develops a system; an enthusiast for outlandish theories (Brinsley le Poer Trench) who constructs his own eclectic model; and another (John Michell) whose enthusiasms lead to a geometric revelation of his own. The variety of methods is matched by the variety of Atlantises thus received. The alert reader will notice repetitions, echoes, and leitmotifs running through the entirety of our material, and also stark contradictions that are equally instructive.

ATLANTIS IN THE INNER LIGHT

As told in chapter 3, the proclamation of Krishnamurti as the coming World Teacher shattered the already shaky unity of the Theosophical Society, but it did not shatter Theosophy. The preceding chapters are evidence for the staying-power of the Theosophical myth of prehistory, and much more will appear before our survey is done. Rudolf Steiner accepted it; so did Alice Bailey, to mention two of the most influential vehicles for the Theosophical current outside the parent society. A third was Dion Fortune, the initiatic name of Violet Mary Firth (1890–1946),[1] whose Society of the Inner Light combined Theosophical doctrines with the magical current of the Golden Dawn.

Born to a solicitor's family with progressive ideas, Dion Fortune qualified as a psychotherapist before gravitating to occult and magical circles. Unlike many of our subjects, who were unprepared when voices or visions suddenly broke in on them, she had been psychic since childhood and deliberately cultivated trance mediumship as a way of access to inner worlds. Later she found that she could obtain images in the waking state and no longer required an amanuensis. Medium she may have been, but she was anything but passive. Her early training and appreciation of Carl Jung gave her esoteric writing a psychological dimension rare in the genre. In short, she is a force to be reckoned with.

In her early book *The Esoteric Orders and Their Work* (1928), Fortune sketches a prehistory that is basically Blavatskian, but with an emphasis on the Seven Rays that brings her closer to her contemporaries Besant, Leadbeater, and Bailey. She tells of three great emigrations of those who foresaw the three great cataclysms of Atlantis and links these with three later occult schools. The first of these moved across Europe and Asia "until it finally contacted the remains of the Lemurian culture in the Pacific, from which it derived some of those elements which render it to-day a dangerous and polluted current."[2] The second crossed central Europe and reached the Himalayas; the third, leaving just before the final cataclysm, founded the Egyptian civilization, which became the parent of the Western esoteric tradition, including its Greek, Hebrew, and Gnostic strains.[3] This being Fortune's own tradition, she pays little attention to the other two currents. She advised her students and readers that the magical methods of the first emigration, being on the Ray of Power and working from physical operations upward, were too dangerous. Those of the second, being on the Ray of Wisdom and working with the higher mind alone, were too abstracted. Westerners should renew their link with the third emigration, which, being on the Ray of Love and Devotion, "had brotherhood and compassion for its ideals and socialisation for its task."[4]

Fortune's psychic experiences convinced her that she had lived before as a priestess in Atlantis. These inspired her novel, *The Sea Priestess* (1938), which is about modern people reliving their past lives in Atlantis's final days. It is no surprise to discover a City of the Golden Gates on the island of Ruta, that Atlantis fell through black magic, or that the Azores are its last remnants. But there is an original touch. While most of our sources consider only the solar cult and compete in florid descriptions of the Sun Temple, Dion Fortune's heroine had been a priestess of the Sea Temple, dedicated to a cult more ancient still: "They hailed the sea as the oldest of created things, older even than the hills, and the mother of all living. But they bade the sea remember that the moon is the giver of magnetic life, and that it was from the moonlight on the sea that living forms arose."[5]

What is fictionalized in *The Sea Priestess* had been directly given through Dion Fortune's mediumship, as was evident when the transcripts were finally published.[6] One of the most powerful ideas in the novel was that the legends of King Arthur, Merlin, and the Knights of the Round Table record characters and events from the end of Atlantean civilization. King Arthur's mother was a sea-princess of Atlantis and Merlin a priest who accompanied the Atlantean tin merchants to Britain;[7] the whole action, in fact, took place thousands of years before Christ. The various characters and events in the Camelot saga represent momentous events in the evolution of consciousness, connected with the transition from the fourth to the fifth root race.[8]

Upon Dion Fortune's unexpected death, the leadership of her initiatic society passed to Margaret Lumley Brown, who was if anything a more gifted medium for "inner plane communications."[9] Already as a young woman she had corresponded with Colonel Percy Harrison Fawcett (1867–1925?) about Glastonbury, Atlantis, and the occult hierarchy.[10] In dream, she had been shown "elaborately drawn maps of what one might call the esoteric geography of England in which were marked various centres which had held the Atlantean descent of power first introduced by colonisers from Atlantis and from them, handed down through the Druids."[11] Upon taking up Ouija board sessions, she received enough Atlantean material to fill a large volume of notes. Her communicators were apparently a teaching fraternity on the astral plane quite distinct from the Theosophical masters and Christian rather than Eastern. They told her of the customs, magic rituals, and way of life that she had lived in her Atlantean incarnation.

One would think that religious differences dissolve in the afterworld, but Brown's sources were a brotherhood dedicated to the Twelve Apostles and the Virgin Mary. All the more surprising, then, that the Atlantis they showed her was standard issue. It had advanced understanding of nuclear physics, a lighting system that we have not yet discovered, a science of genetics that started out well but "became a means of some of the blackest magic ever known," and clairvoyant contact with far-off planes exceeding anything possessed by psychics today.[12] The Atlanteans also had a mastery of sound and its applications that we cannot imagine. They had instruments played not by the hand but by electric mechanism, and they also had different vocal cords from ours, which enabled them to produce more efficacious vibrations.[13] This appealed to Brown, who as a poet and mistress of ritual had a special interest in the qualities of words and their mantric and magical power.

In her Atlantis there was the familiar City of the Golden Gates on the Island of Ruta, with its Sun Temple. This was only the exoteric face of

Atlantean religion; the esoteric side was cultivated by high initiates in the Sea Temple, also called the Withdrawn Temple.[14] Brown's sea cult seems to have been broader visioned than Fortune's lunar cult, for it linked humanity "not only to the Solar Logos as does the Sun but to the Worlds beyond, to the other Solar systems—to the great Cosmic whole."[15] On a homelier scale there were connections with the places that Brown loved. Cornwall, Wales, Brittany had all been Atlantean outposts with strong sea cults, whose aura is still detectable to the sensitive. In Brown's mythic world the Atlantean mythology merged into that of faërie, Avalon, and the Holy Grail.

Both Dion Fortune and Margaret Lumley Brown made their own clairvoyant investigations into Atlantean realms, and these produced the material that circulated within the Society of the Inner Light as "Atlantean Scripts."[16] There it remained until the appearance of a novel by Peter Valentine Timlett, *The Seedbearers* (1974).[17] We have the witness of Gareth Knight, the authority on Dion Fortune and her movement, that Timlett passed through the society.[18] Even without knowing that, every page (except the ones given over to sex and violence) is redolent of the occult Atlantis traditions. Leadbeater's black Rmoahals, yellow Akkadians, and red Toltecs are crammed in uneasy coexistence on the small island of Ruta as the kingdom approaches its end. The Sun Temple and its priesthood have degenerated into political cat's-paws, but the Withdrawn Temple still keeps its integrity. There the heroes plan the last-minute exodus of the "seedbearers," destined to make a new start in Egypt. Occasionally the action flags so that the reader can get a crash course in Theosophical cosmogenesis, root races, and so on.[19] As in Dion Fortune's own cosmos, Theosophical doctrines are blended with ceremonial magic, and Timlett describes the rituals with a sense of occasion and psychology that suggests experience. When the "Atlantean Scripts" were published, Timlett's debt became apparent, but so did the novelistic quality of the revelations themselves, with details of Atlantean waterworks, mating habits, garbage disposal, and so forth.[20]

Colonel Fawcett, briefly mentioned above, returns to this web in a curious manner. In 1925, soon after writing to Margaret Lumley Brown, he left for an expedition in the Brazilian jungle from which he never returned. Over the following decades, several mediums claimed to have received messages from him. They were unclear about whether he was still alive, suspended in a coma, or already dead, but it hardly mattered as he was so communicative. In 1948, through the automatic writing of Geraldine Cummins, he spoke of how he had discovered ruins that dated back to Atlantean days. Near the lost cities there were white towers, relics of the Atlantean technology for drawing electricity out of the atmosphere and storing it in underground reservoirs. The Atlanteans used this electricity for cooking, heating, lighting, cleaning, lifting weights, healing—and waging war. That, said Fawcett, was their undoing, for they overfilled their reservoirs. The "chambers of compressed electricity" exploded and brought on a vast cataclysm.[21]

Everyone consulted agreed that this had to be Fawcett himself communicating. Perhaps encouraged by his eager audience, in 1949 he dictated a yarn worthy of Fortune's or Timlett's fiction. Dramatic and filled with punchy dialogue, it told about his life with the Indian tribes and adventures in the jungle. He met not only anacondas but also a "Pythoness" or virgin oracle, with whom he was invited to father the future guardian of her tribe.[22] (He says he declined.) On the whole, the ex-Fawcett was of one mind with the Fortune circle, but he differed on one significant point. Instead of Avalon and Glastonbury, which he had commended in his letters to Margaret Brown, he now held that it was *Ireland* that was a colony of the lost continent. That, he explained, is why the Irish have never become integrated into Britain. "It is not from hatred of England, it is from the fundamental aristocratic feeling of the Atlanteans, from their sense of innate superiority as regards other races that this feeling springs. The magic ray of the distant Atlantean past stretches across the gulf of time and kindles, in the deeper sense of this little people, the old pride of the Atlanteans—a terrible cold pride that led to their downfall."[23]

THE REVELATIONS OF A NORMAL LAD

Unlike Dion Fortune and Margaret Brown, attuned to the psychic world from childhood, Hugh Clayton Randall-Stevens (1896–?) assures us that he started out as a "normal lad." He began studying medicine, then was presumably called up, for he served with the RAF in both world wars. In between he worked in the West End theatrical world, where his wife was a "well-known musical star."[24] In February 1925 he was surprised, as several of our subjects have been, by a Voice. It told him first to write, then two days later to draw, though he had had no training in either. In short order he completed *The Book of Truth, or The Voice of Osiris,* together with sixty-eight pencil drawings of Egyptian-style heads and objects. The book was published, like many occultist works, by Rider of London, and was followed three years later by *The Chronicles of Osiris.* Instead of the author's name, the title pages proclaim the books as "Set down in the House of El Eros-El Erua, they being male-female, born according to the laws governing the Dhuman-Adamic race, this being their fourth incarnation."

The Book of Truth opens with a kind of Gnostic theology. There is a trinity of a Father-Mother God, plus God the Son, which emanated a series of demiurgic powers, beginning with El Daoud. All dual-sexed like the Godhead, these took on the task of creation. From them came the Dhuman-Adamic race, also known as ray-children, a superior humanity who at first dwelled in immaterial bodies. They were responsible for developing the Yevahic race of potential humans, by integrating divine sparks into material bodies. Reproduction was nonsexual and took place only with divine consent.[25]

Besides the Gnostic creation myth, with its Demiurge and hierarchy of creative powers in pairs, the existence of two human types, one radically superior to the other, echoes the Ariosophists. The voluntary migration of the divine sparks into subhuman bodies, mentioned in the next episode, occurs in the Theosophical system, as does the nonsexual reproduction of earlier stages of humanity.

As Osiris's narrative continued, the evolutionary scheme was upset by a divine being first known as Eranus, later as Satanaku. His ambition was to create material beings independently of the divine plan, who could reproduce without permission of the Godhead. The result was a population of monsters, on an Earth that was cut off from communication with other spheres.[26] In time, Satanaku succeeded in getting the divine sparks to incarnate in his creations, where they practiced "the most terrible sex depravities."[27] This was the situation on the continent of Sarkon (better known as Lemuria), which came to be such a sink of iniquity that El Daoud intervened and destroyed it by condensing its atmosphere.[28]

The Chronicles of Osiris, dictated in 1926, takes up the story from this point. Just before the end of Lemuria, one of the Adamics named Ptah gathered a select group to escape and make a fresh start in Sardegon (Atlantis), where the Yevahic race could develop in conformity with its divine sparks. Ptah built twenty-four temples whose symbol of divinity was the sun disk, the mediator between humanity and the triple God.[29] For thousands of years the Atlanteans lived as vegetarians in a simple, mainly outdoor life, divided into twenty-four clans each ruled by initiate ray-children. Trouble began when a priest called Itheboleth founded a secret sect called Initiates of the Lowlands. Falling under the will of Satanaku, Itheboleth built sanctuaries of initiation and underground chambers. He led his devotees to perform animal and human sacrifices under the belief that they would gain occult powers thereby. When his sect had grown sufficiently strong, he made war on Ptah's people and plundered their temples. Ptah, "standing between the paws of the great Sphinx of the Highlands, cried unto the Cosmos." The earth trembled and split, fires leaped forth, and thousands were swallowed up.[30]

The insurrection of Itheboleth had resulted in his death and that of many of the initiates. Osiris's son, Horus, was left to reorganize Atlantis with the help of an Adamic called El Erosuphu or El Eros, whose significance will become apparent. El Erosuphu acted as judge and lawgiver to the entire continent, aided by his twin and wife El Erosuphua. Another long period of peace ensued, during which Atlanteans colonized the shores of the Sahara Sea and Central and South America. But eventually there was again a demand from the unqualified for knowledge of the Mysteries. The cult of Itheboleth revived, and Satanaku threw all his energies behind it. With genocidal intention he demanded especially the elite Adamic children for human sacrifice.[31]

To cut a now familiar story short, the capital of Atlantis, the Golden City of Chekon, was destroyed, though not before another Adamic group, led by Horehetop, had escaped to Egypt. This was around 15,000 BCE. Most of them traveled by boat, but some initiates left in their immortal bodies, one of them carrying tablets of stone that were dematerialized for the trip, then rematerialized on arrival. The wicked Atlanteans could not escape, as the sea became a mass of molten lava.[32]

In Egypt, Horehetop and his people worked intermittently over a period of 1,050 years to build the Sphinx, the pyramids, and an underground complex of passages and chambers. But this was not all. Osiris says: "The Pyramids never formed the Inner Circle of the divine Initiation, they being only stones of remembrance to keep the people in the knowledge of the Cosmos until such times as the sacred House of my Father should be ready, which was not till about the year 10,000 BC."[33] The true House of Initiation was constructed at an undisclosed location in Upper Egypt by a group led by the second incarnation of El Erosuphu.[34] *The Book of Truth* describes it in minute detail,[35] and many of the drawings in that book illustrate its furnishings and sacred objects. There are floors of mother-of-pearl; gold and silver tapestries; heptangular columns of crystal; self-opening doors; a theater; a fountain of alabaster; and towers, pylons, and pyramids bearing signs, symbols, and inscriptions. Osiris assures us that it will all be rediscovered at the appointed time.[36]

For a long period Upper and Lower Egypt were ruled by kings, always chosen from among the Adamic race, rather than from the subservient Yehavic people. There was social mobility, however, thanks to reincarnation, so that an evolved Yehavic man or woman could be born to Adamic parents.[37] Meanwhile, in the colonies of Atlantis, Satanaku and his entities from the astral planes were at work perverting the people. To make them distinguishable from the people of Khemu, "the Cosmos had spoken unto Eil Daudu [El Daoud] and had commanded him to cause them to have coloured skins; so that those of Central America had reddish skins, whilst those of Africa and the East had some bronze skins and some black. The black and lowest race have survived to-day as the negroes of South Africa."[38] Then came the inevitable miscegenation of the higher with the lower races. In 7600 BCE the people of Nubia invaded the two kingdoms of Egypt, initiating a state of war that continued for about a thousand years. Finally around 6600 BCE the two lands were united under Mentos, wearer of the double crown.[39]

There is no need to continue with Osiris's history of Egypt, except to say that much weight is given to the reformer Pharaoh Akhnaton, who was the third incarnation of El Erosuphu. Osiris calls his rule disastrous because "firstly, the material side of life was forgotten, and religious ideas were forced upon the people to a fanatical degree."[40] He then addresses his scribe directly:

They, the figures in that ancient tragedy are incarnate again, and must work out their Kharmic debts afresh. The circumstances are familiar to thee, twain El Erosuphu-El Erosuphua—therefore, I say unto thee, go forward and, knowing the past, strive to bring the future to a successful conclusion.[41]

This explains the cryptic mention of a "fourth incarnation" in the subtitles of *The Book of Truth* and *The Chronicles of Osiris*. Randall-Stevens had to accept that he was Akhnaton reborn, though he purported to be none too happy about it.[42]

After World War II, Randall-Stevens returned to print with *Atlantis to the Latter Days,* "inspirationally dictated to H. C. Randall-Stevens (El Eros) by the Masters Oneferu and Adolemy of the Osirian Group." The book sported a frontispiece photograph and offered the scraps of biography given above. Later editions appeared under the imprint "Order of the Knights Templars of Aquarius," based in London and the Channel Island of Jersey, which still awaits its chronicler.

Besides repeating much of the material from the earlier books, *Atlantis to the Latter Days* gives a revelation from 1927 about the initiations that took place in the Temple of the Sphinx, that is, the Great Pyramid. These are remarkably similar to the account of Paul Brunton, the traveler and philosopher, who wrote of his own experiences during a night spent in the King's Chamber.[43] In both cases the subject leaves his body and sees it lying there, then follows a guide and passes through various ordeals or illuminations. He is warned that our civilization, if it continues on its present path, will suffer the same fate as Atlantis; then he reenters his body.[44] While *The Book of Truth* had an apocalyptic tone, with frequent mention of the coming "great day of Aquarius," *Atlantis to the Latter Days* continues with material on time cycles and current Earth changes, and a long moralizing conclusion. This elaborates on the theme announced at the beginning of the book: "The 'Latter Days' are come, the days of the Co-Adamics and Gentile Divine Sparks, when they must choose between light and darkness—God and Anti-God."[45]

I have treated Randall-Stevens's work at some length because of its multiple correspondences with other accounts of Atlantis and Egypt, with Gnostic theology, and with Theosophical prehistory. One naturally wonders whether these were actual influences on it, or whether some other explanation has to be found. *The Book of Truth* carries an introduction by one Peter Miles, whose address at 4, Upper Wimpole St., London, suggests that he may have been a medical man of repute. Miles had often watched Randall-Stevens producing the "so-called inspirational writings and automatic drawings," and noted the speed and lack of erasures on them. His careful inquiry into Randall-Stevens's life showed that he had no previous talent or interest in such matters. Miles concludes:

> Having regard to the complete ignorance of the writer, at the time of writing the following pages, of Egyptian history and Egyptology generally, it does not appear to me that the writings and the book as a whole can adequately be accounted for as the product of what is commonly termed the subconscious mind, as understood by psy-

chologists. A more tenable hypothesis is that the work is that of a Superior Intelligence coming from beyond and using the writer as a medium.[46]

While the scene of initiation in the Great Pyramid could have been plagiarized from Brunton's work of 1936, and predated to 1927, an author who practiced that sort of fabrication could have done much more to enhance his work. There is a naivety to Randall-Stevens's revelations, as well as to his drawings, that inclines me to the same conclusion as Peter Miles, though "superior" is not the word I would use.

Having mentioned Paul Brunton (1898–1981), I here include his small contribution to the Atlantis myth. Brunton was a professional journalist before he became a bestselling author of books on travel, meditation, oriental philosophy, and the conduct of life. *A Search in Secret Egypt* contains vivid firsthand accounts of his meetings with fakirs, magicians, spiritual masters, and tricksters. More to the point, he also writes of visions that arose before his inner eye while meditating in places where the genius loci was strong.

Sitting in meditation by the Sphinx, Brunton had a vision of its makers, scurrying to and fro with baskets, climbing up flimsy ladders, chipping away at the rock. "The faces of all these men were long and hard, the skins tinted reddish brown, or greyish yellow, and the upper lips, also, were noticeably long." Once their work was complete, there was the gigantic human head set on a lion's body, with a disk of solid gold above its headdress. Then the vision continued with a wall of water overwhelming the monument, as the Deluge struck. The waters ebbed away, leaving the yellow desert in their place.[47] Brunton comments: "It was a tremendous and astonishing thought that the Sphinx provided a solid, visible and enduring link between the people of today and the people of a lost world, the unknown Atlanteans." As his musings continue, it becomes plain to him that the Temple of the Sphinx is nothing other than the Great Pyramid, so that both were built in Atlantean times.[48] He mentions the well-known date of 2170 BCE that Sir John Herschel, the astronomer, proposed for the Great Pyramid, based on the orientation of its main passage to the former pole star Alpha Draconis, and makes a point that the pyramid's date might as well be a whole precessional cycle earlier. H. P. Blavatsky had already suggested this, with a date of 28,868 BCE.[49] Brunton's date, based on a different precessional figure, is 27,997 BCE; we can add these to the many dates that have been affixed to these monuments, keeping in mind that they are only as good as Herschel's proposal. The Egyptian builders may have had entirely different criteria for the angle of the ascending passage.

The warning that our civilization is heading for imminent doom is a favorite refrain of Atlantologists. To a certain cast of mind, often shared by Superior Intelligences, it always seems that the present day is on the brink of catastrophe, because everyone is so wicked (except of course the writer and his or her readers). Nonetheless, there are times when a general crisis—physical, moral, or spiritual—affects virtually everyone. One of these was the Second World War.

PSYCHOMETRY ON THE BRINK OF WAR

Lieutenant Colonel John Foster Forbes (1889–1958) came from a similar background to that of William Scott-Elliot: the minor Scottish aristocracy.[50] He attended Cambridge University, served as intelligence officer in World War I and as British vice-consul in Munich, then spent some years schoolmastering. A severe illness interrupted his career, from which he emerged a changed man. He joined the Order of the Cross, a Christian pacifist and vegetarian movement founded by John Todd Ferrier, and by the 1930s was involved in what we would call psychic archeology. This did not impair his standing in respectable quarters, for in 1936 he became a fellow both of the Royal Anthropological Institute and of the Society of Antiquaries of Scotland.

As Forbes relates in his book *The Unchronicled Past,* he set himself the task of filling in the gap between the earliest traces of humans in Europe (which to him were the Aurignacians, around 20,000–25,000

BCE) and the intrusion from the West around 10,000 BCE, possibly from an Atlantic continent.[51] He called his method psychometry, and his collaborator was Olive Pixley, a noted "conscious medium." It sounds as though she had talents similar to those of Leadbeater or Steiner, in that she could see past events while still conscious of the present, but preferring it to be focused by an object or a place.

In her unpublished work on psychometry, Pixley records that in 1930 she and Forbes visited Glastonbury Tor, a steep oval hill just outside the historic Somerset town. She saw that on top of the Tor there had once been a stone circle, and that winding upward to it was a host of people performing a dawn ritual, which she knew to derive from Atlantean traditions. Singing and drumming as they went, they created a serpentine path of etheric energy. As the sun rose, "the raised spiral of serpent power fused with the sun's light through the agency of the stone circle. The resultant energy then shot outwards through the 'alignments' over the land. This was for the benefit of the plant and butterfly realms. The key to the ritual, Pixley thought, was the vibration of sound and light."[52]

John Michell's *View over Atlantis* was the first postwar book to draw attention to this group of researchers into ancient mysteries that included Pixley, Forbes, and Major F. C. Tyler. Tyler was the secretary of the Straight Track Club (the original ley-hunters), founded by Alfred Watkins.[53] He worked with Pixley and recorded her psychometric impressions, then made them available to Forbes. Out of these came *The Unchronicled Past,* in which Forbes interprets the psychically obtained material in his own way.

The book strikes a Masonic tone from the beginning, as Forbes writes: "Psychometry has revealed that the whole of Britain at these early ages was controlled most perfectly by the masters and past masters of ancient Masonry, which is the science of the cosmos and the one-time science of the world."[54] An unorthodox attitude to the famed secrets of Freemasonry emerges when he discusses the huge menhirs of Brittany. Whether or not he had read Sinnett or Leadbeater, Forbes was sure that there had been no need for physical force to raise them, because the priests of the time "were adepts in the science of sound and rhythm to which the elements in the hand of a master mason become responsive"(22).* Other relics of those ancient times were the seven Tors of Dartmoor, massive piles of granite generally thought to be natural formations. Pixley, on the contrary, saw them as the remains of gigantic walls, adding a statement reminiscent of her vision on Glastonbury Tor: "They used the forces of Nature as one, for the *Combination of Sound and Light is the Essence of Creation!*"(39).

From here, the road to Atlantis was plain. Forbes wrote: "In Atlantean times and even *before that* not only was the element of which stone was composed responsive to the law even of sound when properly applied, but that in conditions long prior to an age of *fixity* or earth conditions, the substance now called stone was malleable, or even pliable"(46).

Other information on the Atlanteans follows, though it is impossible to tell what came directly from Olive Pixley's clairvoyance, and what was Foster Forbes's conjecture as he filled in the gap of his original question. It is certainly he who concurs with Theosophists that the Atlanteans had trekked East and West long before the final subsidence in 9650 BCE. The Azilians may have been their last wave, meeting an earlier one of Cro-Magnons coming West again (64–65). Then two great cultures started in Egypt and Babylon. The Great Pyramid was built prior to 10,000 BCE by a highly advanced people and later found there by the proto-Egyptians. The builders then came West via the Mediterranean and made the dolmens and other megalithic monuments (68–69).

These early settlers in southwestern Britain were worshippers of sun and stars, their rituals labyrinthine and spiral, without sacrifice. Here Forbes adds another allusion to Freemasonry, which he evidently saw as spiritually linked to the old religion. He says that it is the worship of God, of whom the sun is the symbol, and that there is no Christian doctrine in it—one needs only to believe in God; and geometry forms the basis of its creed (45). In contrast to this ancient pure religion and its modern counterpart is the epoch embracing most of dynastic Egypt, Greece, and

---

*Page numbers in parentheses are from *The Unchronicled Past*.

Rome. All of that, Forbes says, belongs to the "occult age" when wrong forces were set in motion for base ends. But, he adds, there really was a Golden Age, and it can still be sensed in Britain (49).

This was 1938, and the storm clouds were gathering. Forbes took comfort from his studies.

> I feel that England has been awaiting this hour [of revelation of the truth]. Despite the infinite tragedy and sorrow that has marked the ages; despite the efforts of all her enemies to mar and scar the face of this truly magic land, that the true worth has been preserved not only in the heart of the country, but in the hearts of her wonderful people. Here twenty thousand years ago or even more, who can tell? men and women of great spiritual might have trod her green hills and valleys and wherever they went they left the indelible impress of an influence that has never been dispersed, that has withstood all things, and is as strong today as ever it was, for surely that which is of good and of God belongs to the imperishable elements that stand altogether outside the range of the powers of destruction. [28–29]

LEWIS SPENCE'S OCCULT TRILOGY

The powers of destruction were soon unleashed on Britain as never before. The elderly Lewis Spence, whom we last met in chapter 1, was certain that Germany had been taken over by satanic forces. Spence had always been hovering on the threshold of occultism as a fascinated but uncommitted observer. Now he crossed it, with *The Occult Causes of the Present War* (1940), *Will Europe Follow Atlantis?* (1942), and *The Occult Sciences in Atlantis* (1943), all published by Rider. The first of these was mainly based on anecdotes about Hitler, on Alfred Rosenberg's *Mythos des 20. Jahrhunderts,* which had been published in English,[55] and on the "Deutsche Glaubensgemeinschaft," an attempt to create a "German Faith-Community" with allegiance to the Nazi state rather than to Christian leaders. With the outbreak of war the movement was moribund, while, as mentioned in chapter 5, Rosenberg was no longer a force to be reckoned with. Spence lacked the rich material that a study of the Ariosophists could have provided. Instead, he cataloged all the atrocities committed on German soil over the centuries, to prove that the Germans have always had satanic tendencies.

Will Europe Follow Atlantis? is a more substantial book. It covers the literary and traditional evidence for the destruction of Atlantis and surveys the mass of Atlantological literature that had appeared in the fifteen years since Spence had last addressed the subject. Otherwise it is a moving testimony to the spirit of Britain in the darkest days of the war.

Spence's opinion of the Germans was not improved by what he had learned about the Weimar Republic, when "Berlin became the centre of excesses so outrageous and so depraved that the whole chronicle of Roman and Byzantine beastliness could scarcely have suggested new avenues of unnatural experiment to its abandoned devotees."[56] If the Nazis purged that Sodom and Gomorrah, it was only to replace them with homicide, terror, torture, and the rule of the grotesque Adolf Hitler: "not so much the leader of Germany as the spiritual projection of her evil desire and intention, a furious emanation directed against the last community in Europe which bears aloft the torch of righteousness"[57]—that is, Britain, blamed by Germany for its defeat in the First World War.

Spence looks back into the myths and legends with which his mind was so well stocked and finds evidence that whenever humans become excessively wicked, God intervenes, or to put it another way, nature reacts. Writing in the summer of 1941, he finds not only Germany but much of Europe nearing the moral breaking point. Few countries are spared his censure of their morals and their abandonment of Christian principles and belief, but still he does not envisage a total destruction of the continent. In the chapter "How Europe May Follow Atlantis," he speculates on what might occur, and settles on a local subsidence of the earth's crust as the most likely or desirable outcome. The prospect excites him:

Down the Valley of the Rhine will pour the relentless fury of the North Sea, the most terrific earthquake the world has seen will convulse Western Germany, the proud and beautiful land of the New Prussia. From Hanover to Karlsruhe the agitated crust of the earth will rock, will sink into the pit of the magma, and ocean will submerge for ever the broad lands between Cologne and Cassel, and from Emden to Baden. . . . All that is presently industrial Germany will be eternally lost in a waste of waters. France will forever be cut off from her ancient foe by an inland sea half as great as the Black Sea, broader than the Adriatic.[58]

And so on, with the wretched survivors left to reenact on each other the horrors of the Thirty Years War. Britain, untouched by the catastrophe, will lead the New Europe and, with the aid of her Commonwealth, will "pursue her illustrious destiny as the standard-bearer of world-freedom and justice. . . . The altruism which has always been implicit in the genius of our people will at last come to its full flower, and the nations savour the perfume thereof to the enduring good of the whole earth."[59] But this will only happen under a renewal of the Christian faith in the spirit of the Grail tradition, assisted with study of the mystics and the wisdom religions of all nations. Spence names Freemasonry, Theosophy, and the Rosicrucians among those who will be called upon to help form a new Christian religion without schisms or sects. Thus humanity may discover the "great secret of co-operation with God."[60]

The third of Spence's wartime works was *The Occult Sciences in Atlantis,* a title that raises expectations of bizarre scenes in the style of Steiner or Leadbeater. Quite the contrary: Spence dismisses the Theosophical, clairvoyant, and spiritualist revelations at a stroke. His distance from them can be judged by how he treats the famous myth of the rebel angels and their mating with human women: it merely concerned "the rebellion of the lower caste in Atlantis against its more civil inhabitants."[61] Having one hand, as it were, tied behind his back, Spence struggles to squeeze out sufficient material from classical authors, antediluvian legends, and folklore. However, he has another source: "a very considerable body of traditional matter [that] exists in the records of occult fraternities, known generally as 'The Arcane Tradition', which deals with occult history in its entirety. This is partly written, partly communicated by word of mouth"(13).* It takes the form of manuscripts shown at the time of initiation, then withdrawn, so that initiates have thereafter to rely entirely on memory. Spence finds this an annoying situation, but he will not name the one society he has had contact with. Its manuscripts date from the late Middle Ages through the mid-seventeenth century and are written in English, Latin, French, or Spanish. Some are damp-stained and barely legible, others overconcerned with occult grades, and many evidently derived at third or fourth hand from the original source (33–36). A typical example is called *The Tale of the Barcelona Shipper,* which tells stories that a Spanish sailor heard in Algeria while he was enslaved there in the 1540s. Some of these describe the black magic practiced in Africa by devil worshippers from Atlantis, after Allah had overthrown their land (58). In later manuscripts Spence detects an overhaul of the tradition in the spirit of the Enlightenment, and even detects the influence of Jean-Sylvain Bailly (110). All in all, it is a very unsatisfactory situation both for the writer and the reader.

Far from regarding the Atlanteans as great wielders of occult powers now lost to humanity, Spence thinks that they were quite primitive in their beliefs, and that their occult sciences were in a vestigial state (131). One exception was the Mysteries practiced by the elite, in which the initiate was hypnotized and led through the experience of death and rebirth into immaterial realms (114). Here at last Spence reveals his own conviction that the whole goal of the occult sciences is to recapture the prelapsarian state—and that it is futile. "For the one manner of perfecting it is to seek piously that fellowship and at-one-ment with God, of which divine marvel and supernatural vision are merely the concomitants and ancillary effects, or background, and not the reality" (133).

---

*Page numbers in parentheses are from *The Occult Sciences in Atlantis.*

In this rejection of occultism (whose existence is not denied) for mysticism, there is more than a suspicion of A. E. Waite, and not just in the prose style. In *Will Europe Follow Atlantis?* and *The Occult Sciences in Atlantis,* the only contemporary spiritual authority quoted with approval is Waite, the twentieth century's most prolific writer on the Holy Grail, the Rosicrucians, alchemy, the Tarot, magic, Christian mysticism, and so forth. Waite belonged to numerous secret and occult orders, beginning with the Golden Dawn, and founded more than one of them himself. This may be the place to look for the Arcane Tradition that initiated Spence, as he admits, only into a lowly degree, and was so miserly in giving him access to its precious manuscripts.

THE MESSAGES OF HELIO-ARKAN/ARCANOPHUS

Since Lewis Spence, in the end, disappointed his readers, it was left to a more obscure figure, Daphne Vigers, to make a direct connection between the present crisis and the distant past. Her publisher was Andrew Dakers, who had already published the works of the American Theosophist and architect Claude Bragdon, as well as Vera Brittain's controversial pacifist books. Dakers himself introduced *Atlantis Rising* with the words: "The author asks us to believe that she has gone back into the remote past on many occasions, and that she has witnessed the scenes and met the people described in these pages."[62] He adds that when he read the material, he thought it beyond the competence of a girl of twenty-six to invent. He consulted an author of several books on the astral who had the same gift of "backseeing" (possibly Vera Stanley Alder, whom Dakers also published). She told him that much of what she had seen was identical to what Vigers's manuscript described, and on these grounds *Atlantis Rising* got its imprimatur.

The point of the book is that Britons are the good Atlanteans reborn, and, in Dakers's words, that "the future of civilization depended in 1940 uniquely upon the spiritual strength of the British people."[63] Vigers situates Atlantis between 10°–50°N and 17°–40°W, with the Azores as the remains of its highest peaks. The scenes of an earthly paradise with children romping with lions, chariots of ebony and ivory, and so forth recall Edmund Dulac's or Maxfield Parrish's book illustrations. Atlantean religion occupies a large part of the work. We are given a tour of the Temple of the Sun in the holy city of Khekon, reached by crystal steps through a golden archway. Helio-Arkan, the chief priest, is white with dark eyes, short hair, a white robe with purple trimming, and bare feet, his eyes gentle but firm. He has a pet leopard.[64] The religion is a worship of Life and Light (though there are others who worship Darkness); the winged sun is their symbol, as well as a seven-rayed eye. From the temple we proceed to the Sanctuary of Healing, where mead and sweet cakes are served, and learn about artificial limbs, etheric sciences, herbs, and sound vibrations. Then in the Place of Science the narrator's guide ushers her into Nezhualtyl, the Room of Discoveries.

First there was the compass very delicately and precisely made. Then there were rock cutters and levitating machines which lifted the great blocks of stone by magnetism, both driven by direct solar power. The copper thought-form recorder made me ask Nezhualtyl many questions. Then there were rainfall regulators, astro-gravitational power deflectors. Crystals that "caught" and recorded the music of the spheres. Flying chariots with birds' wings of thin metal, also driven by direct solar power. Vibro-engines that picked up the psycho-magnetic energy of the person who wished to work them, making them able to drive a chariot without horses.

Cotton, linen, and wool spinners and tiny mechanisms on which silk was woven from the cocoons.

Nezhualtyl picked up a disc of crystal which was actually a powerful lens. "We use this to look upon other worlds," he smiled.[65]

But all this came to an end, in a not-unfamiliar way: "Those whom we call the Thokhartens, the ones who are fully developed psychically, but not counterbalanced intellectually, have been allowed to exercise their powers unlimited for the benefit of the priests who believe material gain is a better prize than spiritual attainments."[66] This evil priesthood persecuted and tortured the good Atlanteans, labeling them heretics. Some escaped before the final destruction, and so their tradition was preserved in the Puranas and by the Egyptians, Mexicans, and Persians.[67]

Helio-Arkan now gives his guest a vision of Atlantis arisen as a future Utopia, in which our lives will be our religion and cruelty the only sin. The sun will provide the power; machines will do all the work. First, however, there is a war to be won over the so-called Aryans, whose qualities Vigers, or her source, tabulates as follows:

Characteristics of Atlanteans	Characteristics of So-Called Aryans
1. Magnetic power projection	1. Dominating power lust
2. Positive courage in achieving a sane objective	2. Sadistic brutality arising from loss-of-power fear
3. Use of so-called supernatural powers	3. Fear of so-called supernatural powers
4. Power of individual action	4. Innate desire for regimentation
5. Power of leadership in each individual	5. Lack of individual initiative
6. Sharply discriminating intellect	6. Easily influenced by a flow of words

The book ends on what I suppose was intended as an optimistic and patriotic note, though it reads now as a manifesto for genocide:

> The Atlantean race type, the highest psychic development, is in every way, physical, mental, spiritual, superior to the so-called "Aryan" sub-race type, and is destined to establish Atlantean rule throughout the world, beginning in the isles of Britain; the so-called "Aryans" being eliminated by psycho-cetric [*sic*] powers known only to the Atlanteans.[68]

The name of Daphne Vigers's informant, Helio-Arkan, is suspiciously like Helio-Arcanophus, who has been sending messages since

1955 through the mediumship of Anthony Neate. Mr. Neate was already practicing psychometry but was unaware of Daphne Vigers's obscure work when the voice of Helio-Arcanophus came to him.[69] Since then Neate and "H-A" have been a fixture of the British New Age scene with lectures, workshops, retreats, and a healing center. Here we will concentrate on *Atlantis Past, and to Come* (1959), an early booklet produced by Neate's group of "Atlanteans," into which Helio-Arcanophus packed his prehistoric scenario.

The first inhabited landmass, he tells us, was Mu or the Motherland, called "Lemuria" in the nineteenth century. It stretched from the Mideast to China and much of the Pacific Ocean and flourished for thousands of years, leaving remains in South Asia to this day. China, Tibet, predynastic Egypt, and Easter Island were all "Mu-an" lands. Then the axis of the earth tilted, with reversion of the poles and equator, and the first Ice Age began.[70]

Shortly before the destruction of Mu, where a large gap had arisen between evolved and bestial human types, some more highly evolved spirits from Venus incarnated and made their way to a new continent of Atlantis. At first this was a cold and damp region; then another planet passed close to the earth and upset its orbital balance, leaving Atlantis warm and sunny. It became a Garden of Eden, a home to monotheistic sun-worshippers. The winged disk was their symbol, referring to the priests' ability of astral projection. The high priest was also the ruler of the state, but not as our priesthood is, for the Atlantean clergy was selected under occult guidance. There was no army. The capital city, in the Central Zone, was called Chalidocean, and there, besides the government, were art galleries and colleges of science and occultism.[71]

In Atlantean society no one lived in want. The diet included fish and fowl, but no red meat. Messages were sent telepathically, and many of the priests could levitate. Tarsias, horselike animals, were used for riding. The houses were built with the help of sonic gongs, so that huge stone blocks could be raised without machinery or human effort. All the power came from the sun. Lions were kept as pets, for felines are good for psychic work and "protection against the lower astral." When a person died, the body was "disintegrated by the occultist priests by the use of certain cosmic forces."[72]

Helio-Arcanophus was the ruler of Atlantis from the year 1134 after the beginning of Atlantean civilization, which began around 14,697 BCE. His people were a fair race, many with black hair and violet eyes. Evolved spirits from other planets (Venus, Uranus) were drawn to incarnate there. Women were equal in status to men. Children were judged at the age of three for their future professions. The main fault of the Atlanteans was that they were too philosophical and unworldly. When immigrants came from less evolved lands they became interested in the Atlanteans' psychic powers and learned occult secrets. They conjured evil spirits from the lower astral and did terrible things. Black magic spread, and the people became debauched.[73]

Then Lucifer, brightest of the planets, moved nearer the earth. There was general panic, and small bands of the good people left. Lucifer, now known as Luna, was captured by the earth's gravitational field. The earth's axis tilted, putting the poles where the equator had been, and lands sank while others rose. Atlantean civilization had lasted about 9,840 years "in today's years: they were shorter before the capture of the Moon."[74] The deva of Lucifer now has control of the earth.

Before the fateful day, though, the high priest "called together all the powers which were used by the Priests of Righteousness on the Atlantean Occult Vibration. By the use of a certain Ritual, he concealed and sealed these rays so that none could call upon them until the time came when there would be people on a similar evolutionary vibration as the Sealer. The key to this Seal he placed in a certain country in the world—the land you call England. Its symbol is the sword of St. Michael, or the Excalibur of Arthur, and its withdrawal signifies the birth of the new Atlantean race."[75]

Helio-Arcanophus concludes with a prophecy. He says that the planet Uranus will soon leave its orbit and restore the axis of the earth to where it was in Atlantean times. The seasons will go haywire, volcanoes and earthquakes will rend the world, and Atlantis will rise again. It will be up to the survivors to make a fresh start there, once the influence of Lucifer is removed and Michael resumes his position as ruling deva.[76]

When one compares the details of Helio-Arcanophus's account with those of Helio-Arkan, there are several coincidences, such as the communicator's name and status, the friendly lions, the winged disc, solar power, the levitation of stones, the white-skinned and dark-eyed race, the influx of black magicians, and the special destiny of Britain as heir to Atlantis. Mr. Neate claims to have been the first person to channel the High Priest Helio-Arcanophus, but now simply calls him (or it) a "source of higher consciousness."[77] This may reflect a weariness, even on the part of believers, with high-flown claims, and a more philosophical attitude on the part of channelers in general. A couple of other points stand out. The date that Helio-Arcanophus gives for Atlantis's destruction, 4,857 BCE, is unique in the literature and unusually recent (discounting the Thera hypothesis and the counting of Plato's 9,000 years as months). Unusual, too, is the cause given for the catastrophe: the capture of the moon. It is the leitmotif of Hans Hörbiger's *Welteislehre*, which Hans Schindler Bellamy and Denis Saurat were promoting at this very time (see chapter 1). Moreover, the radical tilting of the earth's axis was what Imanuel Velikovsky had claimed in *Worlds in Collision* (1950), as a result of Venus and Mars passing close to the earth. Let us say at least that such notions were in the air in the 1950s. Astronomers, geologists, and paleoclimatologists would have severe objections to make to them, but Neate's group is unswayed: the capture of the moon and the toppling of the earth were still part of their teaching in 2008.[78]

THE RETURN OF STAINTON MOSES

There must have been many back-parlor channelers between the wars, each attracting a handful of believers. One of these published some pamphlets and booklets between 1946 and 1954 under the imprint of the Golden Triangle Fellowship. Showing no influence whatever from Theosophy or the magical tradition, it connects itself to the Spiritualist movement of the previous century.

> The Leader today who has traveled up through the ages, who has taught in many lands, felt the Guiding Hand in 1921 and obeyed the Call. Teachers from Jupiter came to instruct always following the plan of the Guiding Hand. Through the early stages many gifts were offered and calmly accepted.
>
> The great doors of the Spirit world were first opened by Imperator, our King in Them [name of the holy city in Atlantis], Mancept. The fine teachings he brought by the hand of Stainton Moses, "Spirit Teachings" in 1870 is a book of true wisdom and brought the first knowledge of the Spirit world into the opening door which has led to the foundation of the Fellowship today.[79]

William Stainton Moses (1839–1892) was an ordained clergyman and schoolmaster who published his spirit communications under the pseudonym of M. A., Oxon. His method was automatic writing, which he could do while thinking and even talking of something else. His chief control, first contacted in 1873, signed itself as Imperator +. Moses was well connected socially and friendly with the early London Theosophists, but Blavatsky's hostility to Spiritualism and Christianity alienated him. His *Spirit Teachings* are not concerned with prehistory, but with a broadly Christian spiritualist philosophy.[80]

According to "Diana," founder of the fellowship, the Guiding Hand had by 1954 given well over 1,200 "little pictures of life."[81] What method was used by Mandasoran the Recorder is not told, but the description is an apt one for the scenes and anecdotes of Atlantis. At the start it is announced that the "great message" to be communicated is reincarnation (contrarily to the Spiritualist wing to which Stainton Moses belonged), and that the Atlanteans had atomic energy for peaceful use, airplanes, wireless, and other "gifts from the mechanical country of Mars."[82]

The narrator goes in spirit to the Holy City of Them in the province of Eclata (which is the Golden Triangle), and there to the Palace of Mancept, "known to you today as Imperator." Mancept himself is seven feet tall, dressed in a long cream-colored robe with an embroidered robe of purple over it, and gold sandals. He has a noble face with a high forehead, blue eyes, and gold shoulder-length hair and beard. His queen is Estarnyamo, an Egyptian.[83] We are shown the Hall of Agriculture, the schools, and the Colony of the Manus. These Manus were trained and sent out to South America, Egypt, and Tibet, where their handiwork can still be seen. "You don't know," says the guide in an aside, "that the Master Jesus traveled to India, Egypt, and Tibet between the ages of 12 and 30." The tour continues around facilities for healing, gardens, and temples, in which reverence is paid to the sun as symbol of the Tao, the divine source of life.[84] Temple maidens sing hymns to the rising sun, and at sunset a single male server sends out a farewell. The Temple of Tao has a domed roof, reflecting the rays from the planets, and a Bowl of the Luos upheld on the wings of three figures, filled with fluid supplied from spirit. Much description of its worship, festivals, and the high morality of the people follows.

More unusually, we learn that the Jews are Atlanteans who still carry their badge of the double triangle.[85] Jesus, whose real name was Suyamo, was sent from the Dhuman Spheres to carry the first teaching to Earth, and he has never ceased through the ages. Many of those who once lived in Them are coming into the fellowship. Also, "John Wesley took the early training and began his writing in 1922. . . . With John's wise writing was next added music coupled with inspired lyrics. John Keeble [sic] gave some beautiful songs later to be joined by Mendelssohn."[86] The fellowship acquired a duplicator in 1936 and was able to start a magazine, which continued through the war. It now has 84 Triangles with three flowers to each, many of them overseas.[87]

As always, this summary may misrepresent the depth, breadth, and earnestness of the original, for it is always a temptation to choose the most striking or absurd incidents, as well as the most telling ones that give clues about their sources. When one reads about a Manu called Merrifumanptah from the Temple of Ptysis,[88] one wonders who is teasing whom. Worse, from the last quotation I suspect that members of the Golden Triangle Fellowship believed themselves to be reincarnations of noted figures from the past. There was John Wesley, the founder of Methodism; John Keble, whose ritualistic Oxford Movement was Methodism's polar opposite; and the composer Felix Mendelssohn. One shudders to think of the poetry and music that now passed under their names.

Mandasoran the Recorder, whoever he or she was, is of a piece with Randall-Stevens, Daphne Vigers, and Anthony Neate. Like Stainton Moses, all four were chosen, more or less to their own surprise, as vehicles for a named entity, and—which is the sticking point—they all believed what they were told. Their communications about Atlantis differed from those of the Theosophists, sometimes radically. Certainly there is a Leadbeateresque feel to much of the scenery, to say nothing of the clichés of Atlantean fiction—the sun temples, the white-robed sages, the high technology. But Randall-Stevens's Satan-figure, Vigers's evil Aryans, or Neate's Lucifer-moon plainly contradict the Theosophical or Anthroposophical system. Someone or something, whether internal or external to the channel, was making a deliberate effort to put across a certain version of prehistory, and one can only wonder why.

Olive Pixley and Paul Brunton, who was briefly mentioned above, are of an entirely different type. They were not so much passive receivers as active users of their psychic powers, stimulated by the spirit of place. But this does not eliminate contamination from their own fund of knowledge and belief, nor in Pixley's case from benevolent editing by Foster Forbes. Brunton was a Theosophist, in fact if not in name, before he went to Egypt. What he saw there in the inner clarity of meditation was probably what he expected to see, only in more fascinating detail.

THE SKY PEOPLE AND THE AVALONIANS

A year before Olive Pixley saw a ritual procession winding up Glastonbury Tor, the first intimations of the "Somerset Zodiac" saw the light. The seer responsible for these was Katharine Maltwood (1878–1961), a sculptor and painter in the Symbolist style.[89] In 1929 she was drawing a map of the Glastonbury area for the Everyman edition of *The High History of the Holy Grail,* a translation of a medieval French romance.[90] She superimposed the legendary locations (Isle of the Elephants, Hermitage of the Fountain, etc.) on a modern map and, as a hint, added two intersecting circles six miles in diameter marked "equator" and "ecliptic," together with a shaded figure marked "Leo" that somewhat resembles a lion. The edition gave no explanation of this curious detail. Maltwood later wrote: "I shall never forget my utter amazement when the truth dawned on me that the outline of a lion was drawn by the curves of the Cary river below the old capital town of Somerset. So that was the origin of the legendary lion that I had been questing! A nature effigy and a god of sunworshippers! Leo of the Zodiac. . . . Obviously, if the lion was a nature effigy then the dragon, griffon and the giants and so on, must be likewise; perhaps this was the most thrilling moment of my discovery."[91]

It remained for Maltwood's own *Guide to Glastonbury's Temple of the Stars* to show how the hedges, ditches, fields, and paths outlined Orion, Phoenix, and the signs of the zodiac, though with strange variants from the modern version.[92] Having ample financial means through her husband, John (managing director of Oxo, Ltd.), she commissioned aerial photographs to confirm her intuitions.

Skeptics may regard the Glastonbury Zodiac as a kind of Rorschach blot, like the giant faces seen in the Externsteine (see chapter 5) or the Lemurians in Richard Shaver's agates (see chapter 10). They may doubt, for example, that prehistoric landscape artists would have outlined Virgo as a frumpy figure in a crinoline, wielding a broom or fan; they are rightly suspicious of the excuses made for the strange variants and missing constellations.[93] But rational objections cannot impair the power of an archetype. Maltwood's revelation was perfectly attuned to the loosely connected group already mentioned, which shared a mystical enthusiasm for Glastonbury, the Grail, and the legendary Avalon, and believed that these marked a special destiny for Britain.[94] Besides Dion Fortune's circle, they included the architect Frederick Bligh Bond, who discovered through automatic writing the lost chapels at Glastonbury Abbey (and was promptly sacked by the church commissioners).

Another Avalonian was Major Wellesley Tudor Pole (1884–1968), who had been involved with spiritualism and the Bah'ai World Faith before being drawn to Glastonbury as the spiritual center of Britain. When World War II broke out, he persuaded the BBC to institute a "silent minute" every evening after Big Ben struck at 9:00 p.m., in which all listeners would focus their thoughts or prayers. There is a legend that a German officer, under interrogation, admitted that the Nazis suspected some secret weapon connected with the chimes of Big Ben but never found out what it was.[95] In 1959 Tudor Pole founded the Chalice Well Trust to preserve the sacred sites of Glastonbury, under whose Chalice Hill he and many others believed that Joseph of Arimathea had buried the cup used at Jesus's Last Supper. Soon afterward he wrote:

> I believe that the Cup or Chalice is destined to become the symbol for the new age now dawning, and it is my hope that Chalice Well may once more fulfil the inspiring mission of acting as a gateway through which revelation for coming times may flow, radiating from there across Britain and the world.
>
> It is my conviction that the people of our island will be given the opportunity once more to lead humanity out of the present darkness into the Light.[96]

This statement appeared in an afterword to *Men Among Mankind* (1962) by Brinsley le Poer Trench (1911–1995). The same book carries a foreword by Leslie Otley, who was the secretary of the Tyneside UFO Society and editor of its journal, *Orbit,* and the two contributions neatly frame Trench's interests. In between is a curious and sometimes breathless mixture of historical speculation, British patriotism, Avalonian ideals, and Atlantean lore.

Trench was a friend of Desmond Leslie (see chapter 10), who collaborated on the first book by the UFO contactee George Adamski. Between them they launched the "alien intervention" or "ancient astronaut" theory of human prehistory. Trench published his version in 1960 as *The Sky People,* in the same year as Jacques Bergier and Louis Pauwel's *Le Matin des magiciens* (see chapter 2) and eight years before Eric von Däniken's *Erinnerungen an die Zukunft* (*Chariots of the Gods?*). Trench later inherited the Irish title of Eighth Earl of Clancarty, which gave him a seat in the House of Lords. Careless of mockery, he urged his peers to a serious consideration of the UFO phenomenon and succeeded in 1979 with a full-scale debate that was recorded verbatim in the parliamentary proceedings.[97]

Here, extracted from *Men Among Mankind,* is Trench's historic scenario in its main outlines: The Atlanteans were a highly developed people, possessing spaceships, communicating with other planets, and commanding forces even more destructive than nuclear weapons. It is said that between about 30,000 and 25,000 BCE there was a terrible conflict among them (75–76),* ending with a tremendous seismic upheaval of the earth's surface and the destruction of most of Atlantis. A second cataclysmic period began around 13,000 BCE when Luna, the third planet outward from the sun, approached the earth. This caused the uplifting of the great mountain ranges and further catastrophic events lasting until 9500 BCE, when Luna was finally captured and the earth settled into its present form. At that time the remaining island of Poseid was destroyed, and the length of the year increased from 360 days to its present value (29–30). However, "One part of Atlantis had not gone under. The lands now known as the British Isles—the Fortunate Isles—remained high and dry, and it was from there that the world was once more to receive civilization"(31).

Britain was sacred even in Atlantean times. It was there that the Glastonbury Zodiac was created as a landmark for the Sky People, who

---

*Page numbers in parentheses are from *Men Among Mankind.*

have always had a concern for the human race and a role in its evolution, education, and care. There is no suggestion of their being aliens, but rather Atlanteans who had left before the catastrophe of 25,000 BCE and taken refuge on other planets, where they fared better than their fellows left on earth (66). Thereafter they were regular visitors and the originals of many myths of gods and demigods. After the event of 9564 BCE, which reduced the human race to a Stone Age struggle for mere survival, they stopped coming openly to earth (53). About 4,000 years later, stirred by ancestral memories of Atlantis, they returned to see if any humans were fit to receive their assistance in restarting civilization. As we can guess, they spied the Glastonbury Zodiac and knew that Britain was the place to start (58–59). They remained until civilization was set on a safe path of development, then around 4700 BCE they gradually withdrew, leaving the priesthood to take on its role as lawgivers and instructors (79).

In the fifth millennium BCE, Britain was still the chief center of initiatic knowledge. Egyptian priests had journeyed there to learn its secrets at a time when the seas were 400 feet lower and England was joined to the continent of Europe (98). Their civilization, too, was developed with the help of the Sky People, who left them the Great Pyramid as a parting gift about 3434 BCE (105). The other pyramids were built later in imitation of it, much as the Egyptologists maintain, but the Sphinx is much earlier. It originally had a female face and probably dates from the Age of Virgo around 15,000 BCE (107).

Besides acknowledging Blavatsky and Hörbiger by name, Trench often refers to Freemasonry and uses its coded language. Perhaps there was a group of British Freemasons who shared these ideas and dated the birth of their Craft not just to Solomon's Temple but to prehistoric times. Trench also hints at a cult of the Archangel Michael, who figured in Tudor Pole's mythology and plays a vital role in Trithemius's system of time cycles (see chapter 11).

"St Michael is a most interesting figure," remarks John Michell (1933–2009) in his first book, *The Flying Saucer Vision* (1967), and continues:

He is the leader of the host of angels who received Enoch on his journey to the heaven and told him of the 'word' by which the universe was created. It is he who Daniel says will appear at that time of chaos preceding the Millenium. In Christian hagiology Michael seems to be the descendent of some former revered being, associated with high places and with the killing of a dragon. The number of churches dedicated to St Michael which stand on hilltops and pre-Christian mounds is remarkable. Evidently all their sites were once associated with the memory of a being from the sky and of the dragon disc.[98]

Michell's book, too, belongs to the ancient astronaut genre, though it is a highly sophisticated example, drawing on Jungian archetypal psychology as well as on an encyclopedic knowledge of "Fortean" or anomalous phenomena. Michell mentions the many locations that have been suggested for Atlantis and allows that there may have been a mid-Atlantic continent engulfed by the sea. But that is of little moment to him. "It was not from some lost continent that civilization reached America and elsewhere, but from somewhere outside the earth, the land from which Quetzalcoatl, travelling on the serpent raft or flying disc, brought the vision of the gods to men."[99]

Near the end of the book, Michell makes the connection between high hills, places dedicated to St. Michael, and the gods from space. One of the most famous is the ruined tower of a former St. Michael's Church on the top of Glastonbury Tor. Katharine Maltwood's vision of the Glastonbury Zodiac is mentioned approvingly, but it was in Michell's next and more famous book, *The View over Atlantis* (1969), that this theme came to fruition. Atlantis barely appears beyond the title, but we would classify the book as one of those that place the lost land "everywhere." It is an accumulation of evidence for a prehistoric worldwide civilization whose accomplishments included the accurate measurement of the earth's dimensions and its distance from the sun and the moon; the establishment of a system of measures based on these; the knowledge of subterranean energies that could be channeled, or that moved, in straight lines across the landscape, perhaps supporting flight and moving megaliths; and the persistence of these traditions in megalithic and Gothic architecture, Chinese geomantic science, and Greek sacred writings, especially the New Testament. Most influential was Michell's revival of Alfred Watkins's work on the "old straight track" and the resultant "ley lines," still detectable in ancient trackways and by connecting the dots of prehistoric monuments (stones, tumps, barrows, dolmens) and churches dedicated to St. Michael.

The View over Atlantis created a new generation of Avalonians. In the 1970s it sent them traipsing around the English countryside, Ordnance Survey maps in hand, looking for alignments and communing with the spirits of place and of the past. When the energy faded from that activity, it was renewed by the phenomenon of crop circles. Southwestern England was again the main theater, and Michell again a prominent commentator. He kept the Avalonian spirit alive with such works as *New Light on the Ancient Mystery of Glastonbury* (1990) and *The Measure of Albion* (with Robin Heath, 2004), ever more certain that an ancient canon of knowledge was reemerging in our time. "The instrument of all human enlightenment is an educated mind illuminated by revelation,"[100] he had written on the first page of *The View over Atlantis,* and in all humility he admitted to being a case in point. His own revelation came in the difficult form of a numerical and geometrical canon, without history and without occult baggage, but with the promise that the problems besetting us would solve themselves if we were again to order our lives according to it.[101] Such a thing is hardly imaginable in the present state of the world, but for those responsive to his work, Michell brought to life a tradition infused in the very soil and stones of Britain by ancestors, who might as well be called Atlanteans as anything else.

EIGHT

Some Independents

——— ✳ ———

MAYAN CONNECTIONS

Of the three main feeders of Atlantology during the later nineteenth century, we have already treated the speculations of Ignatius Donnelly (see chapter 1) and the revelations of Sinnett and Blavatsky (chapter 3). The third source was the contribution to Mayan studies by two Frenchmen: Charles Étienne Brasseur de Bourbourg (1814–1874) and Augustus Le Plongeon (1826–1908): adventurous and ingenious characters long since discarded by the learned world, but whose ghosts are still nourished by believers.

Brasseur de Bourbourg was an "abbé" whose work for the church in Quebec, Boston, Rome, Mexico, and Guatemala allowed him to pursue a parallel career as a pioneering scholar of ancient America. In the collection of a Guatemalan bibliophile he found a manuscript of the Popol Vuh, the mythological book of the Mayas, which he translated into French and published in 1861. The dusty shelves of the Royal Academy of History in Madrid yielded the abridged but only version of Diego de Landa's *Relación de las cosas de Yucatán* (ca. 1566), and Brasseur published that, too, in 1864. Thereupon, as the eminent Mayan scholar Michael Coe remarks, the world of Mayan scholarship changed forever.[1] After this a Madrid collector produced a manuscript that Brasseur recognized as Mayan. He named it the Troano Codex, after its owner, and published a magnificent facsimile of it with some specimen translations.[2] The few pages he attempts turn out to be all about volcanoes, gas bubbles, lava, flying stones, gods, and genies, for Brasseur's Mayans are obsessed by memories of the cataclysm that destroyed Atlantis and about 160 million inhabitants.[3] He believed it to have been in the Caribbean and its refugees to have founded the civilizations of Central America and the Yucatan. Michael Coe, with affectionate exasperation, calls Atlantis Brasseur's hobbyhorse, and his interpretations of Mayan writing nonsensical.[4]

For all that, Brasseur de Bourbourg is still part of "rational" Atlantology. Not so the contribution of Augustus Le Plongeon. A Freemason, commercial photographer, and M.D. of dubious provenance, Le Plongeon spent years in the land of the Incas (Peru), then in that of the Mayas. He and his American wife, Alice (Dixon), made photographs and documentation of archaeological sites that are still of value, since so much has been altered since their discovery. At Chichen Itza, they found the famous reclining statue of Chacmool. Le Plongeon's biographer, Lawrence Desmond, praises his practical methods but deplores his interpretations.[5] Ironically, Le Plongeon writes that Brasseur de Bourbourg's preconceived opinions led him to see analogies and similarities where none existed,[6] then proceeds to follow the abbé's example, just with different opinions. His particular hobbyhorse was the Mayan origin of the Old World civilizations—Chaldean, Egyptian, Indian, Greek, and the rest. In pursuit of it, he built a mighty house of cards out of spurious etymologies and fantastic translations wrested from the Mayan glyphs, to which he had the wrong key, and from the Troano Codex, which he read backward.

Publishers of occult literature still keep Le Plongeon's books in print, for he and the Theosophists quoted each other, and his approach was in broad agreement with theirs. For instance, in *Queen Moo and the Egyptian Sphinx* he cites Blavatsky's translation of the *Stanzas of Dzyan* as corroboration of his Mayan cosmology[7] and draws Theosophical-looking diagrams of circles and six-pointed stars to show the parallels between the Mayan and Kabbalistic systems.[8] They were bound to correspond, because in his reconstruction of history, the Mayan colonists made their way up the Euphrates to Babylon, the City of the Sun,[9] where the Kabbalah originated. In the case of Egypt it was Queen Moo and her brother, Chacmool, who arrived as refugees and rose not merely to become its rulers but afterward to be deified as Isis and Osiris. In India it was Mayan adepts who became the highly civilized people called the Nagas, who ruled all of Hindustan until the Aryan invasion.[10] The Greeks learned of Atlantis from Plato's authentic account of the Land of Mu and its destruction.

Not only Mayan cosmology, but their language permeated the Old World civilizations. It is not by chance that the Hindus call the material world *Maya*! The famous words of Jesus expiring on the cross, *"Eli, eli, lama sabachthani,"* do not mean "My God, my God, why hast Thou forsaken me," words that Le Plongeon considered inappropriate for a Godman. If we realize that Jesus was "speaking pure Mayan," we can translate them correctly as, "Now, now I am fainting. Darkness covers my face."[11] I have often seen this "translation" presented as a great discovery by amateur mythologists and occultists. Some of them follow Robert Stacey-Judd, who thinks Jesus meant (still speaking Mayan), "My wounds will be kept open by those who defame me."[12] Another favorite is the number sixty-four million that Le Plongeon gives for the inhabitants of Mu, falsely attributing it to Brasseur de Bourbourg.[13]

Alice Le Plongeon (1851–1910), a skilled photographer, feminist, and author in her own right, made her own contributions to the Mayan theory, suggesting that Indian elephant worship was an outgrowth of American mammoth worship.[14] When she took to writing fiction, the circle was complete. Her last work, *A Dream of Atlantis,* was published in the Theosophical magazine *The Word.*

RALEIGH AND THE YUCATAN BROTHERHOOD

The theme of the Mayas as teachers of the Egyptians recurs in the work of Dr. Albert Sidney (A. S.) Raleigh. Based in Chicago, he was a prolific writer on Hermetic and Theosophical subjects but almost totally unknown as a personality. He had a group to which he gave private instruction, and I trust that they addressed him by his preferred name of "Hach Mactzin El Dorado Can," and respected his title of "Hierophant of the Mysteries of Isis." The relevant work is his commentary on the first treatise of the *Corpus Hermeticum,* called the *Poimandres,* or, in English, *The Shepherd of Men* (1916). In the Preface he styles himself the "High Priest of the Heart of Heaven" and says that since none of his Egyptian brethren are initiates into this mystery, he is "the one person on the earth today who can speak with absolute authority with reference to the subject matter of this Sermon [the *Poimandres*]." He adds a warning to doubters: "Any interpretation that may differ with the following in the slightest degree is, to the extent of such difference, erroneous."[15]

Raleigh/Hach writes that, given the many disputes about the source of the Hidden Wisdom, it is time to show that it came originally from Atlantis. It was the Mayas who brought it from there and passed it on to their colonies in Egypt, Akkadia, Chaldea, India, and Persia. Therefore the place to seek it nowadays is not in any of those countries, but in the Medicine Lodge of the American Indians, and above all in Mexico.

This is the first we have heard of present-day Native Americans, not just ancient ones, as a repository of wisdom. It connects with a minor tradition within the Theosophical Society concerning a Yucatan Brotherhood.[16] Several post-Blavatskians mention this as a group of Atlantean adepts incarnated into the bodies of American Indians. They were allegedly responsible for the "Rochester rappings" of 1848, the phenomenon that launched the Spiritualist movement. Their object in doing so was to counteract the materialistic tendencies of the time, though in the opinion of Blavatsky and most Theosophists, the project went badly wrong, as the phenomena were mistaken for communications from the spirits of the dead.

Evidently Raleigh did not get along with the Theosophists. Although (or because) much of his material is indebted to them, he had to find other publishers for his numerous works. He also relies heavily on Le Plongeon, whom he occasionally acknowledges, along with Gerald Massey. But he would prefer us to believe that his information on the inner life of the Atlanteans is from the "secret archives of the Hermetic Brotherhood" and "authentic in every detail."[17]

Raleigh's classification of the Atlanteans is a blend of the Theosophical system (he mentions sub-races) with the French tradition of four races distinguished by color. He calls the first sub-race very spiritual and "moon-colored," the second golden-hued, artistic, and philosophical. The third was a red race whose members were great occultists but became degenerate; the fourth, a black race, were given to black magic and conquered almost the entire world. With the whites banished to North America, the black Atlanteans in Poseidonia ran a very materialistic and utilitarian civilization through the exploitation of the ether, the odic force, the astral light, and so forth. They had airplanes that ran on regular schedules, but the people were kept in a semihypnotized state by the ruling class.[18] Perhaps Raleigh was seeing into the near future, rather than the distant past.

This material imbalance upset the earth, which sank as and when recorded by Plato. Before the catastrophe, around 13,000 BCE, there had been a great migration of pure Red Atlanteans into the Yucatan. Their totem was the mastodon (sanctified by Le Plongeon, who saw proboscids everywhere), their society a gynarchy, and their whole nation an expression of the cult of the Great Mother. They also practiced mathematics, augury, and biology, and believed humans to be descended from apes. In time these Maya (the name meaning "womb people") became expansionist and aggressive and planted colonies in the Old World. One of these was Akkad, the sacred land of the Babylonian theocracy, patterned after the heavens in its government and geography.[19]

As for Egypt, it was first settled by a primitive people from Libya and Ethiopia. In 11,800 BCE a party of Chaldean Mayas settled there with their superior civilization, and the two races amalgamated. When Atlantis fell in 9600 BCE they were isolated and lost their sacred language. Thoth (the second of that name) translated the books from sacred Mayan into the Egyptian tongue.

Other Mayans went West, crossing the Pacific and spreading from

Burma as far as Afghanistan. In Kabul, Raleigh assures us, Mayan was still being spoken in 1879.[20] It was the Persian and Indian Nagas who introduced human sacrifice through tearing out the heart. The purpose was partly for the astral nourishment of the Serpent Deities, and partly to further the victim's reincarnation, which can occur only when the body is deenergized. While cremation is one way of doing this, heart sacrifice is even more effective. Despite this disagreeable practice, Raleigh adds that the Nagas were still a highly civilized people.[21]

Not so the Aryans, in his opinion. About 5,000 years ago they left their Bactrian home and invaded India. They were a materialistic, mentally mediocre, religiously intolerant race of barbarians who later became the Hindus. Raleigh warns us not to believe their modern descendants who extol the wisdom of the Vedas: those are just rites for the worship of mundane gods, and the Atharva Veda is for black magic. Only under Naga influence did these people develop the philosophic religion that we find in the Upanishads and the Laws of Manu.[22]

Rama, the first Aryan leader to introduce ethics, was born about 600 years after the Aryan invasion, in 2433 BCE. The Ramayana is the story of the extermination of the cultured Nagas of Ceylon. Hanuman, Rama's monkeylike henchman, was really the chief of an Aryan tribe that took the monkey as their totem. The war had already been going on for a thousand years when Krishna sided with his fellow Aryans to crush the last Naga power. The solar cult was abolished, and the philosophical Nagas were finally absorbed into the superstitious Hindus. Their religion only really started at this point, so it was a thousand years before Sakyamuni (Buddha) that the Aryans at last became a civilized people.[23]

A. S. Raleigh has yet to find the scholar patient enough to research and study him, but something can be deduced from what we have before us. The absurd names, titles, and claims to absolute authority tell their own psychological tale. With more imagination than erudition, no gift for clarity, and drawing on sources that he does not trouble to name, Raleigh/ Hach still has a claim to our attention. His description of the sub-races seems to embody the usual color prejudice of his time, but as it turns out, the heroes of his story are the Mayans, members of the Red race, while the Aryans are the villains, and the Blacks (as in Fabre d'Olivet) once came close to conquering the whole world. This sets Raleigh apart from his Anglophone contemporaries and starts the anti-Aryan strain already met in Daniélou and the Britons.

THE CHURCHWARDS AND MU

At a time when Brasseur de Bourbourg and Le Plongeon were the only source of translations from the Mayan (the professionals having temporarily admitted defeat), it is understandable that amateur mythographers depended on them. Among these were the Churchward brothers, Albert (1852–1925) and James (1851–1936). They grew up in difficult circumstances, for their father, a "scrivener" (secretary or scribe) living on the edge of Dartmoor, died in 1854, leaving his widow with nine children.[24] Nonetheless, Albert became a (genuine) M.D., fellow of the Royal Geological Society, high-degree Freemason, and author of several ponderous books on Primordial Man. He did not agree with the Frenchmen's theories, but only because he was sure that the influence had gone the other way.

> We fail to see the utility of *Ignatius Donnelly*'s comparison of the Maya alphabet with the *Egyptian Hieratic,* to try and prove that the Maya was "the older" and original, and not the Egyptian. He must go back further than the "Solar Mythos" to prove this, and take the above into consideration, and the other proofs we have brought forward in this work; then he will find that the Mayas obtained their characters from the "Egyptian Hieroglyphics," and all their astronomy, learning, and religious doctrines and ceremonies, pyramids, and so forth from the Egyptians.[25]

Albert Churchward had a semispiritual philosophy, with a theory of "corpuscles" as living elements functioning both in the material state and out of it: "the Alphabet of all things living or dead."[26] Somewhat like his friend Gerald Massey, his theories were Freemasonic, Egyptophile, evolutionist, and politically aware, with Christianity reduced to one mythology among others. He does not enter into our discussion except as providing a springboard for his brother's works.

James Churchward is a more elusive character. In reconstructing his biography, all one can trust is official records such as census reports and facsimiles of patent registrations. For example, the thirty years he is said to have spent in the (British) Indian Army[27] conflict with the London census of 1881 that records his occupation as "East India Planter," and with his arrival in Brooklyn by 1889, there called an engineer.[28] He lived thereafter around New York City and became a U.S. citizen in 1913. His patents, at least, were real, mostly concerning steel, as were the lawsuits for infringement of them. His various addresses suggest that like many inventors, he led a life of fluctuating fortunes.

Churchward waited until he was over seventy years old before bursting on the world with the story of Mu. Some newspapers carried a press release announcing: "Tablets Tell of Great Continent with 64,000,000 White Inhabitants That Was Swallowed Up by Pacific."[29] Now he was called "Lieutenant-Colonel," "formerly of the British Army, educated at Oxford."[30] The sixty-four million is the giveaway, for this was Le Plongeon's number for the inhabitants of Mu/Atlantis. Also from Le Plongeon is the "Cosmic Diagram of the land of Mu," of which both Albert and James Churchward made so much (though with different interpretations),[31] and the determination to show that the ancients were fully conversant with the symbols and rituals of Freemasonry—because they invented them.

When *The Lost Continent of Mu* appeared in 1926, Churchward assured his readers that fifty years before, he had been befriended by an old Indian high priest who chanced to be one of only two in the whole country who knew the primordial language of mankind. This priest spent two years teaching the language to the colonial greenhorn, then revealed to him a collection of clay tablets that just happened to be in the archives of his temple. The priest had never dared open them, but for his young protégé he broke the rules and let him read them. And would you believe it?—the very first tablets turned out to be the genuine records of Mu! The following ones completed the story with the creation of the earth and man, so that Churchward could at last elucidate this eternal problem.

How many second-rate works of fiction have begun in the same vein? Needless to say, no one has ever seen these tablets or anything resembling them. Churchward must have enjoyed the hobby of his old age, as an eager readership devoured one Muan book after another. He boasted of travels all over India, to Burma, Angkor, Tibet and the Himalayan monasteries, Central Asia and the Gobi Desert, the South Sea Islands, the Malay Islands, New Zealand, Mexico, New Mexico, and Arizona. Everywhere he sought, and sometimes found, the guardians of secret knowledge concerning Mu.[32] He was a reasonable draftsman and illustrated his books with many a picture and sketch, most of them carefully dated. Around 1910–12, he was painting prehistoric animals,[33] then from 1924–26 created a large body of Muan maps, symbols, and scenes of destruction. They remind me of the invented world and languages of J. R .R. Tolkien, also a stylish watercolorist and calligrapher.

As for Churchward's sources, perhaps it was true that the Le Plongeons had been dear friends of his and that Augustus had left him his unpublished work.[34] Albert Churchward also called Le Plongeon his friend,[35] though he reversed his whole scheme, placing the source of all civilizations in Egypt. James relocated it to a vanished island in the Pacific and drew appropriate conclusions. He never doubted that any transoceanic similarity means diffusion and influence, nor that any geometrical figure has metaphysical intention. To supplement the 2,500 "Naacal" tablets that Churchward and the Indian priest had deciphered were the "Lhasa Records" of Paul Schliemann, a famous hoax that he swallowed whole. The second edition of *The Lost Continent of Mu* (1931) gave much space to the equally dubious Mexican tablets discovered by William Niven and subsequently lost. Then there was the fund of information in his brother's books, on which James had no compunction in drawing after Albert's death.

To some readers, Churchward must still sound learned and authoritative, but he made glaring mistakes that were never corrected. For example, in three of his books he reproduced photographs of two bronze statuettes which had been looted from China, sold to a sailor, and ended up in a friend's garret. They look like Tibetan work of mediocre quality depicting Bodhisattvas or Dhyani Buddhas.[36] Not so to Churchward: they are priceless, their workmanship equal to any of today's jewelers, and they come from Mu. One of them he captions "A Bronze Statuette of Mu Receiving Man's Soul from The Creator";[37] the other "One of the two oldest known bronzes in the world—a symbolical figure of Mu as the mistress and ruler of the whole earth."[38] About their dating, he writes: "If Uighur [Central Asian], it is about 18,000 or 20,000 years old. If from Mu, the age cannot be estimated."[39] He also reproduces two paintings of similar iconography that he found in an illustrated newspaper, certain that they are a king and queen of Mu, and equally ancient.[40] Had he never been in a museum?

Churchward's Mu was an island in the South Pacific, over 5,000 miles from east to west and over 3,000 from north to south. About 200,000 years ago it was the cradle of the human race, not brought about by evolution but as a "special creation."[41] Mu was idyllic, fertile, and without mountains, benevolently ruled by a priest-king. There were no theologies or dogmas: the Muans worshiped the deity through the solar symbol, knowing that it was only a symbol, and believed in the immortality of the soul. Since all people on Earth were under Mu's suzerainty, there was no conflict anywhere. The dominant race on Mu was white, and they were "exceedingly handsome people, with clear white or olive skins, large, soft, dark eyes and straight black hair. Besides this white race, there were people of other races, people with yellow, brown or black skins. They, however, did not dominate."[42]

Mu's magnificent civilization had already reached its zenith 50,000 or more years ago.[43] Its fall was both moral and physical, but we do not read anything about vile practices on the part of the inhabitants: the corruption came through religion. The Churchward brothers shared the anticlerical, and especially anti-Catholic attitude common to Theosophists and mythologists, James writing as follows:

> At various times in the history of man unscrupulous priesthoods have caused the downfall of religion by introducing into it vicious systems of theology made up of inventions, extravagances and immorality; omissions and false and vicious translations from the Sacred Inspired Religion of Mu from which all religions have sprung.
>
> These systems were invented by priesthoods for the purpose of inspiring superstitious fears in the hearts of the people, to ensnare them, body and soul, into slavery to the priesthood. Having accomplished this, it did not take long for these priesthoods to acquire wealth and become all powerful. . . . The accumulation and concentration of wealth invariably ruins a country. There are at least a dozen historical records of it.[44]

Churchward adds that the first of these "outrages to religion" occurred in Atlantis 22,000 years ago, after which the true religion was restored in Egypt by Osiris. Atlantis itself does not much interest him, since it was only a colony of Mu, but the two lands went down at the same time, around 12,000 years ago, and for the same reason: "both lands were being upheld above water by isolated gas chambers, both lay over the pathway of a forming gas belt. In both cases the isolated chambers were tapped by the forming belt and blown out, in both cases the land went down and was submerged, and, strange to say, the same belt was the double assassin."[45]

These gas belts and chambers, honeycombing the earth's interior, were the basis of Churchward's geological theory and catastrophism. His late book, *Cosmic Forces of Mu,* has a complete analysis, with diagrams and maps, of how the chambers are linked by the belts and how the latter run around the earth, their path usually marked on the surface by earthquake zones. When a gas chamber blows out, the earth or water above it sinks into the hole, and one can imagine the catastrophic results. In addition to this geophysical theory, Churchward also has a theory to rival his brother's "corpuscles," of cosmic forces that merge the material with the spiritual. One of these was known to the ancients as the "cold magnetic force," and it can nullify gravity. Jesus knew how to use it: that is how he walked on water, for he too studied the Sacred Inspired Writings of Mu during his twelve years in a Himalayan monastery.[46] With this, Churchward conflates the popular "lost years of Jesus" theory[47] with Paul Schliemann's "Lhasa Records."

After the fall of the Motherland of Mu, it was India that maintained its civilization, its learning, and its technology, including the inevitable flying machines.[48] This golden age of India and the great vanished island to its southwest lasted 8,000 years, until the coming of the Aryans about 5,000 years ago. Almost all Atlantologists have something to say about the Aryans, whoever they mean by the term. Churchward, like Raleigh (whom he may have skimmed), is no fan of theirs. "They were just hardy mountaineers," he says, "uncouth and uneducated. The Nagas, the most highly educated race in the world, took compassion on them, welcomed them into their schools and colleges, educated and advanced them." Little thanks they got for it. "In time these Aryans dominated the whole of the Northern parts of India including their schools and colleges. Thinking they had leant from the Naacals all there was to be learnt, they proceeded to drive their gentle, kindly instructors out of the country into the snow-capped mountains of the North."[49]

Enough has been said to show how much Churchward shares with our other writers, both in specifics like the airships and in the general conviction of his unique access to the truth. As it turns out, he also shared some of the occult aspects. We discover this at the end of *The Children of Mu,* when Churchward accedes to the many requests for more information about the priest who taught him to decipher the tablets. In a chapter called "Intimate Hours with the Rishi" he recounts the miracles or tricks that the old man demonstrated to show his mastery of the various forces. The two of them spoke of visitations from the dead, especially loved ones, and why these sometimes cease. The Rishi wisely admits that we cannot know whether they have gone to other worlds, been reincarnated on earth, or returned to the Great Source.

The conversation also touches on masters no longer incarnated, who may reveal themselves by lowering their vibrations to our level. Churchward asks why we do not see these visitors. The Rishi replies:

> Because their vibrations, although close enough in unison with yours to cause your brain to receive them, are not sufficiently in unison to produce vision; and sometimes it would appear that they did not wish you to see them. Personally, I have come to the conclusion that those who do not wish to be seen are *great masters who are using you as an instrument for communication and information to this world from the world beyond.*[50] [emphasis mine]

Finally, on the eve of the young Churchward's leaving India, the Rishi takes him on a journey "to *look at ourselves* during *our* last incarnation" (emphasis in original). The former Churchward falls in battle, and the former Rishi, now his father, mourns him. Afterward the author refuses to say whether he believes it was real, or a mesmeric vision, and leaves the reader to decide. This too is a device not unknown to fiction writers, but by the end of Churchward's five books, I fear that he had come to believe his own tall tales and to regard himself as the instrument for a higher revelation.

THE ROSICRUCIANS

Many groups today wear the label of "Rosicrucian," implying identity with the mythical fraternity that proclaimed itself in 1614 with the *Fama Fraternitatis Rosae Crucis* (The fame of the Fraternity of the Rosy Cross), the *Confessio Fraternitatis* (1615), and the fantastic novel *The Chemical Wedding of Christian Rosenkreuz* (1616). Some pretend to be the one and only true Rosicrucian order, with consequences like the "War of the Roses" in the 1930s between the rival claimants Reuben Clymer and Harvey Lewis. If one thing is certain about modern Rosicrucians, it is their lack of any such linkage with the group of Swabian Lutherans who concocted the original documents. On the positive side, all groups share something of the aspirations of Johann Valentin Andreae, Tobias Hess, and their circle for the spiritual renovation of the whole world.

The original Rosicrucians were not concerned with prehistory, but almost all the modern ones have something to say about our subject. The Internet is a boon to them, and it is from there that I have taken their current self-descriptions; the material on Atlantis comes from their older books. Issues of authenticity and priority may remain murky, but some of their roots are easy to discern from what follows.

Societas Rosicruciana in America

One of the more senior orders is the Societas Rosicruciana in America (SRIA[51]), whose most successful period began after 1909 under the leadership of George Winslow Plummer (1876–1944). The SRIA calls itself "the American organization formed by properly qualified initiates to propagate the Ancient Wisdom Teachings in the western world." It pictures its leader in dog collar and pectoral cross, for he was an archbishop, no less, though only in a breakaway Anglican sect. While this sends a reassuringly Christian message to prospective initiates, Plummer's writings bear the clear stamp of turn-of-the-century occultism. Writing as "Khei," he published books on psychometry, clairvoyance, and reincarnation, as well as on Rosicrucianism.

Plummer's idea of "Rosicrucian fundamentals" includes the scheme of seven root races, each with seven sub-races, plus Rudolf Steiner's names for the three periods yet to come: Jupiter, Venus, and Vulcan. Turning to earth's early history, Plummer, like many of our authorities, puts the beginnings of organic life at the North Pole.[52] His Lemurians are just like the Theosophical image of them: they had no vision, only two "sensitive centers," and no memory, but lived in a half-dreaming state. Lemuria was destroyed around 10,417,000 BP by volcanic action. It was the Atlanteans who obtained the sense of sight and for the first time knew the physical world as an objective reality.[53] They were coeval with the giant reptiles, but those are not our ancestors. The dinosaurs came to earth from another life wave and will become human later.[54]

All of this, though unacknowledged, is standard Theosophical doctrine. More interestingly, Plummer writes that "Rosicrucian science" teaches that the earth has four distinct motions:

1. Revolution around the sun
2. Rotation around the polar axis
3. A revolution of the earth's axis at the rate of about 50 seconds a century, the whole cycle taking about 2,592,000 years
4. Nutation (variation in the angle of axial inclination)

The third of these, he adds, explains such things as the vestiges of tropical flora in polar regions.[55] This cycle, lasting 100 times the traditional precessional period of 25,902 years, is unknown to science, but must be akin to that proposed by the Norwich cobbler Sampson Arnold Mackey (treated at length in my previous books[56]). Its principle is that the inclination of the axis increases until, at 90° from the vertical it lies in the same plane as the ecliptic. This brings on what Mackey calls the "Age of Horror," because one half of the globe faces the sun, day and night, for half a year, causing intolerable heat, then for the other half of the year faces away from the sun, causing perpetual darkness and cold. As the cycle continues, the axis moves away from this alignment toward the opposite pole, and the earth becomes habitable again. When it reaches the perpendicular position, that is the Golden Age because there are no seasons, only a perpetual spring. Then the process resumes, until after another million or so years, and another Age of Horror, the earth is back where it started.

Mackey's system was part of the teachings of the Hermetic Brotherhood of Luxor (see chapter 12), with which most of the modern Rosicrucians had some relationship. Plummer's version is a little different; he says of this cycle that the North Pole has many times faced the sun (which is true of the Mackey system), that the buildup of ice on the opposite side causes a sudden reversal, the South Pole taking the position of the North. But equilibrium is then achieved, as is the case at present.[57]

A sudden reversal does not seem to agree with a cycle of regular period; it resembles more the theory of "punctuated equilibrium" that has the earth periodically adjusting its axis as ice builds up and distributes its mass unevenly. I do not know whether this is part of the teachings that the SRIA divulges to its initiates, but cosmology is certainly not emphasized in its publicity materials.

The Rosicrucian Fellowship

The Rosicrucian Fellowship calls itself "An Association of Christian Mystics." By its own account, its founder, Max Heindel (1865–1919), "was selected by the Elder Brothers of the Rose Cross to publicly give out the Western Wisdom Teachings in order to help prepare mankind for the coming age of Universal Brotherhood, the Age of Aquarius." Heindel had met both Leadbeater and Steiner, and admired them, before emigrating to California and founding his order, also around 1909.

Heindel adopts Steiner's system of ages but asserts his independence by saying that the Hyperborean Age came after the separation of Mars, not the Moon, as Steiner has it (see chapter 4).[58] Lemuria was where sexual division began, and the human ego first developed under the influence of Mars.[59] Volcanoes destroyed that continent, whereupon a new one appeared in the Atlantic Ocean. In Atlantis it was always misty; no sun was visible, only a halo in the sky. Humans had heads but almost no faces, and no frontal development to their brains. They were giants with huge arms and legs, and they did not walk, but jumped. Heindel adds some curious physical details here. The hairs of the Atlanteans, he says, were round in section, and this is still the case among their descendants, whereas the hair of Aryans is oval in section. The Atlanteans also have their ears further back than the Aryans.[60] As for the latter, they descended from the fifth Atlantean sub-race, the Original Semites, migrating East through Europe to the Gobi Desert, where the seed of the new race was prepared.

The Rosicrucian Fellowship sprouted from Rudolf Steiner's early teaching just as the latter had sprouted from Theosophy, and like Steiner it maintained a strong Christian orientation. It has long served the cause of astrology by publishing the standard ephemerides (tables of planetary positions). In conformity with the original Rosicrucians, alternative methods of healing play a large part in its activities.

The Lectorium Rosicrucianum

Jan van Rijckenborgh (1896–1968) was a member of Heindel's group before striking off on his own in the 1930s to found the Netherlands-based Lectorium Rosicrucianum. This group keeps a low profile, claiming no pompous lineage but identifying with the Christian esoteric tradition and especially the theosophy of Jacob Boehme. It also has a strong spiritual link to the Gnostics and Cathars.

In 1950 Van Rijckenborgh wrote pessimistically that with the coming of the atomic bomb, the tragedy of Atlantis was repeating itself. That race perished through interference with the divine foundations of cosmic order. Then it was the priesthood who were responsible; now it is dialectical science. In a memorable phrase, he declares that we should lock up our scientists as criminally insane! But it is too late. The destruction of the world order is already a fact, and will take just a few hundred years.[61]

Van Rijckenborgh admits that there are various theories about Atlantis, but little precise knowledge. We can sense Theosophical and Anthroposophical influences in a few of his statements, such as that the earth may have changed from the Atlantean to the Aryan period through a process of "natural dialectics." Like many others, he implies a division of humanity into two groups, but absolutely not according to race or color. He just says that one group now lives with the consequences of the sin of Atlantis, but obliviously, while the other has great new possibilities. Finally, when the "new Jupiter era" dawns, he foresees a further rearrangement of the continents in which all matter in its present form will vanish; and this will separate the two human types.[62]

Fraternitas Rosae Crucis

Reuben Swinburne Clymer (1878–1966) founded the Fraternitas Rosae Crucis (FRC) around 1920. Far from dating back merely to 1614, "It justly claims to be the oldest association of men on earth, dating from the sinking of the New Atlantis isle, nearly ten thousand years anterior to the days of the Greece of Plato." Clymer's sources were overtly non-Theosophical, claiming instead a pedigree from Paschal Beverly Randolph (1825–1875) and the Hermetic Brotherhood of Luxor.[63]

The official line of the FRC on Atlantis is contained in William P. Phelon's *Our Story of Atlantis* (written in the 1890s, published 1905), which this Rosicrucian order has continued to reprint and sell. Eichner and de Camp classify it as fiction, but it is on the borderline. Phelon begins in nonfictional mode by crediting modern science and anthropology with solving the Atlantis enigma. Like many Atlantologists of his time, he is convinced by Le Plongeon and the identification of Plato's Atlantis with the lost cities of the Americas. Phelon also defends "astral presentation and perception" as a valid source of information on the past, "especially as the books of Wisdom of the Past declare, that automatic books of record are kept of all deeds and manifestation, upon the earth."[64] Consequently he says: "I do not doubt the authenticity of my information, nor the statements given as facts, by those who were so kind and courteous as to make the writer their mouthpiece in this re-collection of the ancient memories"(9).* Apparently the author believes in the Theosophical notion of the Akashic Records, and would have us believe that he has access to them, though the description of his methods is obviously fictitious.

Phelon gives as the reason for the modern awakening of interest in Atlantis the great number of reincarnated Atlanteans now living. He sees these souls as the motive force for human progress, in which he is a firm, even ruthless, believer. In whichever nation they throng to reincarnate, that nation has always risen to splendor, and after the British it is the turn of the Americans:

---

*Page numbers in parentheses are from *Our Story of Atlantis*.

As soon as the Anglo-Saxon speaking races were sufficiently developed out of savagery, the Atlantians, [*sic*] commenced re-appearing, startling the whole world ever and anon, with their great strides toward wisdom and knowledge, as they slowly paved the way by conquest and discovery, for the settlement and re-occupation of that which belonged to them [i.e., the Americas]; and for the utilization of all their old resources, under new conditions of added strength and experience. (33)

Therefore, Phelon adds, any sympathy we may have for the Red man is wasted, because he did not know how to exploit the mineral and other resources of the land he usurped (34). In a hundred years' time, Atlantis itself will be above the waves again, and in five hundred, Lemuria will have risen too, and the bulk of the earth's population will live south of the equator (39–40).

The fictional part of the book opens with the author sailing out of New York in 1872. A shipboard acquaintance tells him Plato's Atlantis story almost verbatim, then caps it with quotations from Koot Hoomi (via Sinnett). During a dead calm, the two pals explore a peculiar-looking island, which is really a ruined obelisk or tower 150 feet in circumference, and the first evidence for Atlantis's new rising. Clambering up, then down inside it, they take possession of a stone casket containing the records that they themselves had secreted 29,000 years ago, during their previous incarnations.

Phelon repeats many of the usual clichés: that the Atlanteans lived in a utopian, socialist, theocratic state, and that they were vegetarians and had technology (in this case, a network of tramways) driven by a secret force that only the magi understood (96). Some of his suggestions are novel. For instance, it is the subjugation of women by men that has gradually made the female body inferior in strength and stature, whereas in Atlantis the sexes were equal in both (107). One detail seems to have been taken straight from Samuel Butler's satirical novel *Erewhon* (1872): everyone in Atlantis took the utmost trouble to maintain perfect health, because to be crippled or diseased, or to have such a member in one's family, was regarded as a crime against the people (116).

More clichés follow: a magnificent temple dedicated to solar worship, with morning hymns à la *Aïda;* a perfect system of education, done partly through thought-transference; and a tour of the secret chambers, where the technological wonders include a mirror made from marble and gold through which initiates can view all the past, present, and future (161–62). For all their attention to the body, the Atlanteans are rigorously antisex: "Oh, if you of this day and generation could only understand and perceive the treachery of the physical embrace. . . . The body is nothing! The soul of the Ego is everything!"(159–60). Some of the descriptions recall *The Chemical Wedding of Christian Rosenkreuz,* such as the chamber "permeated by the light which knows no obstruction," with seven columns of different metals attuned to the planets and producing musical and color vibrations (166–67). The same source of inspiration might be searched for the complex geometrical designs on the floors and for the underground laboratories where gold and jewels are manufactured "under primal conditions" through the agency of the elementals: Salamanders, Sylphs, Undines, and Gnomes.

Ghostland, the mysterious occult novel published in 1874, may be the inspiration for the theater in which the council of the "Forty-five" meet, one being an Elder Brother visible only on the psychic plane (174). The adepts work to affect the affairs of the world by imposing their ideas on the Great Astral Record, using, among other things, a great transparent blackboard on which events of past and future are made to appear (184–85). As for what the future, thus manipulated, holds for us, besides the rising of the lost continent, we should expect a new messiah. However, this time it will not be an individual like Buddha or Jesus, but a collective messiah formed from "all who are looking toward the light, all who are seeking unselfishly for wisdom" (209).

One can see why the FRC liked this book. It is a complete course in the Atlantean myth, from the Platonic legend to its supposed verification by modern science. The notion that many Atlanteans are being incarnated in America today is tailor-made for a Rosicrucian order in search of members. What aspirant could fail to hope that he or she was one of this elect group of souls?

AMORC

The Ancient and Mystical Order Rosae Crucis (AMORC) was founded in 1915 by Harvey Spencer Lewis (1883–1939). Until the crisis following the death of Lewis's son in 1987, it was by far the most successful of the modern Rosicrucian orders, with a grand Egyptian compound in San Jose, California, and branches all over the world. A number of today's serious esotericists received their first introduction to this order of ideas through it.

Chapter 2 introduced the grand master of the AMORC in France, Raymond Bernard, and his response to the excitement aroused by the Planète group. Here we turn back to Lewis's own writings, which include the first full-length book about Lemuria. For *Lemuria: The Lost Continent of the Pacific*,[65] Lewis scrambled the syllables of his name into "Wishar Spenle Cervé." Unlike Clymer and Heindel, Cervé/Lewis owes nothing to the Theosophical scheme of prehistory. His sources are anthropologists and travelers, especially in the Americas; sacred books; "the works of Plato"; "the Rosicrucian records and historical writings"; and so on. Without mentioning Wegener, he is a firm believer in continental drift but thinks that it happens on a rapid scale, as can be seen from this compilation of his chronology. (All years are Before Present, and approximate.)

> From time unknown, Lemuria occupies most of the Pacific Ocean, and is probably where all land creatures, including man, began.
> 200,000: The Americas, Europe, Africa all contiguous but semi-submerged.
> By 150,000: these partially submerged lands known, described, and mapped, but uninhabited.
> By 100,000: great earth changes; mountains begin to form.

82,000: Lemuria reduced in size, remains adjacent to Southeast Asia. The other lands rise.

75,000: the Americas begin to drift away from Europe, Africa, and Greenland.

50,000: the westward drift of the Americas stops as they meet Lemuria and Asia. Lemuria sinks further; Atlantis begins to rise.

25,000: Atlantis rises further, mountains form in all lands. Lemurians forced to emigrate to Asia, Americas, Atlantis.

18,000: Atlantean civilization at its height.

15,000: the western part of Atlantis sinks.

12,000: over 12 years, the remainder of Atlantis sinks, leaving only its mountain peaks as the Atlantic islands. All that is left of Lemuria is the West Coast of North America (71–95).*

Lemuria was characterized by a tropical climate and a consequent hypertrophy of all life-forms. Its ants were two inches long, the eponymous lemurs six feet tall, and as for the dinosaurs:

> These creatures grew to be over a hundred feet in length, and some much longer, according to some authorities, and they were undoubtedly the greatest destroyers of life, animal and vegetable. Their strange grumblings, made by a form of gurgling in the throat, which always preceded one of their wild rampages in search of flesh, or the crackling of vegetation as their huge, bulky forms moved through the high growth of grass and wild bushes, were sounds for which the natives constantly listened and of which they lived in dread. [99]

The natives in question were not egg-layers, androgynes, etheric-bodied, giants, perverts, or any of the other things alleged about the Lemurians. They were hearty six- or seven-footers, tanned but not dark-skinned, with muscular arms, long necks, large heads, and hair cascading

---

*Page numbers in parentheses are from *Lemuria: The Lost Continent of the Pacific.*

down the back of the skull that they braided in many ornamental ways "if we are to judge from pictures carved in stone or drawn or painted upon leather" (124). The only feature that might stand out on a Californian beach was a large bump in the center of the forehead. This housed the organ of a sixth sense, enabling the Lemurians to use telepathy and clairvoyance, communicate with animals, and even "attune with the Cosmic and . . . receive direct information of a dependable, reliable nature on all subjects and covering the entire field of knowledge" (130). Thus blessed, the Lemurians lived for 50,000 years in their tropical paradise free from social hierarchy, money, metal tools and weapons, disease, and fear of death (since reincarnation was an open book to them). They dwelled in simple huts and built large stone monuments. Their only troubles came from the larger animals, and, later, from the breakup of their continent.

Dr. James W. Ward, styled "Eminent Disciple of Oriental Mystery Schools," contributes a chapter titled "The Spirituality of the Lemurians" in which he claims to have personally viewed historical records of the Lemurians in the Oriental Monasteries, fifty-three years ago. One of these records related how twelve Lemurians once went exploring in an airship "which looked just a little like our modern blimp." They landed in Atlantis and were well received there, and on their return left a map of their travels that Dr. Ward wishes he had photographed when he saw it. It was in the shape of a coconut, with the countries visited drawn on its surface (145). This contributor, who writes in a style alternately sermonizing and ludicrous, may have been Dr. James William Ward (1861–1939) of San Francisco, who had been president of the American Institute of Homeopathy in the early years of the century.[66] Why he should have wanted to court ridicule with this parody of Leadbeater's famous globes, I cannot imagine.

When Cervé resumes the tale, it is with more about the Lemurian way of life, and especially their success in harnessing the forces of nature efficiently and without complex machinery. Besides propelling their ships and airships with "the energy that radiated from a stone," they had mastered both solar and atomic energy, there being "sufficient stored-up energy in one atom to cause a terrific explosion, if we only knew how to use this energy and apply it safely" (171). There is nothing here about misusing such powers, but perhaps that was reserved for the Atlanteans. Cervé is keen to give the Lemurians a good press, because he has reserved for the end of his book the astonishing news that they are still with us.

The coasts of California, Oregon, and Washington are the only remnant of the Lemurian continent and "the oldest inhabited, cultivated, civilized land on the face of the earth that is still in practically the same physical form, and in the same environment, as when God first created it" (217). Not only have the Lemurians left their writing on the rocks; they are hiding out there, and this accounts for the innumerable reports of mysterious lights seen in the region, especially in the mountains of California. Nowhere is this more certain than around Mount Shasta, where the astronomer Edgar Lucien Larkin saw through his telescope three golden domes among the trees of the mountain—or "such is the story told by Larkin's friends" (252–55). Then there are the odd-looking persons who still come into the lowlands to make purchases, always paying in gold dust or nuggets and never accepting change. Their foreheads, down to the nose, are always covered with a special decoration—obviously to hide the psychic bump. Other denizens are sometimes spotted on the highway, "garbed in pure white and in sandals, with long curly hair, tall and majestic in appearance," but impossible to photograph or talk to because they just vanish (256).

More suspicious yet is the tendency of automobiles, when brought too close to the haunted mountain, to suffer seizure of their electrical systems and loss of power. Hundreds of people have seen oddly shaped boats fly high in the air and over the ocean, then continue on the sea as vessels. "Only recently a group of persons playing golf . . . saw a peculiar, silver-like vessel rise in the air and float over the mountaintops and disappear. It was unlike any airship that has ever been seen and there was absolutely no noise emanating from it" (260). The silent, boat-shaped, silver objects resemble Scott-Elliot's Atlantean airships (see chapter 4), but before dismissing this as fantasy, I would point out that the effects on automobiles anticipate by several decades a stock element of UFO encounters.

AMORC had a strong distribution network, and the publication of *Lemuria* in 1931 caused a worldwide stir. According to an appendix added to the second edition (1935), many people wrote either to corroborate or deny the reports of lights and other phenomena around Mount Shasta. The third-hand report of Larkin's discovery was especially doubted. We will return to this matter in the next chapter.

BEELZEBUB'S DESCENTS TO PLANET EARTH

George Ivanovich Gurdjieff (1866?–1949) included quite an extensive Atlantis story in his book *All and Everything,* otherwise known as *Beelzebub's Tales to His Grandson.*[67] He wrote its 1,200 pages during the 1920s in Russian and Armenian and had it translated roughly into English by pupils who knew those languages. The literary critic and editor A. R. Orage, who was teaching Gurdjieff's methods, improved the English.[68] For many years Gurdjieff presided over readings from it, and money was collected for a publication fund, but it was not until 1950 that the book reached the public.

All and Everything is a notoriously unreadable work. The sentences are interminable, the humor leaden. It is full of outlandish words, some with recognizable components like Theomertmalogos (756: "Word-God"), others without, like Ooissapagaoomnian (455: "pertaining to moral philosophy"?).* Only someone already captivated by Gurdjieff's teaching would read it through once, let alone the three times prescribed as a minimum for understanding it. I make no such claim. That said, there is material in it worth extracting, including a coherent account of human prehistory. I now summarize this, omitting all strange words and clumsy circumlocutions, and, more regrettably, all the asides and fascinating digressions.

The narrator is Beelzebub, who has been banished from his home planet for agitation against authority. He and his comrades have been exiled to the solar system, where they are based on Mars but can travel

---

*Page numbers in parentheses are from *All and Everything.*

by spaceship to the other planets of the system (52). All the planets have intelligent life, in bodies appropriate to their conditions. Those on Mars have stout trunks, wings, huge bulging eyes, and claws on their feet (61). Those on the moon resemble large ants and have tunneled the entire planet to provide shelter from its extremes of hot and cold (62).

We begin with the origin of the moon. Long ago, owing to a miscalculation by the individual responsible, a comet collided with the earth and struck off two fragments (82). One of them was the moon; the other was known to the Atlanteans, but is so small and remote that it is now forgotten (85). After a while, the two fragments settled down in orbit around the earth, but they were still unstable. To avoid future trouble, the commission that takes care of such things arranged that the earth should constantly send to the moon a certain type of vibration, generated when beings die (84).

As the human race evolved in intelligence, the commission worried lest it should discover this arrangement. If humans realized that the purpose of their existence was merely to feed the moon, they might rebel and destroy themselves out of spite. The commission therefore caused a special organ to grow at the base of the human spine that prevented this (88). Although this organ was afterward withdrawn, its effects remained, including the tendency of humans to kill one another. No other planet's intelligent beings behave like this (91).

Beelzebub made six descents from Mars to Earth. The first time, he was deposited by a spaceship on the shores of Atlantis, where a young member of his species had meddled in government and caused a constitutional crisis (112). The solution was to replace the country's officials with members of Beelzebub's own species, in disguise. Shortly after this, the earth suffered its second serious catastrophe. The cause this time was local, not cosmic (177). The expulsion of the moon had left Earth's center of gravity misplaced, and now it shifted to its true center, causing the disappearance of Atlantis and the rising of many lands that still exist (179).

Humans were already multiplying on the new lands when Beelzebub landed for the second time, in the Caspian Sea (184). His mission now concerned a religious mania that sought divine favor from animal and even human sacrifices. Apart from the humanitarian outrage, these unnecessary deaths were overloading the moon with the vibrations necessary for its maintenance (182). Beelzebub's efforts to stop this were partially successful, though the evil effects of the spinal implant seemed ineradicable. His third descent was for the same purpose (207). This time his center of activity was a city in what is now the Gobi Desert. Its founding went back to Atlantean times, when a learned society called the Akhaldans, foreseeing the coming catastrophe, had sent one of their members there with his servants, to study natural phenomena (211). Later a group of Atlantean hunters arrived at the Gobi Sea, seeking a universal panacea found in the antlers of a certain deer. The two groups blended, multiplied, and in time built a city on its shores (212).

Beelzebub's fourth descent was into the Red Sea, with a commission to collect African apes for experimental purposes (284). Despite the heated debates over whether humans have evolved from apes or vice versa, the truth is that they originated after the fall of Atlantis, when living conditions were unnatural and fostered unnatural intercourse. Some human females, lacking partners, mated with animal species. This does not usually result in conception, but on this occasion it did, and the apes were the result (275–80).

All the members of Beelzebub's own species had left Atlantis before the catastrophe and had founded a center of culture in central Africa, near the source of the Nile (302). The Akhaldan society, looking for a place where they could continue their work in isolation, had settled in Egypt. The extraterrestrials then joined them there and remained in friendly contact with the Akhaldans until their final departure from Earth (301–3). Beelzebub was interested in seeing their center, and especially the pyramids that had been planned by the Akhaldans before leaving Atlantis (292). Their purpose was to observe "remote cosmic concentrations" by looking through five long tubes that met in a chamber deep underground. In former times, these concentrations had been perceptible through extrasensory means, but that perception had been lost (306–7). The apparatus also served for controlling the climate (308). After viewing the pyramids and the Sphinx, Beelzebub went south, caught his apes, and shipped them to Saturn (314).

The third earthly catastrophe was again caused by the moon. The satellite had by now acquired an atmosphere, but it was not in harmony with Earth's. The consequence was abnormally strong winds, flattening high lands and filling depressions with sand. The Sahara and the Gobi became deserts, and all the cultural centers that Beelzebub had known on his fourth descent disappeared (315). This catastrophe led to the migrations of races: the Caspian group went to Persia; the Gobi group split, one part going east to China and the other west, eventually reaching Europe. The Africans spread from the center throughout the continent (318).

During these vicissitudes, human life span had become much reduced, and it was to discover the cause that Beelzebub made a fifth and brief descent. He landed in the Persian Gulf, then sailed to Babylon, now the center of learning for the whole planet (321). Here he found the human race in further decline. Its psyche, under so-called learned guidance, was losing its fundamental impulses of Faith, Hope, and Love (321). Wisdom had atrophied, replaced by rote learning (323).

Beelzebub's sixth and final descent left him on Earth for 300 years (equal to one of his own) (524). The spaceship landed him in Afghanistan, then went on to the North Pole to be moored out of sight and danger of the increased human traffic. Beelzebub had come to observe the new methods of war, in which humanity's strange compulsion to destroy its own kind was being carried on with long-distance weaponry (528–29). During this visit he was pardoned for his former dissidence and given permission to leave the solar system (524).

Beelzebub's knowledge of Earth's history is based partly on his own experiences, and partly on the "thought tapes" in the atmosphere created by highly developed people. The tapes last almost indefinitely (293) and can be accessed and read by anyone who can enter a certain level of contemplation (294).

With this we leave our summary of Beelzebub's descents and add a few comments. It is for the reader to judge the genre of the work. Of course, much of it qualifies as fiction, even science fiction, as in the description of how the spaceship works. But much more of it is a serious treatise on human psychology from an esoteric viewpoint, together with an equally esoteric explanation of how that psychology evolved. Through the persona of Beelzebub, Gurdjieff expounds his own system of cosmic correspondences, the "law of octaves." There are hundreds of pages of opinionated writing on society, national characteristics, customs, ethics, religions, and philosophies. There are anecdotes, rants, and quips from the Sufi sage Mullah Nassr Eddin. Whoever rewrites the work in sensible language and at half its length will be doing a service to humanity and, in my opinion, to Gurdjieff himself.

The reader will have noticed many of the favorite Atlantean motifs. They include the impact of a comet and the extrusion of the moon, followed by its capture; a pole shift as cause of Atlantis's fall; the "sin of the mindless" as the origin of apes; groups of Atlantean initiates forewarned of the cataclysm and escaping to build new centers; the Gobi Sea as one of these; the pyramids as Atlantean devices with a special cosmic purpose. Much of this agrees with Theosophy (about which Gurdjieff has harsh words[69]), while the overall theme of human devolution conforms to the pattern of the Yugas. More unusual for its time, recalling that this was written in the 1920s, is the theme of alien intervention. True, science fiction was already full of "men from Mars," but Beelzebub's story resonates with more recent claims. The implantation of the Kundabuffer (the organ at the base of the spine, obviously based on "kundalini") sounds like current rumors of genetic manipulation with sinister intent. The takeover of administrative posts by Beelzebub's "tribe" is an early instance of the theme of alien "walk-ins" disguised as humans. And the picture he draws of the Martians, with their wings and bulging eyes, is terribly like the Mothman!

NINE

Channeling in the
New World

———— ✳ ————

WE HAVE ALREADY met a number of people who attribute their information on prehistoric times to some source outside themselves. Before the term *channeling* was coined, there was the classic example of Alice Bailey taking dictation from "The Tibetan." By her own admission, this was different from someone like Leadbeater or Steiner, who developed a capacity to read the Akashic Records; or from Swedenborg, who was shown the heavens but reported on them in his own words. Channeling, in the broadest sense, includes many different methods and at least two clear divisions: conscious and trance. The first type, conscious channeling, includes methods like automatic writing, typing, drawing, and using an Ouija board. It also includes speaking under direct inspiration, either immediately or after an inner voice has spoken. Some channels are also psychically gifted, in which case the boundaries with clairvoyance and visionary experience become very hazy.

In the second type, trance channeling, the entranced, hypnotized, or sleeping channel is not conscious of what he or she is saying and requires an amanuensis or recording device to capture it. On returning to normal consciousness, the channel usually does not know what has come through him or her. But the possibility of interference from the person's subconscious mind or telepathic influences from others present complicates the situation. Beyond this, and setting aside the whole question of fraud or self-deception, there is the vexed question of how the communicating entities, who may claim to be angels, Atlanteans, Venusians, and so on, can do so in the vernacular. Perhaps they borrow the channel's linguistic equipment, but that also opens the door to contamination. In short, there is no absolutely pure, egoless channel. That is why skeptics can make a good case that the phenomenon is phony from beginning to end, and even sympathetic critics reduce it to the channel's subconscious mind.

Evaluating channeled material can be a delicate matter, for one person's channeling is another person's scripture. On the one hand are modern works that define the genre, such as Jakob Lorber's *Great Gospel of John,* Joseph Smith's *Book of Mormon,* John Ballou Newbrough's *Oahspe,* the anonymously channeled *Urantia Book,* Jane Roberts's *Seth Material,* and Helen Schuchman's *Course in Miracles.* On the other are sacred books, notably the Bhagavad-Gita (purporting to be the words of Krishna), the Mosaic Law (words of Yahweh), the *Asclepius* (words of Hermes Trismegistus), the Chaldean Oracles (attributed to Zoroaster), the Book of Revelation (channeled by John the Divine), and, last but not least, the Quran (words of Allah, via Muhammad). All these came through men or women who sincerely believed themselves to be mouthpieces for an exterior and superior entity; and none of them agrees with any of the others. Traditionalists will say, "By their fruits ye shall know them," to which the cynic in me observes that at least the first group have not yet caused any inquisitions, persecutions, or wars of religion.

Leaving others to argue their respective and rival claims, I do notice that in modern times, channeling has become a specialty of the English-speaking world, and more particularly of the United States. France and Germany have a history of mesmeric mediumship and Christian mystics whose effusions border on channeling, and France was once a hotbed of Spiritualism, but it is rare to find a straightforward modern case there. The only one that comes to mind is Oskar Schlag, channel for Atman, whose séances in the 1930s were attended by Carl Jung.[1] The French and

Germans that we have met in previous chapters tend either to use clair-voyance of some kind (e.g., Guido von List's ancestral memory, Saint-Yves d'Alveydre's astral travel), or to speak ex cathedra without revealing their sources and methods (e.g., Fabre d'Olivet, Peryt Shou). The obvious rea-son for this is the openness of America to new religious movements of every kind. It was no chance that Mormonism, Spiritualism, Theosophy, Adventism, Christian Science, and New Thought all began there before spreading worldwide. If for a moment we accept the channels' belief that they have been chosen to give a message to the world, perhaps their control-lers are sensible to use English. But we are still left with the problem that supposedly wise, even omniscient entities cannot agree with one another. They all go on about the "Fatherhood of God and the Brotherhood of Man," the God Within, and the empowerment of the individual, but the devil is in the details. Our investigation of what the channels have to say about human origins, lost lands and races, cataclysms, and prehistoric high civilizations reveals a glaring lack of consensus. It also uncovers some of the entangled roots that feed these exotic growths.

We will begin in that fertile period of the 1880s, in which Spiritualism, hitherto the dominant alternative religion, felt its foundations sapped by Theosophy and occultism.

OAHSPE: A KOSMON BIBLE

This famous work was published in 1882.[2] There is no mystery about its origin, which was explained the following year in a letter to the Spiritualist journal *The Banner of Light*. John Ballou Newbrough (1828–1891) was a dentist in New York City, an educated man, who gives a clear and self-aware account of his experience:

> Briefly, then, Oahspe was mechanically written through my hands
> by some other intelligence than my own. Many spiritualists are
> acquainted with this automatic movement of the hands, independ-
> ent of one's volition. There are thousands and thousands of persons

who have this quality. It can also be educated, or rather, the susceptibility to external power can be increased. In my own case I discovered, many years ago, in sitting in circles to obtain spiritual manifestations, that my hands could not lie on the table without flying off into these "tantrums." Often they would write messages, left or right, backward or forward, nor could I control them in any other way than by withdrawing from the table. Sometimes the power thus baffled would attack my tongue, or my eyes, or my ears, and I talked and saw and heard differently from my normal state.[3]

Like Emanuel Swedenborg, who was peremptorily ordered to "Eat less food!" before the heavenly arcana were opened to him, Newbrough made a complete reform of his habits. He gave up all stimulants, became a vegan, rose early, bathed in cold water, and after six years of this regime had lost seventy pounds.

Then a new condition of control came upon my hands; instead of the angels holding my hands as formerly, they held their hands over my head (and they were clothed with sufficient materiality for me to see them) and a light fell upon my hands as they lay on the table. In the meantime I had attained to hear audible angel voices near me. I was directed to get a typewriter, which writes by keys, like a piano. This I did, and I applied myself industriously to learn it, but with only indifferent success.

It took him two more years to master the typewriter. Then in 1880–1881, over fifty weeks of daily dictation (not affecting his dental practice), the *Oahspe* book came through. Newbrough was forbidden to read any of it until it was finished. Was he surprised to discover that he had written hundreds of pages in the following vein?

Hear My voice, O ye H'monkensoughts, of millions of years standing, and managers of corporeal worlds! I have proclaimed the uz and hiss of the red star in her pride and glory. Send word abroad in the high-way of Plumf'goe to the great high Gods, Miantaf in the etherean vortices of Bain, and to Rome and to Nesh'outoza and Du'ji.[4]

No one, to my knowledge, has made an objective study of *Oahspe,* though it has sold consistently and even given rise to a small cult, the Faithists.[5] The first books (it is divided into "books," like the Bible) are mostly in an exultant tone as they tell of precosmic happenings among the gods and angelic hosts. There is much coming and going in "ships of fire," glorious pageants that seem less like anything in Western literature than like Hindu theophanies, with their *crores* of gods and goddesses, multicolored radiances, heavenly orchestras of gandharvas, and so on. Whatever generated this material had a powerful imagination and an incapacity for boredom. Some chapters are filled with names and numbers that make the "ship catalog" of Homer's *Iliad* seem succinct.

In *Oahspe*'s cosmogony, as in Lurianic Kabbalah, there have been multiple creations, some of them failures. In conformity with Spiritualism, the purpose of life on earth is to generate mortal beings worthy of progressing to the heavenly spheres, and at each epoch the god or goddess in charge of the earth tallies up the "harvest of souls." The universe is run like a bureaucracy, with hierarchies of administrators and incessant council meetings. God even wields a gavel to call them to order![6] Beneath the gods are orders of spirits, good and evil, who fasten onto mortals. The whole system is coherent according to its own rules, and this coherence extends to its scientific theories that deny gravity and magnetism in favor of "vortices."

Among the gems worth extracting from the dross is this verse, rightly singled out in the *Encyclopaedia of Religion and Ethics:*

And Jehovih caused the earth, and the family of the sun to travel in an orbit, the circuit of which requireth of them four million seven hundred thousand years. And he placed in the line of the orbit, at distances of three thousand years, etherean lights, the which places, as the earth passeth through, angels from the second heaven come

into its corporeal presence. As Embassadors they come, in compa-
nies of hundreds and thousands and tens of thousands, and these are
called the etherean hosts of the Most High.[7]

We can make two associations, one scientific, the other not, that
would not have occurred to earlier readers. That the sun has its own
orbit accords with the later discovery of its revolution, and consequently
that of the solar system, around the galactic center. Secondly, those
familiar with the "alien intervention" or "ancient astronaut" theory will
recall that in the books of Zecharia Sitchin, the Twelfth Planet comes
close to Earth every 3,600 years, and thereupon the Nefilim descend
to intervene in human affairs.[8] These are the sort of coincidences that
occur in studying channeled works, and I have no idea of how significant they are.

Other details that correlate with the lingua franca of Atlantology are
a theory of races, less color-based than most of those we have seen. *Oahspe*
is closer to the present-day theory that there have been multiple species
of hominids, of which one eventually became dominant.[9] There is, naturally, an Atlantis episode, but it is placed on an island occupying most
of the western Pacific, called Pan or Whaga. The map supplied does not
resemble Leadbeater's and Scott-Elliot's Lemuria, but rather anticipates
Churchward's Mu. *Oahspe* tells us little about the ways of the Whagans
for good or ill, only that they had become degenerate.

> Now it had come to pass on earth that the time of a generation of
> mortals had risen from twelve years to eighty years. And there were
> many who lived to be three hundred years old. And they had become
> very large; twice the size of men of this day. But they were without
> judgment and of little sense. Hardly knew they their own species.
> And they mingled together, relatives as well as others; so that idiocy
> and disease were the general fate of the tribes of men; and they were
> large and strong and prolific.[10]

From the point of view of the celestial bureaucracy, there was only one solution. Like Zeus in Plato's story, Jehovih called a council of the gods and lodged his complaint before them.

How can ye bequeath the administration of the earth and her heaven to the earth-born, till she is made suitable as a gift from My hand? Now hear Me, O My sons and daughters: Five great divisions [continents] of the earth have I made, and they have all been inhabited over and tilled by mortals. Yea, on all the divisions of the earth have there been great cities and nations, and men and women of great learning. And as oft as they are raised up in light, so are they again cast down in darkness, because of the great desire of the spirits of the dead to return back to the earth. These druj [spirits uninterested in progress, who stay on earth] return to mortals and fasten upon them as fetals [unborn children?] or as familiars, and inspire them to evil. Go now to the earth, O My beloved, and find the division of the earth where most of these druj congregate, for I will uproot their stronghold; I will break them from their haunts and they shall no longer carry My people down to destruction.

And now the council deliberated, and after a while caused the records of the earth and her atmospherea to be examined, and they discovered that the heaven of the land of Whaga (Pan) was beyond redemption because of the great numbers of the spirits of the cannibals and of the multitude of fetals. It was as if a disease in the flesh be healed over externally, leaving the root of the disease within. So was Whaga and her heaven; the redemption of the cycles remained not with her, but evil broke out forever in a new way.

So Jehovih said: Now will I prune the earth and her heaven. Behold, the division of Whaga shall be hewn off and cast beneath the waters of the ocean. Her heaven shall be no longer tenable by the spirits of destruction, for I will rend the foundation thereof and scatter them in the winds of heaven. Go ye, therefore, down to the earth and provide nets and vanchas [not defined] for receiving the spirits of darkness, and for receiving the spirits of mortals who shall perish in the waters. And provide ye a place in My exalted heavens suitable for them; and ye shall wall them about in heaven that they cannot escape, but that they may be weaned from evil. And when ye are come to the earth and its heavens, acquaint My God and his Lords with My decree. And say to them: Thus saith Jehovih: Behold, behold, I will sink the land of Whaga beneath the waters of the ocean, and her heaven will I carry away to a place in My firmament, where she shall no longer engulf My people in darkness. And Jehovih saith: Go thou, O God of heaven, and thou, O Lord of Whaga, down to My chosen, the I'hins [the superior race], and say to them: Thus saith the Great Spirit: Behold, behold, I will sink the lands of the earth beneath the ocean, because of the evil of the spirits of darkness. Hear Me, O My chosen, and heed My commandments: Fall to, all hands, and build ships in all places, even in the valleys and on the mountains, and let My faithful gather together within the ships, for My hand is surely stretched over the earth.[11]

The heavy work was entrusted to Aph, son of Jehovih. He assembled a fleet of 250,000 etherean fire-ships in a line from Chinvat (near the moon) down to Earth. Then "every ship was contracted ten thousand fold, which was the force required to break the crust of the earth and sink a continent."[12] Beforehand he had constructed a special tube to allow the 24,400 million souls thus released to rise to the etherean regions. With a humanitarian concern that I have seen nowhere else in the literature, care was taken that women with babies who died in the cataclysm should be reunited and given a new home.[13] For all that the book borrows from the Old Testament, *Oahspe*'s gods are touchingly benevolent: Universalists, perhaps, if not Unitarians. For example, on another occasion evil spirits, fairies living in caves and waterfalls, and "lusters" that haunt battlefields and old castles were troubling the earth, and it needed to be purged of them. The solution was to ship them off to another planet, where they could have their own kingdom and god and be educated to become better cosmic citizens.[14]

Two years before the cataclysm, angels had warned the few "faithists" of Pan and told them to build boats. This was not just Noah's Ark: 12,420 escaped. Some landed in Ja-pan (the only part of Pan remaining), others on the other continents, from which they peopled the world.

The rest of this fascinating book does not concern us, except for a single detail occurring much later, where it is said, "Every portion of the earth hath been to the east, to the west, to the north and to the south. Which is proven in the rocks, and boulders, and mountains of the earth."[15] This seems to refer to the wandering of the poles, or alternatively to the changing angle of the axis of rotation, which several of our authors have proposed as agents of epochal change. We will hear William Colville's "inspirational lecture" touch on it, but before continuing with our theme, a word needs to be said about the channeled work that most resembles *Oahspe: The Urantia Book.*[16]

The origins of *Urantia* are less clear-cut, but the source was probably a trance medium called William Custer Kellogg, whose information, given out in the 1920s, was edited for publication by William Sadler, a physician.[17] It was not published until 1955, but it belongs with the rash of channeled works from the period between the two world wars. The themes shared with our other sources include a celestial bureaucracy that oversees events throughout the universe; an explanation of the origins of humans and apes (from mutations in opposite directions) and of the differently colored races (here including green, indigo, and blue); the evolution of consciousness and language; Noah's Flood (just a river overflow); the origins of Egyptian civilization and of the Nordic race (both very much played down). The *Urantia Book* has a strong contribution from early twentieth-century science and a 700-page biography of Jesus, but nothing about Atlantis, Lemuria, Hyperborea, Mu, or even Whaga.

PHYLOS THE TIBETAN

A year or two after *Oahspe*'s publication, a seventeen-year-old Californian, Frederick S. Oliver (1866–1899), found himself in a similar predicament to that of Dr. Newbrough. A mysterious preceptor began instructing him through "mental talks," which in the course of a year became so overwhelming that he told his parents about them. Far from reacting as most parents would today, they formed a circle in which Oliver would repeat what his preceptor said to him. He also wrote it down, edited it under his preceptor's guidance, and by 1886 had produced the manuscript that would be posthumously published as *A Dweller on Two Planets,* by "Phylos the Tibetan."[18] In his preface, Oliver wrote:

> In these days of doubt, materialism, and even rank atheism, it requires all the courage I possess to assert, in clear unequivocal terms, that the following book, *A Dweller on Two Planets,* is absolute revelation; that I do not believe myself its Author—but that one of those mysterious persons, if my readers choose to so consider him, an adept of the arcane and occult in the universe, better understood from reading this book, is the Author. Such is the fact. The book was revealed to me, a boy, and a boy, too, whose parents were mistakenly lenient to such a degree that he was allowed to do as he chose in most things. Not lacking in inclination to study, but very lacking in will-power, continuity and energy, I gained little in educational triumphs, and was pointedly criticised by my teacher as "lackadaisical, even lazy." Hence, when a little past seventeen years of age, "Phylos, the Esoterist," took me actively in charge, designing to make me his instrument to the world, that profound adept showed what seems to me a rare faith, for I was without any solid education, as generally so considered, was minus any special religious trend, and for my sole commendation, had willingness, love of the remarkable, and an uncolored mind.[19]

Phylos's story is set in 11,160 BCE (92) in a well-governed, socialistic society under an elected emperor. We presume that it is in the Atlantic Ocean, and later editions confirm this with maps. The architecture is stupendous, and we are assured that it was built without slave labor. Instead of the gold commonly lavished on the Atlantean cityscape, this one uses the wonderful metal aluminum, which is made out of clay by an advanced technical process (85). Atlantean technology uses the "Night-Side forces" of gravitation, the sun, and light (48). Public transport includes electro-odic trains and airships for hire (50). There is wireless transmission of sound, images, and heat (66).*

On the cultural front, higher education is open to all irrespective of race, color, or sex at the institution called the Great Xioquithlon (28). Criminals are cured through mesmerism, or in extreme cases by magnetic applications to phrenological points (98). The Atlanteans' religion is "virtually Essenianism" (90), with an explicit division between exoteric and esoteric. There is a kind of nonidolatrous solar cult.

Lemuria is merely one of many colonies founded by the Atlanteans. Part of it remains as Australia, the rest having perished in the same cataclysm as Atlantis (84). The native Lemurians are an uncivilized, brutish folk (408). On the other hand there are civilizations contemporary with Atlantis called Suern and Necropan that lack high technology but possess superior occult powers. The Atlanteans would never dare attack them, because physical weaponry is no match for the thought-power of the Suernian adepts (107–8). Later Atlantis followed them in some respects but not in others: "One by one the scholars found that those things which had always been possible only through mechanical contrivance were more easily accomplished by purely psychic means; they learned it was possible to divest themselves of the flesh, and in astral body go whither they would and appear, instant as the electric current, at any distance" (411–12). This led to a neglect of the technology that had sustained Atlantean civilization and to a widening rift between the "scholars" and the masses. Left without guidance, the latter degenerated into superstition and sacrifice of animals and eventually humans, along with every other vice (404). A Noah's Ark story follows, in which one man is warned of the coming cataclysm, builds a ship, loads it with animals, and joins up with pockets

---

*Page numbers in parentheses are from *A Dweller on Two Planets.*

of survivors whom he finds in other lands. The book ends with the usual warning as the author issues a final call to America, the new Atlantis: "Will it meet similar woe?" (417).

All through *A Dweller on Two Planets* are references to events such as the War of Secession, the discovery of Pompeii, even to Cornell University (notable at the time for coeducation). There is a strong sense of the American landscape and its geology, many quotations from the English poets, and a substratum of Spiritualist and Theosophical ideas. In accordance with these, the individual is a compound of physical, psychic, and spiritual elements, of which the "I Am" or ego is the highest (224). Evolution (89) and reincarnation (72) are taken for granted, and there is even mention of the Theosophical system of Rounds (349). A long section is set in the state between rebirths, called the Summerland (in Spiritualist terminology) or Devachan (in Theosophy). All this is enclosed within an esoteric Christianity whose principle is expressed as follows: "Will is the sole Way to esoteric, or occult Christian knowledge. Whosoever will, shall have Eternal Life. But the *will* to overcome must replace our will of desire, as the fresh air replaces the exhalations of our lung" (189).

The other planet of the title is Venus, which Phylos visits in his spiritual body. He goes there after induction into an esoteric society that lives inside Mount Shasta, which was about thirty miles southeast of the home of the Olivers in Yreka. This excerpt gives a flavor of the whole:

> What secrets perchance are about us? We do not know as we lie there, our bodies resting, our souls filled with peace, nor do we know until many years are passed out through the back door of time that that tall basalt cliff conceals a doorway. We do not suspect this, nor that a long tunnel stretches away, far into the interior of majestic Shasta. Wholly unthought is it that there lie at the tunnel's far end vast apartments, the home of a mystic brotherhood, whose occult arts hollowed that tunnel and mysterious dwelling: "Sach" the name is. Are you incredulous as to these things? Go there, or suffer yourself to be taken as I was, once! See, as I saw, not with the vision

of flesh, the walls, polished as by jewelers, though excavated as by giants; floors carpeted with long, fleecy gray fabric that looked like fur, but was a mineral product; ledges intersected by the builders, and in their wonderful polish exhibiting veinings of gold, of silver, of green copper ores, and maculations of precious stones. [248]

I can accept Oliver's account of how his channeling began, but the waters are muddied by the long interval between revelation in 1883–86 and publication in 1905. *A Dweller on Two Planets* is written in the heavy style of a didactic novel, reaching its nadir in a long romantic episode. This, together with all the topical references, suggests input from the more conscious levels of someone's mind. The fact that at the time of writing, Frederick was surveying the boundaries of the mining claim of the Olivers,[20] and that the first thing the hero of the novel does is to strike gold, is rather telling.

In 1899, the year of Oliver's early death, the work was framed with an "Amanuensis' Preface" and a "Note by the Author." In the first, Oliver describes the manner of writing, which involved many drafts, rewritings, and rearrangements of the text. He assures us that the manuscript was finished in 1886, though he does admit that it was (afterward?) "thoroughly edited by a literary expert." He is keen to establish priority in describing, as Atlantean technology, things as yet unknown such as X-rays and the application of electricity to the telescope, which by the time of publication had become fact. Oliver was apparently still in contact with Phylos, for the source appears at the end to announce that publication of the book has deliberately been delayed so that prophecy can be fulfilled, and to issue his warning to America, now at the end of the Sixth Cycle: "Stand from under! Get into the shelter of that Cross" (420). One wonders at Phylos's popping up again after thirteen years' silence. The book was finally published under the care of Oliver's mother, and unless the manuscript is discovered, there is no telling what she may have done to it.

None of this matters much to our studies, but I have set out the facts because of the book's influence on later channeled material. Four points to note are the importance of America at this point of cyclical history; Mount Shasta as its spiritual center; travel by spaceship; and inhabitants of Venus concerned with earthly affairs. While Lemuria is mentioned, there is no sign of the mysterious Theosophical teachings about ethereal androgynes, the Lunar Pitris, the division into sexes, and so on. Phylos's Lemurians and Atlanteans, like his Venusians, resemble ourselves, only cleverer, or more brutish, as the case may be.

AN INSPIRATIONAL LECTURE

Another example from the same year is utterly different in style and content, though its manner of delivery—inspired speech—may have been similar to that of Frederick Oliver in his family circle. The channel here is William Juvenal Colville (1862–1917), who, early in his career as a prolific Spiritualist medium and writer, gave an inspirational lecture on *The Lost Continent of Atlantis* (1884). Of him Emma Harding Britten wrote: "*Petite* in person, and with no special educational or natural advantages, this young gentleman when on the rostrum and under control of his Spirit friends, is capable of dealing with, and mastering any point of science, metaphysics, or history, that may be spontaneously presented to him."[21] Emma herself was noted for this talent.

According to Colville, the end of Atlantis was due to a fact in the history of the earth, described as

a change in the polar axis, gradually brought about through long periods of time, and reaching a culmination at the close of every grand cycle of over 25,000 years. These vast periods of time, during which mighty changes and upheavals are outwrought, were computed by the Ancients with the same accuracy as that which attends your determining the solar year, which you know to be between 365 and 366 days. The grand year of the Pleiades occupies nearly 26,000 years of earthly time, during which the Sun accomplishes its journey through the twelve zodiacal signs. . . . During half the cycle, the south pole advances and the north pole retreats; during the other half, the south pole retreats and the north pole advances. At the present time the North Pole is slowly, but surely, creeping toward you, while the South Pole is retreating. The equator is travelling southward, and therefore, in northern latitudes the climate is steadily becoming more and more inhospitable. Certain scientists deny this.[22]

Colville, or his inspirer, says that there are strong reasons to believe Donnelly. He cites Allan Kardec, Volney, and Plato, and suggests that Bulwer-Lytton's futuristic novel *The Coming Race* can be read as a picture of the *past*. Colville's Atlanteans had aerial navigation, had outgrown warfare, and worshiped the All-Good. They knew no poverty or disease, but when the time came they were prepared to quit the earth and for their spirits to be transported to another planet. Their land sank somewhat over 11,000 years ago, whereupon some survivors came to Egypt.

Most of this is standard stuff, requiring only familiarity with half a dozen books such as *Isis Unveiled*. We could give Colville the benefit of the doubt and say that it came from his unconscious. The one originality is the matter of cycles. Obviously the 25,000- or 26,000-year cycle is the precessional one, and Colville gives a date of 11,000 years ago for its last culmination. He then calculates in epochs of 2,150 years, pointing out that we are at the dawn of the sixth epoch of the present cycle. Thereupon "the world will attain to a civilization matchless in its importance and results" and give to the northern hemisphere a power and supremacy unknown to the Ancients.[23] (Compare Phylos and *Oahspe*'s prophecies.) However, Colville or his inspirer sees the precessional cycle as accompanied by a slippage of the earth's surface relative to its axis of rotation. If this is what is meant, the equator cannot just "travel southward." If it moves to the south on one side of the globe, it must move north on the opposite side. Likewise, the retreating and advancing of poles is a relative matter: if the North Pole is moving toward England, it will be moving away from Japan, and no generalizations can be made about the

Northern Hemisphere. Eventually the movement would deliver Colville's audience (whether English or American) to the North Pole itself, not a propitious place for civilization. In short, his inspirers have not thought the matter through, and neither has he, on allowing it to be printed! But whether inspired, invented, or regurgitated by the unconscious mind, his lecture points to an interest in astrological ages and their connection with geophysical cycles. It was also timely. The year 1884 was also the year in which the Hermetic Brotherhood of Luxor began its public work, which included readings on exactly this topic.

The early 1880s are a fascinating period for students of modern occultism. A number of different groups had looked forward to 1881 as marking the end of the world, or, after the event, as beginning a new era (see chapter 12). In 1882, Donnelly's book on Atlantis drew the public mind to our subject as never before, and as though in response, information poured forth. Beside the examples of *Oahspe* and Phylos, these were the years of the Mahatma Letters (see chapter 3) and A. P. Sinnett's books based on them. I would not be surprised if our next example also dated from this decade, though its publication was somewhat later.

RĬN-GÄ'-SĔ NŬD SЇ-Ї-KĔL'ZĒ

Meaning "links and cycles," this is one of over 3,000 terms of prehistoric and nonhistoric nomenclature revealed by Alem Prolex, one of four Atlantean spirits who provided data for J. Ben Leslie's book, *Submerged Atlantis Restored, or Rĭn-gä'-sĕ nŭd Sї-ї-kĕl'zē. Links and Cycles: A Short Treatise on the Over-Spirit as the Cycle Supreme* (1911). The spirits communicated through clairvoyant and clairaudient methods, giving two-thirds of this material at private séances through Mrs. C. C. Van-Duzee. The remainder was received directly by Mr. Leslie from a Phoenician spirit named Kū-lī-ú'thüs.[24]

Thus Leslie sets the scene for a book monstrous not so much in size (for our field contains even longer works, alas) as in the old sense of something unnatural or malformed. Its 805 pages, peppered with these outrageous terms, must have been a compositor's nightmare. There are maps, alphabets, Atlantean musical notation, and, not least, photographs of the recipients. Mr. Leslie looks like a normal businessman, while the rather older Mrs. Van-Duzee (b. 1828) is typecast for the role of Mrs. Grundy, her sour expression framed in lace and bombazine. Some of her material came in long, unrhymed lines, like Walt Whitman at his worst. I cannot imagine how she dictated the 3,000 terms, peppered with diacritics, or how anyone could have taken the thing seriously.

The work begins in Swedenborgian style with a matter-of-fact account of the principles of the universe, the qualities of the planets, and the spirits' progress thereon. Then it moves to Atlantis. We learn that 22,000 years ago, a large portion of it, called Lost Lontidri, was submerged. Then 3,125 years later there began a series of ten mighty convulsions that changed the land and sea, but the main portion of Atlantis lasted until it was washed away in the final convulsion, 16,500 years ago.[25]

The rest of the book is filled with information on every aspect of Atlantis. First come its ceremonies, plants, trees, animals, and birds, and there are few surprises there. Then come its alphabet and punctuation (suspiciously like English), its calendar and architecture. Here the spirits insert some information about Egypt, whose greatest glory was from 12,000 B.C.E. to 10,000 BCE. The building of pyramids started when that civilization was already in decline; the Step Pyramid of Saqqara was begun after 6000 BCE, the Pyramid of Cheops in 4000 BCE.[26] (This, incidentally, reverses the usual occult order, which prefers to put the Great Pyramid or the three Giza pyramids first, built by Atlanteans, then the rest of them built by the Egyptians as poor imitations.) The spirits, or the author, did not stop at that. They go on for pages, telling the entire history of architecture from the Egyptians up to the present day. Then they move on to printing, which the Atlanteans invented a few years before the last convulsion. They even had metal type, made by electrically driven machines.[27] This leads into a potted history of world literature up to the present day; then we move on to Atlantean music. Curiously enough, their notation was just like ours, only with different signs for the note values, clefs, accidentals, and so on. The Atlanteans had a great music factory that turned out many odd types of instruments, which deserve more attention than I can give them here.[28] A history of music follows, culminating with Franz Liszt, then it is the turn of painting, sculpture, flags, religions, social structure, costume, ethnology, migrations, and a general course in geography. After treating China, the rest of Asia, North America, and Mexico, the exhausted author apologizes: he has had to leave out South America because the book is already too long. And there it ends.

Having no independent information on J. Ben Leslie, I suspect that he was a Rochester businessman who, on the one hand, could finance this expensive project (published by the specialist house of the Rev. Benjamin Fish Austin), and on the other was so culturally ignorant as to fill it up with extracts from popular encyclopedias. He somewhat resembles his contemporary Cyrus Teed, owner of mop-making factories in nearby Syracuse and Utica, who founded the religion of Koreshanity on the belief that the earth is a concave sphere. Another parallel is with *Oahspe*. Without attributing any veracity to either book, I do see a patent difference in quality. Some channeled works, like Leslie's, are obviously rubbish; others may still be rubbish, but are works of art. However boring, displeasing, or absurd (like some works of art I could name), they have style, consistency, and form. There is an intelligence behind them. The question is whose intelligence it is, whether that of the channel or partly or wholly external to him or her. The latter possibility is intolerable to the skeptic, while the religious fundamentalist knows that it's the devil's work!

EDGAR CAYCE

The gentle Edgar Cayce (1877–1945) was a fundamentalist Christian when he began his trance channeling in 1901, and for a time he wrestled with doubts over what was speaking through him. He was more disconcerted still when the "Source" started talking about people's past lives, a concept repugnant to Christian orthodoxy, but with the Source's help he was able to reconcile even this with biblical authority. Reincarnation also turned out to be his road to Atlantis.

When people consulted Cayce for readings, the Source often mentioned former incarnations that were responsible for, or at least explained, their present difficulties. Beginning in 1923, Cayce gave the first of around 2,500 life readings, "whose single purpose was to define and describe a person's present incarnation in relation to previous lives."[29] Over the next twenty years, no fewer than 700 of these mentioned a former life in Atlantis. Nor were these vague references. Cayce's son Edgar Evans, who was the subject of the first life reading, tabulates them according to whether the person lived at the period of the first, second, or third destruction.[30]

Another path to Atlantis lay through Cayce's lesser-known work for patrons who used his readings for stock market investment, treasure hunting, and oil prospecting.[31] In 1927 he himself went to Bimini on a hunt for buried gold, and a reading from that period identified the island as the location of a temple of the "Poseidians," that is, Atlanteans.

Finally, in 1932, to satisfy the curiosity of his son and others, Cayce consented to give a series of thirteen readings specifically on the past. It is not helpful to quote directly from these because the Source employs a tangled syntax, full of archaisms and circumlocutions. We begin by summarizing its version of anthropogenesis:[32]

+ The first ancestors of humanity were sexless spiritual entities, with the ability to project forms into the physical world.
+ The physical world had already evolved as far as the animal kingdom. The spiritual entities, curious to experience physical life, projected physical forms that were monstrosities. This resulted in evolutionary chaos and alienation from God for the spiritual entities caught within those bodies.
+ A being called Amilius (later identified as the Christ Consciousness) took matters in hand and projected a more suitable vehicle for spiritual entities to inhabit: the human one.

+ Humans appeared on earth in five places simultaneously: the Yellow race in the Gobi, the White in the Carpathians, the Red in the Atlantean and American lands, the Brown in the Andes, and the Black in Africa. This occurred more than 10,500,000 years ago.

One of the most impressive things about Cayce's Atlantean dicta is their consistency. It enables his followers and scholars to collate readings from years apart and reconstruct a coherent history from them. Drawing on these, we continue:

+ The five races were the "Sons of God" mentioned in the Bible. The "Daughters of Men" with whom they made the mistake of mating were the monstrous forms left from the early projections. The result was a race of hybrids.
+ Early on in Atlantean civilization, a difference arose concerning these hybrids. One group, "Children of the Law of One," wanted to keep the human race pure but help the hybrids regain their position as creatures of God. The other group, "Sons of Belial," believed in sensual gratification alone and treated the hybrids as "things" or slaves.[33]
+ Atlantis became a great civilization with high technology, some of it in advance of our own. This included airships that could also become submarines, a "firestone" that gathered cosmic energy, and a crystal that used both solar and geothermal power.[34]
+ Lemuria, also called Mu, was a continent in the Pacific Ocean whose westernmost portion was the coast of South America. It disappeared before Atlantis in a series of cataclysms lasting 200,000 years.[35]
+ Atlantis itself disappeared in three separate cataclysms around 50,000 BCE, 28,000 BCE, and 10,000 BCE.
+ The first of these followed the use of advanced technology for destructive purposes, to exterminate the enormous carnivorous

animals that were overrunning the earth. These were the result of creation by the "sons of men," who had lost control over them.[36] God changed the poles, and the animals were destroyed, along with part of Atlantis.[37]

+ The second destruction was preceded by struggles between the two factions. Followers of the Law of One emigrated to Peru, the Yucatan, Nevada, Colorado, the Pyrenees, and Egypt. The cataclysm of 28,000 BCE was caused by misuse of the firestone by turning its power up too high. It was probably accompanied, again, by a pole shift and a change in climate.[38]

+ During the last period of Atlantis, Egypt reached a high level of civilization. The pyramids and Sphinx were built around 10,500 BCE by Ra Ta (a past incarnation of Cayce), levitating the stones through the application of occult laws.[39]

+ Ra Ta also built two temples, the Temple of Sacrifice and the Temple of Beauty. The latter was devoted to the arts and crafts, and the Temple of Sacrifice to genetic improvement by removing the animal components from those who still had them. "These bodies gradually lost, then, feathers from their legs. . . . Many began to lose their tails, or protuberances in various forms. Many paws or claws were changed to hand and foot."[40]

+ On Poseidia, the last remaining island, the two factions continued in strife, and the Sons of Belial instituted oppressive government. Some of the followers of the Law of One, seeing the coming cataclysm, escaped, making the first transatlantic flights as well as sailing to various safe lands.[41]

+ As its end approached, Atlantis was a morass of violence and depravity. Crystal power was used for coercion and torture. There was human sacrifice, and [reading between the lines] the hybrids were used for sexual purposes. The third and final destruction took place through gigantic land upheavals and was complete by 9500 BCE.[42]

Not many people were aware of Cayce's Atlantean readings until the 1960s, when a wave of interest in alternative spiritualities drew attention to him. In 1940 his Source had said: "Poseidia will be among the first portions of Atlantis to rise again—expect it in '68 and '69—not so far away!"[43] The discovery in 1968 of the "Bimini Road" seemed to fulfil the prophecy, and controversy continues over whether the underwater row of giant stone blocks is natural or man-made.[44] Predictably, those studying Cayce's readings divided into the debunkers and the true believers. Only with the publications of Sidney Kirkpatrick and Paul Johnson (see endnotes 29 and 34) did a middle ground appear, allowing for possibilities beyond those of materialism but not making a religion out of the readings.

From Cayce's point of view, the readings on the past were a minor distraction from his life's calling of helping people with problems of body, mind, and soul. Besides his own altruism, wearing himself out in response to overwhelming demand for readings, the Source deserves respect. Much of its medical and psychological advice was ahead of its time, in a good sense. As Paul Johnson writes, "Edgar Cayce played a pivotal role in the transition from New Thought healing to the New Age holistic health movement."[45]

This makes it all the more problematic when the Source's history of the past is transparently borrowed from contemporary Atlantology.

Cayce was not an intellectual or much of a reader—though, significantly, he had read *A Dweller on Two Planets*[46]—but once his extraordinary gift was known, he was consulted by many an educated Theosophist and New Thought type. Paul Johnson draws some conclusions from this that might apply to some of our other subjects.

This range of plausibility indicates that whatever genuine information might have come through Cayce was heavily contaminated with materials from unreliable sources. Chief among these seems to be Madame Blavatsky's *The Secret Doctrine,* with its scheme of root-races and great Lemurian and Atlantean civilizations. Cayce appears to have adopted much of the anthropogenesis of Blavatsky without having read her work, which seems most likely to have occurred due to the belief of many of the readings' recipients in Theosophy or its derivatives. Through conversation and correspondence if not through telepathy, Cayce acquired a striking amount of Blavatskianism. Like her, he asserts that human souls descended into bodies that had been gradually evolved for that purpose, and that after this occurrence humans mated with animals, producing viable but monstrous offspring.[47]

While the "monstrous offspring" and the activities of the Temple of Sacrifice are discreetly ignored, Cayce's other revelations about ancient Egypt have had a considerable impact. The Association for Research and Enlightenment (A.R.E., the foundation that carries on Cayce's work) has funded archaeological projects in Egypt and helped the careers of the Egyptologists Mark Lehner and Zahi Hawass.[48] Cayce devotees are close followers of the New Archaeology and still hope for a payback in the promised discovery of the Hall of Records beneath the Sphinx of Giza.

MOUNT SHASTA AGAIN

Phylos's myth of Mount Shasta was tailor-made for cult leaders working the West Coast.[49] We have already mentioned Edgar Lucien Larkin (1847–1924), an astronomer with mystical inclinations (see chapter 8). In 1913 he published an editorial in *The San Francisco Examiner* that asserted the truth of Atlantis and paraphrased Oliver's account of Mount Shasta.[50] In the year after the astronomer's death, Harvey Spencer Lewis (writing as "Selvius") published an article in the magazine of his Rosicrucian order (AMORC).[51] The bibliography compiled by the nearby College of the Siskiyous calls this "the single most important document in the establishment of the modern Mt. Shasta-Lemuria myth" and quotes the following passage from Lewis: "Even no less a careful investigator and scientist than Prof. Edgar Luci[e]n Larkin, for many years director of Mt. Lowe Observatory, said in newspaper and magazine articles that he had seen, on many occasions, the great temple of this mystic village, while gazing through a long-distance telescope. He finally learned enough facts to warrant his announcement that it was the last vestige of the works of the Lemurians." The bibliographer adds that no such statement by Larkin exists. Lewis repeated most of the article in the book already treated in chapter 8, *Lemuria: The Lost Continent*. After that there was no going back.

The rumor of Mount Shasta as an active spiritual center surviving from Lemurian times was thus circulating in esoteric and Rosicrucian circles by the time the mining engineer Guy Warren Ballard (1878– 1939) was hiking on its slopes in 1930. In his book *Unveiled Mysteries*,[52] authored under the symbolic pseudonym Godfré Ray King, he writes of his unexpected encounter there with the "ascended master" Comte de Saint-Germain, who takes his spiritual education in hand. Ballard is shown his past lives and scenes from history. He journeys in "projected consciousness" to the Sahara, and to a series of locations in the Americas including the Grand Tetons, Yellowstone, the land of the Incas, buried cities of the Amazon, and a secret valley in Arizona. In the most baroque scene of all, a group of handsome Venusians is entertained in an under-ground complex beneath Royal Teton Mountain. Everywhere the narrator goes, transcendent experiences are joined with moral lessons and messages to the human race.[53]

As such works go, *Unveiled Mysteries* is among the more readable and intriguing. The influences that stand out are those of Theosophy, *Oahspe*, *A Dweller on Two Planets*, Phelon, Churchward, and Cervé's *Lemuria*. There is also Masonic symbolism and a possible Rosicrucian subtext (evoking the *Chemical Wedding of Christian Rosenkreuz*). The motiva-tion behind it was the same as caused Spencer Lewis to write a book on Lemuria, a seemingly incongruous subject for a Rosicrucian. It was to cre-ate an esoteric order that would appeal to Americans: one whose sacred sites and living masters were not in Egypt, Tibet, or even in Europe, but in America itself.

Here is the account of Atlantis, which Ballard witnesses in a sort of cin-ema where the Akashic Records can be projected on a screen (an updated version of Phylos's "blackboard"). The punctuation, if little else, is original.

The first scenes portrayed the continent of "Mu"—the activity and accomplishment of its people, and the height to which that civilization attained. This covered a period of thousands of years. Then came events that surely must have been—a reign of terror—to the inhabitants of that land. A cataclysm occurred which tore the surface of the earth—until all collapsed within itself. The ancient land of Mu sank beneath the waves—of what is now the Pacific Ocean. . . . Next, came the growth to beauty, wisdom, and power of Atlantis, a great continent covering a large part of what is now the Atlantic Ocean. At that time, there existed solid land between Central America and what today is Europe. The things accomplished in that age—were tremendous—but again the people's misuse—of the Mighty God Energy—overwhelmed them and, as things were thrown more and more out of balance—the tearing apart of the earth's surface by cataclysmic action was re-experienced.

It left but a small remnant of Atlantis—merely an island in mid-ocean—cut off from close contact with the rest of the civilized world. The east and west portions of the land had sunk beneath the Atlantic Ocean—leaving only the island called Poseidonis. It had been the heart of the then known civilized world, and preparation was made—to protect and preserve—its most important activities—as a central focus—to carry forward certain unfinished work. In that period very great attainment was reached both—spiritually and materially.

The mechanical development of this cycle reached a very high state of achievement, and one of its most remarkable expressions was the perfection of their aerial navigation. The air-transportation of our modern life is—as yet—very crude and primitive—compared to what was then on Atlantis. . . . A large portion of these people became aware of the—Great Inner God Power—within the individual but as before—the human side of their nature or outer activities again usurped—the Great Energy. Selfishness and misuse of this transcendent wisdom and power gained the ascendency to even

greater height than before. The Masters of the Ancient Wisdom—
saw the people were building another destructive momentum—and
that a third cataclysm was threatening. They warned the inhabitants—again and again as previously—but only those who served the
"Light" gave heed.

Great buildings were constructed—of imperishable material—
where records were placed—that have been preserved through the
centuries. These remain in a state of perfect preservation—now—on
the bed of the Atlantic Ocean—hermetically sealed. They will be
brought to the light of day—by the Great Ones—who directed their
preparation—and control their protection.

In them are recorded humanity's advance and accomplishment of
that period, so there has been no permanent loss to mankind of the
activities of the Atlantean civilization. . . . As time goes on indisput-
able proof—of its existence and the height of its attainment—will
be revealed by oceanography, geology, and other scientific data.[54]

After this, Ballard declared himself to be the Messenger of the Great
White Brotherhood for the Seventh Golden Age. Returning to his base
in Chicago, he and his wife, Edna, founded the I AM Religious Activity,
which began public work in 1934 with a ten-day class in which Ballard
channeled messages from the Ascended Masters.[55] The movement was an
immediate success. Many ex-Theosophists were hungry for such contact,
which had ceased within their splintered movement. With I AM, the
thrilling early days of Theosophy seemed to have returned, with the masters again actively involved.

The most communicative of them, Saint-Germain and the Master
Jesus, had been dormant in the old days of Blavatsky and the Mahatma
Letters. It was Charles Leadbeater, followed by Alice Bailey, who had
included them in what they called the Great White Brotherhood or, more
masonically, the Great White Lodge. Early Theosophical writings had
mentioned, in passing, a Hungarian Master,[56] whom Leadbeater identified with the Comte de Saint-Germain: a real if enigmatic person who

died in 1784 and may have descended from the Hungarian princely house of Rakoczy. As with the other masters, Leadbeater supplied him with a reincarnational genealogy. It began with St. Alban and continued with Proclus, Roger Bacon, Christian Rosenkreuz, Hunyadi Janos (Hungarian leader), a monk called Robertus, and Francis Bacon, before the final and deathless incarnation as Saint-Germain/Prince Rakoczy.[57] All this the Ballards took on board as I AM doctrine and published at least twenty volumes of teachings under Saint-Germain's name. The Ascended Masters became the cornerstone of several later movements, notably the Church Universal and Triumphant of Mark and Elizabeth Clare Prophet, which acknowledges its roots in the work of the Ballards.

While the term *I AM* stems from the words of Yahweh to Moses (Exod. 3:14), Phylos the Tibetan had used it to mean the highest element of the human individual. The I AM philosophy resembles the Hindu doctrine, beloved of the Theosophists, of the identity of Atman (the soul) with Brahman (the Absolute). In variously simplified forms, it would become a slogan of the New Age. Concerning the latter, Ballard's Seventh Golden Age implies that the turn-of-the-century crisis (Phylos's Sixth Age) is now past. America has heeded the order to "get into the shelter of that Cross!" and now, under the guidance of the Master Jesus and his brethren, is ready to become the new Atlantis.

WE ARE ALL STAR GUESTS

Later scholarship identifies another and darker influence on the I AM cult: that of William Dudley Pelley (1890–1965). The self-educated son of a clergyman, Pelley had multiple careers as a journalist, fiction and screenplay writer, and newspaper owner. He was always prone to conspiracy theories and to blaming the world's evils on the Jews. In 1933, in a petty imitation of the fascist movements of Europe, he founded a militant group called the Silver Shirts. After the war in Europe began, Pelley's opposition to America's entry and his abuse of President Roosevelt passed the limits of free speech and brought a conviction for sedition. He was sentenced to fifteen years' imprisonment, of which he served eight, from 1942 until his release on parole in 1950.

Like many extreme right-wingers, Pelley also had a mystical side. It seems to have begun in May 1928, when he was taken unawares by a classic out-of-the-body experience. He published an account of it in the popular *American Magazine* under the title "Seven Minutes in Eternity." According to Pelley's biographer, Scott Beekman, the magazine had over 2 million subscribers, and with further circulation in pamphlet form the article became "one of the most widely read accounts of paranormal activity in American history."[58] The second crucial experience came a few months later, when Pelley and the magazine's fiction editor started automatic writing, she holding a pencil and he lightly holding her hand. He soon graduated from this clumsy method, on finding that he was "adept in what is known as Clairaudience." Consequently, as he says, "I had only to speak the words orally that I saw mentally, and have a stenographer take them in shorthand."

Like other channelers, Pelley found the process addictive, and by his own account produced well over a million words of revelation.[59] Beekman admits that his "writings and lectures from this period represent a formidable, albeit flawed, theology. He read widely in metaphysics, and his Liberation Doctrine possesses a clear spiritualist undergirding. Upon this foundation Pelley added layers of Theosophy, Rosicrucianism, pyramidism, Jainism, and harmonialism, all topped with a peculiar Christocentric millenarianism."[60] For a while he attracted subscribers, first to a magazine, then to a mail-order course in mysticism and a pseudocollege. But after 1933 many followers, alienated by his praise of Hitler and increasingly grating anti-Semitism, defected to Ballard's I AM.[61] It was not until Pelley's release from jail in 1950 that he resumed the mantle of spiritual master, purging his works of their more offensive content.

In 1950 Pelley published his key work, *Star Guests*. It tells a dual story: of how he became a medium in 1928–29, and the history of the human race as it was then revealed to him. The main theme is that all humans are "Star Guests on this planet who find ourselves encased in bodies of primates in order to learn something spiritually ennobling."[62] This came about as follows. Through natural evolution, much as science has explained it, the earth had developed the animal kingdom up to the level of the cat and ape families. Then, as Pelley explains,

> somewhere back in the Eocene or Oligocene periods, fifty to thirty million years ago, there came a great migration of alien spirits to this planet from some other world in interstellar space, who settled down here and began to cohabit with the animal forms it discovered developing here, producing a hybrid race of beings, half-celestial and half-bestial that gave us the unspeakable Sodomic period described in the Bible.[63]

Elsewhere, Pelley writes that these spirits came from the system of Sirius.[64] The "Great Avatar Himself," in the stilted prose favored by higher beings, describes the hybrid of feline and bird forms and the peculiar reproductive system of these monsters.

> Head was first bird-like, as I have disclosed to you. His hands were like claws, conceived for destruction. Feet were reversible, making him able to locomote forwards or backwards. Conception was two-fold: by physical contact yet lacking organs of generation externally. Also he did create by thought, clothing his thought in etheric covering and calling it Material. Contact creation was made cell by cell, male and female embracing and leaving on the ground excretions which when developed became new life. Understand ye this?[65]

Clearly, the educational project had gone so badly wrong that intervention was called for. In compassionate response to the earth's need, the Spirit of Christ came with another host of spirits to cleanse the planet, separate the animal from the human streams, and set their respective evolutions on track.[66] With Christ came about 144,000 Christ People, elsewhere called the Goodly Company, Radiant Beings, or Sons of Light.[67]

Mankind was forever separated in evolution from the animal kingdom, but it continued in its beastly ways, with the result that "the physical world wobbled, and it wobbles today."[68] (This presumably refers to the axial tilt.) For almost a million years the good and bad forces were held in balance, until the Master of the Host (presumably Christ) decreed that earth had to be purged anew. This time it was achieved through melting the ice caps. Good and bad perished alike in the deluge, but "physical death meant nothing to Sons of Light."[69] They would return voluntarily incarnated in fresh bodies to help the human race in its more laborious task of regaining its spiritual nature.

As with many of the works treated in the present book, my summary has oversimplified the complexities and overclarified the muddle of *Star Guests* to bring out the parallels with other channeled teachings. The correspondences with Theosophy are too obvious to need underlining. Pelley's description of the depraved hybrids as "Sodomitic" makes one wonder if his Nazi sympathies had brought him into contact with the theories of Lanz von Liebenfels (see chapter 5). A study of his unsanitized prewar writings might reveal evidence of such a link.

The most striking parallel is with Edgar Cayce, whose Atlantean readings, as explained above, emerged piecemeal during the period 1923–32. Pelley's information on prehistory was given in 1928 and the years following. Both came to general notice only after World War II, when it turned out that Cayce and Pelley had channeled almost identical stories of spiritual beings creating clawed monstrosities through the power of thought, then becoming trapped within them. Cayce's source reveals much more than Pelley's about the Atlantean period, but the earth responds to human depravity in the same way: in Cayce's terms, with a pole shift, in Pelley's, with a wobble.[70] Both men felt the need to reconcile their channeled information with the Bible and with some form of Christianity. In both narratives, Christ is a cosmic being who came to earth to sort things out and redeem the unfortunate hybrids. He continues as a perpetual companion to humanity, and his more dramatic return is expected soon. Finally, both Cayce and Pelley humbly (?) accepted that in past lives they had been companions of Christ, when he lived as Jesus of Nazareth.[71] I can think of only one idea more unlikely than this, and it is that identical fantasies arose simultaneously out of the unconscious minds of such utterly different personalities.

TIBETAN PRETENSIONS

In the same year as the movement of the Ballards began (1934), the *Los Angeles Times* announced the foundation of a grandly styled Royal Order of Tibet.[72] Its leader was the resourceful George Adamski (1891–1965), at the time a lecturer, broadcaster, and mail-order guru.[73] A contemporary notice says that he also peddled oil consecrated by the Masters of Tibet to remove facial blemishes, raise the dead, and so forth, and that his followers were largely "disgruntled Besantists."[74] That he claimed his order had been a front for a Prohibition-evading manufactory of "sacramental" wine is beside the point.[75] We have one production from this period of his work: "Satan, Man of the Hour," first issued as a brochure in 1937, then reprinted with minor changes in *Flying Saucers, Farewell* (1961).[76] It is a pessimistic allegory of the modern era, which, like all previous ones, shows how successful Satan has been in perverting the human race. Besides the expected reproaches (that religion has become a symbol of oppression, science knowledge without wisdom), it tells briefly of the lost lands.

> There were races of highly intelligent men upon this planet at one time. In fact, the first perversion of cosmic principle took place in Lemuria, that great land that existed in the Pacific Ocean, connected with what is now the western coast of the United States. It was an Edenic garden where the inhabitants walked the flowery paths of life in a state of perpetual youth. . . . Then gradually Satan began to insinuate strange ideas into the consciousness of those children that had never known any guidance but that of the Great Spirit. . . . They engaged in the work of creating objects to please the senses—likes and dislikes were born. They became self-conscious.[77]

A teacher was sent to recall the Lemurians to virtue, but they spurned him, and their land was destroyed by earthquakes and tidal waves. Then there was Atlantea. "Whereas Lemuria had turned to the selfish worship of beauty and art, Atlantea became a worshipper of commercialism. Competition was born, and individual enterprises divided men in thought and action."[78] Atlantea too was destroyed, as was Egypt, and Rome. The essay leaves us with a picture of modern humans repeating the mistakes of the past, ignoring the call to a life of wisdom and kindness.

This jejune variation on the Atlantis theme belongs with the body of fiction that only Sprague de Camp and Henry Eichner have taken pleasure in reading.[79] But in view of its authorship, it is worth a moment's attention. It is amusing to see the Lemurians, usually painted as monstrous and brutish, punished for being Wildean aesthetes. Far from being Theosophical or the least bit Tibetan, Adamski's Lemuria reflects the West Coast paradise of Phylos and the Ballards, throwing in the Indians' Great Spirit for good measure. Lemuria's glory in its harmony with nature; the urban splendors and high technology of Atlantis, to which other authors have dedicated their purplest passages, get no praise here. Understandably, this son of poor Polish immigrants wished for a more friendly and socialistic America. In the next chapter, we will see him transported to lands beyond his wildest dreams.

Tibet and Mount Shasta came together in the mythology of another American cult leader of the 1930s, Maurice Doreal (died 1963). He was born at an unknown date as Claude Doggins and in 1929 founded the Brotherhood of the White Temple in Denver, Colorado.[80] Doreal claimed to have spent eight years in Tibet and to be in contact with the Great White Lodge. Beside a large quantity of spiritual teachings that were distributed to members, Doreal published a periodical that took the name of a famous Theosophical work, *Light on the Path* (itself channeled by Mabel Collins in 1884). He was basically a neo-Theosophist who accepted the existence of the Masters but, like Alice Bailey, claimed independent contact with them and found it more advantageous to run his own movement.

Walter Kafton-Minkel, in his delightful and erudite book *Subterranean Worlds,* tells us that Doreal also claimed to have visited the secret city inside Mount Shasta, but in his version it was Atlantean, not Lemurian. Doreal's Lemurians are an evil group of priest-kings and nobles imprisoned in huge underground cities that they had built beneath the Caroline Islands (north of New Guinea). Their crime had been to discover a destructive force far worse than the atomic bomb, and the Atlanteans of Mount Shasta act as their jailers, shuttling to and fro by spaceship, to prevent this dreadful weapon from being used.

Doreal had also traveled in his astral body to "Shamballa," which he places under the Himalayas. Earlier we have heard about the confusion between Shambhala and Agarttha (see chapter 2) and between underground, surface, and spiritual locations. Doreal had an ingenious explanation of why Shambhala is now underground: when the Himalayas were raised in the last great cataclysm, they simply piled up over it. Just like Phylos's and Ballard's secret cities, Doreal's Shambhala contains libraries storing all knowledge through technology that seems to be a struggling attempt to describe cyberspace, computers, and holographic projection.

Since most of Doreal's writings date from the 1940s or 1950s, they cannot be considered more than a hodgepodge of existing themes. For example, he too has a pole-shift mythology, a race of Serpent People in Antarctica, a white race in the Gobi Desert, and Sons of God who are always trying to keep the evil races under control. Equally derivative is the story he tells about his best-known work, *The Emerald Tablets of Thoth the Atlantean.*[81] According to the preface, Thoth was an Atlantean priest-king who had achieved immortality, taking and leaving the physical body only when he chose. The fifteen Tablets are in a saga-style metrical prose, more powerful in effect than most channeled works. In the beginning, the Children of Light look down on the poor Children of Men and decide to create humanlike bodies for themselves and help raise them "from the Earth to the Sun" (Tablet II). They make themselves a dwelling inside the earth, beneath Atlantis, and teach humans. Over the millennia a great civilization evolves, but eventually some of its elite became corrupt:

Proud they became because of their knowledge,
proud were they of their place among men.
Deep delved they into the forbidden,
opened the gateway that led to below.
Sought they to gain ever more knowledge
but seeking to bring it up from below. [Tablet V]

These are presumably the same as the Lemurians mentioned in Doreal's other writings. The Dweller who lived in etheric form, watching over the civilization, decided that Atlantis must be destroyed: "Called he then on the powers the Seven Lords wielded; changed the Earth's balance. Down sank Atlantis beneath the dark waves" (Tablet V). But before the destruction was complete, Thoth was ordered to gather the "sons of Atlantis" and all his records and magical instruments, load them onto a spaceship, and take them to Egypt.

The Translator's Preface adds some dates and continues the history. The exodus from Atlantis happened around 50,000 BCE, and Thoth ruled in Egypt until 36,000 BCE. Before leaving, he constructed the Great Pyramid as a temple of initiation and a repository for his records, and the Sphinx. We fast-forward to 1300 BCE, when a group of Egyptian priests brought the tablets to the Mayan lands, placing them beneath a solar temple in Yucatan. The story then gets exciting:

The writer (who has a connection with the Great White Lodge which also works through the pyramid priesthood) was instructed to recover and return to the Great Pyramid the ancient tablets. This, after adventures, which need not be detailed here, was accomplished. Before returning them, he was given permission to translate and retain a copy of the wisdom engraved on the tablets. This was done in 1925 and only now [1939?] has permission been given for part to be published. It is expected that many will scoff. Yet the true student will read between the lines and gain wisdom.

He is right. I scoff at Doreal's pyramid adventures, but the *Emerald Tablets of Thoth* seem to me better than their scribe. They contain some quite occult ideas concerning ceremonial magic, and also strange resonances with the Shaver Mystery, which will be our next port of call.

TEN

Channeling in the New Age

─────────── ✳ ───────────

REMEMBERING LEMURIA

Richard Sharpe Shaver (1907–1975) was an artist, welder, sometime Communist, and inmate of Ypsilanti State Hospital.[1] Already in 1936 he was hatching theories about the primordial language. In March 1945 he burst upon the readers of the fantasy magazine *Amazing Stories* with the declaration, "I Remember Lemuria!"

The hero of the story thus titled is Mutan Mion, a native of Sub Atlan, which is in one of the giant caverns just below Surface Atlan or Atlantis. To further his artistic training, he travels to the caverns at the center of Lemuria (also called Mu or Pan). But like Shaver himself, his life takes a different turn. He is lectured on high technology and learns that increased radiation from the sun is making the earth uninhabitable. There are plans for mass evacuation to Venus and other planets. He also finds that, thanks to "variform breeding," Mu is full of beings with four or six arms, snake-legged anguipeds, dwarves, and giantesses. Only the snow-white race of Nors or Nortans have forbidden miscegenation and remain aloof in their sunless land.

Mutan Mion, no racist, falls for Arl, a girl of pale purple hue with dainty, clicking hooves and an expressive, furry tail.[2] The couple is charged with the awesome responsibility of preserving Atlan's science on plates of imperishable telonium, to be placed both on and beneath the surface of Mu where future humans will discover and profit by them.³ Needless to say, they go through many adventures, in this story and in others.

The only amazing thing about "I Remember Lemuria!" is Shaver's denial that it was fiction. This was either a blatant untruth with the editor's connivance, or else Shaver meant it, as other channels have meant claims little less absurd. Shaver says that he was "what science chooses to very vaguely define as the racial memory receptacle of a man (or should I say a being?) named Mutan Mion, who lived many thousands of years ago in Sub Atlan, one of the great cities of ancient Lemuria!"⁴ David Hatcher Childress, world traveler and publisher, explains: "Shaver claimed that he could hear voices being projected into his head through the welding equipment he was using at a Ford assembly plant in Michigan. The voices were those of a civilization living beneath the surface of the earth. Shaver claimed that he remembered part of his past lives as Mutan Mion and his various escapes, 12,000 years ago, from this civilization's caves beneath the earth."⁵

Through voices, visions, and memories, Shaver reconstructed not only a language and a cosmology that holds an honored place in the hollow-earth literature;⁶ he also discovered the history of the Elder Gods, a race of beings like ourselves who came from another solar system and settled on the planets of our own system. Long ago, for the cause already mentioned, they were forced either to leave the planet or to move underground and dwell in subterranean cities. In time they degenerated into two groups: the evil Deros and their opponents, the Teros. These are the beings whose voices Shaver first heard. He also learned that most of the misfortunes of us surface dwellers are maliciously caused by the Deros.

The editor of *Amazing Stories,* Ray Palmer, befriended and fostered his unusual contributor, editing and probably rewriting Shaver's material and building it up into "The Shaver Mystery." Not only did the magazine's sales leap, but thousands of readers wrote in to confirm Shaver's memories and that the caverns and Deros were no fiction. After three years, Palmer's publishers responded to complaints that the magazine was meant to carry *stories,* not purported facts. Palmer took the Shaver Mystery with him as he moved on to found other magazines including *Fate,* the popular occult magazine still running today. Always with his finger on the collective pulse, Palmer featured in the first number Kenneth Arnold's epoch-making UFO sighting.[7]

During his later years, Shaver answered skeptics by actually producing pictures of the underground world, created aeons ago by the skilled denizens. His first technique was to slice agate stones with a diamond saw so as to reveal the patterns in them, which his imagination easily resolved into significant faces and figures. He declared these to be artifacts, made by "masters who first discovered a way of making agate, and of mixing photo-sensitive chemicals with liquid stone and impressing upon the stone their very thoughts, their art and their history."[8] To help others share his vision and thus his worldview, "he projected the stone slices onto large pieces of cardboard with an opaque projector. He treated the cardboard with dye and laundry detergent, and painted over them with oils so everyone could see what he saw."[9] Kafton-Minkel, summarizing Shaver's technique in these words, continues with an appreciation of the results as "little masterpieces of *Art Brut* [outsider art]."

Of all Shaver's themes, I would single out those of genetic manipulation and racial purity. The first links up with all the instances we have met of human-animal mixtures, from Lanz-Liebenfels through Pelley to Edgar Cayce's Temple of Sacrifice. But there is a difference: alone of all our sources, Shaver does not deplore or pity these hybrids, but rejoices in them, as with Arl, the sexy satyress. At the same time, he is friendly to their antithesis, the race of Nors, who seem to look both backward to Ariosophical myths of Arctic Aryans, and forward to the class of handsome blond-haired space visitors who would later be christened Nordics.

MEETING ORTHON

It was George Adamski who had the first encounter with a Nordic: a Venusian to whom he gave the pseudonym of Orthon. This was on November 20, 1952. The next year he published the book that made him famous, *Flying Saucers Have Landed.*[10] It was not all Adamski's work by any means. The first two-thirds was by Desmond Leslie (1921–2001), a son of the Irish writer and diplomat Sir Shane Leslie and a pioneer in both ufology and *musique concrète.* Leslie prefaced Adamski's fifty-five-page narrative with a well-documented account of UFO sightings through the ages. This includes much Atlantean lore, crediting Blavatsky, Donnelly, the Mahatma Letters, Sinnett, Scott-Elliot, Besant, Leadbeater, Spence, Bailey, Harold Wilkins, James Churchward, and Hindu myths of *vimanas* or flying chariots. Being also an acoustical engineer, Leslie writes interesting thoughts about the occult powers of sound, which Sinnett and others had already connected with Atlantean technology. While it was Adamski's astonishing claim of contact, complete with photographs of saucers and ships, that made the book a bestseller, Desmond Leslie's contribution had a more subtle and lasting influence. It integrated the new myth of extraterrestrial contact with the occult Atlantis myth. The theme was taken up by his countryman Brinsley Le Poer Trench (see chapter 7), with whom Leslie later founded the *Flying Saucer Review,* and laid the foundations on which Charroux, von Däniken, and Sitchin would build. More than that, as Colin Bennett explains in his entertaining and moving biography of Adamski, it "quite overwhelmed the provincial and conservative British scientists at the time"[11] and anticipated the countercultural flood of the next decade.

One of Adamski's informants, a Saturnian whom he calls Ramu, told him the following story about human origins.

> The first inhabitants of Earth were brought to it from the other planets. But it was not long before something unexpected took place in the atmosphere surrounding the Earth, and the transplanted people realized that within a few centuries living conditions on this globe would not be favorable. As a result, the first inhabitants of Earth, with a few exceptions, packed up all of their belongings into space ships and left for other worlds. The few who chose to remain had permitted themselves to deteriorate amidst the lush

beauty and abundance of this new world and sought nothing different. Gradually, they became content to live in natural caves and were
eventually lost in the annals of time.[12]

This is almost exactly what Shaver said. To continue Ramu's narrative, severe Earth changes followed, as foreseen, with many lands rising
or sinking. Earth also acquired a single moon, which was regarded as an
unbalanced state of affairs. But at least the place was habitable again.
The "teachers of wisdom on many planets" held a meeting, at which it
was decided to use the earth as a reformatory for "trouble-makers" from
both inside and outside the solar system. These recalcitrants were gathered in spaceships and dumped on earth without any resources but their
previous knowledge. "These are your Biblical 'fallen angels'," said Ramu.
"Our people of many worlds visited them often, helping and guiding
them as much as they would permit." After a difficult start, they succeeded in making a paradise of Earth and living in peace and happiness.
"Then, as your Bible relates it, man ate of the fruit of the tree of 'knowledge of good and evil,' and divisions entered where before there had
been none."[13] First the different races became hostile to each other, then
nations were formed and no longer lived by the Divine Law. Since then,
there have been ups and downs, but humanity persistently deprives itself
of the paradise that Earth could be.

Ramu explains that Satan is no independent entity, but the inhar-
monious conditions that humans themselves create, and that, once corrected, "Satan becomes an angel of light." He adds some details about
cloudy planets that recall what Steiner and others have said about the
Lemurian and Atlantean epochs. Apparently a clouded atmosphere,
such as Venus has, is more conducive to long life, and that was once the
condition on Earth. Moreover, there is a catastrophe in the making.

It may interest you to learn that a gradual tilting of your Earth is
even now taking place. If, as could happen at any moment, it should
make a complete tilt in order to fulfill its cycle, much of the land

now lying under water will rise. For years to come, this water-soaked soil will be in a process of evaporation which will once more cause a constant cloudy formation, or "firmament" around your Earth. In which case, the life span will again be increased.[14]

Adamski and other contactees fall under the broad definition of channeling, since they presented themselves as chosen mouthpieces for alien entities. Even more than the usual cautions apply concerning their motivation, veracity, and reliability, and possible contamination by their own prejudices, by magazine editors, and so on. Rather than trying to solve these conundrums, I am interested in the way their statements about Atlantis and lost civilizations fit with the larger web that we have been unfolding. Here, without specific mention of Atlantis, are the familiar themes of a deliberate implantation, rather than evolution, of humanity; a cosmic bureaucracy in charge of such things; cyclical changes on the earth's surface and in the human psyche, implying a causal connection between them; the moon as a recent acquisition; and the possibility of a shift of Earth's axis.

After this, why Adamski should have dragged up his old essay, "Satan, the Man of the Hour," is one of many puzzles surrounding his personality. As his biographer, Colin Bennett, points out, at one moment Adamski seems crass beyond belief; at another, he is being listened to by the top military brass of Britain and invited to audiences, certainly with Queen Juliana of the Netherlands and possibly with the pope.[15]

OTHER FLESH, SECRET PLACES

George Adamski was not alone on that memorable encounter in 1952. Six others drove out into the California desert with him: two women friends and two couples from Arizona, the Williamsons and the Baileys. Afterward they all signed notarized statements reading: "I, the undersigned, do solemnly state that I have read the account herein of the personal contact between George Adamski and a man from another world, brought here in his Flying Saucer 'Scout' ship. And that I was a party to, and witness to the event as herein recounted."[16] Whatever that means!

George Hunt Williamson (1926–1986) was an aspiring anthropologist, though he never held the degrees he would afterward claim. At this time he was working in William Dudley Pelley's movement, having been attracted to it through reading *Star Guests* or introduced by Adamski.[17] However, neither Adamski nor Williamson showed any symptom of sharing Pelley's aggressive right-wing and anti-Semitic views.

Earlier in the year, Williamson and his wife, Betty, had started experiments with a sort of Ouija board, together with Alfred and Betty Bailey, which resulted in communications from beings on Mars, Saturn, and Uranus. Next came messages in Morse code via shortwave radio, and finally direct telepathic contact. The messages, when not banal or nonsensical, expressed concern at the H-bombs recently exploded on earth and at the prospects for humanity. Alluding to the clock face on the *Bulletin of Atomic Scientists,* the beings warned, "The world is now close to the Midnight Hour!"[18]

In *Other Tongues—Other Flesh,*[19] published by Ray Palmer's Amherst Press, the message is more encouraging, saying that the space visitors "are now making themselves known to the world as a whole to lead mankind thereby into a New Age as the Earth enters the more intense vibrations of Aquarius."[20] In this complicated book Williamson documents the UFO sightings and encounters of the 1890s, expounds a theory of universal magnetism, reveals the symbols of the original language, and issues more warnings about humanity's peril. There are visible influences from the I AM movement, from the scientific revelations of *Oahspe* (e.g., that the sun is cold[21]), and from Churchward. Williamson then analyzes the footprints left on the desert sand by Orthon's shoes, which he finds full of symbols and portentous meaning. Next comes an account of human origins, with quotations from an Elder Brother who seems to be a close cousin of Pelley's and Cayce's informants:

The human race in its present pattern has been upon this planet anywhere between seventeen million and ten million years. . . . A great migration of souls known as the "Sons of God" arrived on Earth when the evolution of its indigenous life was progressing and incarnated in certain animal forms.

When he first arrived on Earth he had no body as we think of a body, so he looked upon beast and bird and chose the physical vehicle most likely to give him attributes producing qualities of spirit. The various cat forms were attractive to *The Migrants,* but the ape form was the form most suitable for their Earth environment and experience. The ape form gave them a more flexible and better-controlled hand with the all-important opposable thumb. Without the thumb man couldn't have produced a civilization. The cat form was discarded.[22]

The "Sons of God" made wives of the ape creatures and the progeny was antediluvian man, or prehistoric-primitive man. The physical attributes belonged to the anthropoid apes and the spiritual attributes belonged to the migration, which came from the planets of the star-sun Sirius.[23]

The abomination was so vast that forms were fusing together into monsters having no purpose but self-destruction. Men and animals were growing interchangeable of spirit and structure. Man was beastly and beast was manlike. Spirit knew not itself, whether it were divine or whether it were experiment of Thought Incarnate. They had so interchanged that they could no longer be accepted by the Host on the Sirian planets as divine. All physical forms had to be cleansed. "Pure beast must be preserved as beast; pure angel-man must be preserved as angel-man. Therefore, a vast catastrophe was decided upon. Ice from polar seas was melted and released upon continents of monsters." The Elder Brother tells us: "No longer could life make physical vehicles by thought. Forms existing in purity were preserved. Monsters and anomalies were destroyed. No longer could they propagate. Pure species were saved and pronounced sterile unto all but themselves."[24]

Other Tongues—Other Flesh has much more to say, especially on the interpretation of the Bible in light of the above, but its account of Atlantis is brief and to the point. There is a hint at *Oahspe*'s universal salvation as Williamson says, "It is believed that the good people escaped from Atlantis by spacecraft and went to the planet Mars while the evil destroyers lost their physical equipment in the sinking of the Lost Continent and migrated to Orion in spiritual form."[25]

In his third book, *Secret Places of the Lion,* Williamson surprised his knowing readers in the very first chapter.

> Many thousand of years ago in the eastern section of the Motherland Lemuria, in a land known as Telos, the first trade-ships arrived from the planet Hesperus (Venus). This land is now in the vicinity of the Grand Canyon of Arizona.
>
> A prominent student of the mysteries, and historian of Mu . . . was known as "Lady of the Sun" and had been commissioned by the ruling prince to locate the visitors and welcome them to the land of the children of men. The first thing discovered in the wilderness by the historian were strange footprints in the sand, not unlike those made by the Venusian who walked in the sand near Desert Centre, California, on November 20, 1952.[26]

This encounter lasted only a short time before evil priesthoods caused the almost total destruction of Mu. But before that, the Lady of the Sun had spent time with the visitors and recorded what they told her on tablets of Lemuria's imperishable metal, telonium. As catastrophe approached and the cities fell into rampant crime, the prince led the good people to a rendezvous with the Venusian ships, which took them to safety. Just a few remained behind, including the Lady of the Sun and another historian by the name of Mutan Mian. The two worked frantically to complete and deposit the telonium tablets. This was about 12,000 years ago, when Mu was submerged, leaving only part of California, Arizona, and other parts of the American Southwest, Australia, and Easter Island.[27]

Mutan Mian? Telonium? This is not Cayce or Pelley, but pure Shaver!

Williamson hints that some of the ancient records have been rediscovered, but why this should be necessary when there is direct access to higher entities is not made clear. The main purpose of *Secret Places of the Lion* is to propound a new version of Egyptian and Hebrew history and chronology, an esoteric version of the life of Jesus, and an account of later concealments of secret records. Incidentally, receiving tedious and contradictory accounts of Jesus's life is an occupational hazard of channeling. Virtually all those named did so, whether to satisfy their own curiosity through unconscious fantasy, to attract an audience with residual Christian allegiance, or in obedience to some discarnate prankster. A comparative study of such lives might repay the patience it would take to read them all.

Underpinning Williamson's work is a system of reincarnations, tabulated after the manner of Leadbeater's "lives." For example, the Lady of the Sun who met the spaceman Merk and interpreted his footprints was later the wife of Joseph; Bathsheba, the wife of David; the wife of Pharaoh Ahmose I; the second wife of Aaron; Elizabeth, mother of John the Baptist; and lastly a male Indian who met Merk as he returned to Earth, landing at Mesa Verde in 1200 CE.[28] It would take too long to list all Ahmose I's incarnations, but they include Daniel; Joseph, the father of Jesus; Merlin the magician; Montezuma; and Joseph Smith.[29]

In this most eclectic book, Williamson adopts the mythology of the *Emerald Tablets of Thoth* (see chapter 9). He or his source has considerable respect for the founder of the Latter Day Saints, whose wisdom likewise came from buried tablets.[30] There are hints at Rudolf Steiner's Christology, including the extraordinary significance that Steiner and Williamson accord to Jesus's physical blood as it fell on the earth at Golgotha.[31] And for Jesus's last words, uttered in "pure Mayan," Williamson confirms Stacey-Judd's translation (see chapter 9) as absolutely correct.[32]

Among the persons acknowledged in *Secret Places of the Lion* is "Brother Philip, O.A. [Amethystine Order], of a monastery in the Peruvian mountains who worked tirelessly amidst Cyclopean masonry translating original, ancient records in the scriptorium there."[33] Three years later, Brother Philip would appear as the author of *Secret of the Andes,* and no one doubts that he was Williamson himself. His order was now called the Brotherhood of the Seven Rays, and its seat was in Peru, on the northern side of Lake Titicaca.

Secret of the Andes completes and clarifies Williamson's version of prehistory. Lemuria is not a synonym for Mu, but the name for the last part of that great Pacific continent. The destruction and submergence of Mu lasted from 30,000 BCE to between 12,000 BCE and 10,000 BCE, and shortly after that Poseidonis, the last remnant of Atlantis, was also destroyed. The cause was "diabolic experiments" by "those working on the Left Hand Path."[34]

These worldwide catastrophes caused the rise of the Andes and lifted the seaport of Tiahuanaco 12,000 feet into the mountains. Thither came Lord Aramu-Muru, one of those charged to preserve the Lemurian wisdom, riding not a spacecraft but a needle-like airship. Nearby, in a valley with an anomalous, semitropical climate, he founded the Monastery of the Brotherhood of the Seven Rays. It was built from gigantic blocks of stone, cut using the "energy of primary light force." Among the treasures Muru brought from Lemuria was the Golden Sun Disc of Mu, a symbolic and also scientific instrument. Among its powers were healing, transdimensional travel, and causing Earth changes. It was made of transmuted gold, similar to the almost translucent metal of UFOs. Thanks to this device, the Masters from the new mystery schools throughout the world could teleport to meet in council. The disc remained in the Sun Temple until Pizzaro's Spaniards landed. Thereupon it was hidden in a subterranean temple, where it will remain until humans are ready to use it again.[35]

Unlike Williamson's previous books, this one has many long channeled messages, some of them precisely sourced and dated. For instance, on January 21, 1956, the Archangel Michael gave an address in Banff, Canada. (Incidentally, Michael was one of the very few named communicators who periodically interrupted the usual Source of Edgar Cayce.[36])

Other messages, even sermons, come from the Archangels Uriel, Raphael, and Gabriel, from Joseph of Arimathea, Sanat Kumara, Koot Hoomi, Morya, and Aramu-Muru himself. "Their words are recorded by means of voice channeling of a telepathic nature," explains the author.[37] Saint-Germain is called an Ascended Master, Chohan of the Seventh Ray, and the head of the Amethystine Order.[38]

One would like to know much more about the Brotherhood of the Seven Rays. What if it was they who renewed the Cross of Urcos, so memorably discovered by Weidner and Bridges?[39] (See chapter 12.) Like most of Williamson's later life, the Peruvian connection remains obscure. Standard reference sources agree that he changed his name to Michael d'Obrenovic and migrated from the world of flying saucers to that of minor churches with major pretensions. He was ordained in the Liberal Catholic Church, the Orthodox Church of the East, and the Eastern Catholic Syro-Chaldean Church.[40] Like Leadbeater, he died a bishop.

SETH SPEAKS

Of all the channels of the later twentieth century, Jane Roberts (1929–1984) is the most sophisticated and fascinating. She was a Skidmore-educated writer who tumbled into mediumship in 1963 while she and her artist husband, Robert Butts, were experimenting with an Ouija board. Many sessions had no more audience than the two of them, but gradually word got out, and a small group started meeting at the Buttses' apartment in Elmira, New York. For all her subsequent celebrity, Jane Roberts was content to live a modest, provincial life, never going on tour or exploiting her contact beyond the printed word.

The communicating entity, Seth, presented himself as a being who had lived many lives on Earth but had now moved on to a discarnate state. Over many hundred sessions, Seth expounded through Jane Roberts's voice a metaphysical system that became one of the pillars of New Age thought. Wouter Hanegraaff writes, "It is hardly an exaggeration to regard Jane Roberts as the Muhammad of New Age religion, and Seth as its angel Gabriel."[41] Moreover, unlike most angels, Seth was able and willing to describe his own perception of the situation and the people present, insofar as he could make them comprehensible to more limited forms of consciousness.[42] Whether he was "only" Jane Roberts's subconscious mind, or her Oversoul, any study of channeling must come to terms with the Seth phenomenon and the highly principled and articulate woman who delivered it.

While Jane Roberts wrote books ranging from Seth-inspired novels (e.g., *The Education of Oversoul 7*) through speculative studies of psychology (*Psychic Politics*) and parapsychology (*The Afterdeath Journal of an American Philosopher*) to summaries of Seth's teachings (*The Seth Material*), from January 1970 to August 1971 Seth dictated a book that was all his own, published as *Seth Speaks*. He outlined its chapters from the beginning, and at each session took up from the point at which he had left off. Besides some listeners' questions and Robert Butts's helpful notes, the book is a coherent digest of Seth's view of reality.

From Seth's perspective, Atlantis and other past civilizations are not of great interest or importance. One reason is that being outside time as we know it, he does not see human evolution, either collective or personal, as linear. Instead of a sequence of incarnations linked by karma, Seth sees the simultaneous experiences of a single, timeless Oversoul, all co-present and able to affect each other in both directions. This gives him a more relaxed attitude to world history, as comes out in the following statement:

> It seems to you that you have, perhaps, but one chance as a species to solve your problems, or be destroyed by your own aggression, by your own lack of understanding and spirituality. As you are given many lives in which to develop and fulfill your abilities, so has the species in those terms been allotted more than the single line of historical development with which you are presently acquainted. . . . Groups of people in various cycles of reincarnational activity have met crisis after crisis, have come to your point of physical development and either gone beyond it, or destroyed their particular civilization.[43]

Seth continues by explaining that some such groups have solved the problems that a physical incarnation has to offer and have "evolved into the mental entities they always were."[44] (This resonates with the many teachings we have heard about spirits coming into incarnation, then returning to the spiritual state the richer for their experiences.) Some such beings, who were once human, continue to take a benevolent interest in Earth life, and we might think of them, says Seth, as Earth gods. Here he gives out a crumb or two of information on prehistoric civilizations, which I summarize.

There were three civilizations long before the time of Atlantis, and incidentally three long periods when the earth's poles were reversed. All three prior civilizations were technologically superior to ours. The first of them, having followed a course of development somewhat like our own, ended when most of its members decided to leave the earth for planets within other galaxies. A group that elected to stay behind built the second pre-Atlantean civilization. It was called Lumania (Seth carefully spelled out the name), and it was based in what are now Africa and Australia.

No one else talks about Lumanians. Seth's lecture about them is like a report from an explorer of a remote and hitherto unknown tribe, overlooked in the great tides of history. He tells us that the Lumanians were scientifically brilliant but timid and introverted, not sharing their knowledge with the less-developed native peoples surrounding them, and regarding any type of violence with horror: "They did send out members of their own group, however, to live with the natives and intermarry, hoping peacefully to thus alter the physiology of the species."[45] (Here Seth hints at the familiar story of a separate, indigenous race, less developed than the one with extraterrestrial ancestry.) The Lumanians had telepathic gifts and ways of manipulating and understanding sound far beyond anything we can conceive of. They used sound to create brilliant images before the inner eye, and also as their main source of physical energy.[46]

Outside their homeland, the Lumanians had outposts in the form of cleverly engineered cave and tunnel systems, which they had excavated using sonar power. From these havens they observed the native peoples and made a profound study of astronomy and geology. The caves were adorned with symbolic paintings and sculptures that would in some manner "speak" to this paranormally sensitive people. Many of these outposts were in present-day Spain and the Pyrenees. They served later as homes for Stone Age peoples, who imitated the decorations they found there.[47]

Seth never described the third pre-Atlantean civilization, because he turned to other subjects and his hearers never thought to remind him of it.[48] Regarding Atlantis itself, he seems to have taken its existence for granted, as well as the survival of some of its knowledge into archaic times. He tells one of the auditors that around 1200 BCE he (the auditor) was a member of an esoteric group that traveled through Asia Minor, carrying in their memories elaborate codes of ethics that originated from Atlantis and ultimately from a "race from another star."[49] Seth also speaks of the Atlanteans' understanding of certain "concentrated energy points" in space and time, where other realities are more easily perceived. He mentions the pyramids as being at one such point, and says that the great religions all had their births at these places where "ideas and emotions are propelled into physical actuality with great vigor."[50] The Atlanteans used their knowledge of energy points to achieve stability for their roads and building projects. (Here Seth comes close to the idea of ley lines and Earth energies that had just reached a wide public through John Michell's work.) But Seth's concern is less to satisfy curiosity about the past than to give out knowledge useful for the present. Near the end of the book he sums up the situation:

Ancient Rome exists, and so does Egypt and Atlantis. You not only form the future, as you think of it, but you also form the past. You have been told simple tales, and they are delightful ones; but if you were not ready to hear more you would not be in this room.

You and your reincarnated selves, or personalities, are not imprisoned in time. There is a constant interchange going on between what you think of as your present self, and your past and future selves. . . . Time has open ends in all directions or such a thing as probabilities would not exist. Therefore, actions that you make now can help a so-called past personality; and a so-called future personality may step in and help you along your weary way.[51]

TOM AND THE NINE

With the publications of Jane Roberts's books, the third modern channeling wave began, and it has not yet crashed. Self-help gurus proclaim that "anyone can channel," and many are the books with mauve covers that reveal centenarian platitudes about Atlantis (and everything else). A few stand out from the mass, and to complete this chapter I have chosen *The Only Planet of Choice* for its prickly originality, Ramtha for his notoriety, and James Merrill's *The Changing Light at Sandover* because some think it the greatest American poem of the century.

In 1974 the medium Phyllis Schlemmer (born 1929) began giving trance sessions in Ossinning, New York. The auditors included the psychical researcher Andrija Puharich (discoverer and defender of Uri Geller) and Sir John Whitmore, an English baronet who had tired of car-racing and other rich people's pursuits. The material that came through Schlemmer was so remarkable that several other people paid attention to it, none of them fools. They included Gene Roddenberry, creator of the mythic science fiction series *Star Trek,* and the writer Stuart Holroyd, for whom this would start a fresh career as a New Age chronicler. Holroyd published the first book based on Schlemmer's channeling in 1977.[52] A second selection appeared in 1993 as *The Only Planet of Choice,* and it is from this that I extract the story of Atlantis and the early races.

The source that spoke through Schlemmer's voice calls itself Tom and uses an odd, stilted English that sometimes sounds exactly like Edgar Cayce's Source (see the quotation at the end of the next paragraph). Tom is supposedly one of The Nine. The editors call them "beings with origins earlier than the human race, and with intelligence which encompasses the Universe. Among other things they oversee progress on our own planet."[53] But they are not the only ones, and their plans are always in danger of being foiled by extraterrestrial meddlers.

Tom's prehistory is not told in linear fashion, and there are ambiguities and contradictions that I cannot resolve. But the outlines are plain. It starts around 20 million years ago, when a group of advanced beings came to Earth and prepared its energy fields and ley lines for future life-forms. Evolution proceeded naturally up to the human level, producing the Neanderthals, who died out, and humans of the Black race. Then some outside entities were curious to see what would happen if they "seeded" the planet. They placed "outcasts" on it (very much as Adamski's directors dumped recalcitrants), and these too evolved into humans. In 32,400 BCE an extraterrestrial known as the Hawk came with his people and interbred with these "seeds," producing three new races: Yellow, White, and Red.[54] Thus the Black race is aboriginal, whereas the other races are hybrids, or mongrels. Things were further complicated when yet another group came to Earth looking for a place to live and got stranded. Tom says, "They in turn developed other beings through their reproduction, and there were those also that reproduced with the aboriginals, and they produced groups of darkened exterior, with non-negroid features."[55]

Such statements about racial origins were common earlier in the century, but by the 1970s they were sorely out of place. Yet this is what the source said, and the editors, to their credit, did not suppress it despite their evident embarrassment.

Hawk and his people had landed their spacecraft in central Asia. To avoid frightening the natives, he dressed like a shaman in a bird costume. (Readers of Andrew Collins will immediately think of the feather-clad Watchers.[56]) During a thousand-year residence, Hawk brought language, knowledge, and science and raised the human life span from an average of 20 to 150 years.[57] After him came another "space being," who is remembered as the Adam of the Hebrew Bible. Being lonely, he requested a companion of his own kind, and this was supplied, but the entities in charge forbade him to have sex with her. The reason seems to be that at his level of evolution, he did not need sexual bliss to remind him of his oneness with the Creator. However, he saw the earthlings mating, both human and animal, and lusted to follow their example. We don't need Tom to tell us the rest: a malevolent archangel tempted Adam to disobey; he "fell," and put the blame on Eve, to the lasting detriment of the female sex.[58]

As with Tom's account of racial origins, it is disconcerting to meet the old doctrine that Adam and Eve's sin was sexual intercourse. But now we come to his Atlantis, which was another effort by well-meaning aliens to upgrade the human gene stock, beginning between 26,000 and 21,000 BCE. The beings responsible were Alteans: unisexual humanoids from another system who had fair, iridescent skin, blue eyes, and no hair. Being dumb, they simulated speech through a computer.[59] (An irreverent thought occurs: was Orthon an Altean in a wig?) They used aircraft and perhaps teleportation to get around their vast land, which stretched from North America to Greece. Lemuria or Mu, in the Pacific, was part of the same civilization, and Egypt and the Maya lands were colonies.[60]

The Atlanteans who developed from the Alteans' continuous seeding program fell in love with physical existence, living as they did in a kind of paradise with high technology. Among their achievements were enlarging their sexual organs and creating animal-human hybrids, hoping for more physical pleasure thereby.[61] Hawk returned in 11,000 BCE to try to improve matters but failed. The Atlanteans' romance with technology got completely out of hand. Through some misapplication of hydrogen-derived power, they created storms and brought about the melting of the ice caps. Their end came overnight.[62]

Tom's narrative passes to Egypt, where the Great Pyramid had been started 150 years before Atlantis's destruction in 9,000 BCE. Its function was to bring energy to the planet and to rejuvenate cells. Its building, which went on until 5,000 BCE, was done "with the benefit of vocal sound tuned to crystal, with the sound of OM."[63] The other Giza pyramids were built a millennium or so later, in early dynastic times.

I leave the interested reader to discover what Tom has to say about Abraham, the Jews, Jesus, Satan, and the problems of the Middle East. He also obliges his listeners' curiosity about UFOs, crop circles, the Gray aliens, and plans for a public landing of our extraterrestrial keepers. (The one scheduled for 1979 was canceled.) While Tom challenges his listeners' assumptions and moral codes, he gives little advice beyond telling us to behave better toward one another and the earth. *The Only Planet of Choice* is not a comfortable work, but then neither is the earth a comfortable planet. As the title signifies, it is the only one in the universe where humans can exercise free will, and, given preceptors who are conflicted or plain incompetent, things can go catastrophically wrong.

RAMTHA THE LEMURIAN

The career of JZ Knight (born 1946) is as different as could be from that of Jane Roberts or Phyllis Schlemmer. While Seth and Tom spoke to private groups, Ramtha holds forth to audiences of hundreds on Knight's former stud ranch in Yelm, Washington. Yet there are similarities, especially with Seth. In both cases, the communicating entity uses the voice and body of the channel while she is to some degree entranced. Jane Roberts could light a cigarette or fetch a drink while Seth was speaking through her and was sometimes conscious of what she was saying. Knight does not remember Ramtha's words after she emerges from her trance, but while possessed by him she strides around speaking, like Seth, in a sonorous, masculine tone. Both entities, while declaring themselves beyond the need for physical vehicles, enjoy vicariously the pleasures of the human senses, such as drinking wine.[64] They both teach a no-nonsense, unsentimental method of self-realization that has no respect for the great religions or for human hierarchies. Neither one is tinged by the racist doctrines that were commonplace in earlier Atlantean revelations.

Ramtha tells his own story in a book familiarly known as "The White Book" and entitled simply *Ramtha*.[65] It bears no resemblance to that of the hero of the Ramayana who inspired the Ram of Fabre d'Olivet's and Saint-Yves' epics. From the start, it is a gift to the skeptics, for Ramtha claims to be a 35,000-year-old Lemurian. He was born a slum child in Onai, the greatest port city of Atlatia, "the land you call Atlantis." The Lemurians were a religious, sensitive race, lacking technology but with great spiritual understanding and a loving devotion to what they called the Unknown God. The Atlatians, in contrast, were a highly accomplished, scientific race, proud of their inventions, which included the generation of energy from light. They had, of course, airships, and with these had pierced the cloud cover that then enshrouded the planet. This was a big mistake: it caused a deluge that inundated most of Lemuria and northern Atlatia, so that the survivors of those lands were forced to take refuge in the southern regions of Atlatia (by implication, India). Now deprived of most of their technology, the degenerate Atlatians lived under a tyranny and took out their resentments on the dark-skinned Lemurians, whom they held in the lowest contempt.[66]

Ram changed all that. After a mountaintop epiphany he raised a rebellion, then an army, and, in his words, *"created* war. I was the first conqueror this plane ever knew."[67] In the course of sixty-three years he built an empire covering three-quarters of the known world. He also found the time to transform his body and "gradually changed the programming in every cellular structure to increase the vibratory rate within them." People noticed that his body was starting to glow; he found that he could turn it at will into the substance of wind or light. Instead of dying (as even Rama the avatar was content to do), he just vanished from this plane, thus becoming the first human being to "ascend" and become a god.[68] Ramtha's essential teaching is that we too are gods. Not only do we make our own reality, but creation is what we have made of it. We came to Earth eons ago and created its living organisms.

> You must understand that you did not *labor* to create these things, for as light beings you were without an embodiment to labor with. Whatever you desired to create, you simply *became* it. In order to give substance to matter, to give personality to it, to give intelligence and design to it, you became a part of everything you created. Once each creation became a living thing of the intelligence of its creator, you withdrew from your creation—always searching for *greater* creations.[69]

The physical human being was the result of long experimentation by a group of gods. Their first efforts reproduced through cloning were ill adapted to the rigors of physical existence and "were continuously made a meal of by the animals about." Among the improvements they introduced was the separation into sexes. By about 10,500,000 years ago the gods were satisfied that they had made a perfect vehicle for their own self-expression and joy.[70]

None of this was meant to be permanent; it was "simply a game to participate in."[71] But these gods became so immersed in matter, so identified with their human bodies, that they forgot their true nature. This brings us to our present condition, from which Ramtha's School of Enlightenment offers an uncompromising, and for some an efficacious, remedy.

J. Gordon Melton, the encyclopedist, scholar, and defender of alternative religions, has paid Ramtha the compliment of a book-length study. He sees the teaching as a modern revival of Gnosticism, and Knight's organization as an "esoteric Gnostic school."[72] In 1996–97, Melton organized a panel of experts from different disciplines to witness and comment on the phenomenon.[73] The participants were willing to say what Ramtha *wasn't* (absolving Knight from accusations of fraud or playacting), but not what he *was*. So little progress was made in solving the conundrum of what exactly is going on in channeling.

Ramtha's Lemurian and Atlatian reminiscences remain problematic. One feels that he could have done a better job of making them plausible, but for all his insights and the palpable force of his presence, Ramtha is not an erudite god. The "White Book" seems to have picked up fragments from Blavatsky, Steiner, Jung, Crowley, Ballard, Bailey, Brunton, Gnosticism, Hinduism, and Tibetan Buddhism. In a more specialized study of the apocalyptic talks that Ramtha gave during the 1980s, I found similar evidence of derivation from popular New Age, ufological, and conspiracy-theory literature, and a very poor record of prophecy.[74] In some fields Ramtha seems not so much a teacher as a learner, through JZ Knight's own reading and conversation. Recalling what Jung said about

The Tibetan as Alice Bailey's higher self (see chapter 4), we might reverse the whole process. If we are all gods, then we have no need to channel external entities. The channel's own godhead could be using the more-or-less flawed loudspeaker of his or her current personality, in which case JZ Knight has every right to register Ramtha as her personal trademark!

THE CHANGING LIGHT AT SANDOVER

James Merrill (1926–1995) was twentieth-century America's most favored poet: born rich, then winning every prize and honor short of the Nobel. Only in such circumstances could he have spent twenty years writing an epic poem of Dantean dimensions and gotten away with admitting that much of it came through an Ouija board.[75] Merrill's *Changing Light at Sandover* raises a nice problem of intellectual property, which channels like JZ Knight have settled in their own way. First, credit might be given to the discarnate sources, whose poetry the honest Merrill distinguished from his own by setting it in capital letters. Much of it purports to be the voice of the late English poet Wystan Hugh Auden (1907–1973), putting it in a category well known to students of Spiritualism: that of literary and musical works dictated by dead poets and composers. Refusing to believe that only makes for further difficulty. If such messages derive from the unconscious mind alone, equal credit for authorship might have gone to Merrill's companion, David Jackson, whose hand was also on the teacup as it skittered over the alphabet board. The Pulitzer Prize Committee evidently had no such qualms, probably regarding the whole Ouija matter as a sophisticated Proustian pose.

Mirabell's Books of Number, the second of the three books of *The Changing Light at Sandover,* has much to say about human origins and the various catastrophes that have marked Earth's history. The source speaks as representative of an ancient, quasi-human, bat-winged race. It seems as well informed as Merrill and Jackson about music, poetry, art, culture, and history (which is saying a lot), but it does admit that the conversations come from Merrill's and Jackson's memory or word banks (140,

237), and that it and they are each other's dream (117).* Here is the most cogent story I can patch together from its messages.

One of the gods of the galactic pantheon, God B (standing for Biology), came and built the solar system as his "greenhouse," with its central atomic power in the sun (199). The earth went through the recognized stages of cooling, the coming of water, and the beginning of organic life (166). A species of intelligent beings evolved, resembling centaurs. They were mild and pastoral, grazing on the grassy flats of Atlantis (167). God B, disappointed by them, tried to extinguish the centaurs by growing forests that would crowd them out of their grasslands (201). But the wily critters bred a servant species to fly above the treetops and spot feeding grounds, also acting as messengers (167). This species began as mutant flies that were fed with uranium and sped through 6,000 generations a year. Due to their atomic genesis, they evolved on a different track from the natural-born centaurs, and in time evolved to be the size of their creators, black, winged, and nearly human looking. Soon they were organizing the centaurs' civilization. They ran their heating and lighting systems, built them silos, arenas, and cities ringed with towers in radial patterns (169–70).

The centaurs themselves had mastered solar energy and were able to control the climate. Then they went too far. They discovered how to clone themselves, thereby achieving immortality and unchecked population growth (167). Their solution was to kill off their elderly population, and they deputed the winged species to do the job, using "atomic blast." The centaurs then turned on their servants and set out to destroy their "ray centers." War broke out between the two species, in which the winged ones were easily victorious, henceforth reversing the roles of master and slave (168).

The narrator, a former member of the winged species, wonders whether God B had planned the centaurs' destruction from the start and implanted the disastrous idea of breeding his race (200). The question is

---

*Page numbers in parentheses are from *The Changing Light at Sandover.*

emblematic of one of the philosophical undercurrents in *The Changing Light at Sandover,* regarding the role of destiny versus free will.

After their victory, the winged species decided to leave Atlantis and its forests behind and build a new atomically powered world in the stratosphere. It was a network of antigravitational platforms, anchored to Earth at fourteen points by glowing radioactive stones (168, 125). The only survivors of the centaur extermination were the slaves charged to maintain the anchor points by keeping them clear of vegetation. After about 1,000 years, these workers had changed into a long-necked reptilian form and were shirking their duties. The winged species was perturbed but lacked volunteers to go down and spend their lives in the jungles doing the slaves' maintenance work. Consequently the system began to collapse, the first mooring snapped, and in short order all the latticelike cities were shredded (168–69, 134). God B angrily dismissed the winged beings and charged the archangels Michael and Gabriel with building him a new greenhouse (121).

Another thread of revelations in *The Changing Light at Sandover* tells of multiple human creations, but like the clay tablets of the Gilgamesh Epic, they are but tantalizing fragments of a lost whole. At one point we read that there were three Edens, each one ending in fire or flood (131); at another, that there were three incarnations of the worlds prior to this one (275). Was the epoch of the centaurs and batlike beings one of them? Is the "we" that speaks and claims to be managing human evolution the same as told that story? Unable to answer, I offer some significant fragments.

As in many of our histories, the moon is a recent acquisition, but with a new twist. It was made from a crust of nongravitational matter that the winged beings had forged for their floating world. As that collapsed, the crustal material was swept up and spun off into space to become the moon, a monument to their failure (133). At the same time, the landmass in the southern Atlantic sank (167). A later phrase implies that the moon had gathered the debris from the three previous creations, making it heavy enough to tilt the earth (477).

Another fragment of cosmic history speaks of a pre-Edenic world, which may be the same as the "vast civilization in China" that followed Atlantis (121). It was the home of the first humans, also winged, who busied themselves out of God's sight. They carved the plain with their machines and built a vast city of obsidian. Here again, atomic power seems to have brought about its end. God threw up the Himalayan range as a shield (459). The waters rose to cool the radium-heated Earth, froze, and withdrew. The areas of land and sea were defined, and the poles established (presumably meaning in their present positions) (245).

The human soul was an invention of the third world. While the angels worked on part of it, "we" claim to have made a serviceable soul for the rest. It was first slipped into an ape fetus, which produced a pair of twins very different from their parents. Their pituitary glands secreted the elements needed to pass soul on to their children (236). In some incomprehensible way, the revival of sentient life was subsequently in the "seed of the Jew," from which all the races followed (133).

Since then, humans have run amok, defying the natural equilibrium that keeps their numbers in check (244). The source makes some flippant remarks at this point: that only 2 million cloned humans listen to each other, while the rest "howl and prance so recently out of the trees"; that the politicians' sentiment of "all for all" makes for a fool's paradise; and that the excess millions should be killed off (247). This upsets some readers, who forget that a fictional character (or a channeled source) does not necessarily voice the author's sentiments. Time was when moralizers would have been more disturbed by the homosexuality celebrated by poet and source alike.

A final episode, post-Atlantean but well within our purview, is the source's wonderful history of the heretical pharaoh Akhnaton and his twin and wife Nefertiti. Not only did they institute a solar cult in place of the traditional polytheism of Egypt—everyone knows that—but in this version they harnessed solar energy through crystals. Over eighteen years they transformed the world, curing disease, inventing light storage, controlling the ebb and flow of the Nile Delta, and even pushing up the

African coastline at the Straits of Gibraltar, to regulate the Mediterranean (225–27). Their grand finale was to create a pyramid of rock crystal fifteen meters high, honed to a degree of geometrical exactitude that would focus the sunlight and (somehow) make them masters of the world (126). In fact, it would have destroyed the earth, but God B ensured that there was a tiny imperfection in its geometry (227). As it was, there were two perfect diamonds a seventh of a millimeter across whose power was sufficient to create an explosion, set off the eruption of Thera a thousand miles to the north, and make Thebes a barren land for 1,200 years (127). The effects were even felt in the Caribbean, Russia, and north of the Grand Canyon (146). Akhnaton and Nefertiti, devastated by the failure of their experiment, cut their wrists and perished, but that was not the end of them. His soul was the first to be cloned; Alexander the Great got a fifth of it (179). Nefertiti, who had proposed the crystal pyramid, remains the patron of the beings in charge of human development (128).

The Changing Light at Sandover reflects the worries of any serious person in the 1970s (and not much has changed since): the consequences of overpopulation and the threat of nuclear war. As always in the epic genre, the human and superhuman worlds interact along the lines of the current belief system, irrespective of whether the author shares it. Homer's heroes lived shoulder to shoulder with the gods; Dante's comedy depicted the eternal consequences of earthly deeds. Merrill's has an updated Gnostic god, UFOs, Atlantis, and reincarnation. In compensation for its seriousness, the poem's surface sparkles with high-camp repartee and the furnishings of Merrill's enchanted world: opera, poetry, friends, wine, travel, and the wallpaper in which, Shaver-style, he first saw the faces of his bat-winged mentors.

It is a rare literary critic who can handle all this. One such is John Chambers, who visited Merrill in 1978 and was immediately welcomed to a Ouija-board session. He quotes a broadcast by Merrill in 1985.

> I worked very hard in putting the poem together to try to persuade
> a reader that these things actually happened. Not to persuade him

of the truth of the messages, but to persuade him of the actuality of the experience. I don't mind if people doubt what we were told, if people look at the page and say, "Huh, they call this revelation, you know, these are just banalities that anybody could stitch together." What does rather sadden me are the critics who think that we were pretending that we didn't have the experience.[76]

In the poem itself, Merrill humbly acknowledges that even the most fragmentary message that he and David Jackson received was "twice as entertaining, twice as wise,/As either of its mediums."[77] So where did it come from? Chambers wonders whether it "represents the interface of the poet's creative genius with deep and unknowable truths emerging from some ineffable multidimensional universe. The Edgar Cayce stories as well may be the amalgamation of a different creative genius—yielding up still different parables—with the same unknowable structures of the universe."[78]

Chambers's proposed solution to the channeling phenomenon is not for the metaphysically timid or the dogma-bound. Nor is this development of it, which combines Buddhist doctrine with the allegory of cyberspace. It goes as follows. When sentient beings die, they release mental energies that may form congelations of intelligence, perhaps combining with other free-floating energies in resonance with them. (N.B.: Buddhism has no immortal soul to keep them together.) These act like files containing a mishmash of information, memory, dogma, and speculation, ordered as in life by a logical program akin to language. Given a suitable recipient, they download into it, blending with the recipient's own information, beliefs, and so forth. The way it emerges—through trance, automatic writing, and so on—is merely a matter of style.

In former times, possession by a god, demon, spirit, and so forth, was the only explanation for this phenomenon. Once those were eliminated, it seemed that everything had to come from the channel's subconscious mind. What is proposed is akin to the occultists' idea of the "egregore," a wandering influence that takes on a pseudopersonality and may be nourished by attention, belief, and sacrifice. This could explain the amazing fund of knowledge that some channels draw on, the consistency and personality of their sources, and the variation of the results from ponderous nonsense like *Oahspe,* through playfulness like Merrill, to profound insights like Seth, and an earnest wish to help and heal, like Cayce. Whatever theory one prefers, it is fortunate that the vast majority of people are not "suitable recipients."

ELEVEN

The Four Ages

──────── ✳ ────────

432,000, THE UBIQUITOUS NUMBER

As we float on our one-way journey down the river of time, how we would love to freeze it in midflow and examine its ripples and currents! All chronologies and timelines are efforts of this kind. They try to turn time into space, so that the past, like a musical score, can be present to the eye. Then they can set markers, plot curves, and project them into the future.

Stratigraphy can take a slice of the earth's crust and read downward to discover the evidence of previous epochs. From ice cores one can date volcanic eruptions and falls of cosmic matter and discern cyclical changes of the climate. It is much more difficult to chart human history, let alone prehistory, and to know whether there is any sense to its direction, any meaning to its ripples. This and the next chapter will examine two claims that such patterns exist. One of them is based on the myth of the Four Ages, the other on the astronomical fact of precession.

The earliest European witness to the myth of the Four Ages is Hesiod (eighth century BCE). In his *Works and Days* (lines 109–201) he actually described five ages, inserting an Age of Heroes after the Golden, Silver, and Bronze Ages and before the Iron Age. This seems to have been his compromise with Greek history, in which the Trojan War and its heroes loomed so large; later purveyors of the myth, such as Ovid in his *Metamorphoses* (I, 89–150), did not follow his example. Hesiod's account has the usual (but not quite universal) view of the Four Ages as describing a downward curve, with the present time as the nadir of misery and immorality. Not only human life, but the after-death state changes accordingly. The people of the first two ages, when they died, became spirits who watch over and benefit the human race. The people of the Bronze Age had no such immortality, but went down to Hades, as well we know from Homer. The Age of Heroes hardly stemmed the degeneration, but a few of them crossed the ocean to enjoy a private Golden Age under Cronos himself. As for the people of the Iron Age, it is too soon to tell their fate, but things are not looking good for them.

Hindu tradition tells a similar story, and it was probably from there that it reached the Greeks and other Indo-European peoples. The names of the ages are Krita Yuga (fortunate age; also called Satya Yuga), Dwapara Yuga (second age), Tretá Yuga (third age), and Kali Yuga (age of conflict), the four together constituting a Maha Yuga or Great Age. Whereas Hesiod considered only a single set of ages, Hinduism has multiple sets in cyclical repetition, and it dates them. Here is the version found in the Vishnu Purana, translated by the great Sanskritist Horace Hayman Wilson:

> Brahmá is said to be born: a familiar phrase, to signify his manifestation; and, as the peculiar measure of his presence, a hundred of his years is said to constitute his life: that period is also called Param, and the half of it, Parárddham. I have already declared to you, oh sinless Brahman, that Time is a form of Vishńu: hear now how it is applied to measure the duration of Brahmá, and of all other sentient beings, as well as of those which are unconscious, as the mountains, oceans, and the like. Oh best of sages, fifteen twinklings of the eye make a Káshthá; thirty Káshthás, one Kalá; and thirty Kalás, one Muhúrtta. Thirty Muhúrttas constitute a day and night of mortals: thirty such days make a month, divided into two half-months: six months form an Ayana (the period of the sun's progress north or

south of the ecliptic): and two Ayanas compose a year. The southern Ayana is a night, and the northern a day of the gods. Twelve thousand divine years, each composed of (three hundred and sixty) such days, constitute the period of the four Yugas, or ages. They are thus distributed: the Krita age has four thousand divine years; the Tretá three thousand; the Dwápara two thousand; and the Kali age one thousand: so those acquainted with antiquity have declared. The period that precedes a Yuga is called a Sandhyá, and it is of as many hundred years as there are thousands in the Yuga: and the period that follows a Yuga, termed the Sandhyánsa, is of similar duration. The interval between the Sandhyá and the Sandhyánsa is the Yuga, denominated Krita, Tretá, &c. The Krita, Tretá, Dwápara, and Kali, constitute a great age, or aggregate of four ages: a thousand such aggregates are a day of Brahmá, and fourteen Menus reign within that term. Hear the division of time that they measure. Seven Rishis, certain (secondary) divinities, Indra, Manu, and the kings his sons, are created and perish at one period; and the interval, called a Manwantara, is equal to seventy-one times the number of years contained in the four Yugas, with some additional years: this is the duration of the Manu, the (attendant) divinities, and the rest, which is equal to 852,000 divine years, or to 306,720,000 years of mortals, independent of the additional period. Fourteen times this period constitutes a Bráhma day, that is, a day of Brahmá; the term (Bráhma) being the derivative form. At the end of this day a dissolution of the universe occurs, when all the three worlds, earth, and the regions of space, are consumed with fire. The dwellers of Maharloka (the region inhabited by the saints who survive the world), distressed by the heat, repair then to Janaloka (the region of holy men after their decease). When the three worlds are but one mighty ocean, Brahmá, who is one with Náráyaña, satiate with the demolition of the universe, sleeps upon his serpent-bed—contemplated, the lotus born, by the ascetic inhabitants of the Janaloka—for a night of equal duration with his day; at the close of which he creates anew. Of such days and nights is a year of Brahmá composed; and a hundred such years constitute his whole life. One Parárddha, or half his existence, has expired, terminating with the Mahá Kalpa called Pádma. The Kalpa (or day of Brahmá) termed Váráha is the first of the second period of Brahmá's existence.[1]

From this we can extract the following "ice core" of the past, showing one Great Age (Mahayuga) with its durations in divine years (left-hand columns) and human years (right-hand column):

Krita	Yuga	4000		1,440,000
	Sandhyá	400		144,000
	Sandyásana	400		144.000
	subtotal		4800	1,728,000
Treta	Yuga	3000		1,080,000
	Sandhyá	300		108,000
	Sandyásana	300		108,000
	subtotal		3600	1,296,000
Dwapara	Yuga	2000		720,000
	Sandhyá	200		72,000
	Sandyásana	200		72.000
	subtotal		2400	864,000
Kali	Yuga	1000		360,000
	Sandhyá	100		36,000
	Sandyásana	100		36,000
	subtotal		1200	432,000
	total		12,000	4,320,000

We need one more piece of information to align these durations with known history. The Hindu astronomers agree that the Kali Yuga began at midnight between February 17 and 18, 3102 BCE.[2] Consequently it is due to end about 427,000 CE, whereupon a new Golden Age will dawn.

One might dismiss these as fantastic figures intended to impress with the majesty of the created universe, or even as intimations of its true age. But the numbers are not casual, nor limited to the sacred texts of Hinduism. Here is Berossus (or Berosus) in his *Chaldean Chronicle,* reported thirdhand by the church historian Eusebius:

> Apollodorus says that the first king was Alorus, who was a Chaldaean from Babylon, and he reigned for 10 *sars.* He divides a *sar* into 3,600 years, and adds two other [measures of time]: a *ner* and a *soss.* He says that a *ner* is 600 years, and a *soss* is 60 years. He counts the years in this way, following some ancient form of calculation. After saying this, he proceeds to list ten kings of the Assyrians, one after the other in [chronological] order; from Alorus, the first king, until Xisuthrus, in whose reign the first great flood occurred, the flood which Moses mentions. He says that the total length of the reigns of the [ten] kings was 120 *sars,* which is the equivalent of 432,000 years.[3]

Berossus, a priceless witness to Babylonian chronology, was a priest of Bel and had a school of astronomy on the island of Kos in the third century BCE. His figure is exactly the duration of the Kali Yuga. The reign of Xisuthrus, which ended with the reestablishment of civilization under a new dynasty, was eighteen *sars,* equivalent to 64,800 years: another number we should note.

The plot thickens as we turn to the Chinese chronicles, and to the French scholar-missionaries of the eighteenth century who studied material that even now remains untranslated. One of them, Père Prémare, writes (his italics):

> I will not digress to explain the period of *Tchao-kang-tsie,* which comprises a great year that he calls *Yuen,* and which is composed of twelve parts, like so many months, that he calls *Hoei,* of 10,800 years apiece; which makes 129,600 years for the entire *Yuen.*[4]

Obviously there is some relation to the Babylonian chronology, as

129,600 is 64,800 × 2, or 432,000 × $^3/_{10}$. Prémare's sources continue with an account of prehistoric dynasties:

> The Dynasty of Tien-hoang had thirteen Kings of the same name; that is why they are called brothers, and each of them is assigned 18,000 years, either of life or of reign.[5]
>
> [In the Ti-hoang dynasty] there are eleven Kings of the same name. . . . Each of these eleven Kings ruled or lived 18,000 years, which makes 19,800 for all of them together.[6]

Prémare, a Jesuit and obligatory believer in the Judeo-Christian creation date, did not trouble himself further with these absurd numbers. A later Sinologist, Thomas Fergusson, noticed them and did the simple sum:[7]

> 13 + 11 reigns of 18,000 years = 432,000 years.

As a fourth example, the Icelandic saga called the Poetic Edda describes the preparations for the apocalyptic battle at the end of time, when Valhalla's warriors issue forth against the Fenris Wolf.

> *There Valgrind stands, | the sacred gate,*
> *And behind are the holy doors;*
> *Old is the gate, | but few there are*
> *Who can tell how it tightly is locked.*
>
> *Five hundred doors | and forty there are,*
> *I ween, in Valhall's walls;*
> *Eight hundred fighters | through one door fare*
> *When to war with the wolf they go.[8]*

Any numerate listener will be intrigued enough to calculate: 540 × 800 = 432,000. So the number of warriors gathered in Valhalla on the last day is again the number of years in the Kali Yuga, the last age of the Maha Yuga cycle. No wonder the authors of *Hamlet's Mill* found it a "remarkable and disturbing coincidence."[9] Incidentally, they add that 432,000 is also the number of syllables in the Rig Veda.[10]

The occurrence of the same number in four widely separated cultures (Hindu, Chaldean, Chinese, and Icelandic) has long been noticed. While it is quite possible that it passed from one to the other, the exact process stretches the imagination. It must have involved an elite group of mathematicians, present in every culture, who grafted it onto whatever legendary support lay to hand, whether world cycles, king-lists, or warrior tales.

What is special about 432,000? Granted, it is the product of two numbers important to geometry: 360 (the number of degrees in a circle) and 72 (a fifth of this, producing a pentagon), but these in turn belong to a family of numbers that fascinated ancient mathematicians: numbers generated from powers of 2, 3, and 5 alone. The Kali Yuga number, analyzed in this way, breaks down into the following factors:

$$432,000 = 2^7 [128] \times 3^3 [27] \times 5^3 [125]$$

It was not difficult to manipulate large numbers of this kind, using a chessboard or layout of pebbles with the powers of 3 along one axis, the powers of 5 along the other, and the powers of 2 calculated mentally or on the fingers. To multiply by 10, one coefficient is added to the 2s and one to the 5s. Thus the total duration of one set of Yugas (Maha Yuga) is:

$$4,320,000 = 2^8 [256] \times 3^3 [27] \times 5^4 [625]$$

The reign of king Xisouthrus:

$$64,800 = 2^5 [32] \times 3^4 [81] \times 5^2 [25]$$

Ernest McClain, in his books on music theory in ancient cultures, has revealed a multidisciplinary game, reminiscent of Hermann Hesse's "Glass Bead Game,"[11] based on such calculations (see chapter 1). It was played by esoteric groups in the cultures already named, by contributors to the

Hebrew Bible, and by Plato. Strange as it may seem, the object of the game was the search for mathematically satisfying tuning systems. For example, McClain interprets the Arks of Babylonian and Hebrew legend as multistory diagrams that enclose, or "save" from the flood of possible numbers, those necessary for calculating the calendar and the musical scale. In the case of the Hebrew Ark, the highest number is 432,000.[12]

McClain's discovery warns against any attempt to read the Yuga figures as historical. As Wilson says in his translation of the Vishnu Purana, "It does not seem necessary, to refer the invention to any astronomical computations, or to any attempt to represent actual chronology."[13] Yet to accomplish these two things is the Grail Quest of esoteric chronology.

GUÉNON REVEALS THE CODE

Even Traditionalists, who respect the authority of sacred texts, find the Puranic numbers forbiddingly large. They have no doubt that we are presently in the Kali Yuga or Iron Age, but they cannot help hoping that the next Krita Yuga or Golden Age is just around the corner. The Hindu texts, taken literally, have no comfort to offer. The prospect can be improved only if one can justify manipulating the figures.

For some reason, it is the French who have taken this matter most to heart. René Guénon was the first.[14] He accepted the doctrine of the Four Yugas and their proportionate lengths of 4:3:2:1, but he thought that the actual durations have been deliberately altered by adding zeros. He writes:

> This precaution may seem strange at first sight, but is easily explained. If the true length of the Manvantara were known, and if besides its starting point were exactly determined, anyone could, without difficulty, make deductions allowing them to predict certain future events. But no orthodox tradition has ever encouraged the methods by which man can know the more or less distant future, because in practice, such knowledge brings many more problems than advantages.[15]

Consequently, as Guénon explains, most of the zeros on the Puranic figures are simply there to mislead. The essential thing, he says, is the number 4,320. It should be taken as representing the Maha Yuga: the set of four Yugas that embraces the entire history of present humanity, but 4,320 years is obviously too short a period, just as the 4,320,000 given in the above extract from the *Vishnu Purana* is too long. By what number should 4,320 be multiplied to arrive at the true length of the Maha Yuga? Through logical and erudite arguments Guénon concludes that the proper multiplier is 15. This gives the following durations for the four Yugas:

Krita Yuga	25,920
Dwapara Yuga	19,440
Treta Yuga	12,960
Kali Yuga	6,480
total	64,800

To confirm the matter, the total for the Maha Yuga is exactly the duration of the reign of Xisuthrus (see above), "who is manifestly identical to Vaivaswata, the Manu of the current era."[16]

The Maha Yuga and the Manvantara, terms that cause such confusion to all students of the subject, now coincide. All that remains, if the age-long secret is to be revealed, is to anchor it in historical chronology. Guénon had already given the vital clue in an article of 1931, but it was not, as one might expect, the traditional date of 3102 BCE.

We think that the duration of the Atlantean civilization must be equal to a "Great Year," understood as half the period of the Precession of the Equinoxes. As for the cataclysm that brought it to an end, certain concordant data seem to indicate that it took place 7200 years before the year 720 of the Kali Yuga: a year which is itself the departure point of a familiar era, but one whose origin and significance are no longer known to those who currently use it.[17]

Guénon's commentator, Jean Robin, explains:

> If one knows that the era in question is none other than the Jewish one, whose beginning is traditionally placed 3761 years before the Christian era, it is easy to deduce . . . the "theoretical" end-date of the cycle. The beginning of the Kali Yuga would thus be in the year 4481 BCE (3761+720), and its end would have to come 6480 years later, i.e. in the year 1999 (6480–4481).[18]

Robin, writing in the early 1980s, reminds us that 1999 is the one date specifically mentioned by Nostradamus, as the coming of the "Great King of Terror." If we wish, we can add one year to replace the nonexistent "AD Zero," bringing the end-date to 2000 CE. In either case, the Kali Yuga has gone the way of the Y2K scare, and we are now in the dawning of a new Krita Yuga or Golden Age. But it is hard to imagine the author of *The Reign of Quantity,* if he were living now, agreeing with that.

ALAIN DANIÉLOU'S PURANIC CHRONOLOGY

The orientalist and musicologist Alain Daniélou (1907–1994), who knew the Hindu tradition from the inside, approached the problem of dating the Yugas from a different angle. Daniélou shared many attitudes with Guénon, with whom he had some correspondence, and in some ways was also a Traditionalist. He became a Shaivite (devotee of Shiva) and a defender of traditional peoples and their cultures against the decadent influence of the modern West and the monotheistic religions, these being as he said "intolerant by nature."[19]

Daniélou, like Guénon, cannot accept the extremely large figures given in the Puranas, but he reduces them in a different way. He mainly cites the Linga Purana, which we now consult, though on this subject it hardly differs from the Vishnu Purana as quoted above.[20] Not knowing Sanskrit, I fear to criticize such a great scholar, but Daniélou's treatment of the data and terminology is quite contrary to the sources.

According to *Linga Purana,* ch. 4, v. 24–36
1 Maha Yuga (set of 4 Yugas) = 4,320,000 human years
1000 Maha Yugas = 1 Kalpa or Day of Brahma = 4,320,000,000
years and comprises 14 Manvantaras of 306,720,000 years
Therefore 1 Manvantara contains a little over 71 Maha Yugas

Comment. The Puranic mathematician followed the tradition that there are 14 Manvantaras to a cycle (though later [ch. 24, v. 6–140] he enumerates 28 Manus). However, he took that cycle to be not the Maha Yuga of 4,320,000 years but a Kalpa or Day of Brahma, 1000 times greater. He divided *that* by 14 to find the duration of a Manvantara. Then, to see how many Maha Yugas there were in each of the 14 Manvantaras, he found "a little over 71." This stands to reason, since he had multiplied the Maha Yuga by 1000 and was now trying to get back to it by division! 1000 ÷ 14 = 71.4285714.

Daniélou starts with the same figure of 4,320,000, but he proceeds in the opposite direction, applying the division by 71 to a single Maha Yuga. Daniélou's interpretation:

1 Maha Yuga or Great Year = 4,320,000 human years
This contains 71.42 Manvantaras of 60,487 years
Each Manvantara contains a set of 4 Yugas

Comment. Daniélou's system rests on the following quotation from *Linga Purana:* «*Le Mahâ-Yuga, durant lequel apparaît et disparaît l'espèce humaine est divisé en un peu plus de 71 cycles de 14 Manvantarä*» (*Lingä Purânä 1.4.7.*)[21] That is, "The Maha Yuga, during which the human race appears and disappears, is divided into a little more than 71 cycles of 14 Manvantaras."[22] However, this passage does not appear in the English translation of the *Linga Purana,* which states, on the contrary, "A little over 71 sets of four yugas—Krita, Treta, Dwapara and Kali—constitute a Manvantara."[23] The *Vishnu Purana,* quoted above, concurs: "the interval, called a Manwantara, is equal to seventy-one times the number of years contained in the four Yugas, with some additional years."

Leaving the experts to resolve these contradictions, I now present Daniélou's chronology. Its peg is the traditional date for the beginning of the Kali Yuga, 3102 BCE, which "represents a cosmological reality linked with an alternation in influx from the planetary spheres; it is not an arbitrary date."[24] The right-hand column shows the beginning dates of each period, accurate (as he says) to within fifty years.[25]

Krita	Dawn	2,016.24		58,042 BCE
	Yuga	20,162.40		56,026 BCE
	Twilight	2,016.24		35,864 BCE
	subtotal		24,194.88	
Treta	Dawn	1,512.10		33,848 BCE
	Yuga	15,121.80		32,336 BCE
	Twilight	1,512.10		17,215 BCE
	subtotal		18,146	
Dwapara	Dawn	1,008.10		15,703 BCE
	Yuga	10,081.20		14,695 BCE
	Twilight	1,008.10		4,610 BCE
	subtotal		12,097.4	
Kali	Dawn	504.06		3,606 BCE
	Yuga	5,040.60		3,102 BCE
	Twilight	504.06		1939–2442 CE
	subtotal		6,048.72	
	total		60,487	

Daniélou does not mention Atlantis by name, but he says that the present cycle began with a great flood, recorded by all civilizations (and different from the flood that Sumerian sources date to around the beginning of the Kali Yuga). In anthropological terms, the cycle seems to have begun with the appearance of Cro-Magnon Man. The human species of the previous cycle, dating back to 118,000 BCE, was probably the Neanderthal. As an antievolutionist, Daniélou reminds us that the Neanderthal's brain box was considerably bigger than our own. Concluding his study of cycles with a significant footnote, he strays into territory familiar to us, though perhaps not to his academic readers.

> Vaivasvata Manu (the Noah of the Bible), survivor of a previous human cycle, was saved by Vishnu who, in the form of a fish, pulled the ark to dry land. The descendants of Manu's companions, intermingled with the new races then still in semi-animal form (the Nephilim of Genesis), constitute the present humanity.*

We now have three suggested dates for the end of the Kali Yuga, and with it the end of the present set of four ages. The Puranic figures, taken literally, place it about 427,000 years in the future. Guénon invites his reader to figure out that it ends in 1999 or 2000 CE. Daniélou calculates that the Kali Yuga is now in twilight phase and that "the final catastrophe will take place during this twilight. The last traces of this present humanity will have disappeared in 2442."[27]

GASTON GEORGEL AND THE RHYTHMS OF HISTORY

No one has devoted more attention to these matters than Gaston Georgel (1899–?), the author of five books on cosmic cycles. Working independently in the 1930s, he followed current notions about how history does not exactly repeat, but "rhymes," and does so at definite intervals. His first findings appeared in 1937 as *Les rythmes dans l'histoire* (Rhythms in history). Some of the parallels are impressive, such as that of the medieval kings of France with Louis XIV–XVI, at an interval of 539 years (77 × 7), or that of the English and French revolutions, 144 years apart. However, Georgel spreads his net very widely. Considering that he illustrates cycles of the following durations (in years): 11, 22, 33, 44/45, 55, 77, 100, 125,

---

*According to a theory suggested by the Commentaries of the Puranas, the ark may have been a space vessel in which some survivors of the previous human cycle had taken refuge. It would have been they who gave birth to the new humanity and its Golden Age.[26]

130, 144, 150, 154, 288, 300, 515, 539/540, 666, 1000, 1030, 1078/1080, 1100, 1400, 2160, with a few years' deviance permitted, almost any pairing of historical events can be made to fit somewhere.

René Guénon reviewed Georgel's book in the year of its appearance. He agreed that many of the coincidences were extraordinary, but he regretted that Georgel had not worked with traditional figures such as the precessional period of 25,920 years and its divisions. Probably it was Georgel's book that prompted him to write his crucial "Remarks on the Doctrine of Cosmic Cycles" (1938), in which he divulged his interpretation of the Puranic numbers.

In June 1942, the Gestapo knocked on Georgel's door in Belfort and seized all the copies of his book. Someone must have alerted them to passages such as this:

> Today, the masters of Hitlerian Germany, replacing Christian ideals with those of the Viking barbarians, are invoking the ancient Germanic gods Odin and Wotan, and proclaiming: "It is more honorable to fall in combat than to die of arthritis in one's bed," while the youths engrave "Blood and Honor" on their daggers and sing: "Victorious, we'll crush France." So sang the Norse pirates as they sailed up our western rivers.[28]

Finding this "offensive to Germany and the Führer,"[29] the occupiers imprisoned him. After the Red Cross had secured his release, Georgel developed his theories further in the light of Guénon's criticisms, publishing an enlarged edition in 1947.[30] The Second World War and the fall of Germany provided abundant evidence for a 2,160-year cycle linking modern and ancient history, as well as completing the uncanny 130-year parallel between Napoleon's career and Hitler's. Meanwhile Guénon, writing from Cairo, was educating Georgel in traditional doctrines.

In *Les rythmes dans l'histoire*, Georgel makes much of the 2,160-year cycle, which he aligns with the astrological ages (see chapter 12). He renames the Age of Aries the "Cycle of Abraham" and the Age of Pisces the "Cycle of Caesar." He treats each period as a "year" and divides it into four equal "seasons" of 540 years each, beginning with autumn, then into twelve "months" of 180 years, for each of which he finds an appropriate historical tag. For example, in the Cycle of Caesar, the month of "May," running from 1130 to 1310 CE, is the "Apogee of feudal civilization, of the Papacy, and of the Holy Roman Empire."[31] Then he applies a different rhythm for a closer analysis, dividing each season into seven cycles of 77 years each to make his preferred number of 539.

The point of departure is always the crucial key to cyclical studies. Georgel chose to begin his Cycle of Caesar in 130 BCE, and to end it 2,160 years later, in 2030 CE. As for his reasons, he mentions "a deep study of the Christic cycle" and that "according to Virgil's Fourth Eclogue, the sun at autumn equinox then entered the sign of Virgo."[32] This places the "autumnal" season of Roman civilization between 130 BCE and 410 CE, neatly framing the Roman conquest of Provence (122–118 BCE) and the Germanic invasions of Gaul (404–406 CE). The remaining three seasons, right up to 2130 CE, are shamelessly headed *Civilisation Française.*

In reviewing the work, Guénon made the point that the chronologies of different peoples have different points of departure, and that one cannot establish a general synchronism since diverse civilizations do not simply succeed one another, but coexist.[33] Georgel, though invoking universal principles based on Indo-European traditions, remained not only Eurocentric but Francocentric. For example, in listing the significant events of the fourth cycle of the "summer" season, 1721–1798 CE, he does not even mention the American War of Independence.

At this stage of his researches, Georgel treated history as a kind of gearbox containing wheels of many different gauges, each marking a regular rhythm to which historical events, once aligned, tend to mesh. Guénon's tutelage soon led to a total rebuilding of the machine. *Les quatre âges de l'humanité* (The four ages of humanity), first published in 1949, was much more ambitious, as its foreword declares.

After having demonstrated, in our previous study, the objective existence in history of authentically traditional rhythms (notably the period of 2,160 years), we now intend to enlarge our field of research so as to embrace, if possible, the whole of prehistory, insofar as it is identified with the cyclical duration of 64,800 years that certain Chaldean texts attribute to the history of present humanity.

Might we not extend the field even further into the past? Indeed not, for beyond that "barrier" the chronology of modern experts becomes extremely confused, while Tradition teaches us that there existed then a humanity different from ourselves, of which we know practically nothing. It would be the same as if we were to try, in the opposite direction, to cross the firewall that separates the present cycle from the future one. For all sacred Scriptures teach that we are on the eve of a new "age" about which we know only one thing: that it will begin under "new Heavens" and on a "new Earth."

Thus the subject of our study is clearly bounded in time, between the 63rd millennium BC, when Prehistory began in the gardens and the (then) delightful climate of the Hyperborean continent, and the beginning of the coming century, when a new and final world war will bring the history of present humanity, already 65,000 years old, to its conclusion. In other words, we are undertaking the study of the cycle that the Hindus call the "Manvantara," and which we will situate within a greater period, the Kalpa or world cycle.[34]

Already in December 1937, Guénon had been instructing Georgel on the "traditional" theory of the four races and their correspondences:[35]

North	winter	infancy	lymphatic	White race	water
East	spring	youth	nervous	Yellow race	air
South	summer	maturity	sanguine	Black race	fire
West	autumn	old age	bilious	Red race	earth

Guénon was still holding true to the scheme revealed in 1910, during the séances of the Ordre du Temple Rénové (see chapter 2). In conformity with the French esoteric tradition, he adds that there is no superiority of one race to another; they all have their own possibilities and period of supremacy or predominance, following cyclic laws. When his correspondence resumed after the war, Guénon clarified the Hindu terminology.

> [The Kalpa] is the total duration of a world, and it cannot be included in any larger cycle. It is divided into 14 Manvantaras, each of them the complete cycle of a humanity. The matter of the Four Ages belongs within each Manvantara. . . . As for the Christian tradition, it considers nothing beyond the present Manvantara. What it calls the "end of the world" (and would be better called the "end of *a* world") is nothing more than the end of present humanity. . . . Given this, the Earthly Paradise naturally corresponds to the Krita-Yuga or Golden Age of our Manvantara. Since in the first epochs men lived on continents since vanished, it is most unlikely that the "prehistoric" remains that are found go back so far, and in fact they are usually only dated to about 15 or 20,000 years, which is relatively recent. They would have to be nearly three times as old to date from the Golden Age.[36]

Needless to say, this dating of the age of the earth conflicts with the findings of modern science. Neither Guénon nor Georgel had any patience with the "fabulous figures" of billions of years, which, says Georgel, were arrived at through purely materialistic research and served merely to analyze strata for the benefit of the mining industry.[37] They both agreed that since the current Manvantara is the seventh, and each one lasts 64,800 years, the world is less than half a million years old. Georgel develops a curious theory to account for the disparity, based on a geometrical diagram that relates traditional, cyclical time to scientific, rectilinear time.[38] He also has a theory of the evolution of civilizations at points spaced around the globe at 60° apart, each with its own pole, and many other ideas that cannot be treated here.

Les quatre âges de l'humanité reached Guénon in January 1950, and he promised to read and review it. In November, having done so, he took the trouble to quiz Georgel about the cyclical number 10,800—and this from a man with three young children, a pregnant wife, and suffering from ulcerated legs.[39] It was one of Guénon's last letters to anyone; he died a few weeks later on January 7, 1951.

Georgel had been a good pupil, up to a point, but he stuck to his own dating, saying, "To facilitate our research, we will here adopt the date of AD 2030 that was proposed as a working hypothesis in our first book, for the end of the Manvantara."[40] He paid his mentor a dubious compliment in inventing a threefold division of the cycle. Guénon himself pointed out politely that no tradition mentions such a thing,[41] but Georgel felt sufficiently supported by the myth of Agarttha and its threefold rulership (see chapters 2 and 6), which Saint-Yves d'Alveydre had published in *Mission de l'Inde* and Guénon approved in *Le Roi du monde*. The three equal periods, he says, reflect the successive authority of the Brahatma or king of the world, who "speaks to God face to face," then the Mahatma, who is the high priest, and lastly the Mahanga, who is the emperor or temporal ruler.[42] Georgel applies this division in all his subsequent writings and finds it reflected at every level. For example, he divides the "modern cycle" into a "Prophetic or Primitive phase" from 1310 to 1550 CE, when esoteric traditions were still alive; a "Sacerdotal or Religious phase" from 1550 to 1790, ending when the French Revolutionaries seized church properties; and a "Royal or Temporal phase" from 1790 to 2030, when religion was no longer a significant influence.[43]

Georgel considered it portentous that Guénon, in 1938, had broken the "Law of the Mysteries" and revealed the true duration of the Hindu cycles.[44] He defends his master's action by another appeal to Saint-Yves, who declared in *Mission de l'Inde* that in 1877, "after consulting the celestial Intelligences about the meaning of these Signs, the Supreme College of Agarttha, guided by its venerable leader, recognized in them a direct command from God announcing the progressive Abrogation of the Law of Mysteries."[45]

Georgel found confirmation of 2030 CE as the end date of our cycle in a related source: *Beasts, Men and Gods* by Ferdinand Ossendowski.[46] This bestselling book of adventure in central Asia, published in 1922, borrowed much from Saint-Yves' Agarttha (calling it "Agharti"). It culminated with a prophecy that the King of the World is supposed to have made in 1891.

> In the fiftieth year only three great kingdoms will appear, which will exist happily seventy-one years. Afterwards there will be eighteen years of war and destruction. Then the peoples of Agharti will come up from their subterranean caverns to the surface of the earth.[47]

The fiftieth year from 1891 is 1941. The happy period of seventy-one years under three great kingdoms lasts from 1941 until 2012. Then eighteen more years bring us exactly to 2030.[48] As Georgel points out, "we keep landing on these dates of 2030 or 2031, and we have to admit that the present cycle will go no further."[49]

Once Georgel had learned about the Four Ages, he started dividing his historical periods in the proportion of 4:3:2:1. Applied to our current Manvantara or Maha Yuga, this yields the chronology on page 317, which can be compared with the others, above.[50]

As Georgel elaborates his system, every cycle is divisible into three equal periods and also into four ages of diminishing length (as shown above); into five equal "Great Years," and into a symmetrical fourteen-fold division, with seven ascending and seven descending phases.[51] Moreover, the system is fractal: every subcycle or phase is divisible in the same multiple ways, and so on potentially ad infinitum. As with the "rhythms of history," the critic may object that with so many possibilities, there are sure to be enough hits to support any argument. For that reason I will leave aside most of Georgel's subsequent material and concentrate on his analysis of the Four Ages as they manifest in more recent epochs.

Golden Age	25,920 years	Began 62,770 BCE	Reign of Cronos or period of Eternal Spring	Beginning of present humanity. Hippopotamus Epoch, period of "eternal spring" at Spitzbergen
		ca. 50,000 BCE		Glaciation of northern regions. Mammoth Epoch. Far Eastern prehistory, of uncertain chronology
		ca. 40,000 BCE		Neanderthal Race? So-called Mousterian period
Silver Age	19,440 years	Began 36,850 BCE	The "Fall." Reign of Jupiter and appearance of the arts	
		ca. 25,000 BCE		Beginning of the Aurignacian. Reindeer Age in Europe. End of the Solutrean
Bronze Age	12,960 years	Began 17,410 BCE	Corruption of the human race	
		ca. 16,000– 12,000 BCE		Magdalenian
		ca. 11,000 BCE		End of the "Glacial" period
Iron Age	6,480 years	Began 4450 BCE	Confusion of languages. Dark Age	
Total	64,800 years	2030 CE	End of the cycle	

The Dark or Iron Age divides into four phases.[52] (All the dates, Georgel admits, are approximate.)

1st phase, lasting $^4/_{10}$ of the age　　4450 BCE–1858 BCE

Reflection of the primordial Golden Age. Religion is in high regard, literature and the arts are sacred in nature.

2nd phase, lasting $^3/_{10}$ of the age　　1858 BCE–86 CE

Reflection of the Silver Age. Predominance of noble and chivalric values: magnificence, conquest, pride of birth

3rd phase, lasting $^2/_{10}$ of the age　　214 BCE–1382 CE

Reflection of the Bronze Age. Materialism increases, profit and bourgeois values prevail over honor. Atheism and agnosticism appear.

4th phase, lasting $^1/_{10}$ of the age　　1382–2030 CE

Confusion of castes, election of dictators, tyranny of the state, hypertrophy of industry. Hints of the dawn of the coming Golden Age.

Strictly speaking, the division should continue by breaking down each of these phases into subphases in the proportion 4:3:2:1. Instead, Georgel turns to a different scheme for his analysis of "modern times," beginning not in 1382 but in 1310 with the suppression of the Templars.[53] This gives the following fourfold plan:[54]

Golden Age	1310–1598	Late Middle Ages and Renaissance
Silver Age	1598–1814	Absolute monarchies and Revolution
Bronze Age	1814–1958	Capitalist period
Iron Age	1958–2030	Populist (?) or technocratic period

Following the fractal principle, each of these microcosmic ages contains four phases in 4:3:2:1 proportion. Here is Georgel's scheme for the "populist or technocratic" age in which we are now living, which again has its miniature Golden, Silver, Bronze, and Iron Ages:[55]

1st phase	1958–1987	Excess of wealth and power; medical and scientific triumphs; demands for freedom; all the world's wisdom made available
2nd phase	1987–2009	[Fall of communism; globalization; climate change; militant Islam]
3rd phase	2009–2023	
4th phase	2023–2030	

Writing in about 1970, Georgel could only describe what he had seen in its first, relatively "golden" phase, with its potentially dangerous excesses of wealth and power, its scientific and medical triumphs, the hippies' vision of a new age, and the ruder demands of the 1968 student uprisings. He rejoiced in the flood of esoteric literature that was now freely available, especially texts of oriental wisdom almost unobtainable fifty years earlier.[56] Far from being pessimistic, he still hoped for a reconciliation not only between the Christian sects but between Christianity and Guénon's elective faith of Islam. He cited the prophecy of St. Malachy concerning the popes, which ends with the one called *De gloria olivae* (The glory of the olive; now known to be Benedict XVI) and then the return of St. Peter. Would the olive branch in question be extended to the Muslim world, and accepted? Finally, in 1986, aged eighty-six or eighty-seven, he added a sad but not despairing postscript:

> In 1986, the sole lasting result of ecumenism concerns the reconciliation between the two churches, Roman and Orthodox. In contrast, the gulf between Christianity and Islam has deepened since the Iranian Revolution. There is nothing to hope for from the Hindu or Buddhist side, so that it can only be at the End of Time that Christ's prophecy will be realized: "There shall be one flock, and

one shepherd." [John 10:16] At the End of Time, or rather at the start of the future Golden Age?[57]

INTERIM REFLECTIONS

The system of the Four Ages rests on certain assumptions that it would be good to scrutinize before either accepting or rejecting its various components. The first premise is that time, as humans experience it, is not uniform but proceeds in waves. The second is that these waves do not resemble sine curves but have a sawtooth shape. Each one begins with a lengthy state of relative perfection (the Golden Age or Krita Yuga), then curves ever more steeply downward, accelerating and crashing at the end of the Kali Yuga. Whatever was of value (which may include select humans) is preserved by the divine preceptors (Manus) as a seed from which the new Krita Yuga shoots up.

If one has a fundamentally spiritual view of things, then in broad terms this makes sense. Each Maha Yuga begins with a spiritual influence planted in the material world, where it must ineluctably wither and die. For nearly half the cycle, humans "walk with the gods" and thereafter enjoy spiritual awareness to various degrees. Only near the end does this fade to become a matter for mere belief (religion) or denial (materialism). After that, a new spiritual impulse is needed, and the process begins again.

A subsidiary question is whether the transitions between the four ages are punctuated distinctly, as their beginning undoubtedly is, or whether the 4:3:2:1 ratio is just a way of plotting a smooth, accelerating curve. If the latter, then all dates given for the in-between ages are irrelevant. If the former, then the agent of punctuation needs to be identified. We would like to know what exactly happens at the nodal points.

If, on the other hand, spirit and matter are not separate, then the whole process is more a function of time itself. Since time depends on the movement of bodies, there will probably be some astronomical or astrological explanation for these successive waves. (We will see a few examples below.) It may require catastrophes to interrupt the regular revolutions of suns, moons, and planets to create a periodic "new heaven and new earth." Atlantologists have suggested comets, falling moons, near-collisions with passing planets, and pole shifts as some of the possibilities.

Alternatively, one may take the Pythagorean view that the cosmos is harmonious by nature and hence in perpetual complex vibration. This would support Georgel's theories of rhythms and patterns that repeat at all fractal levels. His simultaneous subdivision of periods into 3, 4, 5, and other fractions resembles the harmonic series generated by a vibrating string. Though sympathetic to this view, I find that Georgel protests too much. Like every inspired amateur possessed by a single line of thought, he drives it to extremes, such as according global importance to the Fifth French Republic. If he had been content, as Guénon and Daniélou were, simply to present the basic mechanism of the Yugas, he would have been more persuasive.

The two functions of Yuga theory are to understand the past and to predict the future. The assumptions are again quite weighty ones, depending on what credit one allows to dates and figures. The minimal possibility is that ancient sages, writing the sacred texts, looked around them and saw (as old people tend to see) a world in decline. They projected this onto the deep past and integrated it, as they felt sure it should be, with the numbers of their *Glasperlenspiel.*

Another possibility is that they had some supersensible power of seeing into the past, which enabled them to discern the rhythms in question. They could have understood the currents of time without necessarily attaching numbers to them, then proceeded as above. This assumes, of course, that such rhythms are there for the finding, and that humans possess such powers. Even then we may ask whether they saw truly, or whether they saw only projections of their own fantasies—or an ego-contaminated truth, as seems to be common among seers.

A further possibility is that the system of the Yugas was not obtained through human capability whether rational or suprarational, but revealed by higher beings in the course of humanity's prehistoric education. Many of our occult Atlantologists have agreed with this, specifying what sort of higher beings are intended, how the transmission took place, and who received it.

A bolder assumption is that the rhythms *are* there, that they *were* revealed to those ancients by whatever means, and that the numbers given in the Puranas are absolutely true. This is the fundamentalist position that has gone unquestioned among Hindus for thousands of years. Esotericists modify it, looking as they do for the inner meanings of sacred texts. In a way theirs is the biggest assumption of all. They truly believe that the ancients possessed the chronological key to cosmic and human history, then deliberately published a faulty version of it, either content to keep the truth within an order of initiates, or confident that when the time became ripe, someone (themselves?) would crack the code and make proper use of the information.

What would be proper use, in this case? It is always interesting to learn about how the cosmos works—scientists are telling us more all the time— but the Yuga scheme invites disbelief, because of all the assumptions it requires. Apocalyptic Christians and Muslims have plenty of assumptions of their own. For those who have lost faith in progress, and maybe in the theory of evolution and the materialist paradigm, the Yuga doctrine only confirms what they already know. The one thing that might be useful is to know exactly when life on Earth will become insupportable, so that one can plan one's remaining days accordingly.

Here our authorities fail to agree. It did not matter in Puranic times, but now there is quite a difference between a Kali Yuga that ended in 1999, one that will end in 2012 or 2030, and one that will straggle on until the twenty-fifth century. Whom can one trust, or are all prophets who dare to name the Last Day presumptuous fools? Guénon, who, it will be remembered, never named the day (that was left to his epigones Georgel and Jean Robin), writes in his late work *The Reign of Quantity and the Signs of the Times* that even if one could fix on precise dates (which he rather doubts), one should keep quiet about them, "in order not to run the risk of contributing to a further growth of the anxiety and disorder now [1944] reigning in our world."[58] In any case, he says, what is destroyed at the end of the cycle is only what must be destroyed because its manifestation is finished and exhausted,[59] and in the memorable closing words of the book, "the 'end of a world' never is and never can be anything but the end of an illusion."[60]

Forty years on, Alain Daniélou, a happier character altogether, had no doubt that the Kali Yuga will come to a catastrophic end, but also that humanity has the power to hold it off. He was encouraged by a new cohesion between scientific research and cosmological speculation and "a continuity between physics, metaphysics, and eventually spirituality, in contrast with the dogmatism of the religions coming from Arihat [meaning Buddhism and Jainism, plus Christianity and Islam]."[61] With not a breath of sentimentality, he explains:

> Humankind is destroyed only after it has outlived its reason for existence; from the point of view of both carnal and spiritual beings, this occurs when the lineage is debased by racial mixing and when the tradition of occult knowledge can no longer find any receptacle to receive and pass on its heritage.
>
> The extent to which certain men will be able to reverse the tendencies of the modern world, and rediscover ways of life and thought in keeping with their true nature, will determine for how long the final day can be forestalled, or at least allow some groups of individuals to escape the cataclysm and participate in the formation of the future humanity and of the new Golden Age, which should appear after the next flood.[62]

FABRE D'OLIVET REVERSES THE YUGAS

In his *Philosophic History of the Human Race,* Fabre d'Olivet (already mentioned in chapter 2) took the radical step of reversing the Hindu Yugas. This is what he writes:

The *Satya-youg,* which corresponds to the first age, is that of physical reality. According to what is said in the Pouranas, it is an age filled with frightful catastrophes where the conspiring elements declare war, where the gods are assailed by demons; where the terrestrial globe, at first engulfed by the seas, is every instant menaced with total ruin. The *Tetra-youg* which follows it, is no more fortunate. It is only at the epoch of the *Douapara-youg* that the earth begins to present a picture more smiling and more tranquil. Wisdom, united to valour, speaks by the mouth of Rama and Krishna. Men listen and follow their lessons. Sociability, arts, laws, morals, and religion flourished there, vying with each other. The *Kali-youg,* which has commenced, is to terminate this fourth period by the appearance of Vishnu, whose hand, armed with a glistening sword, will strike the incorrigible sinners and make the vices and evils which defile and afflict the universe disappear forever from the face of the earth.

The Greeks, however, were not the only ones guilty of having reversed the order of the ages and so brought confusion into this beautiful allegory. The Brahmans themselves advocate today the *Satya-youg* and slander the present age, and this despite their own annals which describe the third age, the *Douapar-youg,* as the most brilliant and most fortunate. This was the age of their maturity; they are today in their decrepitude and their attention as that of old people is turned often toward the time of their childhood.[63]

How Fabre d'Olivet extracted this idea from the translations available to him, I cannot say. He seems, at least, to be the only person ever to have interpreted the Four Yugas in this manner. His biographer, Léon Cellier, has a psychological explanation. In brief, it is that the myth of the Golden Age was the myth of Jean-Jacques Rousseau; Rousseau was the cause of the French Revolution; Fabre d'Olivet, implicated by his own testimony in the early stages of the revolution, had become disillusioned with it. Writing now after the Restoration of 1815, he had renounced Voltaire, Rousseau, Diderot, Weishaupt, and all the progressives of the *âge des lumières.*[64] But he had become a disciple of progress of another sort. His interpretation of world history as due to the interplay of the three principles, Providence, Will, and Destiny, had to give precedence to the first: an impersonal deity that desires the best for its creation. The history of the world, as he tells it, is the history of revolutions and restorations. We might plot it as a sawtooth wave in the opposite direction, in which the human condition rises to a plateau, then plunges down again.

Anyone with sufficient command of history can extract examples to support his "grand narrative," whether of evolution or devolution. The next two sections return to ancient sources in which the choice was not either, but both.

BUDDHIST SYSTEMS

The cyclic theories of Buddhism and Jainism, religions that appeared in India long after Hinduism, differ from the Hindu ones in three significant ways. First, they involve numbers so vast as to remove them from human experience or even imagination. This bars any attempt to link the cycles to known chronology. Second, they include the idea of cycles that oscillate up and down, more like sine waves than sawtooth waves.

What passes as the Buddhist system is found not in the original Pali texts but in commentaries that have become canonical teachings of the later, Mahayana sects. I summarize the system from the work of Carl Friedrich Koeppen, a nineteenth-century scholar on whom subsequent encyclopedists largely relied.[65]

> The complete period of a world, from first appearance to final annihilation, is called a Maha Kalpa. These recur eternally.
>
> Each Maha Kalpa divides into four Asankhya (uncountable) Kalpas. Two of these are negative, two positive.
>
> In the first, the universe perishes. In the second, it remains annihilated.
>
> In the third, it is renewed. In the fourth, it remains in existence.

(Koeppen compares this to the Hindu notion of a Day of Brahma as comprising dawn, day, twilight, and night.)

Some say that each of these four Kalpas is divided into twenty periods, making eighty for the Maha Kalpa.

Others count sixty-four destructions. They proceed as follows: seven times the world is destroyed by fire, then once by water. This pattern repeats seven times (bringing the number to fifty-six). Then there are seven more destructions by fire, and a final, sixty-fourth, by wind. The destructions affect billions of worlds, sometimes including the higher worlds of the Dhyanas (sublime states of consciousness), but never affecting the fourth Dhyana, nor the Formless World.

Each destruction is announced 100,000 years before its occurrence by a Deva who warns humanity to improve its behavior.

After the destruction, the world is repopulated by beings who have spent the second (dormant) Kalpa in the unaffected higher realms. They have exhausted their merit and now have to be reborn on earth. But they are free and sinless beings, knowing neither sun nor moon, night or day, seasons, or distinction of sexes.

However, as these beings taste the sweet juices exuded by the earth, desire arises in them. They become physical beings. Some divide into sexes, incurring future rebirths through the womb. Property comes next, then strife. Some are reborn as animals. Depravity becomes so great that the hells are opened, and many go there after death.

At this point an equilibrium is reached, and with it the fourth Kalpa, that of stability. It is during this that the Buddhas take birth.

In the fourth Kalpa the human life span diminishes from 80,000 to 10 years, then increases again to 80,000. This double cycle repeats ten times.

The level of human virtue mirrors its life span. Each time the nadir is reached, most of humanity perishes through war, plague, or famine.

The survivors improve in virtue, and their life span increases.

We are now in a declining phase, as shown by the shortening of our life span.

However, we happen to live in a fortunate period that has already seen four Buddhas, and has one yet to come.

All the above is driven by Destiny, which is the law of nature.

The system seems to derive from a garbled version of Hindu doctrines. The declining periods agree with the descriptions of the Four Yugas. The period of nothingness before the new world receives an influx of higher beings may derive from the notion of *pralaya* or rest between the largest cycles. There is a Gnostic or Neoplatonic resonance in the descent of spiritual beings who become engrossed with material existence, and in early human androgyny. Naturally the Theosophical cosmogony, reputedly derived from "esoteric Buddhism," is similar. But it should be emphasized that this is not *the* Buddhist system. The whole notion of any exterior destiny controlling, predicting, and supervising manifestation is alien to the Four Noble Truths.

Koeppen, writing in the 1850s, makes a wise comment that could have been made yesterday, so relevant is it to current debates over cosmology and consciousness.

We [moderns] believe that living beings are products of nature; the Buddhist believes the reverse. To him, the breathing beings come first, and the exterior world second. The world is not the prerequisite for breathing beings, but they are the basis for it. . . . Only because beings have been sinning from all eternity and falling into matter, does matter exist. And since from all eternity they have been active in the process of purification and liberation, a countless number of worlds has arisen and vanished. The ensouled beings, the individuals, are the marrow [*das Mark:* core, essence] of the world: the outer universe merely the shell, the container that forms around the marrow. But this should not be understood, as we might like to think, as saying that the worlds exist only for the individuals. No! Buddhist opinion goes much further. The universe, in its appearance, its course, its arising and perishing is *a consequence, a result* of the moral conditions and action of breathing beings.[66]

A very different Buddhist system is found in the Kalachakra Tantra, the initiatic doctrine of Tibet.[67] The Kalachakra contains a prophecy of a great war to come at the end of the Kali Yuga, in which the last king of Shambhala will be victorious over the *Mlecchas*. This term referred originally to Muslims but is usually translated "barbarians," and interpreted as all those hostile to the Buddhist Dharma.

Dating this event is not problematic because the Kalachakra prophecy involves a series of twenty-five kings of Shambhala, each of whom rules for one hundred years. To anchor them in known chronology, we have 1927 CE as the date of accession of the twenty-first king of Shambhala, Aniruddha. Improbable as it sounds, the event was celebrated throughout Tibet, as the Dalai Lama confirmed in 1980. Therefore the twenty-fifth and last king, called Raudra Chakri, will assume power in 2327 CE, and after his defeat of the Mlecchas, Buddhism will flourish for another 1800 years. Some sources date the war to the ninety-eighth year of Raudra Chakri's rule (so in 2425); others to about the fiftieth year, while confirming that his victory will bring in the Age of Perfection or Krita Yuga.

THE SYSTEM OF THE JAINS

Jainism, like Buddhism, arose in the sixth century BCE as an outgrowth or reformation of Hinduism. The Jain system of time is based on a cycle of alternating world ages. An ascending age (*utsarpiṇī*) begins with the human condition at its worst and gradually rises to the zenith of well-being. Thereupon it switches to a descending age (*avasarpiṇī*), which drags the human condition down to its nadir, and to the beginning of a new ascending age. As in Buddhism, the cycle repeats infinitely.

Each age has six phases, with durations as follows:[68]

Avasarpiṇī (descending age)

1. 4 *koṭākoṭis* of *sagāropamas*
2. 3 *koṭākoṭis* of *sagāropamas*
3. 2 *koṭākoṭis* of *sagāropamas*
4. 1 *koṭākoṭi* of *sagāropamas* less 42,000 years
5. 21,000 years
6. 21,000 years

Utsarpiṇī (ascending age)

1. 21,000 years
2. 21,000 years
3. 1 *koṭākoṭi* of *sagāropamas* less 42,000 years
4. 2 *koṭākoṭis* of *sagāropamas*
5. 3 *koṭākoṭis* of *sagāropamas*
6. 4 *koṭākoṭis* of *sagāropamas*

While the Buddhists were content to call their cycles "uncountable," the Jains rejoiced in large numbers. A *koṭākoṭi* is 10^{14} years, and a *sagāropama* is $84,400,000^{19}$.[69] The scheme is more familiar than it looks on first sight, being based on the proportions 4:3:2:1, just like the Hindu Yugas. The 42,000 years deducted from the shortest of these (no. 4 of the descending period, no. 3 of the ascending) are compensated for by the twice-21,000 years of the extra periods. To the rationalist, those cycles (nos. 5–6 descending, 1–2 ascending) might as well be eliminated. That would leave a set of four Yugas in the usual descending mode, followed by its mirror image or reversal. Perhaps the small periods exist to provide some orientation in real time. The Jain teaching is that we are currently 19,000 years advanced in the fifth period of an *Avasarpiṇī* (descending age), so that we can expect the worst era to begin about 2,000 years hence.

SRI YUKTESWAR

The Jain system may have influenced that of Sri Yukteswar Giri (1855–1936), who became known outside India through the much-read *Autobiography of a Yogi* by his disciple Paramahansa Yogananda.[70] He was also admired by Walter Evans-Wentz, the scholar of fairy lore and Tibetan Buddhism, who prefaced that work.[71] Sri Yukteswar's book *The Holy Science,* written in 1894, describes an idiosyncratic Yuga theory that has recently come to prominence. Yogananda's Self-Realization Fellowship had always promoted it, but since the turn of the millennium, it has attracted much wider attention. This is largely thanks to the enthusiasm of Walter Cruttenden, who started the annual Conference on Precession and Ancient Knowledge (CPAK), founded the Binary Research Institute, and wrote a book of mythological and speculative astronomy, *Lost Star of Myth and Time.* Consequently Sri Yukteswar's theory has entered the lively forum of ideas about ancient astronomy, the galactic center, the Mayan calendar, and the year 2012. In New Age circles, especially those informed through the Internet, it already passes as *the* Yuga system.

Sri Yukteswar came from the Bengali landowning class and received a college education from British-run institutions. After the early death of his wife, he assumed the role of spiritual teacher and turned his family mansion into an ashram. Through his studies of Hindu astronomy and astrology, he came to the conclusion that the traditional chronology of the Yugas was not only wrong: it had been rigged for political reasons, so as not to let people know that the feared Kali Yuga had begun.[72]

Sri Yukteswar may have had political reasons of his own to proclaim the Kali Yuga at an end, instead of stretching 427,000 years into the future. During the early years of the twentieth century, he was active in a secret anticolonial movement called Yugantar, meaning "new age" or "transition of an epoch," along with another future guru, Aurobindo Ghosh. His two preoccupations come together in this police report of a revolutionary meeting.

Shortly before the publication of the *Yugantar* from Kolkata, early March 1906, Mokhada's friend Preonath Karar of Serampore (later known as Sri Yukteswar Giri) reached Benares and, with the help of Hrishikesh Kanjilal of the Kolkata Anushilan Samiti and Suranath, convened a public meeting as well as a meeting of the pundits: by quotations from the Hindu Astrology and Astronomy, it was announced that the sinful Iron Age was over and it was now the dawn of *Yugantar* or the *dvapar-yuga*. Hrishikesh undertook a tour of pilgrimage to proclaim the advent of the New Age and incite the sannyasis [roving monks] in a rebellion against the English.[73]

For whatever reason, Sri Yukteswar discards the Puranic numbers and the traditional date for the start of the Kali Yuga. Instead, he adopts a 24,000-year period of equinoctial precession. Twelve thousand of these years are given to a set of descending Yugas in the traditional proportion 4:3:2:1. Their durations are exactly those given in the first table of this chapter, but reading human years in place of divine years. On reaching the nadir, however, the cycle does not return to the Krita Yuga but starts an upward set of Yugas in reverse order. It is exactly like the Jain system, only reduced to historical dimensions. The dates are easily calculated from Yukteswar's information.

Satya I	4800	11,501 BCE–6701 BCE
Treta I	3600	6701 BCE–3101 BCE
Dwapara I	2400	3101 BCE–701 BCE
Kali I	1200	701 BCE–499 CE
Kali II	1200	499–1699 CE
Dwapara II	2400	1699–4099 CE
Treta II	3600	4099–769 CE
Satya II	4800	7699–12,499 CE

Each age, as in the Puranic system, consists of the core Yuga with *sandhis* or periods of mutation at its beginning and end, each worth $^1/_{10}$

of the Yuga. Thus a Dwapara Yuga proper lasts 2,000 years, framed by mutation periods of 200 years each. Writing in 1894, Yukteswar said: "In 1899, on completion of the period of 200 years of Dwapara Sandhi, the time of mutation, the True Dwapara Yuga of 2000 years will commence and will give to mankind in general a thorough understanding of the electricities and their attributes."[74]

The idea that humanity is in an upward cycle is so contrary to all traditional ideas that we must look for its source elsewhere. Yukteswar and his friends may have resisted the British yoke, but they had assimilated the European myth of progress. In conformity with this, the sage believed that around 1700, the world had entered an "electrical" age. The discovery of electricity and its uses signified that humans were attaining a finer perception than in the purely materialistic age that had preceded it. Before that, in the dual Kali Yuga, "the intellectual part of man was so much diminished that it could no longer comprehend anything beyond the gross material of creation."[75]

This I find an astonishing idea. The period from 701 BCE to 1699 CE saw the advent of the Orphic, Pythagorean, Taoist, Buddhist, Zoroastrian, Jain, and Vedantic movements; the birth of post-exilic Judaism, Druidry, Christianity, Manicheanism, Gnosticism, Catharism, and Islam; better yet, of Zen and Vajrayana Buddhism, Sankhya philosophy, Kabbalah, Sufism, Theosophy both Neoplatonic and Christian, and the arts of magic, alchemy, and astrology. Reports of miracles were commonplace, and belief in nonmaterial realities such as oracles, curses, the will of God, the devil, transubstantiation, and witchcraft was so intense as to cause major wars and persecutions. The only ones to welcome the post-1700 age as an improvement should be the materialists and atheists who see the human race gradually coming to its senses after an age of religious mania!

Yukteswar's system has a further complication. The sun, he wrote, "takes some star for its dual and revolves round it in about 24,000 years of our earth—a celestial phenomenon which causes the backward movement of the equinoctial points around the zodiac."[76] Cruttenden and others have sought, and found, astronomical justification for this statement. It entails rethinking the cause of equinoctial precession: that it is not the result, as Isaac Newton thought, of the tug of the sun and moon on the oblate spheroid of the earth, but something much simpler: "As the solar system slowly curves through space in its binary motion, it indirectly causes the earth to slowly change orientation to inertial space *without* completing any retrograde motion relative to the Sun."[77] The sun's companion star may be invisible, or it may even be the most mythic star of all, Sirius![78]

Not only is the sun revolving around its dual, in Yukteswar's cosmology, but the pair of them are going around a grand center called Vishnunabhi or Brahma.[79] In 1990 the Vedic scholar David Frawley suggested that Vishnunabhi might denote the galactic center, an idea that the Mayanist and independent researcher John Major Jenkins has developed through several works.[80] Jenkins spreads his net very wide, taking in Mesoamerican, Mithraic, and Egyptian mythologies, Islamic astrology, the legends of Virgo and St. James of Compostela, and the modern authorities Guénon, A. K. Coomaraswamy, and Fulcanelli. The crucial physical phenomenon is the alignment of the solstitial sun with the galactic center, which happens twice during the precessional cycle: once when the summer solstice aligns, and once when the winter solstice does so. In his most recent book, Jenkins shows that Plato himself may have alluded to this in his Atlantis myth. Not only is Plato's date close to the actual alignment of the summer solstice circa 10,000 BCE, but it was at that era that the dark rift in the Milky Way that marks the galactic center "sank" out of sight from Greece.[81]

Jenkins is sympathetic to Yukteswar's dual Yuga system, to which the galactic center alignments supply a plausible rhythm and perhaps explain the changes in human consciousness. However, he is well aware of the anachronisms in Yukteswar's dating, which he adjusts so that the cusp between the two Kali Yuga periods falls not at 499 CE but at 2012. His criticism is to the point:

Sri Yukteswar wanted the end of the descending Kali Yuga to correspond to his historical understanding—based on a nineteenth-century education—of the European Dark Ages and his belief in the elevation of human consciousness beginning around AD 500. He cites scientific advances and Europe's slow emergence from the Dark Ages to support this, but in my opinion, technology has thrust us deeper into material dependency and spiritual darkness. Yukteswar's scenario is Eurocentric and ignores Islamic and Chinese civilization. In addition, his elucidation depends on certain astronomical details of the ancient doctrines that, by his time, had eroded into semantic vagaries. Finally, he was writing before modern science had rediscovered the Galactic Center.[82]

Jenkins's solution places us at the absolute nadir, between the two Kali Yuga periods, at the point where the movement reverses and begins its upward phase. He sees this not in terms of physical causality, nor as a moment of catastrophe, but as the concomitant of a spiritual cycle in which, as the Perennial Philosophy teaches, humanity "progressively forgets its true, multidimensional nature, and later resurrects or remembers this true Self. In this way, we might think of the rise and fall of Atlantis as a metaphor for the forgetting and remembering of the Primordial Tradition."[83]

There is much talk of the galactic center these days. Paul LaViolette, one of the few scientifically trained authorities, presents it both as the place where matter is created and as the agent of periodic catastrophe for the earth.[84] I note one curious experimental finding concerning parapsychological abilities: "When the galaxy's center is below the earth's horizon, human cognitive and anomalous performance, such as remote viewing, dramatically improves by an order of magnitude as compared to when the galaxy's center is above the earth's horizon."[85] This involves only a daily cycle, but it suggests that claims of the center's influence on humans should not be dismissed out of hand.

Beside the traditional Hindu, Buddhist, and Jain systems, this chapter has presented only a few representative authorities: Guénon, Daniélou, Georgel, Sri Yukteswar, Cruttenden, and Jenkins. The reader may be aware of many more, and if not, the sources mentioned can lead to them. What unites them all is the need to honor traditional teachings (already a revolt against the modern world!) and then to adapt them to a particular theory of history. I have said enough above about the assumptions that this entails, and I hope that the reader has read the latter part of this chapter with those reflections in mind.

TWELVE

The Precession of the Equinoxes

———————— ✳ ————————

PRECESSION OF THE RATIONALISTS

Historians of science agree that it was Hipparchus (ca. 190 BCE–ca. 120 BCE), the Greek astronomer and mathematician, who first discovered and measured precession. Working on the island of Rhodes, Hipparchus had access to Babylonian eclipse tables and to Greek observations nearly 200 years old. He noticed that the position of the autumnal equinox had changed since the ancient records and calculated that it was moving west at as much as 1° every century. But he was unsure whether this movement affected all the stars, or just those of the zodiac.

It remained for Ptolemy (ca. 90–ca. 168 CE) to deduce from Hipparchus's and other data that the movement of the equinoctial point around the ecliptic was due to a special motion of the starry sphere around the fixed Earth. The whole body of stars was revolving at a snail's pace around an unmarked point in the northern sky. Progressing (or precessing) 1° a century, their journey back to their starting point took 36,000 years.[1]

Thanks to the dual authority of Plato and Ptolemy, 36,000 long remained the accepted number for the precessional cycle, though it needed an odd movement of "trepidation" (backtracking) to account for a faster observed rate.[2] In the Arab world, which for a time inherited all of Greek learning and science, Al-Battani (ca. 858–929) improved greatly on Ptolemy's figures. He estimated a motion of 1° in 66 years, making the whole cycle 23,760 years. Peter of Abano (ca. 1250–ca. 1316) revised this to 1° in 70 years, for a cycle of 25,200 years. Lynn Thorndike writes: "He regarded this as a matter of great importance because of the vast changes which he believed the revolution of the eighth sphere brought about. Its influence could even change dry land into sea, as the story of the lost island of Atlantis showed." It could also restore a Golden Age to humanity.[3] Nevertheless, Ptolemy's period served to calibrate most celestial coordinates until Danish astronomer Tycho Brahe (1546–1601) swept it away, along with trepidation and any notion that precession was variable. Tycho set the rate at 1° in 71½ years, which gave a period of 25,740 years.[4] This is not far from the present figure of 25,770.

However, that is only a figure, not a fact. All it means is that if the present rate of precession were constant for the whole 360°, that would be the period; but it isn't so. The rate is currently increasing, therefore the period is decreasing. Consequently all the periods mentioned are just extrapolations from a currently observed rate, such as 1° in 100 or 71½ years, and not accurate keys to past positions.

The idea of astrological ages rests on the assumption that changes occur on Earth in accordance with this cycle. The vernal (spring) point moves contrarily from the sun, transiting the constellations in reverse order: Pisces, Aquarius, Capricorn, Sagittarius, Scorpio, Libra, Virgo, Leo, Cancer, Gemini, Taurus, Aries. Apart from the fact that there is no astronomical validity to the concept, there are two ways of reckoning the twelve ages: by constellations and by signs.

The stars sprinkle the firmament like a Rorschach blot onto which viewers project images and gestalts. How this first happened is anyone's guess. Of the zodiacal constellations, only the Lion and Scorpion have any verisimilitude; Sagittarius looks more like a teapot, and there is almost nothing to the Crab. Astronomers, for their own convenience, fence them within arbitrary borders. This makes the zodiacal constellations very disparate in size: Virgo spans 47° of the ecliptic circle, Cancer only 14°. There is even part of the constellation Ophiuchus (the Snake Holder) intruding between Scorpio and Sagittarius, so that the ecliptic passes through not 12 but 13 constellations. To make matters worse, the proper motion of some stars has already distorted the borders that most astronomers agreed upon in the 1930s. There is no universal consensus on where the constellations begin or end. To avoid this mess, astronomers begin where the spring equinox fell on a certain date and plot their longitudes in a single eastward circle from there. In their language, 0° Aries is the celestial prime meridian for the coordinate of right ascension (i.e., longitude, expressed in hours, minutes, and seconds). Due to precession, any coordinate has to be supplied with its date, usually the year 2000.

The twelve signs of the astrological zodiac are much a tidier affair than the constellations, since each contains exactly 30°. They too begin in the first degree of Aries, and planetary positions are calculated by sign and degree (expressed in degrees, minutes, and seconds). This leads many theorists to assign each age an equal twelfth part of whatever precessional cycle they adopt, dividing the Great Year into "months."

Just as with the Four Yugas, theorists can play around with proportions and lengths, but the crux of the matter is the anchor point in physical reality. For the Yugas, this is a date in a universally accepted chronology like the Julian Period. For the astrological ages, it is a location among the (comparatively) fixed stars.

There is no difficulty in specifying the present vernal equinox point. It is in Pisces, at longitude close to the star Omega Piscium, which is even called Vernalis. Pisces is usually imagined as a pair of fishes joined by the tail. It is a straggling constellation, and the equinox still has far to go before it passes the "Head of the Western Fish" and can safely be said to enter the constellation of Aquarius.

Carl Jung considered the matter in his essay "The Sign of the Fishes." He says that the spring point will enter Aquarius in the course of the third millennium, and adds this footnote:

Since the delineation of the constellations is known to be somewhat arbitrary, this date is very indefinite. It refers to the actual constellation of fixed stars, not to the *zodion noeton,* i.e., the zodiac divided into sectors of 30° each. Astrologically the beginning of the next aeon, according to the starting-point you select, falls between AD 2000 and 2200. Starting from star "O" [Omicron Piscium] and assuming a Platonic month of 2,143 years, one would arrive at AD 2154 for the beginning of the Aquarian Age, and at AD 1997 if you start from star "a 113." [Alpha Piscium] The latter date agrees with the longitude of the stars in Ptolemy's Almagest.[5]

Jung was aware of the difference between the astronomical and astrological viewpoints and the consequences of starting from one (an actual star) and calculating from the other (an astrological month). Here is the whole problem of astrology, both as popularly understood and as scientifically denied. The popular understanding is that the constellations have some influence on Earth, especially as the planets pass through them. The skeptics point out that constellations and signs no longer coincide, due to precession, so that when astrology thinks a planet is in the sign of Aries, it is really in the constellation of Pisces, making nonsense of the whole system. The truth, such as it is, lies in the fact that astrological positions have nothing to do with the stars, but only with *the positions of the planets relative to the solstices and equinoxes.* The assumption is that there is something special about the earth's annual orbit, and that it really does divide first into the solsticial-equinoctial cross (4), then into the "signs of the zodiac" (12), then into the decans (36), and finally into the degrees (360), each of which has its own symbol and quality. The underlying model is more akin to musical harmonics than to anything astronomical, and for all I know, it may have been the real basis for the ancient preference for these numbers. Given that, anyone who declares that the Aquarian Age began or will begin on a certain date either does not understand the problem, or has an agenda that overrides it.

BEFORE AND AFTER *HAMLET'S MILL*

Despite the due honor paid to Hipparchus, was there advanced astronomy in earlier times and among other peoples that might have led to knowledge of precession? For the answers I turn to the most eminent academic authorities. Otto Neugebauer thinks not. He writes that apart from the Babylonians and Greeks, "none of the other civilizations of antiquity, which have otherwise contributed so much to the material and artistic culture of the world, have reached an independent level of scientific thought." He adds that the only pieces of prescientific lore that survived did so in astrology: they were the 36 Egyptian decans and the 28 Indian lunar mansions, both derived from "crude observation."[6] Moreover, there is every evidence that the Babylonians themselves did not recognize precession.[7]

John North agrees that all ancient astronomies derived from Babylon. The Hindu Yugas are obviously based on Babylonian figures (360° being "almost as good as a Babylonian signature") and might have been developed as early as the third century BCE.[8] As for the age of the zodiac, by the early fifth century BCE, the Babylonians had divided the zodiac into twelve signs, named after prominent constellations.[9]

William O'Neil puts the roots of the zodiac as far back as 3000 BCE, by which time the Sumerians had recognized four constellations with heliacal risings (i.e., first appearance over the horizon just before sunrise). They were the Bull, whose rise marked the onset of spring around 2500 BCE; the Great Lion, which heralded summer; the Scorpion for autumn; and the Ibex for winter. In time, eight other constellations were added, inserted two by two between these four seasonal markers. However, their concept of the constellations did not coincide with ours. The Babylonian constellation of the Bull shared only a few stars with what we call Taurus.[10]

The archaeoastronomer Anthony Aveni concludes that the Mayas *could* have detected precession and got within a few thousand years of the true cycle.[11] That is to say, their observation was equal to the task, but it does not mean that they did detect it, or, if so, that they did anything about it. The same might be said of the Babylonians. Anton Pannekoek writes that it is surprising that they didn't figure out precession, but gives the reason: they were doing religious rites, not pure astronomy.[12] A third case is the Chinese astronomer Yü Hsi, who discovered precession independently in the early fourth century CE. There again, astronomy served a ritual purpose, and the discovery held no further interest in his milieu.[13] The wise conclusion is that one should examine cultural contexts and probabilities before assuming that knowledge, even it if existed, was put to use.

The stumbling block for historians of astronomy is the reading of *Hamlet's Mill*, the joint work of Giorgio de Santillana of the Massachusetts Institute of Technology and Hertha von Dechend of the University of Frankfurt. No one with a preconceived idea can get through it, for the book is designed to repel such boarders: they drop off long before the end. It is an initiatic book, and after reading it, one's view of these matters is changed.

An early respondent was Harald Reiche. He followed von Dechend's suggestion, in her independent writings as well as in *Hamlet's Mill*, that the myth of World Ages denotes successive equinoctial constellations, separated by catastrophes and each associated with a planetary ruler. Reiche argues that the Atlantis myth is just such an allegory, and that the topography of the island kingdom needs to be transferred to the heavens to be understood.[14]

Subhash Kak, in a history of early Indian astronomy, may be overconfident in saying that since *Hamlet's Mill* it has "come to be generally recognized that ancient myths encode a vast and complex body of astronomical knowledge."[15] His contribution is to push back the date of the Rig Veda, hence its astronomical content. He highlights the recent discovery that the Sarasvati River, which figures so much in the Rig Veda, dried up before 1900 BCE, so that the text must be at least that old.[16] The Mahabharata War, which ended the Vedic age, is dated in the Puranic king lists to 1924 BCE, and that war well have been one of the consequences of the river's drying and associated population shifts. This increases one's confidence in Indian texts as sources of historical record.[17] If we assume that a catastrophic tectonic event was the cause of it, the Kali Yuga could be a memory of the beginning of that dark age.[18]

There is more. Since the prehistory of the Vedic people goes back to the fourth millennium, or even earlier, and archaeological discoveries show a continuity of Indian tradition from 8000 BCE, Kak concludes that the Vedic texts and the archaeological finds may relate to the same reality. He then reminds the reader that there is rock art in India as old as 40,000 BCE.[19] Without quite spelling it out, he is suggesting a prehistoric origin for the Vedic writings, hence for the Yuga concept mentioned in them. He does state that the early stages of Indian astronomy are well prior to the rise of mathematical astronomy in Babylon and Greece.[20] At the end of his article, he mentions the Puranic estimate for the speed of light (2×18^2 greater than the speed of the sun). "It is a lucky chance that the final number turned out to be exactly equal to the true speed. This speed of light must be considered the most astonishing 'blind hit' in the history of science!"[21]

David Kelley's recent encyclopedic work supports another heretical idea, that of worldwide communications in the far past. He illustrates it with myths and images of the Cosmic Turtle from Angkor, Bali, Thailand, the Mayan country, Assyria, India, Tibet, China, among the Algonquin, Shumash, and Pawnee Indians, and in Polynesia. Everywhere the turtle is associated with cosmic events and especially with a shifting axis.[22] Kelley is also convinced that "much of Mesoamerican astronomy is derived in modified form from the Old World." Among many pieces of evidence, he mentions that the sarcophagus of Pacal the Great (603–83) in Palenque shows the seven planets lined up in the Old World weekday order (Sun, Moon, Mars, Mercury, Jupiter, Venus, Saturn).[23] Kelley writes that the theories of William Sullivan deserve a hearing: they take the ideas of *Hamlet's Mill* further, to the astronomical identification of Incan gods.[24] He gives space to David Ulansey's theory that the Mithraic Bull-Slaying icon is an allegory of constellations in a precessional context.[25] These notions all challenge received prehistory, but scholars of the stature of Kelley and Aveni (who writes a foreword to the book) can afford to give them a hearing.

Hamlet's Mill itself does not argue that ancient peoples knew how precession worked. Quite the contrary: its discovery caused them terror and dismay. It was traumatic to learn that the fixed stars, seemingly the ultimately reliable thing in an uncertain universe, were shifting. It was as though the beams of heaven were threatening to collapse, or, in the imagery of a mill, the whole machine breaking asunder. Santillana and von Dechend draw no conclusions. They leave the reader to reflect on the ubiquity of such myths, on a primitive world disconcertingly unified and communicative, with a high level of astronomical observation and imagination. The sea rovers of Atlantis are not far off.

PRECESSION OF THE MYTHOLOGISTS

The study of precession has always been colored by the interaction of its two branches, the empirical and the mythological. Isaac Newton was exasperated by Ptolemy, who presented as observations data that had been selected to fit his mathematical models.[26] Godfrey Higgins (see below) put the matter plainly, writing that "whether the equinoxes preceded after the rate of 72 years to a degree, or something more or less, was a subject of great debate among the ancient, as it has been among modern, astronomers. But the rate of 72 had been finally determined to be sufficiently near for common mythological purposes, though not correctly true."[27]

Hipparchus's estimate of 36,000 years for the precessional cycle was consecrated by the myth of a Great Year derived from two passages in Plato. One is in the *Timaeus* (392d): "The perfect temporal number and the perfect year are complete when all eight orbits have reached their total of revolutions relative to each other, measured by the regularly moving orbit of the Same"—that is, when all the planets have returned to the places of their origin relative to the fixed stars. Johann Kepler was among later astronomers who tried to determine these places and thus to cast the horoscope of the Creation. Plato's other contribution is the Nuptial

Number. A convoluted passage in the *Republic* (546b-c) gives the clues for this number, generally taken to be 12,960,000 = 3^4 [81] × 4^4 [256] × 5^4 [625]. If counted as days and divided by 360, it gives 36,000 years.[28]

Innumerable sources insist that the "Platonic Year" is 25,920 years, as though Plato had stated this somewhere. He did not. The Perfect or Great Year was defined either by the return of the stars to their original positions, as in the *Timaeus,* or to their more easily calculated conjunction. Berossus (already mentioned in chapter 11) held that whenever the sun, moon, and planets line up in the last degree of Capricorn, the world is incinerated; when in Cancer, it is flooded. The myth of the Phoenix is an allegory of this periodic destruction. The bird lives 540 years before building its funeral pyre and being reborn from its ashes. Some natural philosophers reckoned that this was the length of the Great Year. Others, including Aristotle and Cicero, gave it the much larger duration of 12,954 solar years.[29] That is suspiciously close to 12,960, 1/1000 of Plato's *Republic* number and exactly half of 25,920.

The traditional precessional number is so neatly constructed from the first six integers—

$$25,920 = 2^6 [64] \times 3^4 [81] \times 5^1$$

—that it must have been part of the *Glasperlenspiel* described in chapter 11. Since it does not agree with the findings of astronomers, it was of little interest until the golden age of comparative mythography. This lasted from the 1770s, when the first reliable information on Indian and Persian sources arrived in Europe, until the 1830s, when scholarship and mythography went their separate ways. Some of the main contributors were Court de Gébelin, Bailly, Anquetil Duperron, Dulaure, Dupuis, Volney, and Fabre d'Olivet for the French; *Asiatic Researches,* Bryant, Maurice, Knight, Drummond, and Higgins for the English; Herder, the Schlegels, Dalberg, and Creuzer in Germany.[30]

The most important mythographer in our context is Charles François Dupuis (1742–1809). During the brief period of freethinking following the French Revolution, he was able to publish *Origine de tous les cultes, ou religion universelle* (The origin of all cults, or the universal religion, 1794). The main thread of this enormous work is that all religions derive from sun worship. The twelve Labors of Hercules, the Twelve Tribes of Israel, and even the Twelve Apostles symbolize the signs of the zodiac; the myths of Bacchus, Osiris, the Argonauts, and Christ allegorize the sun's path through its solstices and equinoxes. Dupuis placed the invention of the zodiac in Egypt between 14,000 and 15,000 BCE, reasoning that the signs symbolized the qualities and labors of the months, and that in Egypt this only made sense with Libra, rather than Aries, at the spring equinox.[31] He turned back the precessional clock to find when this was the case, and it brought him to an era over half a precessional cycle ago.

Even more significant is Dupuis' observation that the placement of the spring equinox dominated the religious life of antiquity. During the two millennia and more when it was in Taurus, many nations worshiped the Bull. When the equinox precessed into Aries, cults of the Ram or Lamb sprang up. Often the transition was violent, leading to rivalries between the old cult and the new (e.g., Moses's anger at the Golden Calf). The image of Mithras slaying the Bull denoted the end of the Age of Taurus; the "Lamb who was slain," the end of the Age of Aries. Finally, Jesus was only one of the solar saviors "crucified" on the cross of the solstices and equinoxes. The outrage felt by Dupuis' Christian readers can well be imagined.

In writing his *Anacalypsis,* the Yorkshire squire Godfrey Higgins (1772–1833) performed a similar service to Dupuis'.[32] He made a compendium of world mythology and traced themes through it, while treating the Judeo-Christian mythology on a par with the others. However, while Dupuis appears to have been entirely secular in spirit, Higgins was aware of the esoteric dimension of his material. At one place he writes of having found "direct proof that the true esoteric religions of Homer, the Hindoos, and the Jews, were all the same."[33] Addressing the theme of cycles, with more complexity than I can summarize here, Higgins extends the pattern in both directions. He detects signs in south India of a very ancient cult of Twins (Age of Gemini),[34] notes the fish symbolism of early Christianity (Age of Pisces), and states that the equinox is "now [1800] placed in the last degree of Aquarius."[35]

The prolixity and unrevised nature of *Anacalypsis* left some loose ends, such as three different dates for the equinoctial entry into Pisces: 380, 360, and 350 BCE.[36] Higgins also writes: "Julius Caesar fixed the solstice to the 25th of December, about one in the morning, which brings the Equinox, in the zodiacal circle, to the 25th degree of Pisces."[37] That would place the beginning of the Piscean Age at 46 + (5 × 72) = a little before 400 BCE. In his second volume he states, "Caesar and Sosigenes were in a great error in fixing the solstice to the 25th of December; and our globes are equally in error now in fixing the equinox to the first or thirtieth of Aquarius. . . . The sun certainly only entered the sign Pisces five degrees, or 5 × 72 = 360 years BC."[38] On the very next page, Higgins writes, in confessional mood, "I know what I deserve; I fear, I know what I shall receive, from my self-sufficient and ignorant countrymen. But yet, a new æra is rising."[39] This may have been the first announcement of the Age of Aquarius, and certainly Higgins's dates—whether 1760, 1780, 1800, or 1810—are the earliest given to it.

THE AGE OF AQUARIUS

All the French esotericists of the nineteenth century knew Dupuis' work, at least in its abridged version, and all the English ones knew Higgins's. Blavatsky, who knew and admired both, wrote as follows:

> There are several remarkable cycles that come to a close at the end of this [19th] century. First, the 5,000 years of the Kaliyuga cycle; again the Messianic cycle of the Samaritan (also Kabalistic) Jews of the man connected with *Pisces* (Ichthys or "Fish-man" *Dag*). It is a cycle, historic and not very long, but very occult, lasting about 2,155 solar years, but having a true significance only when computed

by lunar months. It occurred 2410 and 255 BC, or when the equinox entered into the sign of the *Ram,* and again into that of *Pisces.* When it enters, in a few years, the sign of *Aquarius,* psychologists will have some extra work to do, and the psychic idiosyncrasies of humanity will enter on a great change.[40]

I do not pretend to understand all of this, quoting it only for the sake of the dates. Notice that Blavatsky does not use the traditional length for the cycle, but the nineteenth-century astronomers' figure of 25,860 years (2155 × 12),[41] and that this gives 1890 CE as the start of the Aquarian period. Her prediction, at least, has held good.

The historian John Benedict Buescher quotes the above passage in his study of Levi Dowling (1844–1911), author or scribe of *The Aquarian Gospel of Jesus the Christ* (1909). This was a channeled book that purported to tell the *true* story of Jesus for the benefit of a new and enlightened age. As Buescher says, "The ideas in it—the Age of Aquarius, the Akashic Record, the Cosmic Christ, Jesus in Asia, and on and on—became an indelible part of the New Age movement itself."[42] The Aquarian meme quickly spread among Theosophists and West Coast Rosicrucians, lay dormant, then in the 1960s sent its spores worldwide.

In France the Aquarian as well as the Atlantean par excellence was Paul Le Cour, who issued his clarion call as *L'ère du Verseau* (The age of Aquarius, 1937). He accepted Dupuis' theory of the precessional ages and the traditional rate of 1° in 72 years. An astronomer told him that on the strength of 40,000 observations, the precessional rate was without a doubt 71.632 years, and the cycle therefore 25,788 years. Le Cour was unmoved, declaring in favor of the figure 72: "This number escapes mathematical and inorganic rigidity; it is, in a way, alive. It is like the pulsation of a heart."[43] To prove it, he quotes from a homeopathic physician, Dr. Lavezzari, that the human heart beats 72 times a minute; that we breathe 18 times a minute, corresponding to the 18-year nutation cycle; and that in 24 hours that makes *25,920* breaths! So Le Cour rejects the findings of one scientist, because the latter's precessional number is too "rigid," then welcomes those of another, who presents a vague average as though it were precise data, because it supports his theory. Such woolly thinking is endemic to the field. Raoul Auclair parrots Lavezzari's figures,[44] as does Jean Phaure,[45] (see chapter 2) and so they circulate as gospel truth on the borderline between Traditionalism and the New Age.

Like Dowling, Le Cour identified himself and his mission with the dawning age. When listing all the important events that have taken place in February (the month of Aquarius), he includes the time (February 1–11, 1924) when the idea occurred to him. He was already interested in Joachim de Fiore's system of the three ages, and his study of the zodiac led him to align the precessional ages with those. Virgo opened the cycle, with the creation of Adam or *Homo sapiens*. The first four ages, from 12,960 BCE to 4320 BCE, were under the Religion of the Father. The next four (Taurus, Aries, Pisces, and Aquarius), are under the Religion of the Son, from 4320 BCE to 4320 CE. The remaining signs will be under the Religion of the Holy Spirit, from 4320 to 12,960 CE. Thus the Piscean Age starts at Christ's incarnation, which is also the center point of a precessional cycle of 25,920 years.[46] This delays the Age of Aquarius until 2160, but more important still was the return of Christ, which Le Cour was sure would occur long before that. We have noted his allegiance to the spirituality and aims of the Hiéron du Val d'Or (see chapter 2); one of these was "to announce and prepare, for the year 2000, the political and social reign of Christ the King."[47] This was understood literally, and all movements toward one-world government were seen to be leading up to it, so that Christ, when he came, could take upon his shoulders the government of the whole world.[48]

Le Cour's friend Pierre Dujols, an "erudite Hermeticist," had prepared him for all this. In a letter of April 1912, Dujols wrote:

> Some immense movement is in preparation which, however it turns out, can only be beneficial for humanity. It may be dreadful from

the point of view of exterior, confessional Christianity, for with it, or despite it, will come an unknown, transfigured religious form, an era of renovation awaited by all the finest individuals of modern times.[49]

The ingenious research of Jay Weidner and Vincent Bridges has recently unveiled Pierre Dujols as one of those responsible for the writings of the twentieth-century alchemist "Fulcanelli," and the likely author of an essay entitled "The Cyclic Cross of Hendaye."[50] They think that Dujols' interest in this cross, which stands in a small town near the Spanish border, was the starting point for the whole Fulcanelli enterprise. Although the essay was not published until 1957, as a supplement to *Le mystère des cathédrales*,[51] it could well have been written early in the century and, for whatever reason, reserved. Picking up the clues carefully laid by Fulcanelli/Dujols, Weidner and Bridges decipher in the cross's iconography a warning about the "end of time," a "double catastrophe," and a "place of refuge."

Another member of this company was Raoul Auclair. We know what to expect when Phaure calls him "a living example of what an ardently Christian and Catholic faith can do in the service of the strictest Hermeticism, completely free from any trace of occultism."[52] Auclair's book *Le livre des cycles* (The book of cycles) treats the universality of the numbers 72 and 25,920 and also favors a precessional cycle centered on Christ's birth and divided into three. Writing of the zodiac as key to the cycle, he mentions especially the four "fixed signs": Leo, Taurus, Scorpio, and Aquarius. These traditionally correspond with the symbols of the Four Evangelists and with the Four Living Creatures with the semblance of Lion, Bull, Eagle, and Winged Man, seen in vision by the prophet Ezekiel and St. John the Divine.[53] In veiled words, Auclair writes that their iconography is "condensed in a sublime manner in the esotericism of the letters I.N.R.I., at the summit of the Cross where the son of man is sacrificed."[54] Fulcanelli brings out some of this esotericism as he analyzes those same letters, "which lend to the [Hendaye] cross its secret meaning: *Igne Natura Renovatur Integra* [By fire Nature is renewed whole]. For it is with the help of fire and in the fire itself that our hemisphere will soon be tried. And just as one separates gold from impure metals with the help of fire, just so, says Scripture, the good will be separated from the wicked on the great Day of Judgment."[55] The implication is that when the spring equinox enters Aquarius, the other points of the "cosmic cross" enter new signs: the autumn equinox enters Leo, the winter solstice Scorpio, and the summer solstice Taurus. The setup in the heavens then matches the apocalyptic vision of the four angels of Revelation, who are always pictured around Jesus in scenes of the Last Judgment.

Another member of Dujols' group was R. A. Schwaller de Lubicz, who told the late André VandenBroeck that he had written at least part of Fulcanelli's work.[56] In *Le roi de la théocratie pharaonic* (The king of the pharaonic theocracy, 1961) he writes that crises occur at the transition points between the astrological ages. Such was the case at the end of the age of Taurus, at that of Aries, "and again we see the beginning of an identical crisis during the present epoch of passage from *Pisces* to *Aquarius*. The same symptoms characterize them: a democratization that casts into oblivion the achievements from the time of the kings and repudiates a religious metaphysics; the social disorder, moreover, is often accompanied by climatological and telluric disturbances."[57]

After Paul Le Cour's death, Jacques d'Arès took over his journal *Atlantis,* and after 1960 brought Le Cour's *L'ère du Verseau* up to date. Political and scientific developments necessitated some corrections but mainly supported Le Cour's basic thesis: that symptoms of the new age are already appearing. Just as Sri Yukteswar believed electricity to be a mark of the Dwapara Yuga (see chapter 11), Le Cour associated it with the Aquarian Age. But d'Arès warns us not to generate it through nuclear energy, an unnatural and perilous procedure. Since Aquarius is the Water-bearer, the proper source is hydroelectric power.[58]

Finally we return to Jean Phaure's *Le cycle de l'humanité adamique,* written under the dual influence of René Guénon and Paul Le Cour.

Everything is there in his tremendous book: spiritual astrology, geometric and alchemical symbolism, Egyptian myths of time, the Hindu Yugas, Pythagoras and the Platonic Year, prehistoric civilizations, anti-Darwinism, modern physics and astronomy. Like the other French esotericists mentioned, Phaure privileges the Judeo-Christian revelation. He sets great store by Hebrew prophecies and the Book of Revelation and takes seriously the apparitions of the Virgin Mary (whether or not approved by the church), the coming of the Antichrist, and St. Malachy's list of the popes.

Phaure's concept of "Adamic humanity"[59] has the same duration as Guénon's, 64,800 years, and is divided in the proportions 4:3:2:1. It begins with the Golden Age in the Earthly Paradise, which lasted for an entire precessional cycle of 25,920 years. Then came the Fall and humanity's involvement in the physical body, as explained in chapter 2. The Silver Age follows for 19,440 years, in which Phaure inscribes the names of Hyperborea, Mu, and Lemuria, leaving it uncertain when (and even if) the latter two existed.

The Bronze Age, 12,960 years, begins with three precessional ages, Scorpio, Libra, and Virgo, assigned to Atlantis, then three more to Atlantean colonies. Then comes Noah's Flood, on the cusp between the Age of Gemini and that of Taurus around 4320 BCE.

Now we have reached recognizable antiquity and the Iron Age, which lasts only 6,480 years and three precessional ages: Taurus, Aries, and the Christian Age of Pisces. This concludes the cycle. What is left is the Aquarian Age, which is in a sense outside time. It witnesses the Millennium, the Second Coming of Christ, and the Last Judgment. Then a new cycle of humanity begins, probably with a reversal of the poles.[60]

Like Gaston Georgel, Phaure admits many overlapping and fractal cycles, notably the division of the Iron Age in the same proportions of 4:3:2:1. Considering these brings him to the question of when exactly the Iron Age began, hence when it will end. He offers two alternatives:[61]

	Version A	Version B
Phase I 2592 years (Antiquity)	4472 BCE Time of the Deluge	4320 . . . of Noah and Deucalion
Phase II 1944 years	1880 Egypt: decadence of the Middle Empire. Abraham	1728 Decadence of the Middle Empire. End of Sumer. Hyksos invasions
Phase III 1296 years (Middle Ages)	64 CE Burning of Rome. Christian martyrs. 70 CE, destruction of the Temple of Jerusalem	216 Beginning of barbarian invasions. Origen. Plotinus
Phase IV 648 years (Modern Times)	1360 Hundred Years War. Treaty of Brétigny. Decadence of Middle Ages. 1312, Templars abolished	1512 End of pre- Columbian America. 1515, battle of Marignan. 1517, Luther's Reformation
	2008 Great Tribulation?	2160

Phaure finds both versions revealing, but he leans toward the earlier one (A), "because despite appearances the 'rupture' of the fourteenth century was more important in the spiritual order than that of the 16th."[62] It also confirms that the twentieth century is the stage for the "tribulations" predicted by the Book of Revelation. The first of these he reckons to have begun in 1917, the year of the Bolshevik Revolution in Russia, the Balfour Declaration heralding the return of the Jews to Israel, and the miraculous appearance of the Virgin at Fatima.[63] The second tribulation, which will witness the coming of the Antichrist, is due about seventy-two years later. Writing a new introduction to his book in 1983, Phaure connected it with a rare planetary conjunction on December 25, 1989.[64] Elsewhere he suggests "as a working hypothesis" the date of 2030 or 2031 for the end of the cycle of popes and the end of the Roman Church (but certainly not of Christianity).[65]

Not everything is negative, though. Like Daniélou, Phaure welcomes the new physics because it makes scientific materialism impossible, and he sees the latest discoveries converging with traditional cosmogony, cosmogenesis, and metaphysics.[66] Moreover,

> for those who retain some power of reflection and spiritual intuition, our times still offer food for Life and Hope. The relative renaissance of esoteric sciences, the unveiling of ancient civilizations, the proclamations of the Virgin Mary: these powerfully aid us in reintegrating our Adamic consciousness and preparing us for the next planetary Tribulations.[67]

THE REIGNS OF THE ARCHANGELS

The sevenfold division of time, of which we saw examples in chapter 11, is a story in itself. Ultimately it may go back to India, where we found the twice-seven Manvantaras, or to the Babylonians, inventors of the seven-day week. The Iranian scholar Seyyed Hossein Nasr writes of how the Ikhwān al-Ṣafāʾ (Brethren of Purity, tenth century) made each planet correspond to a prophet and a period of history.[68] Later, Averroes (Ibn Rushd) borrowed from Hebrew tradition the association of angels with planets, and it was from his avidly studied works that it came to the West.

Peter of Abano, already mentioned, was led by his study of planetary conjunctions to segment history into periods of 354 years and four lunar months, which, as Thorndike says, is the number of days in the lunar year.[69] The seven planets presided in turn over these periods, causing characteristic events. From Averroes, Peter took the associations of "intelligences": Cassiel was the angel of Saturn, Sachiel of Jupiter, Samael of Mars, Michael of the sun, Anael of Venus, Raphael of Mercury, and Gabriel of the moon.[70]

The pieces were now in place for the synthesis of Johann Trithemius (1462–1516), the German abbot, humanist, and teacher of Cornelius Agrippa and maybe Paracelsus. In his *De septem secundeis* (Of the seven secondary [intelligences], 1508), Trithemius adopted Peter's chronology and angelic rulerships and proposed using them for prophetic purposes. Noel Brann writes in his study of Trithemius's magical theology: "Prophecy, being intuitively attuned to the cosmic process governed by the seven secondary intelligences occupying their respective planetary spheres, represents the extension of history into the future. Conversely, history is consummated prophecy."[71]

Trithemius's system puts the planets in reverse order to the days of the week, thus: Saturn, Venus, Jupiter, Mercury, Mars, Moon, Sun. He believed that "Mars first of all governed over the flood, and the second time over the destruction of the Trojans. This time, near the end of the epoch [Brann adds "viz., 1525"], it will watch over the great loss of unity."[72] Luther's Reformation soon seemed to bear this out. The interested reader can calculate the planetary periods going back to the Creation, which Trithemius dated to 5206 BCE.

Trithemius's theory of cycles would have been left for the fleeting amusement of scholars, had not someone, perhaps Eliphas Levi, noticed that the period of Mars's rulership was about to run out, in 1879 to be precise. The people behind the Hermetic Brotherhood of Luxor, a small but influential order that taught practical occultism, set great store by it and revised Trithemius's figures in the light of traditional chronology.

The correct Cycle, or Period, during which each of the Seven Intelligences has chief rule over all worldly concerns, is an 84th part of the Great Solar Period of 25,920 years, or a seventh part of the Sub-Solar Period of 2,160 years, and is equal to about 308 years and 208½ days.[73]

They also changed the order of planets to Saturn, Jupiter, Mars, sun, Venus, Mercury, moon. This matched astrological schemes such as the planetary hours and allowed each astrological age a set of seven angelic rulerships. The Hermetic Brotherhood maintained that the Age of Michael had begun in 1881, adding:

The year 1881 may appear incorrect to anyone conversant with modern astronomy, which maintains that our Sun will not enter the Sign Aquarius until the year AD 1897. This is a difference of sixteen years, but modern astronomers are wrong. The Sun entered Aquarius in February of 1881. This is not the only mistake they have to discover.[74]

A slightly different date comes from Charles Harrison (1855–1933), a High Anglican occultist whose influence was crucial in turning Rudolf Steiner away from Theosophy.[75] Harrison describes the changing of the heavenly guard in dramatic terms.

I have said that all great movements in the external world have their origin in the spiritual world, and that the conflict of ideas which marks the transition period between one historical epoch and another is, as it were, a copy of a battle already fought and won in the spiritual region. On such a transition period we have just entered. The reader may take the following facts for what he thinks they are worth. The year 1879 marked the close of an epoch in the intellectual life of Europe and America. In that year, the hosts of light, under S. Michael the Archangel, obtained a decisive victory over the hosts of darkness, led by Beelzebub and Mammon, in a series of battles extending over a period of thirty or forty years. About the middle of this [19th] century, the fifth root race touched the point known to occultists as the point of physical intellectuality, or the lowest in its evolutionary cycle.[76]

The 1879 or, more often, the 1881 event was not taken lightly in the English-speaking world. Beside the Hermetic Brotherhood, believers included Piazzi Smyth, the astronomer royal whose calculation was based on the Great Pyramid;[77] the forger of a prophecy attributed to Mother Shipton;[78] Freeman Dowd, a Rosicrucian of P. B. Randolph's lineage;[79] Blavatsky's loyal friend Lady Caithness;[80] the cult leader Thomas

Lake Harris;[81] the Christian Hermeticists Anna Kingsford and Edward Maitland;[82] A. S. Raleigh, already noted in chapter 8;[83] and the source of *Oahspe*.[84] A search of the Spiritualist literature would produce many more. It may not be coincidental that in 1881 two important journals were launched, *Light* and *The Theosophist;* Anna Kingsford gave the series of lectures that would become *The Perfect Way;*[85] Koot Hoomi wrote his first doctrinal letter to A. P. Sinnett (Mahatma Letter VIII). Some would find it significant that Tsar Alexander II and President Garfield, both potential reformers, were assassinated in that year.

Anthony Aveni, in *The End of Time,* puts the 1881 event into the political and social context of the time, and uses it to illuminate the expectations and fears of the year 2012.[86] Referencing Guénon's *Reign of Quantity,* Aveni writes: "Cultures that view themselves as waning are usually those most likely to tap into doomsday scenarios, especially when the world's end is followed by universal renewal."[87] But what of the time after the event? When a prophecy fails, the boldest strategy is to declare that what was predicted *did* happen, but on a plane that the scoffers cannot perceive. In 1882, Lady Caithness was cheerfully dating her letters "Anno Lucis [year of light] I."[88] Three years later, Edward Maitland published a book called *How the World Came to an End in 1881*. For those who discovered Theosophy or occultism in the succeeding decades, it was easy to believe oneself living in a new world, or on a higher plane.

Recurrent Themes
of Occult Atlantology

——————— ✳ ———————

THESE LAST TWO CHAPTERS on the cycles of time could well be expanded into another book, though it would not have the entertainment value of lost lands and bizarre visions. Nevertheless, the myth of time cycles is an essential pendant to the Atlantis myth, and not just because of its pretension to mathematical rigor. To be complete and satisfying, the occult or esoteric worldview requires a past, a present, and a future. For the individual, there are doctrines of preexistence, reincarnation, the spiritual path, and so on. *Atlantis and the Cycles of Time* refers instead to the collectivity. The authors we have been studying view the whole "human life-wave," and purport to make sense of it. If they succeed, they make sense of the present and assure us that there will be sense to the future, too, since all is proceeding according to a cosmic plan.

Such a plan is the core assumption of occult Atlantology and most distinguishes it from the so-called rationalists. It may be interesting, in conclusion, to list some of the other recurrent themes, with the names of those in whose works they appear. ("Theosophists" includes all or some.)

RECURRENT THEMES OF OCCULT ATLANTOLOGY

Effect of axial tilt or polar wandering	Fabre d'Olivet, Phaure, Theosophists, List, Wirth, Rosenberg, Neate, Plummer, Gurdjieff, *Oahspe,* Colville, Cayce, Pelley, Doreal, Adamski, Seth, Phaure
Polar or far northern location of early civilization or races	Bailly, Fabre d'Olivet, Phaure, Theosophists, Steiner, List, Zschaetzsch, Wieland, Gorsleben, Wirth, Guénon, Evola, Plummer, Doreal
Different origins for the differently colored races	Fabre d'Olivet, Saint-Yves, Schuré, Papus, Charroux, Theosophists, Lanz, List, Zschaetzsch, Wirth, Rosenberg, Wiligut, Machalett, Evola, Randall-Stevens, Raleigh, Urantia, Cayce, Tom
Root races, sub-races	Theosophists, Steiner, Bailey, List, Gorsleben, Wiligut, Fortune, Raleigh, Heindel, Lewis
Early races were nonphysical	Theosophists, Steiner, Bailey, Williamson
Early races were sexless	Theosophists, Steiner, List, Wiligut, Randall-Stevens, Cayce, Tom, Ramtha
Mating of angels/gods/ ETs with humans	Theosophists, Wiligut, Randall-Stevens, Cayce, Pelley, Williamson
Mating of humans with animals/subhumans	Theosophists, Lanz, Gorsleben, Wiligut, Cayce, Pelley, Shaver, Williamson, Daniélou
Apes descend from humans	Theosophists, List, Gurdjieff
Ram, Rama, Ramtha, Ramu	Fabre d'Olivet, Saint-Yves, Schuré, Papus, Raleigh, Ramtha, Adamski
Gobi Desert center	Saint-Yves, Charroux, Theosophists, Bailey, Guénon, Gurdjieff, Tom
Moon: late birth or arrival	Papus, Steiner, Neate, Trench, Gurdjieff, Adamski, Merrill
Moons: Hoerbiger theory	Pauwels and Bergier, Saurat, Bellamy, Wieland, Wiligut, Peryt Shou, Machalett
Atlanteans were sun worshippers	Bernard, Theosophists, Wirth, Fortune, Brown, Randall-Stevens, Brunton, Forbes, Vigers, Mandasoran, Raleigh, J. Churchward, Phelon, Phylos, Cayce, Williamson

Atlanteans had spiritual or psychic powers	Charroux, Theosophists, Steiner, Lanz, Gorsleben, Wirth, Wiligut, Peryt Shou, Fortune, Brown, Randall-Stevens, Forbes, Vigers, Neate, Michell, Lewis, Gurdjieff, Phylos, Doreal
Atlanteans had technology unknown today	Charroux, Bernard, Theosophists, Steiner, Lanz, List, Gorsleben, Fortune, Brown, Fawcett, Vigers, Neate, Mandasoran, Trench, Seth, Michell, Raleigh, J. Churchward, Phelon, Lewis, Phylos, Doreal, D. Leslie, Seth
Sound used as power source	Theosophists, Brown, Forbes, Neate, D. Leslie, Seth, Tom
Atlanteans had aircraft	Bernard, Theosophists, Steiner, Trench, Raleigh, Lewis, *Oahspe,* Colville, Cayce, Ballard, Williamson, Tom, Ramtha, Phylos, Cayce, Ballard, Adamski, Doreal
Atlanteans were literate	Theosophists, J. Churchward
Atlanteans were vegetarian	Theosophists, Zschaetzsch, Wieland, Randall-Stevens, Neate (partial)
Megaliths are Atlantean	Papus, Le Cour, Sinnett, Machalett
Great Pyramid is Atlantean	Bernard, Theosophists, Machalett, Randall-Stevens, Brunton, Forbes, Trench, Gurdjieff, Cayce, Doreal, Tom
Atlantis fell through misuse of technology	Steiner, Peryt Shou, Van Rijckenborgh, Cayce, Ballard, Williamson, Ramtha, Merrill
Evil forces in Atlantis caused catastrophe	Theosophists, Steiner, Guénon, Fortune, Randall-Stevens, Spence, Vigers, *Oahspe*
Atlanteans are reincarnated today	Theosophists, Steiner, Bailey, Fortune, J. Churchward, Phelon, Williamson, Seth
Space visitors	Charroux, Pauwels and Bergier, Peryt Shou, Trench, Gurdjieff, *Oahspe,* Pelley, Shaver, Adamski, D. Leslie, Tom
Visitors from Venus	Charroux, Theosophists, Neate, Phylos, Adamski, Williamson
Winged humanoids	Lanz, Wiligut, Gurdjieff, Merrill
Giants in early races	Theosophy, Bellamy, Saurat, Steiner, Heindel, *Oahspe*

Notes

———————— ✳ ————————

CHAPTER ONE. ATLANTIS OF THE RATIONALISTS

1. Plato, *Timaeus,* 24e–25a.

2. Athanasius Kircher, *Mundus Subterraneus* (Antwerp: Jansson, 1665), 1:82.

3. See Joscelyn Godwin, *Athanasius Kircher's Theatre of the World* (London: Thames & Hudson/Rochester, Vt.: Inner Traditions, 2009), 223.

4. L. Sprague de Camp, *Lost Continents* (New York: Dover, 1970), 43.

5. Ignatius Donnelly, *Atlantis: The Antediluvian World* (New York: Harper & Brothers, 1882), 477–78.

6. Ignatius Donnelly, *Atlantis: The Antediluvian World,* ed. Egerton Sykes (New York: Gramercy Publishing, 1949).

7. Faber & Faber published Bellamy's *Moons, Myths and Man: A Reinterpretation* (1936); *The Book of Revelation Is History* (1942); *Built Before the Flood: The Problem of the Tiahuanaco Ruins* (1944); *In the Beginning God: A New Scientific Vindication of the Cosmogonic Myths in the Book of Genesis* (1945); *The Atlantis Myth* (1948); *A Life History of Our Earth: Based on the Geological Application of Hoerbiger's Theory* (1951); *The Calendar of Tiahuanaco: The Measuring System of the Oldest Civilization* (1956); and *The Great Idol of Tiahuanaco* (1958), the last two written with Peter Allan.

8. Donnelly, *Atlantis,* 1949 ed., xv.

9. Lewis Spence, *Encyclopaedia of Occultism* (London: Routledge, 1920), 50.

10. Paul Jordan, *The Atlantis Syndrome* (Thrupp, U.K.: Sutton Publishing, 2001), 86.

11. Ibid., 87.

12. Lewis Spence, *The Problem of Atlantis* (New York: Causeway Books, 1974), 230.

13. Donnelly, *Atlantis,* 1949 ed., xviii.

14. Peter James, *The Sunken Kingdom: The Atlantis Mystery Solved* (London: Jonathan Cape, 1995), 166.

15. Nicolas Zhirov, *Atlantis; Atlantology: Basic Problems,* trans. David Skvirsky (Moscow: Progress Publishers, 1970).

16. Ibid., 37.

17. Plato, *Critias,* 116, trans. Desmond Lee.

18. Zhirov, *Atlantis; Atlantology,* 49.

19. The coordinates were given as 31°15'15.53N, 24°15'30.53W.

20. Walter Smith and David Sandwell, at http://googleblog.blogspot.com/2009/02/atlantis-no-it-atlant-isnt.html (accessed May 23, 2009).

21. Jean-Sylvain Bailly, *Histoire de l'astronomie ancienne* (Paris: De Bure, 1781; 1st ed. 1775). See also Joscelyn Godwin, *Arktos: The Polar Myth* (Grand Rapids: Phanes, 1993), 27–30.

22. The correspondence is published in Jean-Sylvain Bailly, *Lettres sur l'Atlantide de Plato* (London: M. Elmesly, 1779).

23. Bailly, *Lettres,* 430 and note.

24. Bailly, *Histoire,* 286, 323.

25. Bailly, *Lettres,* 293–334 (letter to Voltaire of April 20, 1778).

26. David King, *Finding Atlantis* (New York: Harmony Books, 2005).

27. Jürgen Spanuth, *Das enträtselte Atlantis* (Stuttgart: Union Deutscher Verlags-Gesellschaften, 1953).

28. Jürgen Spanuth, *Atlantis: The Mystery Unravelled* (London: Arco Publishers, 1956).

29. Jürgen Spanuth, *Atlantis of the North* (New York: Van Nostrand Reinhold, 1980).

30. Ibid., 62.

31. Ibid., 47.

32. [Henry] Beckles Willson, *Lost England: The Story of Our Submerged Coasts* (London: Hodder & Stoughton, 1902; reprinted as *Lost Lyonesse: Evidence, Records and Traditions of England's Atlantis,* with introduction by John Michell, London: AdCo Associates, 1986).

33. Hans Steuerwald, *Der Untergang von Atlantis* (Berlin: Kulturbuch-Verlag, 1983), 69.

34. Ibid., 83.

35. Ibid., 54.

36. Paul Dunbavin, *Atlantis of the West* (New York: Carroll & Graf, 2003), 113.

37. Ibid., 189.

38. Ibid., 202.

39. Albert Herrmann, *Unsere Ahnen und Atlantis* (Berlin: Klinkhardt & Bierman, 1934), 128–31.

40. Ibid., 6.

41. Ibid., maps in ills. 73–76.

42. Ibid., 44–47.

43. Ibid., 141–42.

44. Ibid., 162–63.

45. I follow James, *Sunken Kingdom,* 58–83, and Cindy (Cynthia J.) Clendenon, *Hydromythology and the Ancient Greek World* (Lansing, Mich: Fineline Science Press, 2009), 423–28.

46. Wilhelm Brandenstein, *Atlantis: Größe und Untergang eines geheimnisvollen Inselreiches* (Vienna: Gerold, 1951).

47. Massimo Pallottino, "Notizie e discussioni: Atlantide," *Archeologia Classica* 4 (1952): 229–40.

48. A. G. Galanopoulos and Ernest Bacon, *Atlantis: The Truth Behind the Legend* (Indianapolis: Bobbs-Merrill, 1969).

49. James Mavor, *Voyage to Atlantis* (New York: Putnam, 1969).

50. J. V. Luce, *The End of Atlantis: New Light on an Old Legend* (London: Thames & Hudson, 1969).

51. Michel de Grèce, *La Crète, épave de l'Atlantide* (Paris: Juilliard, 1971).

52. Rodney Castledon, *The Knossos Labyrinth* (London: Routledge, 1990).

53. Giorgio Grongnet de Vasse, *L'Atlantide,* Ms. 614/5, Biblijoteka Nazzjonali, Valletta.

54. Anton Mifsud, Simon Mifsud, Chris Agius Sultana, and Charles Cavona Ventura, *Malta: Echoes of Plato's Island* (n.p.: Prehistoric Society of Malta, 2000), 49.

55. Ibid., 34–35.

56. Ibid., 24, 42–43.

57. Thorwald C. Franke, "King Italos = King Atlas of Atlantis? A Contribution to the Sea Peoples Hypothesis," presentation to the Atlantis Conference, Athens, 2008 http://atlantis-scout.de/Franke_ItalosAtlas_Atlantis2008_Presentation.pdf.

58. Robert Sarmast, *Discovery of Atlantis: The Startling Case for the Island of Cyprus* (San Rafael: Origin Press, 2004).

59. Eberhard Zangger, *The Flood from Heaven: Deciphering the Atlantis Legend* (London: Sidgwick & Jackson, 1992).

60. Ibid., 170–71.

61. Ibid., 117.

62. Ibid., 118.

63. James, *Sunken Kingdom,* 203.

64. Ibid., 209, 270.

65. Ibid., 286.

66. Emilio Spedicato, "Galactic Encounters, Apollo Objects and Atlantis: A Catastrophic Scenario for Discontinuities in Human History," 3rd rev. version. www.ecn.org/cunfi/spedicgalact.pdf.

67. Andrew Collins, *Gateway to Atlantis* (New York: Carroll & Graf, 2000).

68. Spedicato, "Galactic Encounters," 30.

69. Ibid., 34–35.

70. Ibid., 31–32.

71. Collins, *Gateway to Atlantis,* 249.

72. Ibid., 267–68.

73. Andrew Collins, *From the Ashes of Angels* (London: Michael Joseph, 1996).

74. Ibid., 346–47.

75. Richard Firestone, Allen West, and Simon Warwick-Smith, *The Cycle of Cosmic Catastrophes: Flood, Fire, and Famine in the History of Civilization* (Rochester, Vt.: Bear & Co., 2006).

76. Ibid., 147.

77. Ibid., 140–41.

78. Ivar Zapp and George Erikson, *Atlantis in America: Navigators of the Ancient World* (Kempton, Ill.: Adventures Unlimited, 1998).

79. Ibid., 157–58.

80. Ibid., 376–77.

81. Rafael Requena, *Vestigios de la Atlántida* (Caracas: Tipografica Americana, 1932), 142.

82. Ibid., 69.

83. Ibid., 178–79.

84. Ibid., 190.

85. J. M. Allen, *Atlantis: The Andes Solution* (Moreton-in-Marsh, U.K.: Windrush Press, 1998).

86. Ibid., 97.

87. Ibid., 4, 10.

88. Charles H. Hapgood, *Maps of the Ancient Sea Kings,* rev. ed. (London: Turnstone Books, 1979; 1st ed. 1966).

89. Rand Flem-Ath and Rose Flem-Ath, *When the Sky Fell: In Search of Atlantis* (New York: St. Martin's Press, 1995).

90. Ibid., 49–50.

91. Ibid., 87.

92. Mary Settegast, *Plato Prehistorian: 10,000 to 5000 B.C. in Myth and Archaeology* (Cambridge, Mass.: Rotenberg Press, 1987), 19.

93. Ibid., 67.

94. Robert M. Schoch, "How Old Is the Sphinx?" Paper written to accompany a presentation at the 1992 American Association for the Advancement of Science Annual Meeting, Chicago, 7 February 1992 (Boston: R. M. Schoch, 1992), 2.

95. John Anthony West, *Serpent in the Sky: The High Wisdom of Ancient Egypt* (London: Wildwood House, 1978), 198–212.

96. *The Mystery of the Sphinx,* documentary narrated by Charlton Heston, NBC, 1993, reissued in various media.

97. Graham Hancock, *Fingerprints of the Gods: A Quest for the Beginning and the End* (London: Heinemann, 1995); Graham Hancock and Santha Faiia, *Heaven's Mirror: Quest for the Lost Civilization* (New York: Three Rivers Press, 1998).

98. Graham Hancock: *Underworld: The Mysterious Origins of Civilization* (New York: Crown Publishers, 2002).

99. See Robert Bauval and Adrian Gilbert, *The Orion Mystery* (New York: Three Rivers Press, 1995); and Robert Bauval and Graham Hancock, *Keeper of Genesis* (London: Heinemann, 1996).

100. Paul LaViolette, *Earth Under Fire: Humanity's Survival of the Apocalypse* (Schenectady, N.Y.: Starburst Publications, 1997), 107n.

101. Colin Wilson, *From Atlantis to the Sphinx* (New York: Fromm International, 1997).

102. Rand Flem-Ath and Colin Wilson, *The Atlantis Blueprint* (London: Little, Brown, 2000).

103. Ibid., 311.

104. Hapgood to Flem-Ath, 16 October 1982, in *The Atlantis Blueprint,* 330.

105. Colin Wilson, *Dreaming to Some Purpose: An Autobiography* (London: Century, 2004), 376.

106. Ibid., 377–79.

107. Colin Wilson, *Atlantis and the Kingdom of the Neanderthals: 100,000 Years of Lost History* (Rochester, Vt.: Bear & Co., 2006).

108. LaViolette, *Earth Under Fire,* 35–39.

109. Ibid., 228.

110. Ibid., 222–23.

111. Ibid., 224.

112. John Michell, *The Dimensions of Paradise* (London: Thames & Hudson, 1988).

113. Ibid., 133.

114. Ibid., 35.

115. Ibid., 119.

116. Ibid., 133.

117. Ernest G. McClain, *The Pythagorean Plato: Prelude to the Song Itself* (Stony Brook, N.Y.: Nicholas Hays, 1978). See also McClain's Appendix to Ian Driscoll and Matthew Kurtz, *Atlantis, Egyptian Genesis* (New York: Kali Yug Publishing, 2009), 181–206.

118. McClain, *Pythagorean Plato,* 96.

119. Ibid., 80.

120. Ibid., 95–96.

121. Zdeněk Kukal, "Atlantis in the Light of Modern Research," *Earth-Science Reviews* 21 (1984): 1–225.

122. Ibid., 82–83.

123. Ibid., 76.

124. Ibid., 106–8.

125. Ibid., 115.

126. Ibid., 146–48.

127. Ibid., 167.

128. Ibid., 191.

129. De Camp, *Lost Continents.*

130. For these, see Richard Ellis, *Imagining Atlantis* (New York: Knopf, 1998).

131. De Camp, *Lost Continents,* 277.

CHAPTER TWO. THE FRENCH ESOTERIC TRADITION

1. Delisle de Sales, *Philosophie de la nature,* 3rd ed. (London, 1777), 1:187.

2. Ibid., 1:153.

3. Ibid., 1:186–87.

4. Ibid., 1:265.

5. See Léon Cellier, *Fabre d'Olivet* (Paris: Nizet, 1953), 62.

6. Fabre d'Olivet, *Lettres à Sophie sur l'histoire* (Paris: Lavillette, 1801), 1:42.

7. Fabre d'Olivet, *Lettres,* 1:54. This was Delisle's later theory; see Olivier Boura, *Les Atlantides: Généalogie d'un mythe* (n.p.: Arléa, 1993), 206–13.

8. D'Olivet, *Lettres,* 1:110–12.

9. Ibid., 1:137–38.

10. Auguste Viatte, *Les sources occultes du romantisme: Illuminisme—théosophie 1770–1820* (Paris: Honoré Champion, 1979; 1st ed. 1928), 2:181–82.

11. Fabre d'Olivet, *Hermeneutic Interpretation of the Origin of the Social State of Man* [translation by Nayán Louise Redfield of *Histoire philosophique du genre humain*] (New York: G. P. Putnam's Sons, 1915), xiii.

12. Ibid., 163.

13. Fabre d'Olivet, *The Hebraic Tongue Restored,* trans. Nayán Louise Redfield (New York: G. P. Putnam's Sons, 1921), 1:13.

14. d'Olivet, *Hermeneutic Interpretation,* 180.

15. Ibid., 56n.

16. Ibid., 40.

17. Ibid., 77.

18. Ibid., 168–69.

19. Ibid., 184.

20. Ibid., 185.

21. Cellier, *Fabre d'Olivet,* 97.

22. On Virginie Faure and Saint-Yves' years on Jersey, see Jean Saunier, *Saint-Yves d'Alveydre, ou une synarchie sans énigme* (Paris: Dervy Livres, 1981), 74–97, and Cellier, *Fabre d'Olivet,* 371–81.

23. See Jean Saunier, *La synarchie ou le vieux rêve d'une nouvelle société* (Paris: Culture Arts Loisirs, 1971).

24. "Saint-Yves d'Alveydre," in *Le Rappel,* July 16, 1885; cited in Cellier, *Fabre d'Olivet,* 387.

25. Saunier, *Saint-Yves,* 286.

26. Ibid., 286–90.

27. See my introductions to Saint-Yves d'Alveydre, *The Kingdom of Agarttha,* trans. Jon Graham (Rochester, Vt.: Inner Traditions, 2008) and to Marco Baistrocchi, *Agarttha: A Guénonian Manipulation?* trans. Joscelyn Godwin (Fullerton: Theosophical History Center, 2009); also Godwin, *Arktos,* 79–104.

28. Stanislas de Guaïta, *Au seuil du mystère,* 5th ed. (Paris: Durville, 1915; 1st ed. 1886), 34–35.

29. Edouard Schuré, *The Great Initiates: Sketch of the Secret History of Religions,* trans. Fred Rothwell (London: Rider, 1913), 1:4.

30. Ibid., 159–60.

31. Ibid., 162.

32. Quoted in Michael Ladwein, "Edouard Schuré, eine biografische Skizze," *Novalis* 1–2 (2004). www.ladwein-reisen.de/Aufs9.html.

33. Papus, *Traité élémentaire de science occulte,* 7th ed. (Paris: Dangles, n.d.; 1st ed. 1898), 235–36.

34. See Godwin, *Arktos,* 188, 212, for more on Papus's use of Figanières.

35. Papus, *Traité élémentaire,* 238.

36. Ibid., 237.

37. Ibid., 243–44.

38. Ibid., 244.

39. Ibid., 266.

40. Official biography (in French) of Paul Le Cour on the "Atlantis" website: www .atlantis-site.com/asso/paul_lecour.php?m04.

41. Jean-Pierre Laurant, "Le destin sacré des peuples, race et occultisme au XIXe siècle: L'exemple du Hiéron de Paray-le-Monial," *Politica Hermetica* 2 (1988): 43–49; here cited, 45.

42. Pier Luigi Zoccatelli, "Notes on an Unpublished Correspondence Between René Guénon and Louis Charbonneau-Lassay," CESNUR International Conference, Bryn Athyn, Pa., 2–5 June 1999; www.cesnur.org/paraclet/guenon.html.

43. See Jean-Pierre Laurant, *L'Ésotérisme chrétien en France au XIXe siècle* (Paris: L'Age d'Homme, 1992), 132.

44. Official biography of Paul Le Cour; see note 40 above.

45. Paul Le Cour, *À la recherche d'un monde perdu: L'Atlantide et ses traditions* (Paris: Leymarie, 1926).

46. Ibid., 17–18.

47. Ibid., 54.

48. Louis Pauwels and Jacques Bergier, *The Morning of the Magicians,* trans. Rollo Myers (New York: Avon Books, 1971; 1st ed. 1963).

49. Ibid., 235–39.

50. Ibid., 240–41.

51. Ibid., 243–44.

52. Robert Charroux, *Le livre des secrets trahis* (Paris: Robert Laffont, 1965), jacket.

53. Ibid., 217.

54. Ibid., 164–65.

55. Ibid., 156.

56. Robert Charroux, *Le livre des maîtres du monde* (Paris: Robert Laffont, 1967), 76.

57. Ibid., 86.

58. Ibid., 144–55.

59. Ibid., 98.

60. Ibid., 96–97.

61. Raymond Bernard, *Les maisons secrètes de la rose-croix* (Villeneuve St.-George. France: Éditions Rosicruciennes, 1979; 1st ed. 1970), 215–50.

62. Ibid., 258–59.

63. Ibid., 260.

64. Ibid., 261–62.

65. Andrew Tomas, *Les secrets de l'Atlantide* (Paris: Laffont, 1971); Eng. trans. (unattributed), *Atlantis: From Legend to Discovery* (London: Robert Hale, 1972).

66. On what Roerich was really doing around Tibet, and for whom, see Alexandre Andreyev, *Soviet Russia and Tibet: The Debacle of Secret Diplomacy, 1918–1930s* (Leiden, Netherlands: Brill, 2002), 293–317.

67. Bernard, *Les maisons secrètes,* 264.

68. Jean Phaure, *Le cycle de l'humanité adamique* (Paris: Dervy-Livres, 1988), 485.

69. Ibid., 280.

70. Ibid., 286.

71. Charroux, *Le livre des secrets,* 146.

72. Ibid., 147.

73. Phaure, *Le cycle de l'humanité adamique,* 254.

74. Ibid., 273–74.

75. Ibid., 301–2.

76. Ibid., 317.

77. Ibid., 323.

CHAPTER THREE. H. P. BLAVATSKY AND THE EARLY THEOSOPHISTS

1. Plato, *Critias,* trans. Thomas Taylor (London, 1804), 573–74.

2. H. P. Blavatsky, *Isis Unveiled* (New York: Bouton, 1877), 1:589.

3. Ibid.

4. Ibid., 1:590.

5. Henry S. Olcott, *Old Diary Leaves,* First Series (Adyar [Chennai], India: Theosophical Publishing, 1941; 1st ed. 1895), 208–12.

6. Ibid., Series 1, 213.

7. Blavatsky, *Isis Unveiled,* 1:593.

8. Ibid., 1:592.

9. Ibid., 1:594–95n.10.

10. *The Mahatma Letters to A. P. Sinnett from the Mahatmas M. and K. H.*, 3rd ed. (Adyar [Chennai], India: Theosophical Publishing House, 1979), 69 (Letter no. 12).

11. Ibid., 82 (Letter no. 14).

12. Ibid., 147 (Letter no. 23b).

13. See the important article by James A. Santucci, "The Theosophical Concept of Race," *Nova Religio* 11/3 (2008): 37–63.

14. *Mahatma Letters*, 147–48.

15. Ibid., 151.

16. Ibid., 153.

17. A. P. Sinnett, *Esoteric Buddhism*, 8th ed. (London: Theosophical Publishing, 1907; 1st ed. 1883), 65–66.

18. *Autobiography of Alfred Percy Sinnett* (London: Theosophical History Centre, 1986), 27. See also Boris de Zirkoff's notes in H. P. Blavatsky, *Collected Writings*, vol. 4 (Wheaton, Ill.: Theosophical Publishing House, 1969), 639.

19. "Two Chelas" in the Theosophical Society [Mohini Chatterji and Laura C. Holloway], *Man: Fragments of Forgotten History* (London: Reeves & Turner, 1885), 21–22.

20. Ibid., 25–31.

21. Ibid., 76–77.

22. Ibid., 85.

23. Sinnett's first book, describing Blavatsky's paranormal phenomena.

24. Letter no. 64, *Mahatma Letters*, 354–55.

25. H. P. Blavatsky, *Collected Writings*, vol. 6 (Wheaton, Ill.: Theosophical Publishing, 1975), 412; letter of November 7, 1885.

26. *The Letters of H. P. Blavatsky to A. P. Sinnett and Other Miscellaneous Letters*, ed A. T. Barker (New York: Frederick A. Stokes, n.d.), Letter 120, p. 259.

27. H. P. Blavatsky, *The Secret Doctrine: The Synthesis of Science, Religion, and Philosophy*, 2 vols. (London: Theosophical Publishing, 1888), 2:438; *The Secret Doctrine*, "Adyar Edition," 6 vols. (Adyar [Chennai], India: Theosophical Publishing House, 1971): 3:435.

28. Blavatsky, *Secret Doctrine*, 1888, 2:274–75; Adyar ed., 3:276–77.

29. Ibid., 2:56; Adyar ed., 3:66–67.

30. Ibid., 2:42; Adyar ed., 3:53.

31. Ibid., 2:87; Adyar ed., 3:96.

32. Ibid., 2:113; Adyar ed., 3:124.

33. Ibid., 2:95; Adyar ed., 3:104.

34. Ibid., 2:6; Adyar ed., 3:20.

35. Ibid., 2:138; Adyar ed., 3:146.

36. Ibid., 2:121; Adyar ed., 3:130.

37. Ibid., 2:7; Adyar ed., 3:20.

38. Ibid., 2:138; Adyar ed., 3:146

39. Ibid., 2:289; Adyar ed., 3:291.

40. Ibid., 2:132; Adyar ed., 3:140–41.

41. Ibid., 2:228; Adyar ed., 3:231.

42. Ibid., 2:317–318; Adyar ed., 3:317–18.

43. Ibid., 2:333; Adyar ed., 3:332–33.

44. Ibid., 2:263–65; Adyar ed., 3:266.

45. Ibid., 2:333–34; Adyar ed., 3:333.

46. Ibid., 2:486; Adyar ed., 3:424.

47. Ibid., 2:692; Adyar ed., 4:262.

48. H. P. Blavatsky, *Collected Writings,* vol. 7 (Madras: Theosophical Publishing House, 1975), 125; *The Secret Doctrine,* Adyar ed., 5:256.

49. T. Subba Row, *Esoteric Writings* (Adyar [Chennai], India: Theosophical Publishing House, 1980; 1st ed. 1895), 571.

50. Blavatsky, *The Secret Doctrine,* 1888, 2:636–37; Adyar ed., 4:208.

51. Ibid., 2:330; Adyar ed., 3:329–30.

52. Ibid., 2:149; Adyar ed., 3:157.

53. Ibid., 2:710; Adyar ed., 4:279.

54. Ibid., 2:313–314; Adyar ed., 3:314.

55. Ibid., 2:433n; Adyar ed., 3:431n.

56. Ibid., 2:429; Adyar ed., 3:427.

57. Ibid., 2:760–61; Adyar ed., 4:330.

CHAPTER FOUR. LATER THEOSOPHISTS

1. Autobiography of A. P. Sinnett, 34–35.

2. Ibid., 38.

3. Ibid., 44.

4. A. P. Sinnett, "The Pyramids and Stonehenge," in *Collected Fruits of Occult Teaching* (London: T. Fisher Unwin, 1919), 189–217; here cited, 200.

5. Ibid., 208, 214.

6. Ibid., 212.

7. According to Hugh S. Gladstone, *Record Bags and Shooting Records* (London, 1922), 45, William Scott-Elliot (1811–1901) attended seventy-four successive "twelfths" [of August]. See the standard biographical entries on Walter Travers Scott-Elliot (1895–1977), Labour MP and murder victim, to whom the Atlantis book is sometimes misattributed.

8. Sinnett mentions Count Bubua, Scott-Elliot, Miss Arundale, Mr. and Mrs. Varley, Leadbeater, "Mary," and "one or two others" who surely included his wife, Patience Sinnett. See *Autobiography of A. P. Sinnett*, 44.

9. See Daniel H. Caldwell and Michelle B. Graye, "Mary Unveiled," *Theosophical History*, 1/8 (1986): 205–7.

10. W. Scott-Elliot, *The Story of Atlantis and the Lost Lemuria* (London: Theosophical Publishing House, 1968), ix–x.

11. Gregory Tillett, *The Elder Brother: A Biography of Charles Webster Leadbeater* (London: Routledge & Kegan Paul, 1982), 37.

12. Ibid., 47–48.

13. Ibid., 58.

14. Arthur H. Nethercot, *The Last Four Lives of Annie Besant* (Chicago: University of Chicago Press, 1963), 48.

15. C. W. Leadbeater, letter to Francesca Arundale, August 25, 1895, published as "Dr. Besant's First Use of Clairvoyance," *The Theosophist*, October 1932, 11. www.katinkahesselink.net/other/leadb2.html.

16. Tillett, *Elder Brother*, 56–57.

17. Preface by C. J. Jinarajadasa to C. W. Leadbeater, *The Astral Plane* (Adyar [Chennai], India: Theosophical Publishing House, 1933), 11.

18. W. Scott-Elliot, *Atlantis: A Geographical, Historical, and Ethnological Sketch, Illustrated by Four Maps of the World's Configuration at Different Periods* (London: Theosophical Publishing, 1896).

19. Scott-Elliot, *The Story of Atlantis and Lost Lemuria*, 18–19.

20. Ibid., 25.

21. Ibid., 34.

22. Ibid., 37.

23. Ibid., 57.

24. Ibid., 47–49.

25. *Autobiography of A. P. Sinnett*, 45.

26. Published as W. Scott-Elliot, *The Lost Lemuria* (London: Theosophical Publishing House, 1904).

27. The two books were first published together in 1925.

28. Scott-Elliot, *The Story of Atlantis,* 1968, 78.

29. For Kingsland's biography, see H. P. Blavatsky, *Collected Writings,* vol. 10 (Wheaton, Ill.: Theosophical Publishing House, 1974), 419–24.

30. William Kingsland, ed., *A Child's Story of Atlantis, Book I* (London: Theosophical Publishing Society, 1908).

31. Ibid., 23.

32. Ibid., 19n.

33. Ibid., 25.

34. In 1900, aged nine, Daisy Ashford wrote *The Young Visiters, or Mr. Salteena's Plan* (first published 1919).

35. Kingsland, *Child's Story of Atlantis,* 43n.

36. Annie Besant and C. W. Leadbeater, *Man: Whence, How and Whither: A Record of Clairvoyant Investigation* (London: Theosophical Publishing House, 1913).

37. Ibid., 110.

38. Ibid., 83.

39. See the photograph of a similar session in Tillett, *Elder Brother,* plate 9.

40. Besant and Leadbeater, *Man: Whence, How and Whither,* 102–3.

41. Ibid., 109.

42. Ibid., 114–22.

43. Ibid., 34.

44. Ibid., 6–8.

45. See Mary Lutyens, *Krishnamurti: The Years of Awakening* (London: John Murray, 1974), 23–24.

46. See Paul Newman, *Aleister Crowley and the Cult of Pan* (London: Greenwich Exchange, 2004).

47. Besant and Leadbeater, *Man: Whence, How and Whither,* 120.

48. Ibid., 111.

49. Ibid., 247.

50. Ibid., 263n.

51. Ibid., 311.

52. Ibid., 335.

53. Paul Brunton, *A Message from Arunachala* (London: Rider, 1936), 19.

54. Johannes Hemleben, *Rudolf Steiner: A Documentary Biography,* trans. Leo Twyman (East Grinstead, U.K.: Henry Goulden, 1975), 78–79.

55. Gary Lachman, *Rudolf Steiner: An Introduction to His Life and Work* (London: Penguin, 2007), 160.

56. Rudolf Steiner, *Theosophie: Einführung in übersinnliche Welterkenntnis und Menschenbestimmung* (Berlin, 1904); Eng. trans. *Theosophy* (Spring Valley, N.Y.: Anthroposophic Press, 1971).

57. Rudolf Steiner, "Wie erlangt man Erkenntnisse der höheren Welten?" *Luzifer-Gnosis*, 1904. Eng. trans. by George Metaxa, *Knowledge of Higher Worlds and Its Attainment* (Spring Valley, N.Y.: Anthroposophic Press, 1947).

58. First published in booklet form as *Aus der Akasha Chronik: Unsere atlantischen Vorfahren* (Berlin: Theosophischer Verlag, 1904).

59. Rudolf Steiner, *The Submerged Continents of Atlantis and Lemuria* (London: Theosophical Publishing Society, 1911); enlarged as *Cosmic Memory: Prehistory of Earth and Man,* trans. Karl E. Zimmer (Hudson: Steinerbooks, 1987; 1st ed. 1939).

60. Steiner, *Cosmic Memory,* 1987, 37.

61. Ibid., 38–39.

62. Helmut Zander, *Anthroposophie in Deutschland: Theosophische Weltanschauung und gesellschaftliche Praxis 1884–1945* (Göttingen, Germany: Vandenhoeck und Ruprecht, 2007), 630, n340.

63. Steiner, *Cosmic Memory,* 1987, 39.

64. Rudolf Steiner, *Spiritualism, Madame Blavatsky, and Theosophy: An Eyewitness View of Occult History,* ed. Christopher Bamford (Great Barrington, Mass.: Anthroposophic Press, 2001), 21.

65. Ibid., 126.

66. Ibid., 128–29.

67. Ibid., 215–21.

68. Ibid., 161.

69. Ibid., 153.

70. Rudolf Steiner, *Karmic Relationships,* 8 vols. (London: Rudolf Steiner Press, 1972–1975).

71. Steiner, *Cosmic Memory,* 1987, 67.

72. Ibid., 64n.

73. See Rudolf Steiner, *An Outline of Occult Science* (London: Theosophical Publishing Society, 1914), 123–205.

74. Steiner, *Cosmic Memory,* 1987, 156–64.

75. Ibid., 1987, 116.

76. Ibid., 93.

77. Ibid., 103.

78. Ibid., 82.

79. Rudolf Steiner, *Atlantis: The Fate of a Lost Land and Its Secret Knowledge* (London: Rudolf Steiner Press, 2001), 34–35.

80. Ibid., 90–91.

81. Steiner, *Cosmic Memory*, 1987, 43–55.

82. Ibid., 43–44.

83. Steiner, *Outline of Occult Science*, 262.

84. Steiner, *Cosmic Memory*, 1987, 61.

85. Steiner, *Atlantis: The Fate of a Lost Land*, 41–43.

86. Alice A. Bailey, *The Unfinished Autobiography of Alice A. Bailey* (New York: Lucis Publishing, 1951), 162–63.

87. Ibid., 166.

88. Ibid., 164.

89. John R. Sinclair, *The Alice Bailey Inheritance* (Wellingborough, U.K.: Turnstone Press, 1982), 20.

90. Alice A. Bailey, *Initiation, Human and Solar* (New York: Lucifer Publishing, 1922; London: Lucis Press, 1922).

91. "Lucifer" was soon dropped in favor of "Lucis," already the name of the London branch. The other books were *The Consciousness of the Atom* and *Letters on Occult Meditation*.

92. Tillett, *Elder Brother*, 279.

93. See Tenzin Gyatso, Fourteenth Dalai Lama, *The Kālachakra Tantra*, ed. and trans. Jeffrey Hopkins (London: Wisdom Publications, 1985), 166–67.

94. Bailey, *Initiation, Human and Solar*, 42–43.

95. Ibid., 45.

96. Ibid., 34.

97. Ibid., 35.

98. Ibid., 35.

99. Alice A. Bailey, *The Destiny of the Nations* (London: Lucis Trust, 1949), 13.

100. Ibid., 45.

101. Blavatsky, *The Secret Doctrine*, 1888, 2:303; Adyar ed., 3:304.

102. Wouter J. Hanegraaff, *New Age Religion and Western Culture: Esotericism in the Mirror of Secular Thought* (Leiden, Netherlands: Brill, 1996), 95.

CHAPTER FIVE. GERMANIC ATLANTOLOGY

1. James A. Santucci, "The Theosophical Concept of Race," *Nova Religio* (2008): 51.

2. Nicholas Goodrick-Clarke, *The Occult Roots of Nazism* (Wellingborough, U.K.: Aquarian Press, 1985).

3. Jörg Lanz von Liebenfels, *Theozoology, or the Science of the Sodomite Apelings and the Divine Electron: An Introduction to the Most Ancient and Most Modern Philosophy and a Justification of the Monarchy and the Nobility,* trans. Fam. Viktor and Br. Procursus (N.p.: ONT Study Group, 1985; 1st ed. 1904), 54.

4. Ibid., 69–70.

5. Ibid., 53–54.

6. Ibid., 78.

7. Ibid., 58.

8. Ibid., 39–40.

9. Ibid., 90.

10. Ibid., 92.

11. Ibid., 72.

12. See Goodrick-Clarke, *Occult Roots of Nazism,* 101–2, 243n.

13. See Guido von List, *Die Rita der Ario-Germanen,* 3rd ed. (Berlin: Guido von List Verlag, 1920; 1st ed. 1908), 185n.

14. Goodrick-Clarke, *Occult Roots of Nazism,* 67.

15. List, *Die Rita der Ario-Germanen,* 97.

16. Ibid., 58.

17. Ibid., 35–39.

18. Ibid., 22n.

19. Ibid., 243, citing Mead's *Fragments of a Faith Forgotten.*

20. Guido von List, *The Religion of the Aryo-Germanic Folk, Esoteric and Exoteric* (Smithville, Tex.: Runa-Raven Press, 2005; 1st ed. 1909 or 1910), 9.

21. Ibid., 4, 19.

22. Ibid., 22.

23. Ibid., 8.

24. Ibid., 9.

25. Ibid., 3.

26. Ibid., 37.

27. Ibid., 7, 11, 23–4, 26–27.

28. Ibid., 11, 38.

29. Ibid., 24.

30. Ibid., 23, 27–28.

31. Ibid., 40.

32. Ibid., 48.

33. Ibid., 5.

34. Guido von List, *Die Bilderschrift der Ario-Germanen* (Vienna: Guido-von-List Gesellschaft, 1910), 30.

35. Franz Wegener, *Das Atlantidische Weltbild: Nationalsozialismus und Neue Rechte auf der Suche nach der versunkenen Atlantis* (Gladbeck, Germany: Kulturförderverein Ruhrgebiet, 2001), 21.

36. Ibid., 33.

37. Karl Georg Zschaetzsch, *Atlantis, die Urheimat der Arier* (Berlin: Arier-Verlag, 1922), 7–9.

38. Ibid., 10–12.

39. Ibid., 15–16.

40. Ibid., 44.

41. Ibid., 62.

42. Ibid., 63.

43. Ibid., 66–67.

44. Ibid., 94.

45. Ibid., 96–97.

46. Hermann Wieland, *Atlantis, Edda und Bibel: Das entdeckte Geheimnis der Heiligen Schrift des deutschen Volkes Rettung aus Not und Tod* (Nuremberg: Chr. Karl Wuzel, 1922).

47. Hermann Wieland, *Atlantis, Edda und Bibel: 200,000 Jahre germanischer Weltkultur und das Geheimnis der Heiligen Schrift* (Nuremberg: Chr. Karl Wuzel, 1925).

48. Wieland, *Atlantis, Edda und Bibel,* 1922, 3.

49. Ibid., 8.

50. Ibid., 27n, 35.

51. I have not been able to see the 1925 edition. For an illustration from it of Hörbiger's moon, see Wegener, *Das Atlantidische Weltbild,* 34.

52. Wieland, *Atlantis, Edda und Bibel,* 1922, 141.

53. Ibid., 128.

54. Reference is to the *Wisdom of Jesus Son of Sirach* in the Apocrypha.

55. Wieland, *Atlantis, Edda und Bibel,* 1922, 115.

56. On Gorsleben, see Goodrick-Clarke, *Occult Roots,* 155–59.

57. Rudolf John Gorsleben, *Hoch-Zeit der Menschheit* (Leipzig: Koehler & Amelang, 1930), xvii–xviii.

58. Ibid., 105.

59. Ibid., 464.

60. Ibid., xxi–xxiii.

61. Ibid., 293.

62. Ibid., xxii.

63. Ibid., xxiii.

64. Ibid., 193.

65. Ibid., 539.

66. Ibid., xxiv.

67. This section is partly based on Joscelyn Godwin, "Out of Arctica? Herman Wirth's Theory of Human Origins," *Rûna* 5 (2000): 2–7.

68. On Wirth's musicological work, see Joscelyn Godwin, "Herman Wirth and Folksong," *Tyr* 2 (2004): 263–83.

69. Herman Wirth, *Der Aufgang der Menschheit* (Jena, Germany: Eugen Diederich, 1928), 61–62.

70. Wirth, *Aufgang*, 105.

71. For later corroboration, see Ivan van Sertima, ed., *African Presence in Early Europe* (New Brunswick, N.J., and Oxford, U.K.: Transaction Publishers, 1988), esp. 23–29.

72. Julius Evola, "Nota critica sull'opera de H. Wirth: *Der Aufgang der Menschheit*," *Bilychnis* 20/1 (Jan.–Feb. 1931); reprinted in Evola, *I saggi di Bilychnis* (Padua: Edizioni di Ar, 1987): 139–41; here cited, 141.

73. Herman Wirth Roeper Bosch, *Um den Ursinn des Menschseins: Die Werdung einer neuen Geisteswissenschaft* (Vienna: Volkstum-Verlag, 1960), 84.

74. Eberhard Baumann, *Der Aufgang und Untergang der frühen Hochkulturen Nord- und Mitteleuropas* (Passau, Germany: n.p., 1981), 95.

75. See Eberhard Baumann, *Herman Wirth: Schriften, Vorträge, Manuskripte und Sekundärliteratur* (Toppenstedt, Germany: Uwe Berg Verlag, 1995), 25.

76. *The Oera-Linda Book*, trans. William R. Sandbach (London: Trübner, 1876), 68.

77. Ibid., 70.

78. Arthur Hübner, *Herman Wirth und die Ura-Linda-Chronik* (Berlin: Walter de Gruyter, 1934), 34–35.

79. See Wirth as quoted in Hübner, *Herman Wirth*, 41.

80. Alfred Rosenberg, *Der Mythos des 20. Jahrhunderts* (Munich: Honeneiche, 1936; 1st ed. 1930), 24.

81. Ibid., 135–136.

82. Beauftragten des Führers für die Überwachung der gesamten geistigen und weltanschaulichen Schulung und Erziehung der NSDAP.

83. See Goodrick-Clarke, *Occult Roots of Nazism,* 177–91.

84. Amt für Vor- und Frühgeschichte in the Rasse- und Siedlungshauptamt.

85. See Karl Hüser, Wulff E. Brebeck, Dieter Fölster, Heinz Bittner, and Joachim Jochimsen, *Wewelsburg 1933–1945: Kult- und Terrorstätte der SS* (Paderborn: Deutsches Institut für Bildung und Wissen, 1982), 23–28.

86. On the identification of this with the "Black Sun," see Nicholas Goodrick-Clarke, *Black Sun: Aryan Cults, Esoteric Nazism and the Politics of Identity* (New York: New York University Press, 2002), 148–50.

87. Stephen E. Flowers and Michael Moynihan, eds., *The Secret King: The Myth and Reality of Nazi Occultism* (Waterbury Center, Vt./Los Angeles: Dominion/ Feral House, 2007), 71.

88. Facsimile in Flowers and Moynihan, *Secret King,* 43.

89. Translated in Flowers and Moynihan, *Secret King,* 126–30.

90. See Manfred Lenz, "Leben und Werk des deutschen Esoterikers Peryt Shou," *Gnostika,* 28 (Oct. 2004): 23–40.

91. Ibid., 24.

92. Peryt Shou, *Esoterik der Atlantier in ihrer Beziehung zur aegyptischen, babylonischen und jüdischen Geheimlehre* (Leipzig: Theosophisches Verlagshaus, 1913), 40–42, 59–61.

93. Ibid., 62.

94. Ibid., 8.

95. Ibid., 10, 17.

96. Ibid., 57.

97. Ibid., 57.

98. Lenz, "Leben und Werk," 28, 30.

99. Ibid., 37.

100. Peryt Shou, *Atlantis: Das Schicksal der Menschheit. Die geistige Frühkultur der Atlantier und das gegenwärtige Europa. Nach wissenschaftlichen Quellen* (Graz: Edition Geheimes Wissen, 2008; 1st ed. 1930), 28.

101. Lenz, "Leben und Werk," 36.

102. Shou, *Atlantis: Das Schicksal der Menschheit,* 34.

103. Ibid., 78.

104. Lenz, "Leben und Werk," 39, from the diary of "Fra. Ortwin."

105. Wegener, *Das Atlantidisches Weltbild,* 96.

106. Rüdiger Sünner, *Schwarze Sonne: Entfesselung und Mißbrauch der Mythen in Nationalsozialismus und rechter Esoterik* (Freiburg i. B.: Herder/Spektrum, 1999), 70.

107. Until about 2005 the group was called "Arbeits- und Forschungskreis Walther Machalett für die Vor-und Frühgeschichte der Externsteine im Teutoburger Wald."

108. Heino Gehrts, untitled Memoir of Walther Machalett, *Rückschau der Arbeits- und Forschungskreis Walther Machalett* 28 (1994): 3.

109. Walther Machalett, *Sichtbare Strahlen* (self-published, privately circulated).

110. See the substantial study by two participants in the Externsteine circle: Gert Meier and Hermann Zschweigert, *Die Hochkulturen der Megalithzeit: Verschwiegene Zeugnisse aus Europas großer Vergangenheit* (Tübingen: Grabert-Verlag, 1997), esp. 405–21.

111. Walther Machalett, *Die Externsteine: Das Zentrum des Abendlandes. Die Geschichte der weißen Rasse,* 6 vols. (Maschen, Germany: Hallonen-Verlag, 1970). Despite the given publication date, some illustrations are dated 1952, others 1978. A proper bibliographic report is not attempted here.

112. Ibid., vol. 1, *Atlantis,* 9.

113. Ibid., vol. 1, *Atlantis,* 4.

114. Machalett, *Die Externsteine,* vol. 1, *Atlantis,* 7–9.

115. Ibid., vol. 4, *Salvage,* 145.

116. Ibid., vol. 4, *Salvage,* 138–40.

117. See John Michell, *At the Centre of the World: Polar Symbolism Discovered in Celtic, Norse and Other Ritualized Landscapes* (London: Thames & Hudson, 1994).

118. See John Michell and Christine Rhone, *Twelve-Tribe Nations and the Science of Enchanting the Landscape* (Grand Rapids: Phanes Press, 1991).

CHAPTER SIX. TWO TRADITIONALISTS

1. René Guénon, *The Symbolism of the Cross,* trans. Angus Macnab (London: Luzac, 1958), xiii.

2. Julius Evola, *Revolt Against the Modern World,* trans. Guido Stucco (Rochester, Vt.: Inner Traditions, 1995), xxxiv.

3. For a list of the questions, see Jean-Pierre Laurant, *Le sens caché dans l'oeuvre de René Guénon* (Paris: L'Age d'Homme, 1975), 46–47.

4. *Le sens caché,* 48–49.

5. René Guénon, "Il Re del Mondo," *Atanor* 12 (Dec. 1924): 354–70. Subsequently published as *Le roi du monde* (Paris: Librairie Charles Bosse, 1927).

6. René Guénon, *Le roi du monde* (Paris: Gallimard, 1958), 62.

7. Ibid., 83.

8. Ibid., 1958, 84.

9. Ibid., 1958, 62.

10. Ibid., 1958, 63–64.

11. Blavatsky, *Secret Doctrine*, 1888, 1:204; Adyar ed., 1:253.

12. Ibid., 2:6; Adyar ed., 3:20.

13. Guénon, *Le roi du monde*, 67.

14. Marco Baistrocchi, "Agarttha: Una manipolazione guénoniana?" *Politica Romana* 2 (1995): 8–40; for English translation, see chapter 2, note 27.

15. Julius Evola, *Imperialismo pagano* (Padua: Edizioni di Ar, 1996; 1st ed. 1928), 22.

16. See Renato del Ponte, *Evola e il magico "Gruppo di Ur"* (Borzano: SeaR Edizioni, 1994).

17. Arvo [Julius Evola], "Sulla tradizione iperborea," *Ur,* 2/12 (Nov.–Dec. 1928); reprinted in Gruppo di Ur, *Introduzione alla magia quale scienza dell'Io* (Genoa: Fratelli Melita, 1987), 2:412–22.

18. Ibid., 415–416.

19. Ibid., 418.

20. For Guénon's candid opinions of these, see his letters to Guido de Giorgio in del Ponte, *Evola e il magico "Gruppo di Ur,"* 159–74.

21. René Guénon, "Les pierres de foudre," *Le Voile d'Isis,* May 1929; reprinted in Guénon, *Symboles fondamentaux de la science sacrée* (Paris: Gallimard, 1962), 187–91; here cited, 189n.

22. See René Guénon, "Atlantide et Hyperborée," *Le Voile d'Isis,* Oct. 1929; reprinted in Guénon, *Formes traditionnelles et cycles cosmiques* (Paris: Gallimard, 1970), 35–45; here cited, 36n.

23. Ea [Julius Evola], "Sul simbolismo dell'anno," *Krur,* 6 (June 1929); reprinted in Gruppo di Ur, *Introduzione alla magia,* 3:199–209; here cited, 201.

24. René Guénon, "Place de la tradition Atlantéenne dans le Manvantara," *Le Voile d'Isis,* Aug.–Sep. 1931; reprinted in Guénon, *Formes traditionnelles et cycles cosmiques* (Paris: Gallimard, 1970), 46–51; here cited, 46.

25. Ibid., 49.

26. Ibid., 50.

27. Ibid., 51.

28. See Giovanni Damiano, *Postfazione,* in Evola, *Imperialismo pagano,* 159.

29. Julius Evola, *Rivolta contra il mondo moderno* (Milan: Fratelli Bocca, 1951; 1st ed. 1934), 252; *Revolt Against the Modern World,* 188.

30. *Revolt,* 195; *Rivolta,* 260.

31. *Revolt,* 197; *Rivolta,* 262.

32. Julius Evola, *Il mito del sangue* (Borzano, Italy: SeaR Edizioni, 1995; reprint of 1942 ed.), 20; also 162.

33. *Revolt,* 189n.; *Rivolta,* 253n.

34. On this subject, see Dana Lloyd Thomas, *Julius Evola e la tentazione razzista: L'inganno del pangermanesimo in Italia* (Mesagne, Italy: Giordano, 2008).

35. Evola to Pierre Pascal, quoted in Michel Angebert, *Julius Evola, le visionnaire foudroyé* (Paris: Copernic, 1977), 201.

36. "Le sanglier et l'ourse," *Études Traditionnelles,* Aug.–Sep. 1936; reprinted in Guénon, *Symboles fondamentaux,* 177–83; here cited, 181.

37. René Guénon, *The Reign of Quantity and the Signs of the Times,* trans. Lord Northbourne (London: Luzac, 1953), 316.

38. Ibid., 222–23.

39. Ibid., 143–64.

CHAPTER SEVEN. THE BRITONS

1. See John Selby, "Dion Fortune and Her Inner Plane Contacts: Intermediaries in the Western Esoteric Tradition," Ph.D. diss., University of Exeter, 2008.

2. Dion Fortune, *The Esoteric Orders and Their Work* (York Beach, Maine: Weiser, 2000; 1st ed. 1928), 26.

3. Ibid., 28, 30.

4. Ibid., 31.

5. Dion Fortune, *The Sea Priestess* (York Beach, Maine: Weiser, 1993; 1st ed. 1938), 122.

6. Dion Fortune, Margaret Lumley Brown, and Gareth Knight, *The Arthurian Formula* (Loughborough, U.K.: Thoth Publications, 2006).

7. Fortune, *Sea Priestess,* 149.

8. Fortune et al., *Arthurian Formula,* 45–46.

9. Gareth Knight, *Pythoness The Life and Work of Margaret Lumley Brown* (Loughborough, U.K.: Thoth Publications, 2006). Knight's biography does not give Brown's birth or death dates.

10. Ibid., 10–14.

11. Ibid., 125.

12. Ibid., 126–27.

13. Ibid., 220–21.

14. Fortune et al., *Arthurian Formula,* 165–66.

15. Knight, *Pythoness,* 194.

16. Gareth Knight, writing in Fortune et al., *Arthurian Formula,* 154.

17. Peter Valentine Timlett, *The Seedbearers* (New York: Bantam Books, 1976; 1st ed. 1974). I thank Frank Donnola for bringing this novel and Margaret Lumley Brown to my attention.

18. Gareth Knight, "About Dion Fortune," www.angelfire.com/az/garethknight/aboutdf.html.

19. Timlett, *Seedbearers,* 29–30, 71.

20. See Knight et al., *Arthurian Formula,* 155, 157, 161.

21. Geraldine Cummins, *The Fate of Colonel Fawcett: A Narrative of His Last Expedition* (London: Aquarian Press, 1955), 28–29.

22. Ibid., 76–77.

23. Ibid., 42.

24. H. C. Randall-Stevens, El-Eros, *Atlantis to the Latter Days* (London: Aquarian Press, 1954), 13–14.

25. H. C. Randall-Stevens, *The Book of Truth,* 2nd ed. (London: Rider, 1927; 1st ed. 1925), 3–9.

26. Ibid., 14–15.

27. Ibid., 18.

28. Ibid., 29.

29. H. C. Randall-Stevens, *The Chronicles of Osiris* (London: Rider, 1927), 3–4.

30. Ibid., 18–19.

31. Ibid., 29–30.

32. Ibid., 44–45.

33. Ibid., 55.

34. Ibid., 53.

35. Randall-Stevens, *Book of Truth,* 141–62.

36. Ibid., 142.

37. Randall-Stevens, *Chronicles of Osiris,* 62.

38. Ibid., 63.

39. Ibid., 64–68.

40. Ibid., 99.

41. Ibid., 98.

42. Randall-Stevens, *Atlantis to the Latter Days,* 69.

43. Paul Brunton, *A Search in Secret Egypt* (New York: Dutton, 1936), 57–78.

44. Randall-Stevens, *Atlantis to the Latter Days,* 50–59, 87.

45. Ibid., 5.

46. Randall-Stevens, *Book of Truth,* viii.

47. Brunton, *Search in Secret Egypt,* 20–21.

48. Ibid., 34.

49. H. P. Blavatsky, "Buddhism, Christianity and Phallicism," in *Collected Writings,* 13:322.

50. A biographical article on J. Foster Forbes by Patrick Benham is at the website. www.mybrightonandhove.org.uk/page_id__7448_path__0p117p155p. aspx. See also *Burke's Landed Gentry of Great Britain,* s.v. "Forbes."

51. J. Foster Forbes, *The Unchronicled Past* (London: Simpkin & Marshall, 1938), i–ii.

52. Nicholas Mann, *The Isle of Avalon: Sacred Mysteries of Arthur and Glastonbury* (Woolavington, U.K.: Green Magic, 2001), 64.

53. See F. C. Tyler, *The Geometrical Arrangement of Ancient Sites: A Development of the Straight Track Theory* (London: Simpkin & Marshall, 1939).

54. Forbes, *Unchronicled Past,* 15.

55. Alfred Rosenberg, *Mythus,* 3 vols., var. trans. (London: Friends of Europe, 1936–1937).

56. Lewis Spence, *Will Europe Follow Atlantis?* (London: Rider, n.d. [1942]), 23.

57. Ibid., 24.

58. Ibid., 154.

59. Ibid., 157.

60. Ibid., 184–86.

61. Lewis Spence, *The Occult Sciences in Atlantis* (London: Rider, 1943), 21.

62. Daphne Vigers, *Atlantis Rising: The Records of the Author's Visits, Through an Uncommon State of Consciousness, to Ancient Atlantis* (London: Andrew Dakers, 1944), 5.

63. Ibid., 9.

64. Ibid., 22–24.

65. Ibid., 52.

66. Ibid., 110.

67. Ibid., 137.

68. Ibid., 171.

69. Shirley Andrews, *Atlantis: Insights from a Lost Civilization* (Minneapolis: Llewellyn Books, 2002), 250.

70. Helio-Arcanophus, *Atlantis Past, and to Come* (London: The Atlanteans, 1959), 4.

71. Ibid., 6–7.

72. Ibid., 8–9.

73. Ibid., 10–13.

74. Ibid., 3.

75. Ibid., 11.

76. Ibid., 16.

77. http://spiritualchannelling.com.

78. *Wessex Research Group Newsletter* 3/11 (Nov. 2008). www.wessexresearchgroup .org/newsletters/2008_nov.pdf.

79. Mandasoran, the Recorder, *Atlantis* (London: Golden Triangle Fellowhip, 1954), 51.

80. On Stainton Moses, see Joscelyn Godwin, *The Theosophical Enlightenment* (Albany: State University of New York Press, 1994), 293–300.

81. Mandasoran, *Atlantis,* 53.

82. Ibid., 1.

83. Ibid., 3.

84. Ibid., 6–7.

85. Ibid., 50.

86. Ibid., 52.

87. Ibid., 56–57.

88. Ibid., 5.

89. The University of Victoria (BC), to which Maltwood left her art collection, has a biography at www.maltwood.uvic.ca/k_maltwood.

90. *The High History of the Holy Grail,* trans. Sebastian Evans (London: J.M. Dent, 1929). The map is signed "K. Maltwood, Chilton Polden, Bridgwater, 1929–1930."

91. Katharine Maltwood, "The Discovery of a Prehistoric Zodiac in England," *Journal of the Royal Astronomical Society of Canada* (Sept. 1943): 272.

92. Katharine Maltwood, *A Guide to Glastonbury's Temple of the Stars: Their Giant Effigies Described from Air Views, Maps, and from "The High History of the Holy Grail"* (London, Women's Printing Society, 1934).

93. See Tom Williamson and Liz Bellamy, *Ley Lines in Question* (Tadworth, U.K.: World's Work, 1983), 162–68.

94. See Patrick Benham, *The Avalonians* (Glastonbury: Gothic Image, 2006).

95. I heard this in a lecture by Sir George Trevelyan, who carried the Avalonian ethos up to the close of the century.

96. W. Tudor Pole, "A Note on the Chalice Well at Glastonbury," in Brinsley le

Poer Trench, *Men Among Mankind* (London: Neville Spearman, 1962), 191.

97. See *The House of Lords UFO Debate. Illustrated, Full Transcript with Preface by Lord Clancarty (Brinsley le Poer Trench) and Notes by John Michell* (London: Open Head Press, 1979).

98. John Michell, *The Flying Saucer Vision: The Holy Grail Restored* (London: Sidgwick & Jackson, 1967), 150.

99. Ibid., 130.

100. John Michell, *The View over Atlantis* (London: Garnstone Press, 1969), 1.

101. See John Michell, *The Dimensions of Paradise: The Proportions and Symbolic Numbers of Ancient Cosmology* (London: Thames & Hudson, 1988).

CHAPTER EIGHT. SOME INDEPENDENTS

1. Michael D. Coe, *Breaking the Maya Code* (London: Thames & Hudson, 1992), 99.

2. Brasseur de Bourbourg, *Études sur le système graphique et la langue des Mayas,* 2 vols. (Paris: Imprimerie Impériale, 1869, 1870).

3. Ibid., 1:125.

4. Coe, *Breaking the Maya Code,* 106.

5. Lawrence G. Desmond, "Augustus Le Plongeon: A Fall from Archaeological Grace," in *Assembling the Past: Studies in the Professionalization of Archaeology,* ed. Alice B. Kehoe and Mary Beth Emmerich (Albuquerque: University of New Mexico Press, 1999): 81–90; here cited, 85.

6. Augustus Le Plongeon, *Queen Moo and the Egyptian Sphinx,* 2nd ed. (New York: Author, 1900; 1st ed. 1896), 243.

7. Plongeon, *Queen Moo,* 16.

8. Ibid., 22–26.

9. Ibid., 33.

10. Ibid., 18.

11. Ibid., 38.

12. Robert B. Stacey-Judd, *Atlantis: Mother of Empires* (Kempton, Ill.: Adventures Unlimited Press, 1999; 1st ed. 1939), 278.

13. Le Plongeon, *Queen Moo,* 147, citing folio v of the Troano, but not present in Brasseur's translation.

14. H. P. Blavatsky thought it was the other way about. See her note in *Lucifer,* 1890, in *Collected Writings,* vol. 12 (Wheaton, Ill.: Theosophical Publishing House, 1980), 382.

15. A. S. Raleigh, *The Shepherd of Men: An Official Commentary on the Sermon of Hermes Trismegistos* (San Francisco: Hermetic Publishing, 1916), 6.

16. See Joscelyn Godwin, "The Hidden Hand, Part I: The Provocation of the Hydesville Phenomena," *Theosophical History* 3/2 (1990): 35–43.

17. Raleigh, *Shepherd of Men,* 116.

18. Ibid., 94–97.

19. Ibid., 101–9.

20. Ibid., 132–33.

21. Ibid., 135–36.

22. Ibid., 139–41.

23. Ibid., 142–45.

24. Death of father and names of nine children from Wikipedia, s.v. "James Churchward." Father's profession from National Archives, www.national-archives.gov.uk/a2a/records.aspx?cat=821-178b&cid=-1#-1.

25. Albert Churchward, *Signs and Symbols of Primordial Man,* 2nd ed. (New York: Dutton, 1913; 1st ed. 1910), 243.

26. Albert Churchward, *The Origin and Evolution of Freemasonry* (London: Allen & Unwin, 1920), 15–33.

27. Hans Stefan Santesson, *Understanding Mu* (New York: Paperback Library, 1970), 9.

28. See the James Churchward Timeline at www.my-mu.com/jtimeline.html.

29. James Churchward Timeline, with facsimile of newspaper headline.

30. An Oxford education is unlikely for one who married at twenty and was then listed as a banker's clerk. See documentation in James Churchward Timeline.

31. Compare Le Plongeon, *Queen Moo,* 17 (plate xvii); Churchward, *Lost Continent,* 141; Albert Churchward, *Signs and Symbols,* 24–25.

32. See the list of travels compiled from Churchward's books at www.my-mu.com/jtravels.html.

33. See James Churchward, *Cosmic Forces of Mu,* vol. 1 (Albuquerque, N.Mex.: Be, Books, 1992; 1st ed. 1934), 139–50.

34. James Churchward, *The Lost Continent of Mu, the Motherland of Man* (Albuquerque, N.Mex.: Be, Books, 1994; 1st ed. 1926), 235.

35. Albert Churchward, *The Origin and Evolution of Religion* (London: Allen & Unwin, 1924), caption to plate xlviii, opp. 232.

36. One of them was used as the jacket illustration of Wishar Cervé's *Lemuria* (see below).

37. Churchward, *Lost Continent,* 193.

38. James Churchward, *The Children of Mu* (Albuquerque, N.Mex.: Be, Books, 1988; 1st ed. 1931), opp. 158; *The Sacred Symbols of Mu* (Albuquerque, N.Mex.: Be, Books, 1988; 1st ed. 1933), 160–61.

39. Churchward, *Children of Mu,* 18.

40. Churchward, *Lost Continent,* 108–9.

41. Churchward, *Children of Mu,* 16.

42. Churchward, *Lost Continent,* 25, crediting Troano and Cortesianus Codices.

43. Ibid., 119.

44. Churchward, *Sacred Symbols,* 32–33.

45. Churchward, *Children of Mu,* 113.

46. Ibid., 251–52.

47. See Nicolas Notovitch, *The Unknown Life of Jesus Christ* (New York: R. F. Fenno, 1890); Levi H. Dowling, *The Aquarian Gospel of Jesus the Christ* (Los Angeles: Royal Publishing, 1908).

48. Churchward, *Children of Mu,* 188–89.

49. Churchward, *Sacred Symbols,* 274–75.

50. Churchward, *Children of Mu,* 265.

51. Not to be confused with the older Societas Rosicruciana in Anglia, which uses the same acronym.

52. Khei, *Rosicrucian Fundamentals: An Exposition of the Rosicrucian Synthesis of Religion, Science and Philosophy* (New York: Societas Rosicruciana in America, 1920), 243.

53. Ibid., 221–30.

54. Ibid., 245.

55. Ibid., 170–74.

56. Joscelyn Godwin, *The Theosophical Enlightenment* (Albany: State University of New York Press, 1994), 67–76; *Arktos, The Polar Myth in Science, Symbolism, and Nazi Survival* (Grand Rapids: Phanes, 1993), 199–202.

57. Khei, *Rosicrucian Fundamentals, An Exposition of the Rosicrucian Synthesis of Religion, Science, and Philosophy* (New York: Societas Rosicruciana in America, 1920), 175.

58. Max Heindel, *The Rosicrucian Cosmo-Conception,* 2nd ed. (Seattle: Rosicrucian Fellowship, 1910; 1st ed. 1909), 263.

59. Ibid., 265.

60. Ibid., 276.

61. J. van Rijckenborgh, *Elementary Philosophy of the Modern Rosy Cross,* 3rd ed. (Haarlem, Netherlands: Rozekruis Press, 1984; 1st ed. 1950), 81.

62. Ibid., 82–84.

63. See John Patrick Deveney, *Paschal Beverly Randolph, a Nineteenth-Century Black American Spiritualist, Rosicrucian, and Sex-Magician* (Albany: State University of New York Press, 1997), 140–43, 243–45.

64. William P. Phelon, *Our Story of Atlantis, Written Down for the Hermetic Brotherhood* (San Francisco: Hermetic Book Concern, 1903), 7.

65. Wishar S. Cervé, *Lemuria: The Lost Continent of the Pacific* (San Jose, Calif.: Supreme Grand Lodge of AMORC, 1946; 1st ed. 1931).

66. On James W. Ward, see www.oac.cdlib.org/data/13030/fn/tf8c6009fn/files/tf8c6009fn.pdf.

67. G. I. Gurdjieff, *All and Everything* (London: Routledge & Kegan Paul, 1950), 756.

68. James Webb, *The Harmonious Circle: The Lives and Work of G. I. Gurdjieff, P. D. Ouspensky, and Their Followers* (London: Thames & Hudson, 1980), 310–11.

69. Gurdjieff, *All and Everything*, 249.

CHAPTER NINE. CHANNELING IN THE NEW WORLD

1. See Oskar R. Schlag, *Von alten und neuen Mysterien: Die Lehren des A.,* Bd. 1, ed. Antoine Faivre and Erhart Kahle (Würzburg: Ergon, 1998).

2. *Oahspe: A Kosmon Bible in the Words of Jehovih and His Angel Embassadors* (Boston: Author, 1882).

3. Letter to *The Banner of Light* of Jan. 21, 1883, from *The Internet Sacred Text Archiv.* www.sacred-texts.com/oah/pamphlet.htm.

4. *Oahspe,* Book of Aph, 2:6.

5. *Encyclopaedia of Religion and Ethics,* ed. James Hastings, vol. 9 (Edinburgh: T. & T. Clark, 1917), 429, s.v. "Oahspe."

6. *Oahspe,* Book of Sethantes, 5:24.

7. *Oahspe,* Book of Jehovih, 7:2.

8. See Zecharia Sitchin, *The Twelfth Planet* (New York: Stein & Day, 1976), 224–27.

9. See *Oahspe,* First Book of First Lords; Synopsis of Sixteen Cycles.

10. *Oahspe,* Synopsis of Sixteen Cycles, 2:13.

11. *Oahspe,* Synopsis of Sixteen Cycles, 3:14–19.

12. *Oahspe,* Book of Aph, 3:18. Chinvat is borrowed from Persian cosmology.

13. *Oahspe,* Book of Aph, 4:6.

14. *Oahspe,* Book of Ah'shong, 7:5–7.

15. *Oahspe,* Book of Cosmogony and Prophecy, 1:12.

16. *The Urantia Book* (Chicago: Urantia Foundation, 1955).

17. See Martin Gardner, *Urantia: The Great Cult Mystery* (Buffalo, N.Y.: Prometheus Books, 1995).

18. See John B. Hare, introduction to *A Dweller on Two Planets* in *The Internet Sacred Text Archive.* www.sacred-texts.com/atl/dtp/index.htm.

19. Phylos the Tibetan, *A Dweller on Two Planets* (Los Angeles: Poseid Printing, 1920; 1st ed. 1905), 28.

20. Hare, introduction to *Dweller on Two Planets.*

21. Emma Hardinge Britten, *Nineteenth Century Miracles; or, Spirits and Their Work in Every Country on the Earth* (New York: William Britten, 1884), 554.

22. W. J. Colville, *The Lost Continent of Atlantis; and the Civilization of the Prehistoric World: An Inspirational Lecture* (London: J. Burns, n.d. [1884]), 6–7.

23. Colville, *Lost Continent of Atlantis,* 7.

24. J. Ben Leslie, *Submerged Atlantis Restored, or Rĭn-gä'-sĕ nŭd Sï-ï-kĕl'zē (Links and Cycles). A Short Treatise on the Over-Spirit as the Cycle Supreme* (Rochester, N.Y.: Austin Publishing, 1911), 12.

25. Ibid., 80–82.

26. Ibid., 243–49.

27. Ibid., 298.

28. Ibid., 347–54.

29. Sidney D. Kirkpatrick, *Edgar Cayce: An American Prophet* (New York: Riverhead Books, 2000), 281.

30. Edgar Evans Cayce, Gail Cayce Schwartzer, and Douglas G. Richards, *Mysteries of Atlantis Revisited* (New York: St. Martin's Press, 1997), 25–27.

31. Kirkpatrick, *Edgar Cayce,* 205–36, 366–74, 415–30.

32. Compiled from Cayce et al., *Mysteries of Atlantis;* Edgar Evans Cayce, *Atlantis: Fact or Fiction?* (Virginia Beach: Association for Research and Enlightenment, 1962); Lytle W. Robinson, *Edgar Cayce's Story of the Origin and Destiny of Man* (New York: Coward, McCann & Geoghegan, 1972).

33. Cayce et al., *Mysteries of Atlantis,* 35–36.

34. K. Paul Johnson, *Edgar Cayce in Context. The Readings: Truth and Fiction* (Albany: State University of New York Press, 1998), 63.

35. Johnson, *Edgar Cayce in Context,* 64.

36. Kirkpatrick, *Edgar Cayce, an American Prophet,* 378.

37. Cayce et al., *Mysteries of Atlantis,* 39–40.

38. Ibid., 43, 48.

39. Johnson, *Edgar Cayce in Context,* 66.

40. Robinson, *Edgar Cayce's Story,* 93, quoting reading #294-L-8.

41. Cayce, *Atlantis: Fact or Fiction?* 30.

42. Robinson, *Edgar Cayce's Story,* 61–62.

43. Cayce, *Atlantis: Fact or Fiction?* 35.

44. Cayce et al., *Mysteries of Atlantis,* 165.

45. See Johnson, *Edgar Cayce in Context,* 27; see also 22.

46. Ibid., 131.

47. Ibid., 73–74.

48. Ibid., 66–71.

49. See the annotated bibliography of Mount Shasta legends compiled by the College of Siskiyous, www.siskiyous.edu/shasta/bib/B16.htm.

50. Edgar Lucian Larkin, "The Atlantides," *San Francisco Examiner,* Dec. 31, 1913, 18 [editorial page].

51. Selvius, "Descendants of Lemuria: A Description of an Ancient Cult in America," *Mystic Triangle,* 3 (Aug. 1925): 113–14. Also reprinted in *Rosicrucian Digest,* 9 (May 1931): 495–97.

52. See Ballard, writing as Godfré Ray King, *Unveiled Mysteries* (Chicago: Saint Germain Press, 1934); *The Magic Presence* (Chicago: Saint Germain Press, 1935).

53. For an analysis of such encounters, see J. Gordon Melton, "The Contactees: A Survey"; and John H. Saliba, "Religious Dimensions of UFO Phenomena," in James R. Lewis, ed., *The Gods Have Landed: New Religions from Other Worlds* (Albany: State University of New York Press, 1995), 1–14, 15–64.

54. King, *Unveiled Mysteries,* 92–95.

55. See J. Gordon Melton, ed., *Encyclopedia of Occultism and Parapsychology,* 5th ed. (Farmington Hills, Mich.: Gale Group, 2001), 2:773, s.v. "'I AM' Religious Activity."

56. See Henry Olcott, *Old Diary Leaves,* 1st series (Adyar [Chennai], India: Theosophical Publishing House, 1941), 275–76.

57. Leadbeater, *Masters and the Path,* 269.

58. Scott Beekman, *William Dudley Pelley: A Life in Right-Wing Extremism and the Occult* (Syracuse, N.Y.: Syracuse University Press, 2005), 70. The article was published in March 1929.

59. William Dudley Pelley, *Star Guests: Design for Mortality* (Noblesville, Ind.: Fellowship Press, 1978; 1st ed. 1950), 223.

60. Beekman, *William Dudley Pelley,* 57.

61. Ibid., 87.

62. Pelley, *Star Guests,* 64.

63. Ibid., 65.

64. Ibid., 75.

65. Ibid., 76.

66. Ibid., 66, 80, 90, 101.

67. Ibid., 175–76, 235.

68. Ibid., 236.

69. Ibid., 238.

70. Ibid., 236.

71. Kirkpatrick, *Edgar Cayce,* 487; Pelley, *Star Guests,* 152, 164.

72. See transcription of the article, dated "April 1934," at www.ufodigest.com/ news/0109/adamski-print.html.

73. Colin Bennett, *Looking for Orthon: The Story of George Adamski, the First Flying Saucer Contactee, and How He Changed the World* (New York: Cosimo, 2008; 1st ed. 2001), 23.

74. *The O.E. Library Critic,* 23/6 (Mar.–Apr. 1935): 4.

75. Bennett, *Looking for Orthon,* 18.

76. See the retitled issue, *Behind the Flying Saucer Mystery* (New York: Warner, 1967), 147–59.

77. George Adamski, *Behind the Flying Saucer Mystery* (New York: Warner, 1967), 153–54.

78. Ibid., 155.

79. See L. Sprague de Camp, *Lost Continents* (New York: Dover, 1970); Henry Eichner, *Atlantean Chronicles* (Alhambra, Calif.: Fantasy Publishing, 1971).

80. On Doreal, see Walter Kafton-Minkel, *Subterranean Worlds: 100,000 Years of Dragons, Dwarfs, the Dead, Lost Races & UFOs from Inside the Earth* (Port Townsend, Wash.: Loompanics, 1989), 155–60.

81. Doreal, *The Emerald Tablets of Thoth the Atlantean* (Sedalia, Mo.: Brotherhood of the White Temple, 1939).

CHAPTER TEN. CHANNELING IN THE NEW AGE

1. See David Hatcher Childress and Richard Shaver, *Lost Continents and the Hollow Earth* (Kempton, Ill.: Adventures Unlimited, 1999), 218–20.

2. Ibid., 51.

3. Ibid., 71.

4. Ibid., 1.

5. Ibid., iv.

6. See Walter Kafton-Minkel, *Subterranean Worlds: 100,000 Years of Dragons, Dwarfs, the Dead, Lost Races and UFOs from Inside the Earth* (Port Townsend, Wash.: Loompanics, 1989), 133–53.

7. Childress and Shaver, *Lost Continents and the Hollow Earth,* 230.

8. Kafton-Minkel, cited from *Subterranean Worlds,* 149.

9. Ibid., 150.

10. Desmond Leslie and George Adamski, *Flying Saucers Have Landed* (New York: British Book Centre, 1953), 172.

11. Colin Bennet, *Looking for Orthon: The Story of George Adamski, the First Flying Saucer Contactee, and How He Changed the World* (New York: Cosimo, 2008), 62.

12. George Adamski, *Inside the Space Ships* (New York: Abelard-Schuman, 1955), 178–79.

13. Ibid., 181.

14. Ibid., 238.

15. See Colin Bennett, "Breakout of the Fictions: George Adamski's 1959 World Tour," *The Anomalist* 8 (2000): 39–84.

16. Leslie and Adamski, *Flying Saucers Have Landed,* opp. 192.

17. See Alec Hiddell, "Tracks in the Desert," *The Excluded Middle* 3. www.excludedmiddle.com/tracks%20in%20desert.html.

18. George Hunt Williamson and Alfred C. Bailey, *The Saucers Speak! A Documentary Report of Interstellar Communication by Radiotelegraphy* (Los Angeles: New Age Publishing, 1954), 124.

19. George Hunt Williamson, *Other Tongues—Other Flesh* (Amherst, Wisc.: Amherst Press, 1953).

20. Williamson, *Other Tongues,* 8–9.

21. *Oahspe: A Kosmon Bible in the Words of Jehovah and His Angel Ambassadors,* Book of Cosmogony and Prophecy (Boston, 1882), 1:38; Williamson, *Other Tongues,* 56.

22. Williamson, *Other Tongues,* 197–98.

23. Ibid., 196.

24. Ibid., 199.

25. Ibid., 384.

26. George Hunt Williamson, *Secret Places of the Lion* (Amherst, Wisc.: Amherst Press, 1958), 7.

27. Ibid., 10–11.

28. Ibid., 195.

29. Ibid., 213–14.

30. Ibid., 203–5.

31. Ibid., 155.

32. Ibid., 153.

33. Ibid., 3.

34. Brother Philip, *Secret of the Andes* (Bolinas, Calif.: Leaves of Grass Press, 1976; 1st ed. 1961), 7.

35. Ibid., 13–17.

36. See Sidney P. Kirkpatrick, *Edgar Cayce: An American Prophet* (New York: Riverhead Books, 2000), 397, 459, 498, 516.

37. Brother Philip, *Secrets of the Andes*, 69.

38. Ibid., 34.

39. See Jay Weidner and Vincent Bridges, *The Mysteries of the Great Cross of Hendaye* (Rochester, Vt.: Destiny Books, 2003), 388.

40. See Gordon Melton, *Encyclopedia of Occultism and Parapsychology* (Farmington Hills, Mich.: Gale Group, 2001), s.v. "Williamson."

41. See Wouter J. Hanegraaff, *New Age Religion and Western Culture: Estoricism in the Mirror of Secular Thought* (Leiden, Netherlands: Brill, 1996), 126 and many references throughout this seminal work.

42. See, for example, Jane Roberts, *Seth Speaks: The Eternal Validity of the Soul*. With Notes by Robert F. Butts (Englewood Cliffs, N.J.: Prentice-Hall, 1972), 4–7, 28, 42–43.

43. Ibid., 252.

44. Ibid., 253.

45. Ibid., 254.

46. See Jane Roberts, *The Education of Oversoul 7* (New York: Pocket Books, 1976; 1st ed. 1973), 104–7, for an imaginative account of the use of sound to move rocks.

47. Roberts, *Seth Speaks*, 260–62.

48. See Robert Butts's note in Roberts, *Seth Speaks*, 265.

49. Roberts, *Seth Speaks*, 482.

50. Ibid., 450.

51. Ibid., 486.

52. Stuart Holroyd, *Prelude to the Landing on Planet Earth* (London: W.H. Allen, 1977). Also published as *Briefing for Landing on Planet Earth* and reissued as *The Nine: Briefing from Deep Space: The Controversial Record of a Unique "Encounter" and a Message of Hope for All Mankind* (Flagler Beach, Fla.: Old Kings Road Press, 2003).

53. Phyllis V. Schlemmer and Palden Jenkins, *The Only Planet of Choice: Essential Briefings from Deep Space* (Bath, U.K.: Gateway Books, 1993), 2.

54. Ibid., 163–65.

55. Ibid., 169.

56. See Andrew Collins, *From the Ashes of Angels* (London: Michael Joseph, 1996), 56.

57. Schlemmer and Jenkins, *Only Planet of Choice,* 171.

58. Ibid., 178–80.

59. Ibid., 99–100.

60. Ibid., 184.

61. Ibid., 185–86.

62. Ibid., 194.

63. Ibid., 201.

64. Information on Knight: mainly from conversations and sessions in Yelm, Washington, November 8–10, 1996, and February 7–9, 1997.

65. *Ramtha* (Bellevue, Wash.: Sovereignty Publishers, 1986). "The work consists of edited transcriptions of magnetic tape recordings authored by JZ Knight, with her permission."

66. Ibid., 5–7.

67. Ibid., 11.

68. Ibid., 18–20.

69. Ibid., 84.

70. Ibid., 86–87.

71. Ibid., 146.

72. J. Gordon Melton, *Finding Enlightenment: Ramtha's School of Ancient Wisdom* (Hillsboro, Oreg.: Beyond Words Publishing, 1998), 165.

73. Ibid., 153–57.

74. Joscelyn Godwin, "Ramtha's Apocalyptic Books," unpublished paper read at panel on Ramtha, Yelm, Washington, February 9, 1997.

75. James Merrill, *The Changing Light at Sandover* (New York: Atheneum, 1982).

76. John Chambers, "The Channeled Myths of James Merrill: New Tales of Atlantis and Akhnaton," *The Anomalist* 5 (1997): 41–58; here quoted, 56–57.

77. Merrill, *Changing Light at Sandover,* 7.

78. Chambers, "Channeled Myths of James Merrill," 54.

CHAPTER ELEVEN. THE FOUR AGES

1. Vishnu Purana, 1:3, citing *The Visnu Purana: A System of Hindu Mythology and Tradition,* trans. H. H. Wilson (Delhi: Nag Publishers, 1989; 1st ed. 1840), 1:31–34. The same numbers are given in other Puranas (see especially references to the Linga Purana, below) and in the Laws of Manu, 1:68–82.

2. See *Sûrya-Siddhânta: A Textbook of Hindu Astronomy,* trans. Ebenezer Burgess, *Journal of the American Oriental Society,* 6 (1860): 161–68. Reprinted Minneapolis: Wizards Book Shelf, 1978.

3. Eusebius, *Chaldaean Chronicle,* 1:8, trans. Andrew Smith, 4.

4. Père [Joseph Henri Marie de] Prémare, *Discours préliminaire,* in Joseph de Guignes, ed., *Le Chou-King, un des livres sacrés des Chinois . . .* (Paris: Tilliard, 1770), li.

5. Ibid., lxv.

6. Ibid., lxvi–lxvii.

7. Thomas Fergusson, *Chinese Researches. First Part: Chinese Chronology and Cycles* (Shanghai: n.p., 1880), 84.

8. *The Poetic Edda, Grimnismol,* 22–23, trans. Henry Adams Bellows.

9. Giorgio de Santillana and Hertha von Dechend, *Hamlet's Mill: An Essay on Myth and the Frame of Time* (Boston: Gambit, 1969), 162.

10. This is what the Shatapatha Brahmana states, though those who have counted them find fewer.

11. This was the game played by the initiates of Castalia in Hesse's 1943 novel *Das Glasperlenspiel,* known in English as *The Glass Bead Game.*

12. Ernest G. McClain, *The Myth of Invariance: The Origin of the Gods, Mathematics and Music from the Rig Veda to Plato* (New York: Nicolas Hays, 1976), 149.

13. Vishnu Purana, ed. cit., 1:34n.

14. What follows is summarized from Guénon, *Remarques sur la doctrine des cycles cosmiques,* 22–24.

15. Ibid., 21.

16. Ibid., 23.

17. Guénon, *Place de la tradition atlantéenne,* 48n.

18. Jean Robin, *Les sociétés secrètes au rendez-vous de l'apocalypse* (Paris: Guy Trédaniel, 1985), 67.

19. Alain Daniélou, *The Way to the Labyrinth: Memories of East and West,* trans. Marie-Claire Cournand (New York: New Directions, 1987; 1st ed. 1981), 294.

20. I consulted *The Linga-Purana, Trans. by a Board of Scholars* (Delhi: Motilal Banarsidass, 1982).

21. From the original French edition, *La fantaisie des dieux et l'aventure humaine: Nature et destin du monde dans la tradition shivaïte* (Monaco: Éds. du Rocher, 1985), 17.

22. Alain Daniélou, *While the Gods Play: Shaiva Oracles and Predictions on the Cycles of History and the Destiny of Mankind,* trans. Barbara Bailey, Michael Baker, and Deborah Lawlor (Rochester, Vt.: Inner Traditions, 1987), 193.

23. Linga Purana, ch. 4, v. 24–35; ed. cit., 14.

24. Daniélou, *While the Gods Play,* 16.

25. Ibid., 197.

26. Ibid., 199.

27. Ibid., 197.

28. Gaston Georgel, *Les rythmes dans l'histoire,* 3rd ed. (Milan: Archè, 1981; 1st ed. 1937), 119.

29. Ibid., 6.

30. Guénon reviewed this, too. Both reviews are reprinted in Guénon, *Formes traditionnelles,* 28–31.

31. Georgel, *Les rythmes dans l'histoire,* 166.

32. Ibid., 164.

33. Guénon, *Formes traditionnelles,* 29.

34. Gaston Georgel, *Les quatre âges de l'humanité (Exposé de la doctrine traditionnelle des cycles cosmiques)* (Milan: Archè, 1976; 1st ed. 1949), 25–26.

35. Ibid., 17; letter of Dec. 29, 1937.

36. Ibid., 16; letter of Oct. 4, 1945.

37. Ibid., 16.

38. Ibid., 67, 73.

39. Robin Waterfield, *René Guénon and the Future of the West: The Life and Writings of a 20th-century Metaphysician* (n.p.: Crucible, 1987), 59.

40. Georgel, *Les quatre âges de l'humanité,* 87.

41. Ibid., 21; letter of Nov. 5, 1950.

42. Ibid., 81–83.

43. Gaston Georgel, *Chronologie des derniers temps (d'après la doctrine tradition-nelle des cycles cosmiques)* (Milan: Archè, 1986), 84.

44. Georgel, *Les quatre âges de l'humanité,* 61.

45. Saint-Yves d'Alveydre, *Mission de l'Inde en Europe; Mission de l'Europe en Asie* (Nice: Bélisane, 1981), 212–13; *The Kingdom of Agarttha,* 105.

46. On Ossendowski's part in the Agarttha mystification, see Marco Baistrocchi, *Agarttha: A Guénonian Manipulation?* translated by Joscelyn Godwin (Fullerton, Calif.: Theosophical History Center, 2009).

47. Ferdinand Ossendowski, *Beasts, Men and Gods* (New York: Dutton, 1922), 314.

48. Georgel, *Chronologie,* 19.

49. Gaston Georgel, *Le cycle Judéo-Chrétien, sceau et couronnement de l'histoire humaine* (Milan: Archè, 1983), 34.

50. Compiled from data in Georgel, *Les quatre âges de l'humanité,* 292, and *Chronologie des derniers temps,* 22–23.

51. The fourteenfold division is the mainspring of Georgel's *Le cycle Judéo-Chrétien.*

52. Georgel, *Chronologie des derniers temps,* 29–32.

53. Ibid., 38.

54. Ibid., 90–92.

55. Ibid., 169–71.

56. Ibid., 180.

57. Ibid., 211.

58. René Guénon, *Reign of Quantity and the Signs of the Times,* trans. Lord Northbourne (London: Luzac, 1953), 315.

59. Ibid., 334

60. Ibid., 336.

61. Daniélou, *While the Gods Play,* 223, 224.

62. Ibid., 222.

63. Fabre d'Olivet, *Hermeneutic Intepretation of the Origin of the Societal State of Man,* trans. Nayán Louise Redfield (New York: G. P. Putnam's Sons, 1915), 30–31.

64. Léon Cellier, *Fabre d'Olivet: Contribution á l'étude des aspects religieux du romantisme* (Paris: Nizet, 1953), 274–77.

65. Carl Friedrich Koeppen, *Die Religion des Buddha und ihre Entstehung* (Berlin: Ferdinand Schneider, 1857–59), 1:266–89. For a longer digest, see Louis de la Vallée Poussin, "Ages of the World: Buddhist" in *Encylopaedia of Religion and Ethics,* 1:87–90.

66. Koeppen, *Die Religion des Buddha*, 284.

67. On the Kalachakra prophecy, see Edwin Bernbaum, *The Way to Shambhala* (Los Angeles: Jeremy P. Tarcher, 1980), 231–45; Dalai Lama, Fourteenth, *The Kālachakra Tantra*, 65; Geshe Lhundub Sopa, Roger Jackson, John Newman, *The Wheel of Time. The Kalachakra in Context* (Ithaca: Snow Lion, 1991), 78–79; Baistrocchi, *Agarttha: A Guénonian Manipulation?* 23–24.

68. Helmuth von Glasenapp, *Jainism: An Indian Religion of Salvation*, trans. S. B. Shrotri (Delhi: Motilal Banarsidass, 1999), 272.

69. Helmuth von Glasenapp, *The Doctrine of Karman in Jain Philosophy*, trans. G. Barry Gifford (Bombay: Trustees of the B.V.J. Panalal Charity Fund, 1948), 97, 100.

70. Paramahansa Yogananda, *Autobiography of a Yogi* (Los Angeles: Self-Realization Fellowship, 1983; 1st ed. 1946).

71. See W. Y. Evans-Wentz, *Tibetan Yoga and Secret Doctrines* (London: Oxford University Press, 1958), frontispiece and xix.

72. Jnanavatar Swami Sri Yukteswar Giri, *The Holy Science* (Los Angeles: Self-Realization Fellowship, 1990; 1st ed. 1949), 16.

73. *Terrorism in Bengal: A Collection of Documents on Terrorist Activities from 1905 to 1939*, ed. Amiya K. Samanta (Calcutta: Government of West Bengal, 1995), 1:155. Accessed through Wikipedia article "Mokshadacharan Samadhyayi." See also Arun Chandra Gula, *First Spark of Revolution: The Early Phase of India's Struggle for Independence, 1900–1920* (Bombay: Orient Longman, 1971), 195–96.

74. Sri Yukteswar, *Holy Science*, 15.

75. Ibid., 13.

76. Ibid., 7.

77. Walter Cruttenden, *Lost Star of Myth and Time* (Pittsburgh: St. Lynn's Press, 2006), 115.

78. Ibid., 159–76.

79. Yukteswar, *Holy Science*, 7.

80. See John Major Jenkins, *Galactic Alignment: The Transformation of Consciousness According to Mayan, Egyptian, and Vedic Traditions* (Rochester, Vt.: Bear & Co., 2002), 130.

81. John Major Jenkins, *The 2012 Story: The Myths, Fallacies and Truth Behind the Most Intriguing Date in History* (New York: Tarcher/Penguin, 2009), 304-306."]

82. Jenkins, *Galactic Alignment*, 131.

83. Jenkins, *The 2012 Story*, 305.

84. See Paul LaViolette, *Earth Under Fire: Humanity's Survival of the Apocalypse* (Schenectady, N.Y.: Starburst Publications, 1997).

85. Robert M. Schoch and Logan Yonavjak, *The Parapsychology Revolution: A Concise Anthology of Paranormal and Psychical Research* (New York: Tarcher/ Penguin, 2008), 248, reporting findings of Michael McMoneagle.

CHAPTER TWELVE. THE PRECESSION OF THE EQUINOXES

1. See Nicholas Campion, *The Great Year: Astrology, Millenarianism and History in the Western Tradition* (London: Penguin-Arkana, 1994), 246–47.

2. James Evans, *The History and Practice of Ancient Astronomy* (New York: Oxford University Press, 1998), 248–49, 275–76.

3. Lynn Thorndike, *A History of Magic and Experimental Science,* vol. 2, *The First Thirteen Centuries* (New York: Columbia University Press, 1923), 895.

4. David H. Kelley and Eugene F. Malone, *Exploring Ancient Skies: An Encyclopedic Survey of Archaeoastronomy* (New York: Springer, 2005), 282.

5. Carl Gustav Jung, *Aion: Researches into the Phenomenology of the Self,* trans. R. F. C. Hull (New York: Pantheon Books, 1959), 94n.

6. Otto Neugebauer, *A History of Ancient Mathematical Astronomy* (New York: Springer-Verlag, 1975), 6.

7. Ibid., 369, 543n.

8. John North, *Cosmos: An Illustrated History of Astronomy and Cosmology* (Chicago: University of Chicago Press, 2008), 175–76.

9. Ibid., 51–52.

10. W. M. O'Neil, *Early Astronomy from Babylonia to Copernicus* (Sydney: Sydney University Press, 1986), 17–18.

11. Anthony Aveni, *The End of Time: The Maya Mystery of 2012* (Boulder, Colo.: University Press of Colorado, 2009), 102–3.

12. A. Pannekoek, *A History of Astronomy* (London: George Allen & Unwin, 1961), 75.

13. North, *Cosmos,* 140.

14. Harald T. Reiche, "The Language of Archaic Astronomy: A Clue to the Atlantis Myth?" in Kenneth Brecher and Michael Feirtag, eds., *Astronomy of the Ancients* (Cambridge, Mass.: MIT Press, 1979), 153–89.

15. Subhash Kak, "Birth and Early Development of Indian Astronomy," in H. Selin, ed., *Astronomy Across Cultures: The History of Non-Western Astronomy* (Dordrecht, Netherlands: Kluwer, 2000), 303–40; here cited, 311.

16. Ibid., 303.

17. Ibid., 307–8.

18. Ibid., 321.

19. Ibid., 307.

20. Ibid., 329.

21. Ibid., 336.

22. David H. Kelley and Eugene F. Malone, *Exploring Ancient Skies*, 493–94.

23. Ibid., 362.

24. Ibid., 464–65.

25. Ibid., 251.

26. O'Neil, *Early Astronomy*, 97.

27. Godfrey Higgins, *Anacalypsis. An Attempt to Draw Aside the Veil of the Saitic Isis; or an Inquiry into the Origin of Languages, Nations and Religions* (New York: Macy-Masius, 1927; 1st ed. 1833–36), 1:174.

28. See James Adam, *The Nuptial Number* (n.p.: Kairos, 1985; 1st ed. 1891), 84–85.

29. See Roelof van den Broek and Inez Wolf Seger, *The Myth of the Phoenix* (Leiden, Netherlands: Brill, 1972), 72–75.

30. See "The Super-Enlightenment," an online archive from Stanford University Libraries curated by Dan Edelstein: http://collections.stanford.edu/supere.

31. Charles-François Dupuis, *Origine de tous les cultes, ou religion universelle* (Paris, An III/1794-95). There is an English translation only of the abridged version. For a translation of the passages concerning the zodiac, see Joseph Priestley, "Remarks on M. Dupuis's Origin of All Religions," in *The Theological and Miscellaneous Works of Joseph Priestley*, vol. 17, 327–28. http://books.google.com/books?id=bsRhAAAAIAAJ&dq=priestley+dupuis+theological+works&source=gbs_navlinks_s.

32. See Joscelyn Godwin, *The Theosophical Enlightenment* (State University of New York Press, 1994), 76–91.

33. Higgins, *Anacalypsis*, 1:509.

34. Ibid., 1:763.

35. Ibid., 1:801.The bracketed number is Higgins's.

36. Ibid., 1:194 says 380 BC; 1:760 says 350 BC; 1:836 says 360 BC, as do 2:137–38, 144.

37. Ibid., 1:191.

38. Ibid., 2:144n.

39. Ibid., 2:145.

40. H. P. Blavatsky, "The Esoteric Character of the Gospels," *Collected Writings,*

vol. 8 (Wheaton, Ill.: Theosophical Publishing House, 1980), 174n. First published in *Lucifer* 1:3 (Nov. 1887).

41. Paul Le Cour (see note 43 below) gives this value as the consensus of Francoeur, Biot, and Arago.

42. John Benedict Buescher, *Aquarian Evangelist: The Age of Aquarius as It Dawned in the Mind of Levi Dowling* (Fullerton, Calif.: Theosophical History, 2008), 44.

43. Paul Le Cour, *L'ère du Verseau: le proche avenir de l'humanité,* revised ed. (Paris: Dervy, 1999), 89.

44. Raoul Auclair, *Le livre des cycles* (Paris: Éditions des Portes de France, 1947), 81, 178.

45. Jean Phaure, *Le cycle de l'humanité adamique: Introduction à l'étude de la cyclologie traditionelle et de la fin des temps* (Paris: Dervy-Livres, 1988), 82.

46. Le Cour, *L'ère du Verseau,* 84–85.

47. Ibid., 228.

48. Ibid., 160–64.

49. Ibid., 53.

50. Jay Weidner and Vincent Bridges, *Mysteries of the Great Cross of Hendaye: Alchemy and the End of Time* (Rochester, Vt.: Destiny Books, 2003), 424–31.

51. Fulcanelli, *Le mystère des cathédrales et l'interprétation ésotérique des symboles hermétiques du grand œuvre* (Paris: Jean-Jacques Pauvert, 1964; 1st ed. 1925), 209–19.

52. Phaure, *Le cycle de l'humanité adamique,* 329.

53. Ezekiel 1:10; Revelation 4:7.

54. Auclair, *Livre des cycles,* 85.

55. Fulcanelli, *Mystère des cathédrales,* 216.   See also Weidner and Bridges, *The Great Cross of Hendaye,* 308.

56. André VandenBroeck, *Al-Kemi: Hermetic, Occult, Political, and Private Aspects of R. A. Schwaller de Lubicz* (Great Barrington, Mass.: Inner Traditions/Lindisfarne Press, 1987), 152.

57. R. A. Schwaller de Lubicz, *Sacred Science: The King of Pharaonic Theocracy,* trans. André VandenBroeck and Goldian VandenBroeck (New York: Inner Traditions, 1982), 117.

58. Le Cour, *L'ère du Verseau,* 142–43.

59. Phaure, *Le cycle de l'humanité adamique,* 30, 263.

60. Ibid., 614.

61. Ibid., 333.

62. Ibid., 332.

63. Ibid., 557.

64. Ibid., viii–ix, 571.

65. Ibid., 552.

66. Ibid., xiii.

67. Ibid., xv.

68. Seyyed Hossein Nasr, *An Introduction to Islamic Cosmological Doctrines* (Boulder, Colo.: Shambhala, 1978), 83.

69. Thorndike, *History of Magic,* 2:897, citing *Conciliator differentiarum philosophorum* (1303).

70. Ibid., 2:900.

71. Noel Brann, *Trithemius and Magical Theology: A Chapter in the Controversy over Occult Studies in Early Modern Europe* (Albany: State University of New York Press, 1999), 134.

72. Ibid.

73. *The Key to the Work of Abbot Trithemius,* in Joscelyn Godwin, Christian Chanel, and John Patrick Deveney, eds., *The Hermetic Brotherhood of Luxor: Initiatic and Historical Documents of an Order of Practical Occultism* (York Beach, Maine: Samuel Weiser, 1995), 169–77. Here quoted, 169.

74. Godwin et al., *Hermetic Brotherhood,* 171n.

75. See Christopher Bamford's introduction and notes to C. G. Harrison, *The Transcendental Universe* (Hudson, N.Y.: Lindisfarne Press, 1993; 1st ed. 1894).

76. Ibid., 128.

77. Piazzi Smyth, *The Great Pyramid: Its Secrets and Mysteries Revealed* (New York: Bell Publishing, 1978; reprint of 1880 ed.), 547.

78. See William H. Harrison, "Mother Shipton: The Yorkshire Sibyl Investigated," *The Spiritualist,* 1881. Internet Sacred Text Archive, www.sacred-texts.com/pro/msi/index.htm.

79. Freeman Benjamin Dowd, *The Temple of the Rosy Cross* (Philadelphia: Rue, 1882), 7.

80. See Joscelyn Godwin, "Lady Caithness and Her Contribution to Theosophy," *Theosophical History* 8/4 (2000): 127–47.

81. See letters from Harris to *The Unknown World* 2/1 (Feb. 1895): 29–30.

82. Edward Maitland, *Anna Kingsford: Her Life, Letters, Diary and Work* (London: Watkins, 1913), 2:22, 42.

83. Advertisement for *The Stanzas of Dzyn* [*sic*], appended to A. S. Raleigh, *The*

Shepherd of Men: An Official Commentary on the Sermon of Hermes Trismegistos (San Francisco: Hermetic Publishing, 1916).

84. See Wing Anderson, *Prophetic Years 1947–1953* (Los Angeles: Kosmon Press, 1946), 44, 195.

85. Alan Pert, *Red Cactus: The Life of Anna Kingsford* (Watsons Bay, NSW: Books & Writers Network, 2006), 84.

86. Aveni, *End of Time*, 141–44.

87. Ibid., 160.

88. Edward Maitland, *Anna Kingsford: Her Life, Letters, Diary and Work* (London: Watkins, 1913), 2:50.

Bibliography

———— ✳ ————

Adam, James. *The Nuptial Number.* N.p.: Kairos, 1985. 1st ed. 1891.

Adamski, George. *Behind the Flying Saucer Mystery.* New York: Warner, 1967.

———. *Inside the Space Ships.* New York: Abelard-Schuman, 1955.

Allen, J. M. *Atlantis: The Andes Solution.* Moreton-in-Marsh, U.K.: Windrush Press, 1998.

Anderson, Wing. *Prophetic Years 1947–1953.* Los Angeles: Kosmon Press, 1946.

Andrews, Shirley. *Atlantis: Insights from a Lost Civilization.* Minneapolis: Llewellyn Books, 2002.

Andreyev, Alexandre. *Soviet Russia and Tibet: The Debacle of Secret Diplomacy, 1918–1930s.* Leiden, Netherlands: Brill, 2002.

Angebert, Michel. *Julius Evola, le visionnaire foudroyé.* Paris: Copernic, 1977.

Auclair, Raoul. *Autobiography of Alfred Percy Sinnett.* London: Theosophical History Centre, 1986.

———. *Le livre des cycles.* Paris: Éditions des Portes de France, 1947.

Aveni, Anthony. *The End of Time: The Maya Mystery of 2012.* Boulder: University Press of Colorado, 2009.

Bailey, Alice A. *The Destiny of the Nations.* London: Lucis Trust, 1949.

———. *Initiation, Human and Solar.* New York: Lucifer Publishing, 1922. London: Lucis Press, 1922.

———. *The Unfinished Autobiography of Alice A. Bailey.* New York: Lucis Publishing, 1951.

Bailly, Jean-Sylvain. *Histoire de l'astronomie ancienne depuis son origine jusqu'à l'établissement de l'école d'Alexandrie.* Paris: De Bure, 1781. 1st ed. 1775.

———. *Lettres sur l'Atlantide de Plato.* London: M. Elmesly, 1779.

Baistrocchi, Marco. *Agarttha: A Guénonian Manipulation?* Trans. by Joscelyn Godwin. Fullerton, Calif.: Theosophical History Center, 2009.

———. "Agarttha: Una manipolazione guénoniana?" *Politica Romana* 2 (1995): 8–40.

Baumann, Eberhard. *Der Aufgang und Untergang der frühen Hochkulturen Nord- und Mitteleuropas . . .* Passau: n.p., 1981.

———. *Herman Wirth: Schriften, Vorträge, Manuskripte und Sekundärliteratur.* Toppenstedt, Germany: Uwe Berg Verlag, 1995.

Bauval, Robert, and Adrian Gilbert. *The Orion Mystery: Unlocking the Secrets of the Pyramids.* New York: Three Rivers Press, 1995.

Bauval, Robert, and Graham Hancock. *Keeper of Genesis: A Quest for the Hidden Legacy of Mankind.* London: Heinemann, 1996.

Beekman, Scott. *William Dudley Pelley: A Life in Right-Wing Extremism and the Occult.* Syracuse: Syracuse University Press, 2005.

Benham, Patrick. *The Avalonians.* Glastonbury: Gothic Image, 2006.

Bennett, Colin. "Breakout of the Fictions: George Adamski's 1959 World Tour." *The Anomalist* 8 (2000): 39–84.

———. *Looking for Orthon: The Story of George Adamski, the First Flying Saucer Contactee, and How He Changed the World.* New York: Cosimo, 2008. 1st ed. 2001.

Bernard, Raymond. *Les maisons secrètes de la rose-croix.* Villeneuve St.-Georges, Paris: Éditions Rosicruciennes, 1979. 1st ed. 1970.

Bernbaum, Edwin. *The Way to Shambhala.* Los Angeles: Jeremy P. Tarcher, 1980.

Besant, Annie, and C. W. Leadbeater. *Man: Whence, How and Whither: A Record of Clairvoyant Investigation.* London: Theosophical Publishing House, 1913.

Blavatsky, H. P. *Collected Writings.* 15 vols. Wheaton, Ill.: Theosophical Publishing House, 1966–91.

———. *Isis Unveiled.* New York: Bouton, 1877.

———. *The Letters of H. P. Blavatsky to A. P. Sinnett and Other Miscellaneous Letters.* Ed. by A. T. Barker. New York: Frederick A. Stokes, n.d.

———. *The Secret Doctrine: The Synthesis of Science, Religion, and Philosophy.* 2 vols. London: Theosophical Publishing, 1888.

———. *The Secret Doctrine: The Synthesis of Science, Religion, and Philosophy.*

"Adyar Edition," 6 vols. Adyar [Chennai], India: Theosophical Publishing House, 1971.

Boura, Olivier. *Le Atlantides: Généalogie d'un mythe.* N.p.: Arléa, 1993.

Brandenstein, Wilhelm. *Atlantis: Größe und Untergang eines geheimnisvollen Inselreiches.* Vienna: Gerold, 1951.

Brann, Noel. *Trithemius and Magical Theology: A Chapter in the Controversy over Occult Studies in Early Modern Europe.* Albany: State University of New York Press, 1999.

Brasseur de Bourbourg, Charles Étienne. *Études sur le système graphique et la langue des Mayas.* 2 vols. Paris: Imprimerie Impériale, 1869, 1870.

Britten, Emma Hardinge. *Nineteenth Century Miracles; or, Spirits and Their Work in Every Country on the Earth.* New York: William Britten, 1884.

Brunton, Paul. *A Message from Arunachala.* London: Rider, 1936.

———. *A Search in Secret Egypt.* New York: Dutton, 1936.

Buescher, John Benedict. *Aquarian Evangelist: The Age of Aquarius as It Dawned in the Mind of Levi Dowling.* Fullerton, Calif.: Theosophical History, 2008.

Caldwell, Daniel H., and Michelle B. Graye. "Mary Unveiled." *Theosophical History* 1/8 (1986): 205–7.

Campion, Nicholas. *The Great Year: Astrology, Millenarianism and History in the Western Tradition.* London: Penguin-Arkana, 1994.

Castledon, Rodney. *The Knossos Labyrinth: A New View of the 'Palace of Minos' at Knossos.* London: Routledge, 1990.

Cayce, Edgar Evans. *Atlantis—Fact or Fiction?* Virginia Beach: Association for Research and Enlightenment, 1962.

Cayce, Edgar Evans, Gail Cayce Schwartzer, and Douglas G. Richards. *Mysteries of Atlantis Revisited.* New York: St. Martin's Press, 1997.

Cellier, Léon. *Fabre d'Olivet: Contribution à l'étude des aspects religieux du romantisme.* Paris: Nizet, 1953.

Cervé, Wishar S. *Lemuria: The Lost Continent of the Pacific.* San Jose, Calif.: Supreme Grand Lodge of AMORC, 1946. 1st ed. 1931.

Chambers, John. "The Channeled Myths of James Merrill: New Tales of Atlantis and Akhnaton." *Anomalist* 5 (1997): 41–58.

Charroux, Robert. *Le livre des maîtres du monde.* Paris: Robert Laffont, 1967.

———. *Le livre des secrets trahis.* Paris: Robert Laffont, 1965.

Childress, David Hatcher, and Richard Shaver. *Lost Continents and the Hollow Earth.* Kempton, Ill.: Adventures Unlimited, 1999.

Churchward, Albert. *The Origin and Evolution of Freemasonry.* London: Allen & Unwin, 1920.

———. *The Origin and Evolution of Religion.* London: Allen & Unwin, 1924.

———. *Signs and Symbols of Primordial Man.* 2nd ed. New York: Dutton, 1913. 1st ed. 1910.

Churchward, James. *Cosmic Forces of Mu,* vol. 1. Albuquerque, N.Mex.: Be, Books, 1992. 1st ed. 1934.

———. *The Lost Continent of Mu, the Motherland of Man.* Albuquerque, N.Mex.: Be, Books, 1994. 1st ed. 1926.

Clendenon, Cynthia J. *Hydromythology and the Ancient Greek World: An Earth Science Perspective Emphasizing Karst Hydrology.* Lansing, Mich.: Fineline Science Press, 2009.

Coe, Michael D. *Breaking the Maya Code.* London: Thames & Hudson, 1992.

Collins, Andrew. *From the Ashes of Angels.* London: Michael Joseph, 1996.

———. *Gateway to Atlantis: The Search for the Source of a Lost Civilization.* New York: Carroll & Graf, 2000.

Colville, W. J. *The Lost Continent of Atlantis; and the Civilization of the Pre-historic World: An Inspirational Lecture.* London: J. Burns, 1884.

Cruttenden, Walter. *Lost Star of Myth and Time.* Pittsburgh: St. Lynn's Press, 2006.

Cummins, Geraldine. *The Fate of Colonel Fawcett: A Narrative of His Last Expedition.* London: Aquarian Press, 1955.

Dalai Lama, Fourteenth (Tenzin Gyatso). *The Kālachakra Tantra.* Ed. and trans. by Jeffrey Hopkins. London: Wisdom Publications, 1985.

Daniélou, Alain. *La fantaisie des dieux et l'aventure humaine: Nature et destin du monde dans la tradition shivaïte.* Monaco: Éds. du Rocher, 1985.

———. *The Way to the Labyrinth: Memories of East and West.* Trans. by Marie-Claire Cournand. New York: New Directions, 1987. 1st ed. 1981.

de Camp, L. Sprague. *Lost Continents.* New York: Dover, 1970.

de Guaïta, Stanislas. *Au seuil du mystère.* 5th ed. Paris: Durville, 1915. 1st ed. 1886.

del Ponte, Renato. *Evola e il magico "Gruppo di Ur."* Borzano, Italy: SeaR Edizioni, 1994.

Delisle de Sales [Jean-Baptiste Isouard]. *Philosophie de la nature.* 3rd ed. London, 1777.

Desmond, Lawrence G. "Augustus Le Plongeon: A Fall from Archaeological Grace," in Alice B. Kehoe and Mary Beth Emmerich, eds., *Assembling the Past: Studies in the Professionalization of Archaeology*. Albuquerque: University of New Mexico Press, 1999, 81–90.

Deveney, John Patrick. *Paschal Beverly Randolph, a Nineteenth-Century Black American Spiritualist, Rosicrucian, and Sex-Magician*. Albany: State University of New York Press, 1997.

Dion Fortune, *The Sea Priestess*. York Beach, Maine: Weiser, 1993. 1st ed. 1938.

Donnelly, Ignatius. *Atlantis: The Antediluvian World*. New York: Harper & Brothers, 1882.

———. *Atlantis: The Antediluvian World*. Ed. by Egerton Sykes. New York: Gramercy Publishing, 1949.

Doreal. *The Emerald Tablets of Thoth the Atlantean*. Sedalia, Mo.: Brotherhood of the White Temple, 1939.

Dowd, Freeman Benjamin. *The Temple of the Rosy Cross*. Philadelphia: Rue, 1882.

Dowling, Levi H. *The Aquarian Gospel of Jesus the Christ*. Los Angeles: Royal Publishing, 1908.

Driscoll, Ian, and Matthew Kurtz. *Atlantis, Egyptian Genesis*. New York: Kali Yug Publishing, 2009.

Dunbavin, Paul. *Atlantis of the West: The Case for Britain's Drowned Megalithic Civilization*. New York: Carroll & Graf, 2003. 1st ed. as *The Atlantis Researches*. London: Third Millennium, 1992.

Dupuis, Charles-François. *Origine de tous les cultes, ou religion universelle*. Paris: An III (1794–95).

Eichner, Henry. *Atlantean Chronicles*. Alhambra, Calif.: Fantasy Publishing, 1971.

Ellis, Richard. *Imagining Atlantis*. New York: Knopf, 1998.

Evans, James. *The History and Practice of Ancient Astronomy*. New York: Oxford University Press, 1998.

Evans-Wentz, W. Y. *Tibetan Yoga and Secret Doctrines*. London: Oxford University Press, 1958.

Evola, Julius, writing as "Arvo." "Sulla tradizione iperborea." *Ur* II/12 (Nov.–Dec. 1928). Reprinted in Gruppo di Ur, *Introduzione alla magia* 2:412–22.

Evola, Julius, writing as "Ea." "Sul simbolismo dell'anno." *Krur* 6 (June 1929). Reprinted in Gruppo di Ur, *Introduzione alla magia* 3:199–209.

Evola, Julius. *Imperialismo pagano*. Padua: Edizioni di Ar, 1996. 1st ed. 1928.

———. *Il mito del sangue*. Borzano: SeaR Edizioni, 1995. Reprint of 1942 ed.

———. "Nota critica sull'opera de H. Wirth: *Der Aufgang der Menschheit*. *Bilychnis*

20/1 (Jan.–Feb. 1931). Reprinted in Evola, *I saggi di Bilychnis*. Padua: Edizioni di Ar, 1987, 139–41.

———. *Revolt Against the Modern World*. Trans. by Guido Stucco. Rochester, Vt.: Inner Traditions, 1995.

———. *Rivolta contra il mondo moderno*. Milan: Fratelli Bocca, 1951. 1st ed. 1934.

Fabre d'Olivet. *The Hebraic Tongue Restored*. Trans. by Nayán Louise Redfield. New York: G. P. Putnam's Sons, 1921.

———. *Hermeneutic Interpretation of the Origin of the Social State of Man*. Translation by Nayán Louise Redfield of *Histoire philosophique du genre humain*. New York: G. P. Putnam's Sons, 1915.

———. *Lettres à Sophie sur l'histoire*. Paris: Lavillette, 1801.

Fergusson, Thomas. *Chinese Researches. First Part: Chinese Chronology and Cycles*. Shanghai: n.p., 1880.

Firestone, Richard, Allen West, and Simon Warwick-Smith. *The Cycle of Cosmic Catastrophes: Flood, Fire, and Famine in the History of Civilization*. Rochester, Vt.: Bear & Co., 2006.

Flem-Ath, Rand, and Colin Wilson. *The Atlantis Blueprint*. London: Little, Brown, 2000.

Flem-Ath, Rand, and Rose Flem-Ath. *When the Sky Fell: In Search of Atlantis*. New York: St. Martin's Press, 1995.

Flowers, Stephen E., and Michael Moynihan, eds. *The Secret King: The Myth and Reality of Nazi Occultism*. Waterbury Center, Vt./Los Angeles: Dominion/ Feral House, 2007.

Forbes, J. Foster. *The Unchronicled Past: Being a Brief Account of What Ensued as the Result of the Tragedy of Atlantis, as Well as the Record of Some Remarkable Discoveries Concerning Ancient Britain*. London: Simpkin & Marshall, 1938.

Fortune, Dion. *The Esoteric Orders and Their Work*. York Beach, Maine: Weiser, 2000. 1st ed. 1928.

Franke, Thorwald C. "King Italos = King Atlas of Atlantis? A Contribution to the Sea Peoples Hypothesis." Atlantis Conference, Athens, 2008.

Fulcanelli. *Le mystère des cathédrales et l'interprétation ésotérique des symboles hermétiques du grand œuvre*. Paris: Jean-Jacques Pauvert, 1964. 1st ed. 1925.

Galanopoulos, A. G., and Ernest Bacon. *Atlantis: The Truth Behind the Legend*. Indianapolis: Bobbs-Merrill, 1969.

Gardner, Martin. *Urantia: The Great Cult Mystery*. Buffalo, N.Y.: Prometheus Books, 1995.

Gehrts, Heino. Untitled Memoir of Walther Machalett. *Rückschau der Arbeits- und Forschungskreis Walther Machalett* 28 (1994): 3.

Georgel, Gaston. *Chronologie des derniers temps, d'après la doctrine traditionnelle des cycles cosmiques.* Milan: Archè, 1986.

———. *Le cycle Judéo-Chrétien, sceau et couronnement de l'histoire humaine. Intégré par une brève histoire cyclique de l'Islam: Étude réalisée d'après la doctrine traditionnelle du mouvement cyclique de l'histoire.* Milan: Archè, 1983.

———. *Les quatre âges de l'humanité: Exposé de la doctrine traditionnelle des cycles cosmiques.* Milan: Archè, 1976. 1st ed. 1949.

———. *Les rythmes dans l'histoire. Historique et cycles secondaires. Cycles cosmiques et synthèse de l'histoire: Applications.* 3rd ed. Milan: Archè, 1981. 1st ed. 1937.

Gladstone, Hugh S. *Record Bags and Shooting Records.* London: H. F. & G. Witherby, 1922.

Glasenapp, Helmuth von. *The Doctrine of Karman in Jain Philosophy.* Trans. by G. Barry Gifford. Bombay: Trustees of the B. V. J. Panalal Charity Fund, 1948.

———. *Jainism: An Indian Religion of Salvation.* Trans. by S. B. Shrotri. Delhi: Motilal Banarsidass, 1999.

Godwin, Joscelyn. *Arktos: The Polar Myth in Science, Symbolism, and Nazi Survival.* Grand Rapids: Phanes/London: Thames & Hudson, 1993.

———. *Athanasius Kircher's Theatre of the World.* London: Thames & Hudson/ Rochester, Vt.: Inner Traditions, 2009.

———. "Herman Wirth and Folksong." *Tyr* 2 (2004): 263–83.

———. "The Hidden Hand, Part I: The Provocation of the Hydesville Phenomena." *Theosophical History* 3/2 (1990): 35–43.

———. "Lady Caithness and Her Contribution to Theosophy." *Theosophical History* 8/4 (2000): 127–47.

———. "Out of Arctica? Herman Wirth's Theory of Human Origins." *Rûna* 5 (2000): 2–7.

———. "Ramtha's Apocalyptic Books." Unpublished paper read at symposium on Ramtha, Yelm, Washington, February 9, 1997.

———. *The Theosophical Enlightenment.* Albany: State University of New York Press, 1994.

Godwin, Joscelyn, Christian Chanel, and John Patrick Deveney, eds. *The Hermetic Brotherhood of Luxor: Initiatic and Historical Documents of an Order of Practical Occultism.* York Beach, Maine: Samuel Weiser, 1995.

Goodrick-Clarke, Nicholas. *Black Sun: Aryan Cults, Esoteric Nazism and the Politics of Identity.* New York: New York University Press, 2002.

———. *The Occult Roots of Nazism: The Ariosophists of Austria and Germany, 1890–1935.* Wellingborough, U.K.: Aquarian Press, 1985.

Gorsleben, Rudolf John. *Hoch-Zeit der Menschheit.* Leipzig: Koehler & Amelang, 1930.

Gruppo di Ur, *Introduzione alla magia quale scienza dell'Io.* 3 vols. Genoa: Fratelli Melita, 1987.

Guénon, René. *Formes traditionnelles et cycles cosmiques.* Paris: Gallimard, 1970.

———. "Il Re del Mondo." *Atanor* 12 (Dec. 1924): 354–70.

———. *The Reign of Quantity and the Signs of the Times.* Trans. by Lord Northbourne. London: Luzac, 1953.

———. *Le roi du monde.* Paris: Gallimard, 1958. 1st ed. 1927.

———. *Symboles fondamentaux de la science sacrée.* Paris: Gallimard, 1962.

———. *The Symbolism of the Cross.* Trans. by Angus Macnab. London: Luzac, 1958.

Gula, Arun Chandra. *First Spark of Revolution: The Early Phase of India's Struggle for Independence, 1900–1920.* Bombay: Orient Longman, 1971.

Gurdjieff, G. I. *All and Everything; or Beelzebub's Tales to His Grandson.* London: Routledge & Kegan Paul, 1950.

Hancock, Graham. *Fingerprints of the Gods: A Quest for the Beginning and the End.* London: Heinemann, 1995.

———. *Underworld: The Mysterious Origins of Civilization.* New York: Crown Publishers, 2002.

Hancock, Graham, and Santha Faiia. *Heaven's Mirror: Quest for the Lost Civilization.* New York: Three Rivers Press, 1998.

Hanegraaff, Wouter J. *New Age Religion and Western Culture: Esotericism in the Mirror of Secular Thought.* Leiden, Netherlands: Brill, 1996.

Hapgood, Charles H. *Maps of the Ancient Sea Kings: Evidence of Advanced Civilization in the Ice Age,* rev. ed.. London: Turnstone Books, 1979. 1st ed. 1966.

Harrison, C. G. *The Transcendental Universe.* Hudson, N.Y.: Lindisfarne Press, 1993. 1st ed. 1894.

Harrison, William H. "Mother Shipton: The Yorkshire Sibyl Investigated." *The Spiritualist,* 1881. Internet Sacred Text Archive. www.sacred-texts.com/pro/msi/index.htm.

Heindel, Max. *The Rosicrucian Cosmo-Conception.* 2nd ed. Seattle: Rosicrucian Fellowship, 1910. 1st ed. 1909.

Helio-Arcanophus. *Atlantis Past, and to Come.* London: The Atlanteans, 1959.

Hemleben, Johannes. *Rudolf Steiner: A Documentary Biography.* Trans. by Leo Twyman. East Grinstead, U.K.: Henry Goulden, 1975.

Hermann, Albert. *Unsere Ahnen und Atlantis: Nordische Seeherrschaft von Skandinavien bis nach Nordafrika.* Berlin: Klinkhardt & Bierman, 1934.

Hiddell, Alec. "Tracks in the Desert." *The Excluded Middle,* 3. www.excludedmiddle.com/tracks%20in%20desert.html.

Higgins, Godfrey. *Anacalypsis: An Attempt to Draw Aside the Veil of the Saitic Isis; or an Inquiry into the Origin of Languages, Nations and Religions.* 2 vols. New York: Macy-Masius, 1927. 1st ed. 1833–36.

———. *The High History of the Holy Grail.* Trans. by Sebastian Evans. London: J. M. Dent, 1929.

Holroyd, Stuart. *The House of Lords UFO Debate: Illustrated, Full Transcript with Preface by Lord Clancarty, Brinsley le Poer Trench, and Notes by John Michell.* London: Open Head Press, 1979.

———. *Prelude to the Landing on Planet Earth.* London: W. H. Allen, 1977. Also published as *Briefing for Landing on Planet Earth* and reissued as *The Nine: Briefing from Deep Space: The Controversial Record of a Unique "Encounter" and a Message of Hope for All Mankind.* Flagler Beach, Fla.: Old Kings Road Press, 2003.

Hübner, Arthur. *Herman Wirth und die Ura-Linda-Chronik.* Berlin: Walter de Gruyter, 1934.

Hüser, Karl, Wulff E. Brebeck, Dieter Fölster, Heinz Bittner, and Joachim Jochimsen. *Wewelsburg 1933–1945: Kult- und Terrorstätte der SS.* Paderborn: Deutsches Institut für Bildung und Wissen, 1982.

James, Peter. *The Sunken Kingdom: The Atlantis Mystery Solved.* London: Jonathan Cape, 1995.

Jenkins, John Major. *The 2012 Story: The Myths, Fallacies and Truths Behind the Most Intriguing Date in History.* New York: Tarcher/Penguin, 2009.

———. *Galactic Alignment: The Transformation of Consciousness According to Mayan, Egyptian, and Vedic Traditions.* Rochester, Vt.: Bear & Co., 2002.

Johnson, K. Paul. *Edgar Cayce in Context. The Readings: Truth and Fiction.* Albany: State University of New York Press, 1998.

Jordan, Paul. *The Atlantis Syndrome.* Thrupp, U.K.: Sutton Publishing, 2001.

Jung, Carl Gustav. *Aion: Researches into the Phenomenology of the Self.* Trans. by R. F. C. Hull. New York: Pantheon Books, 1959.

Kafton-Minkel, Walter. *Subterranean Worlds: 100,000 Years of Dragons, Dwarfs, the Dead, Lost Races and UFOs from Inside the Earth.* Port Townsend, Wash.: Loompanics, 1989.

Kelley, David H., and Eugene F. Malone. *Exploring Ancient Skies: An Encyclopedic Survey of Archaeoastronomy.* New York: Springer, 2005.

Khei. *Rosicrucian Fundamentals: An Exposition of the Rosicrucian Synthesis of Religion, Science and Philosophy.* New York: Societas Rosicruciana in America, 1920.

King, David. *Finding Atlantis: A True Story of Genius, Madness, and an Extraordinary Quest for a Lost World.* New York: Harmony Books, 2005.

King, Godfré Ray. *The Magic Presence.* Chicago: Saint Germain Press, 1935.

———. *Unveiled Mysteries.* Chicago: Saint Germain Press, 1934.

Kingsland, William, ed. *A Child's Story of Atlantis, Book I.* London: Theosophical Publishing Society, 1908.

Kircher, Athanasius. *Mundus Subterraneus.* Antwerp: Jansson, 1665.

Kirkpatrick, Sidney D. *Edgar Cayce: An American Prophet.* New York: Riverhead Books, 2000.

Knight, Gareth. *Pythoness: The Life and Work of Margaret Lumley Brown.* Loughborough, U.K.: Thoth Publications, 2006.

Koeppen, Carl Friedrich. *Die Religion des Buddha und ihre Entstehung.* Berlin: Ferdinand Schneider, 1857–59.

Kukal, Zdeněk. "Atlantis in the Light of Modern Research." *Earth-Science Reviews* 21 (1984): 1–225.

Lachman, Gary. *Rudolf Steiner: An Introduction to His Life and Work.* London: Penguin, 2007.

Lanz von Liebenfels, Jörg. *Theozoology, or the Science of the Sodomite Apelings and the Divine Electron: An Introduction to the Most Ancient and Most Modern Philosophy and a Justification of the Monarchy and the Nobility.* Trans. by Fam. Viktor and Br. Procursus. N.p.: ONT Study Group, 1985. 1st ed. 1904.

Larkin, Edgar Lucian. "The Atlantides." *San Francisco Examiner,* Dec. 31, 1913, 18.

Laurant, Jean-Pierre. "Le destin sacré des peuples, race et occultisme au XIXe siècle: L'exemple du Hiéron de Paray-le-Monial." *Politica Hermetica* 2 (1988): 43–49.

———. *L'Ésotérisme chrétien en France au XIXe siècle.* Paris: L'Age d'Homme, 1992.

———. *Le sens caché dans l'oeuvre de René Guénon.* Paris: L'Age d'Homme, 1975.

LaViolette, Paul. *Earth Under Fire: Humanity's Survival of the Apocalypse.* Schenectady, N.Y.: Starburst Publications, 1997.

Le Cour, Paul. *À la recherche d'un Monde perdu: L'Atlantide et ses traditions*. Paris: Leymarie, 1926.

———. *L'ère du Verseau: Le proche avenir de l'humanité*. Rev. ed. Paris: Dervy, 1999.

Le Plongeon, Augustus. *Queen Mu and the Egyptian Sphinx*. 2nd ed. New York: Author, 1900. 1st ed. 1896.

Leadbeater, C. W. *The Astral Plane*. Adyar [Chennai], India: Theosophical Publishing House, 1933.

Lenz, Manfred. "Leben und Werk des deutschen Esoterikers Peryt Shou." *Gnostika* 28 (Oct. 2004): 23–40.

Leslie, Desmond, and George Adamski. *Flying Saucers Have Landed*. New York: British Book Centre, 1953.

Leslie, J. Ben. *Submerged Atlantis Restored, or Rĭn-gä'-sĕ nŭd Sï-ĭ-kĕl'zē. Links and Cycles: A Short Treatise on the Over-Spirit as the Cycle Supreme*. Rochester, N.Y.: Austin Publishing, 1911.

Lewis, James R., ed. *The Gods Have Landed: New Religions from Other Worlds*. Albany: State University of New York Press, 1995.

Linga-Purana. Translated by a Board of Scholars. Delhi: Motilal Banarsidass, 1982.

List, Guido von. *Die Bilderschrift der Ario-Germanen*. Vienna: Guido-von-List Gesellschaft, 1910.

———. *The Religion of the Aryo-Germanic Folk, Esoteric and Exoteric*. Smithville, Tex.: Runa-Raven Press, 2005. 1st ed. 1909/1910.

———. *Die Rita der Ario-Germanen*. 3rd ed. Berlin: Guido von List Verlag, 1920. 1st ed. 1908.

Luce, J. V. *The End of Atlantis: New Light on an Old Legend*. London: Thames & Hudson, 1969.

Lutyens, Mary. *Krishnamurti: The Years of Awakening*. London: John Murray, 1974.

Machalett, Walther. *Die Externsteine: Das Zentrum des Abendlandes. Die Geschichte der weißen Rasse*. 6 vols. Maschen, Germany: Hallonen-Verlag, 1970.

The Mahatma Letters to A. P. Sinnett from the Mahatmas M. and K. H. 3rd ed. Adyar [Chennai], India: Theosophical Publishing House, 1979.

Maitland, Edward. *Anna Kingsford: Her Life, Letters, Diary and Work*. London: Watkins, 1913.

Maltwood, Katharine. "The Discovery of a Prehistoric Zodiac in England." *Journal of the Royal Astronomical Society of Canada* (Sept. 1943). http://adsabs.harvard.edu/full/1943JRASC..37..269M.

———. *A Guide to Glastonbury's Temple of the Stars: Their Giant Effigies Described from Air Views, Maps, and from "The High History of the Holy Grail."* London: Women's Printing Society, 1934.

Mandasoran, the Recorder. *Atlantis.* London: Golden Triangle Fellowship, 1954.

Mann, Nicholas. *The Isle of Avalon: Sacred Mysteries of Arthur and Glastonbury.* Woolavington, U.K.: Green Magic, 2001.

Mavor, James. *Voyage to Atlantis.* New York: Putnam, 1969.

McClain, Ernest G. *The Myth of Invariance: The Origin of the Gods, Mathematics and Music from the Ṛg Veda to Plato.* New York: Nicolas Hays, 1976.

———. *The Pythagorean Plato: Prelude to the Song Itself.* Stony Brook, N.Y.: Nicholas Hays, 1978.

Meier, Gert, and Hermann Zschweigert. *Die Hochkulturen der Megalithzeit: Verschwiegene Zeugnisse aus Europas großer Vergangenheit.* Tübingen: Grabert-Verlag, 1997.

Melton, J. Gordon, ed. *Encyclopedia of Occultism and Parapsychology.* 5th ed. Farmington Hills, Mich.: Gale Group, 2001.

———. *Finding Enlightenment: Ramtha's School of Ancient Wisdom.* Hillsboro, Oreg.: Beyond Words Publishing, 1998.

Merrill, James. *The Changing Light at Sandover.* New York: Atheneum, 1982.

Michel de Grèce. *La Crète, épave de l'Atlantide.* Paris: Juilliard, 1971.

Michell, John. *At the Centre of the World: Polar Symbolism Discovered in Celtic, Norse and Other Ritualized Landscapes.* London: Thames & Hudson, 1994.

———. *The Dimensions of Paradise: The Proportions and Symbolic Numbers of Ancient Cosmology.* London: Thames & Hudson, 1988.

———. *The Flying Saucer Vision: The Holy Grail Restored.* London: Sidgwick & Jackson, 1967.

Michell, John, and Christine Rhone. *Twelve-Tribe Nations and the Science of Enchanting the Landscape.* Grand Rapids: Phanes Press, 1991.

Mifsud, Anton, Simon Mifsud, Chris Agius Sultana, and Charles Cavona Ventura. *Malta: Echoes of Plato's Island.* N.p.: The Prehistoric Society of Malta, 2000.

The Mystery of the Sphinx. Film narrated by Charlton Heston, NBC, 1993. Reissued in various media.

Nasr, Seyyed Hossein. *An Introduction to Islamic Cosmological Doctrines.* Boulder, Colo.: Shambhala, 1978.

Nethercot, Arthur H. *The Last Four Lives of Annie Besant.* Chicago: University of Chicago Press, 1963.

Neugebauer, Otto. *A History of Ancient Mathematical Astronomy.* New York: Springer-Verlag, 1975.

Newman, Paul. *Aleister Crowley and the Cult of Pan.* London: Greenwich Exchange, 2004.

North, John. *Cosmos: An Illustrated History of Astronomy and Cosmology.* Chicago: University of Chicago Press, 2008.

Notovitch, Nicolas. *The Unknown Life of Jesus Christ.* New York: R. F. Fenno, 1890.

Oahspe: A Kosmon Bible in the Words of Jehovih and His Angel Embassadors. Boston: Author, 1882.

The Oera-Linda Book. Trans. by William R. Sandbach. London: Trübner, 1876.

Olcott, Henry S. *Old Diary Leaves, First Series.* Adyar [Chennai], India: Theosophical Publishing, 1941. 1st ed. 1895.

O'Neil, William. M. *Early Astronomy from Babylonia to Copernicus.* Sydney: Sydney University Press, 1986.

Ossendowski, Ferdinand. *Beasts, Men and Gods.* New York: Dutton, 1922.

Pallottino, Massimo. "Notizie e discussioni: Atlantide." *Archeologia Classica* 4 (1952): 229–240.

Pannekoek, A. *A History of Astronomy.* London: George Allen & Unwin, 1961.

Papus. *Traité élémentaire de science occulte.* 7th ed. Paris: Dangles, n.d. 1st ed. 1898.

Pauwels, Louis, and Jacques Bergier. *Le matin des magiciens.* Paris: Gallimard, 1960.

———. *The Morning of the Magicians.* Trans. by Rollo Myers. New York: Avon Books, 1971. 1st ed. 1963. Title in U.K.: *The Dawn of Magic.*

Pelley, William Dudley. *Star Guests: Design for Mortality.* Noblesville, Ind.: Fellowship Press, 1978. 1st ed. 1950.

Pert, Alan. *Red Cactus: The Life of Anna Kingsford.* Watsons Bay, NSW: Books & Writers Network, 2006.

Phaure, Jean. *Le cycle de l'humanité adamique: Introduction à l'étude de la cyclologie traditionnelle et de la fin des temps.* Paris: Dervy-Livres, 1988.

Phelon, William P. *Our Story of Atlantis, Written Down for the Hermetic Brotherhood.* San Francisco: Hermetic Book Concern, 1903.

Philip, Brother. *Secret of the Andes.* Bolinas, Calif.: Leaves of Grass Press, 1976. 1st ed. 1961.

Phylos the Tibetan. *A Dweller on Two Planets.* Los Angeles: Poseid Printing, 1920. 1st ed. 1905.

Prémare, Père [Joseph Henri Marie de]. *Discours préliminaire,* in Joseph de Guignes, ed., *Le Chou-King: Un des livres sacrés des Chinois.* Paris: Tilliard, 1770.

Raleigh, A. S. *The Shepherd of Men: An Official Commentary on the Sermon of Hermes Trismegistos.* San Francisco: Hermetic Publishing, 1916.

Ramtha. Bellevue, Wash.: Sovereignty Publishers, 1986.

Randall-Stevens, H. C. *The Book of Truth.* 2nd ed. London: Rider, 1927. 1st ed. 1925.

———. *The Chronicles of Osiris.* London: Rider, 1927.

Randall-Stevens, H. C. (El-Eros). *Atlantis to the Latter Days.* London: Aquarian Press, 1954.

Reiche, Harald T. "The Language of Archaic Astronomy: A Clue to the Atlantis Myth?" in Kenneth Brecher and Michael Feirtag, eds., *Astronomy of the Ancients.* Cambridge, Mass.: MIT Press, 1979, 153–189.

Requena, Rafael. *Vestigios de la Atlántida.* Caracas: Tipografica Americana, 1932.

Roberts, Jane. *Seth Speaks; The Eternal Validity of the Soul.* With Notes by Robert F. Butts. Englewood Cliffs, N.J.: Prentice-Hall, 1972.

———. *The Education of Oversoul 7.* New York: Pocket Books, 1976. 1st ed. 1973.

Robin, Jean. *Les sociétés secrètes au rendez-vous de l'apocalypse.* Paris: Guy Trédaniel, 1985.

Robinson, Lytle W. *Edgar Cayce's Story of the Origin and Destiny of Man.* New York: Coward, McCann & Geoghegan, 1972.

Rosenberg, Alfred. *Der Mythos des 20. Jahrhunderts: Eine Wertung der seelisch-geistigen Gestaltungskämpfe unserer Zeit.* Munich: Honeneiche, 1936. 1st ed. 1930.

———. *Mythus.* 3 vols. Various translators. London: Friends of Europe, 1936–37.

Saint-Yves d'Alveydre. *The Kingdom of Agarttha.* Trans. by Jon Graham. Rochester, Vt.: Inner Traditions, 2008.

———. *Mission de l'Inde en Europe; Mission de l'Europe en Asie.* Nice: Bélisane, 1981. 1st ed. (suppressed) 1886.

Samanta, Amiya K., ed. *Terrorism in Bengal: A Collection of Documents on Terrorist Activities from 1905 to 1939.* Calcutta: Government of West Bengal, 1995.

Santesson, Hans Stefan. *Understanding Mu.* New York: Paperback Library, 1970.

Santillana, Giorgio de, and Hertha von Dechend. *Hamlet's Mill: An Essay on Myth and the Frame of Time.* Boston: Gambit, 1969.

Santucci, James A. "The Theosophical Concept of Race." *Nova Religio* 11/3 (2008): 37–63.

Sarmast, Robert. *Discovery of Atlantis: The Startling Case for the Island of Cyprus.* San Rafael: Origin Press, 2004.

Saunier, Jean. *Saint-Yves d'Alveydre, ou une synarchie sans énigme.* Paris: Dervy Livres, 1981.

———. *La synarchie ou le vieux rêve d'une nouvelle société.* Paris: Culture Arts Loisirs, 1971.

Schlag, Oskar R. *Von alten und neuen Mysterien: Die Lehren des A.* Bd. 1, ed. Antoine Faivre and Erhart Kahle. Würzburg: Ergon, 1998.

Schlemmer, Phyllis V., and Palden Jenkins. *The Only Planet of Choice: Essential Briefings from Deep Space.* Bath, U.K.: Gateway Books, 1993.

Schoch, Robert M. "How Old Is the Sphinx? A Paper Written to Accompany a Presentation at the 1992 American Association for the Advancement of Science Annual Meeting, Chicago, 7 February 1992." Boston: R. M. Schoch, 1992.

Schoch, Robert M., and Logan Yonavjak. *The Parapsychology Revolution: A Concise Anthology of Paranormal and Psychical Research.* New York: Tarcher/Penguin, 2008.

Schuré, Edouard. *The Great Initiates: Sketch of the Secret History of Religions.* Trans. by Fred Rothwell. London: Rider, 1913.

Scott-Elliot, W. *Atlantis: A Geographical, Historical, and Ethnological Sketch, Illustrated by Four Maps of the World's Configuration at Different Periods.* London: Theosophical Publishing, 1896.

———. *The Lost Lemuria.* London: Theosophical Publishing House, 1904.

———. *The Story of Atlantis and the Lost Lemuria.* London: Theosophical Publishing House, 1968.

Selby, John. "Dion Fortune and Her Inner Plane Contacts: Intermediaries in the Western Esoteric Tradition." Ph.D. diss., University of Exeter, 2008.

Selvius. "Descendants of Lemuria: A Description of an Ancient Cult in America." *Mystic Triangle* 3 (Aug. 1925): 113–14. Reprinted *Rosicrucian Digest* 9 (May 1931): 495–97.

Settegast, Mary. *Plato Prehistorian: 10,000 to 5000 B.C. in Myth and Archaeology.* Cambridge, Mass.: Rotenberg Press, 1987.

Shou, Peryt. *Atlantis: Das Schicksal der Menschheit. Die geistige Frühkultur der Atlantier und das gegenwärtige Europa. Nach wissenschaftlichen Quellen.* Graz: Edition Geheimes Wissen, 2008. 1st ed. 1930.

———. *Esoterik der Atlantier in ihrer Beziehung zur aegyptischen, babylonischen und jüdischen Geheimlehre.* Leipzig: Theosophisches Verlagshaus, 1913.

Sinclair, John R. *The Alice Bailey Inheritance.* Wellingborough, U.K.: Turnstone Press, 1982.

Sinnett, A. P. *Esoteric Buddhism.* 8th ed. London: Theosophical Publishing, 1907. 1st ed. 1883.

———. "The Pyramids and Stonehenge," in *Collected Fruits of Occult Teaching.* London: T. Fisher Unwin, 1919.

Sitchin, Zecharia. *The Twelfth Planet.* New York: Stein & Day, 1976.

Smyth, Piazzi. *The Great Pyramid: Its Secrets and Mysteries Revealed.* New York: Bell Publishing, 1978. 1st ed. 1880.

Sopa, Geshe Lhundub, Roger Jackson, and John Newman. *The Wheel of Time. The Kalachakra in Context.* Ithaca, N.Y.: Snow Lion, 1991.

Spanuth, Jürgen. *Atlantis of the North.* New York: Van Nostrand Reinhold, 1980.

———. *Atlantis: The Mystery Unravelled.* London: Arco Publishers, 1956.

———. *Das enträtselte Atlantis.* Stuttgart: Union Deutscher Verlags-Gesellschaften, 1953.

Spedicato, Emilio. "Galactic Encounters, Apollo Objects and Atlantis: A Catastrophic Scenario for Discontinuities in Human History." 3rd rev. version. www.unibg.it/dati/persone/636/410.pdf.

Spence, Lewis. *Encyclopaedia of Occultism.* London: Routledge, 1920.

———. *The Occult Sciences in Atlantis.* London: Rider, 1943.

———. *The Problem of Atlantis.* Reprinted New York: Causeway Books, 1974, as *Atlantis Discovered.*

———. *Will Europe Follow Atlantis?* London: Rider [1942].

Stacey-Judd, Robert B. *Atlantis: Mother of Empires.* Kempton, Ill.: Adventures Unlimited Press, 1999. 1st ed. 1939.

Steiner, Rudolf. *Atlantis: The Fate of a Lost Land and Its Secret Knowledge.* London: Rudolf Steiner Press, 2001.

———. *Aus der Akasha Chronik: Unsere atlantischen Vorfahren.* Berlin: Theosophischer Verlag, 1904. Enlarged for the Eng. ed.: *The Submerged Continents of Atlantis and Lemuria, Their History and Civilization. Being Chapters from the Akashic Records.* London: Theosophical Publishing Society, 1911. Further enlarged as *Cosmic Memory: Prehistory of Earth and Man.* Trans. by Karl E. Zimmer. Hudson: Steinerbooks, 1987.

———. *Karmic Relationships.* 8 vols. London: Rudolf Steiner Press, 1972–75.

———. *An Outline of Occult Science.* London: Theosophical Publishing Society, 1914.

———. *Spiritualism, Madame Blavatsky, and Theosophy: An Eyewitness View of*

Occult History. Edited by Christopher Bamford. Great Barrington, Mass.: Anthroposophic Press, 2001.

————. *Theosophie: Einführung in übersinnliche Welterkenntnis und Menschenbestimmung*. Berlin, 1904. Trans. by Henry B. Monges as *Theosophy: An Introduction to the Supersensible Knowledge of the World and the Destination of Man*. Spring Valley, N.Y.: Anthroposophic Press, 1971.

————. "Wie erlangt man Erkenntnisse der höheren Welten?" *Luzifer-Gnosis*, 1904. Trans. by George Metaxa as *Knowledge of Higher Worlds and Its Attainment*. Spring Valley, N.Y.: Anthroposophic Press, 1947.

Steuerwald, Hans. *Der Untergang von Atlantis: Das Ende einer Legende*. Berlin Kulturbuch-Verlag, 1983.

Subba Row, T. *Esoteric Writings*. Adyar [Chennai], India: Theosophical Publishing House, 1980. 1st ed. 1895.

Subhash Kak. "Birth and Early Development of Indian Astronomy," in H. Selin, ed., *Astronomy Across Cultures: The History of Non-Western Astronomy*. Dordrecht, Netherlands: Kluwer, 2000, 303–40.

Sünner, Rüdiger. *Schwarze Sonne: Entfesselung und Mißbrauch der Mythen in Nationalsozialismus und rechter Esoterik*. Freiburg i. B.: Herder/Spektrum, 1999.

Sûrya-Siddhânta: A Textbook of Hindu Astronomy. Trans. by Ebenezer Burgess. *Journal of the American Oriental Society* 6 (1860). Reprinted Minneapolis: Wizards Book Shelf, 1978.

Thomas, Dana Lloyd. *Julius Evola e la tentazione razzista: L'inganno del pangermanesimo in Italia*. Mesagne, Brindisi, Italy: Giordano, 2008.

Thorndike, Lynn. *A History of Magic and Experimental Science*. 8 vols. New York: Columbia University Press, 1923–58.

Tillett, Gregory. *The Elder Brother: A Biography of Charles Webster Leadbeater*. London: Routledge & Kegan Paul, 1982.

Timlett, Peter Valentine. *The Seedbearers*. New York: Bantam Books, 1976. 1st ed. 1974.

Tomas, Andrew. *Les secrets de l'Atlantide*. Paris: Laffont, 1971. Translated as *Atlantis: From Legend to Discovery*. London: Robert Hale, 1972.

Trench, Brinsley le Poer. *Men Among Mankind*. London: Neville Spearman, 1962.

"Two Chelas" in the Theosophical Society. *Man: Fragments of Forgotten History*. London: Reeves & Turner, 1885.

Tyler, F. C. *The Geometrical Arrangement of Ancient Sites: A Development of the Straight Track Theory*. London: Simpkin & Marshall, 1939.

The Urantia Book. Chicago: Urantia Foundation, 1955.

Van den Broek, Roelof, and Inez Wolf Seger. *The Myth of the Phoenix.* Leiden, Netherlands: Brill, 1972.

Van Rijckenborgh, J. *Elementary Philosophy of the Modern Rosy Cross.* 3rd ed. Haarlem, Netherlands: Rozekruis Press, 1984. 1st ed. 1950.

Van Sertima, Ivan, ed. *African Presence in Early Europe.* New Brunswick, N.J., and Oxford, U.K.: Transaction Publishers, 1988.

Vigers, Daphne. *Atlantis Rising. The Records of the Author's Visits, Through an Uncommon State of Consciousness, to Ancient Atlantis.* London: Andrew Dakers, 1944.

Visnu Purana: A System of Hindu Mythology and Tradition. Trans. by H. H. Wilson. Delhi: Nag Publishers, 1989. 1st ed. 1840.

Waterfield, Robin. *René Guénon and the Future of the West: The Life and Writings of a 20th-century Metaphysician.* N.p.: Crucible, 1987.

Webb, James. *The Harmonious Circle: The Lives and Work of G. I. Gurdjieff, P. D. Ouspensky, and Their Followers.* London: Thames & Hudson, 1980.

Wegener, Franz. *Das Atlantidische Weltbild: Nationalsozialismus und Neue Rechte auf der Suche nach der versunkenen Atlantis.* Gladbeck, Germany: Kulturförderverein Ruhrgebiet, 2001.

West, John Anthony. *Serpent in the Sky: The High Wisdom of Ancient Egypt.* London: Wildwood House, 1978.

Wieland, Hermann. *Atlantis, Edda und Bibel: 200,000 Jahre germanischer Weltkultur und das Geheimnis der Heiligen Schrift.* Nuremberg: Chr. Karl Wuzel, 1925.

———. *Atlantis, Edda und Bibel: Das entdeckte Geheimnis der Heiligen Schrift des deutschen Volkes Rettung aus Not und Tod.* Nuremberg: Chr. Karl Wuzel, 1922.

Williamson, George Hunt. *Other Tongues—Other Flesh.* Amherst, Wisc.: Amherst Press, 1953.

———. *Secret Places of the Lion.* Amherst, Wisc.: Amherst Press, 1958.

Williamson, George Hunt, and Alfred C. Bailey. *The Saucers Speak! A Documentary Report of Interstellar Communication by Radiotelegraphy.* Los Angeles: New Age Publishing, 1954.

Williamson, Tom, and Liz Bellamy. *Ley Lines in Question.* Tadworth, U.K.: World's Work, 1983.

Willson, [Henry] Beckles. *Lost England: The Story of Our Submerged Coasts.* London: Hodder & Stoughton, 1902. Reprinted as *Lost Lyonesse: Evidence, Records and Traditions of England's Atlantis.* Introduction by John Michell. London: AdCo Associates, 1986.

Wilson, Colin. *Atlantis and the Kingdom of the Neanderthals: 100,000 Years of Lost History*. Rochester, Vt.: Bear & Co., 2006.

———. *Dreaming to Some Purpose: An Autobiography*. London: Century, 2004.

———. *From Atlantis to the Sphinx*. New York: Fromm International, 1997.

Wirth, Herman. *Der Aufgang der Menschheit: Untersuchungen zur Geschichte der Religion, Symbolik und Schrift der Atlantisch-Nordischen Rässe*. Jena, Germany: Eugen Diederich, 1928.

Wirth Roeper Bosch, Herman. *Um den Ursinn des Menschseins: Die Werdung einer neuen Geisteswissenschaft*. Vienna: Volkstum-Verlag, 1960.

Yogananda, Paramahansa. *Autobiography of a Yogi*. Los Angeles: Self-Realization Fellowship, 1983. 1st ed. 1946.

Yukteswar Giri, Jnanavatar Swami Sri. *The Holy Science*. Los Angeles: Self-Realization Fellowship, 1990. 1st ed. 1949.

Zander, Helmut. *Anthroposophie in Deutschland: Theosophische Weltanschauung und gesellschaftliche Praxis 1884–1945*. Göttingen, Germany: Vandenhoeck & Ruprecht, 2007.

Zangger, Eberhard. *The Flood from Heaven: Deciphering the Atlantis Legend*. London: Sidgwick & Jackson, 1992.

Zapp, Ivar, and George Erikson. *Atlantis in America: Navigators of the Ancient World*. Kempton, Ill.: Adventures Unlimited, 1998.

Zhirov, Nicolas. *Atlantis; Atlantology: Basic Problems*. Trans. by David Skvirsky. Moscow: Progress Publishers, 1970.

Zoccatelli, Pier Luigi. "Notes on an Unpublished Correspondence Between René Guénon and Louis Charbonneau-Lassay." CESNUR International Conference, Bryn Athyn, Pennsylvania, June 2–5, 1999.

Zschaetzsch, Karl Georg. *Atlantis, die Urheimat der Arier*. Berlin: Arier-Verlag, 1922.

Index